D1617471

CAUGHT BETWEEN WORLDS

CAUGHT BETWEEN WORLDS

British Captivity Narratives in Fact and Fiction

Joe Snader

THE UNIVERSITY PRESS OF KENTUCKY

Publication of this volume was made possible in part
by a grant from the National Endowment for the Humanities.

Editorial and Sales Offices: The University Press of Kentucky
663 South Limestone Street, Lexington, Kentucky 40508–4008

04 03 02 01 00   5 4 3 2 1

Library of Congress Cataloging-in-Publication Data

Snader, Joe, 1964–
    Caught between worlds : British captivity narratives in fact and fiction /
Joe Snader.
      p.   cm.
    Includes bibliographical references and index.
    ISBN 0-8131-2164-7 (alk. paper)
    1. English prose literature—18th century—History and criticism.
    2. English prose literature—Early modern, 1500–1700—History and criti-
cism. 3. English fiction—18th century—History and criticism. 4. Captivity
narratives—Great Britain. 5. American literature—English influences.
    6. Narration (Rhetoric). I. Title

PR769.S64 2000
828'.50809355—dc21   99-089786

This book is printed on acid-free recycled paper meeting
the requirements of the American National Standard
for Permanence in Paper for Printed Library Materials.

Manufactured in the United States of America.

For Fran, with love and thanks

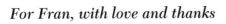

Contents

Illustrations

Acknowledgments

I owe a debt of gratitude first to Vin Carretta, Paula McDowell, and Sue Lanser. The three made for an intriguing combination of divergent perspectives and constructive advice. Also important were the helpful and encouraging contributions of Cal Winton and James F. Brooks. The feedback, insights, and suggestions of Sharon Groves, Eliza Child, and Nancy Shevlin in the early stages of this project helped form some of the deep bedrock within these chapters. An important moment in the evolution of this project was Laura Brown's positive and useful response to the earlier version of chapter 4 that appeared in *Eighteenth-Century Fiction*. Copy editor Noel Kinnamon worked hard and well on converting the notes to fit the chronological bibliography; for this and his other contributions to the project I am grateful.

Introduction

The early modern era witnessed the birth, flowering, and metamorphosis of many Western literary genres. Among these is one that literary scholars have called the captivity narrative, the text devoted extensively or exclusively to documenting a real experience of subjugation in a foreign land. Today, however, we do not think of the captivity narrative as an early modern genre, but rather as an American one, largely because literary scholars have defined the captivity genre in terms of Anglo-American captives and Native American captors. But the captivity narrative, like the novel or the encyclopedia, is a genre whose roots stretch back to the European Middle Ages, and whose initial flowering belongs to the early modern vernacular press.

The captivity narrative became a significant, popular, vernacular genre when European cultures began to explore the rest of the world with an eye to exploiting it. Texts documenting the experiences of British captives held by Native Americans formed one important strand within a larger Anglophone tradition of captivity narratives that began with the earliest British ventures into alien seas, during the late sixteenth century. Throughout the seventeenth and eighteenth centuries, the British press witnessed texts documenting personal experiences of captivity in a variety of lands, from America to Malaysia, from southern Africa to the steppes of Russia. During that era, as the British built two overseas empires and lost one of them, the English captivity narrative became increasingly long, increasingly complex, and increasingly ambitious in its claim to document the differences between allegedly modern and allegedly uncivilized peoples. As the British narrative tradition reveals, the captivity genre, far from belonging to any particular nation of origin, grew out of the tensions surrounding several early modern historical developments of global significance: not only the expansion of European colonialism and trade, but also the rise of liberal individualism and the elaboration of the self-consciously modern intellectual systems of enlightenment. The evolution and variety of this narrative tradition are the focus of this book.

Literary scholarship has often investigated the captivity genre, but it has done so through an exclusive focus on American material. Centered especially on printings from the New England colonies and the fledgling United States, this scholarship has nearly always defined the captivity narrative as a genre whose unique origins were coeval with the supposedly unique origins of Anglo-American culture. In assessing the genre's relationship to Britain, and to the world more generally, scholars have imagined the export of an indigenous American product to an avid Old World readership, the sale within an international literary marketplace of a genre expressing a uniquely American experience or consciousness. In the introduction to a prominent anthology of captivity texts, for example, Alden T. Vaughan and Edward W. Clark have described the captivity narrative as "one of America's oldest literary genres and its most unique," even while acknowledging that the earliest captivity texts with American settings first appeared in European presses.[1] This is a position fostered by generations of American scholarship, especially as it has traced a foundational moment in the genre's emergence to the first extensive English narrative unified by an experience of captivity among Native Americans: Mary Rowlandson's *Soveraignty & Goodness of God* (1682).[2] Under the force of Rowlandson's impressive example, one prominent pattern of critical interpretation has defined the genre in terms of a single narrative formula, built around several key events and characters: a Native American attack on a frontier settlement, the forced journey and consequent introspection of an isolated captive (most often a female), a faceless mass of alien captors, and a return to Anglo-American civilization. According to another prominent pattern of critical interpretation, the captivity narrative furnished uniquely American material for the development of the American novel, especially as represented in the fiction of James Fenimore Cooper, with its myth of cross-cultural brotherhood.

Although scholars have undertaken extensive studies of the American captivity genre, they have not recognized the worldwide scope of British captivity narratives, their place in the English literary tradition, or their impact on their American successors. Nor have scholars recognized the extent to which early British fiction adapted the material of captivity or the varied contribution of the British captivity tradition to the generic evolution of the English novel as a whole. Long before Rowlandson, the British press produced extensive, factual, separately published narratives that were unified by the theme of captivity under a foreign people. Long before Cooper, British novelists adapted and transformed captivity narratives from across the world, developing a broad array of imagined encounters between British characters and various dangerous, exotic, and putatively inferior peoples.

Far from a genre that we can define in terms of any geographical limit, the captivity narrative was an adaptable, expansive genre. Initially the genre expanded by exporting a set of plots and stereotypes that were born in Mediterranean power struggles to a global range of settings. In terms of geographic distribution, the earliest and most significant predecessor for the American setting was the "Orient."[3] Like other early modern forms of Western writing about Eastern lands, the English captivity tradition tended to handle a variety of locations and cultures with the aggressive rhetoric that Edward Said has called "Orientalism."[4] Many early British captivity narratives portrayed North Africa, the Middle East, or southern Asia through a standard set of rhetorical strategies and cultural stereotypes that grew from centuries of religious strife and expanded with Europe's early modern military ascendancy. Throughout the seventeenth and eighteenth centuries, as my first two chapters will show, these strategies and stereotypes migrated from captivity narratives set in the Mediterranean to captivity narratives with more easterly, southerly, and westerly settings, including America. For a little-known setting such as Ceylon or Madagascar, a singular narrative could exert an enormous influence on the scholarship and imagination of Britons at home. Often the captivity narrative's rhetorical appeal lay in its promise of unmediated access to cultures outside the usual run of Western knowledge, but it tended to treat such cultures according to a common set of expectations about foreigners.

In addition to portraying captivity among non-Western peoples, many early modern narratives portrayed British captives confined by other Europeans. Several narratives portrayed captives held in colonial environments by competing European powers. Others portrayed British prisoners of the various Catholic courts of Inquisition. Still others portrayed the experiences of British captives detained by their fellow Britons. One important line of development for this type of narrative was the Protestant martyrology, a narrative form that itself drew heavily from the ancient genre of the saint's life. The most important English martyrology, John Foxe's *Actes and Monuments* (1563), took the form of an extended catalogue, detailing the individuated experiences of various Christian martyrs, beginning with the early history of the church, and concentrating especially on Protestant victims of their fellow Englishmen in the reign of Mary. A more secular subgenre documenting the experiences of Britons captured by Britons arose during the seventeenth and eighteenth centuries, when several texts adopted the personal voices of American indentured servants, the "white slaves" who formed the bedrock of colonial American labor before their replacement by black Africans.[5] All of these varied strands in the captivity tradition relied on the same literary and ideological formulae as British narratives of non-Western captivity; all portrayed the world outside the modern British isles as permeated with subjugation, tyranny, debasement, and transgression.

That this variety of settings and captors exceeds the concept of an "American captivity narrative" is the basis of my title phrase, "British Captivity Narratives." For this study I have chosen to concentrate on texts published initially in the British isles (primarily in London) and organized around the experience of captivity among a foreign people. Thus my title applies not to texts recording experiences of captivity in the British isles, but rather to texts portraying foreign captivity from a metropolitan perspective. I apply the term "British" to texts published well before the 1707 creation of "Great Britain," not because I want to emphasize the place of Irish and Scottish publishing in the creation of the captivity genre, but because I want to emphasize the metropolitan perspective of a tradition that first blossomed in London, as opposed to the creole perspective of the American colonists. The protagonists of these London-based texts returned to Britain after their foreign experiences, received help from British editors who never saw the lands of captivity, and addressed the metropolitan audience of Britain rather than an audience of colonial settlers. My choice of title is guided by both clarity and polemic, since I want to assert the temporal and indeed the logical priority of the British tradition over the American in order to examine how the former influenced the latter as well as the points of divergence between them.

In its range of themes, character types, and rhetorical modes, the British captivity tradition greatly outstrips the abjection and religiosity that scholars have often placed at the heart of the American captivity genre. Whatever its setting, whether New England or Morocco, Ceylon or Madagascar, the captivity narrative was never simply a record of imprisonment. Instead of allowing British captives to waste in dungeons, foreign cultures made them into household servants, family members, gang laborers, or sometimes even government functionaries. As a result of this immersion in a foreign culture, the captive often gained, and certainly claimed, a more intimate experience of the foreign than would a mere jailbird. A captivity narrative would carefully document the abject yet intimate experiences of an isolated European captive and organize these experiences as evidence for the full ethnographic truth about the alien culture of the captors, and about the nature of any cultural interaction on the newly opened global stage. Much of this documentation worked to define non-Western peoples as by nature given to despotism and slavery, while the captive's struggle to escape often defined an inborn liberty within the British people. As British thinkers codified theories of natural rights and the liberal state during the seventeenth and eighteenth centuries, the captivity narrative offered a vehicle for imagining such theories in less abstruse and less incendiary terms. The libertarian individualism of the captive's struggle, furthermore, often seemed to produce concrete economic results. In many a captivity narrative, the isolated protagonist emerged as a man of science, an entrepreneur, or an agent of colonial expansion, a figure of self-consciously modern rationalism whose intellectual skills could turn the abject experiences of foreign captivity to positive account. On the other hand, the captive's heroic potential often seemed to depend on an ability to immerse himself within the alien culture that detained him. In many a narrative, captivity provided a means of exploring both the allures and the perils of culture-crossing, a means of raising and finally rejecting the possibility that captives or other European travelers might abandon civility and redefine themselves within the terms of alien cultures.

The captivity genre's truth claims, heroic paradigms, and cultural tensions became even more complex as metropolitan authors began to fictionalize them. Within the early modern British press, the captivity narrative emerged as a "factual" genre because its authors employed a marked rhetoric of historicity and empirical evidence typical of the era's rapidly changing notions of truthfulness. But even the earliest British examples of the "factual" captivity narrative also revealed a marked tendency towards fictional embellishment. On the other hand, British writers began to introduce episodes of foreign captivity into fictional texts as early as 1665. In the eighteenth century, British authors created a substantial tradition of fictional captivity narratives, texts that mixed the narrative patterns and imagery of the factual accounts with fictional protagonists and plot lines. Experimentation with fictional captivity narratives was especially prominent in the 1720s, a crucial decade for the development of the English novel. Throughout a century when British readers turned first to travel narratives and then also to novels on an unprecedented scale, the specialized subgenre of the captivity narrative was an important conduit for the expansion of both these larger genres. Thus the connection between factual and fictional versions of the captivity experience is much clearer and richer in the British context than in the American.

Based on the transition from factual to fictional captivity narratives, my study argues that the experience of captivity among an allegedly savage or barbarous people posed a fundamental challenge to British concepts of their own national liberty, character, and civility. Captivity was a colonial experience that demanded imaginative revision from Britons at home. One response to this demand was to intensify the captivity narrative's potential as an allegory of freedom, to make the captive into a figure of natural liberty and social oppression in a manner that remains central to Western popular narrative. At the same time, fictional versions of the captivity experience provided a means for eighteenth-century Britons to question and even criticize their rapidly changing relationships with the peoples of the non-European world. While some novels imagined captivity as a crucible for the development of a spectacularly successful colonial heroism, others imagined captivity as a sign of the potential dangers, failures, and iniquities of the colonial project.

In order to analyze the transition from factual to fictional captivity narratives, my study adopts a two-part structure, with the first part devoting three chapters to the factual accounts, and the second part devoting three chapters to the fictions. Chapter 1 follows the emergence of the captivity narrative's generic identity within the London press, tracing the development of varied rhetorical modes for shaping the captivity experience at an aggregate level, the level of titles and organizational patterns. Rather than base the captivity narrative's identity in a foundational text or ideal of generic perfection, this chapter considers the generic flux and epistemological conflicts that resulted as former captives and their editors mixed a set of variable appropriations from other genres. The chapter focuses especially on the captivity narrative's struggle to incorporate two conflicting Western impulses, the first to render personality in terms of abjection, endurance, and salvation, and the second to develop intellectual schema capable of mastering through representation the exotic features of any alien culture. These two divergent impulses led to two incongruous rhetorical modes: the travail narrative, which organizes an individual traveler's experiences as a sequence of abjections, and the ethnographic travel description, which organizes the traveler's observations into a seemingly timeless and impersonal register of an alien space. As my first chapter argues, the captivity experience furnished particularly useful but also particularly troubling and unstable material for both these narrative patterns.

Whereas my first chapter considers the captivity narrative's rhetorical structures at an aggregate level, my second more closely analyzes the content of the local images and events organized within these structures. As Britain gained a wider place on the colonial stage, the captivity genre experimented with a broad and malleable range of methods for representing interactions between captive selves and ruling others. Often the situation of captivity was transformed into an agonistic drama of colonial struggle, and at one level the genre might seem to rest inevitably with an opposition between the captive as isolated Western individualist and the captors as representatives of an amorphous, alien, all-encompassing horde. As my second chapter reveals, a narrative might celebrate a captive's insular resistance to forced proselytism, his transformation into an agent of colonial revenge, or her successful mastery of an alien economy. But many of the captive's heroic behaviors involve some level of participation in an alien culture, and my third chapter turns to a variety of discursive tensions that arise as captives portray their willing or unwilling accommodation within allegedly inferior cultures. The chapter analyzes these tensions primarily through an extensive reading of the narratives of Robert Drury and Thomas Pellow, two of the longest and strangest captivity narratives in the English language. Because these captives spent decades among their captors and attained positions of respect within alien cultures, their narratives throw into particularly sharp relief the captivity genre's inherent tensions between general and particular accounts of experience, between abjection and liberation, between ethnographic aggression and cultural accommodation.

After my first part analyzes tensions within the scientific, individualistic, and colonial ideology of the factual captivity genre, my second part shows how British fictional adaptations sometimes intensified and sometimes disrupted this ideology as they reimagined the captivity experience, linking it to new locations, cultures, and captors, and subjoining episodes of captivity to larger structures of novelistic plotting and social commentary. The second part follows a geographical as well as a thematic plan of organization, so that each chapter concentrates on a particular setting, either the "Orient," America, or sub-Saharan Africa. Each chapter briefly identifies the distinctive features of the factual narratives associated with one of these settings before moving into a fuller account of the fictional narratives that either adapted or resisted those features. For each setting a dominant fictional structure emerged in relation to the dominant mode of British colonial practice in that area. For narratives set in the "Orient," the dominant fictional structure intensified the patterns of plotting and heroism evident in the factual tradition, while for America and sub-Saharan Africa, the dominant fictional structure repressed or criticized the ideological implications of the factual tradition. As I show in chapter 4, "Mastering Captivity," an aggressively handled "Orient" furnished the setting for the first and most popular wave of fictional captivity narratives in English literature, which crested in the 1720s with novels by Penelope Aubin, William Rufus Chetwood, and Eliza Haywood. The first two of these authors produced highly popular male and female versions of self-reliant, adventurous protagonists, who endure slavery in various Middle Eastern lands but then master them mentally, physically, and economically, so that captivity seems to provide an apprenticeship for colonial heroism. In a sharp riposte to this approach, Haywood offered several captivity episodes that reversed her precursors' colonial and sexual ideologies.

My final two chapters turn to novels that further departed from the heroic individualism celebrated within the works of Aubin and Chetwood. After the 1720s British captivity fictions almost always concentrated on the figure of a captive male rather than a captive female, and they depicted him not as a masterful proto-colonist but rather as a passive victim. These fictions, furthermore, often clothed the captive male in a language of emotive sensibility, so that he appeared a man at odds with an aggression that seemed endemic to the colonial landscape, affecting both British colonists and colonized males. This narrative pattern became especially pronounced within the novels that form the basis of chapter 5, "Resisting Americans." There I consider the dominant mode of representing American captivity in British fiction, in novels by such authors as Charlotte Lennox, Henry Mackenzie, and Charlotte Smith. Each of these novels includes an episode that begins by invoking the stereotypical terrors of the factual American tradition but quickly displaces such terrors by focusing on the Native American custom of adopting captives as tribal or family members. From the 1720s to the 1790s, these novels persisted in representing both the failure of Amerindian efforts in cultural conversion and the failure of the adventurous Briton in America. I interpret this emphasis as an ambiguous metropolitan opposition to the colonial project in America, based primarily on fear that the seemingly endemic aggression of the American landscape would transform sensitive British males so that they resembled the land's natives. Although sometimes these novels granted subjective depth to the colonized, they concentrated more thoroughly on recommending British withdrawal from what they represented as a debasing outside world. Through this character and plot structure, eighteenth-century British novelists produced a myth of American cultural interaction that represents nearly a direct opposite to Cooper's influential American myth of cross-cultural brotherhood.

Of all the varied metropolitan responses to the material of captivity, the most paradoxical occurred in three novels that mix African captivity and utopia, by Simon Berington, Robert Paltock, and George Cumberland. My sixth chapter, "Utopian Captivities," investigates how the widely divergent mixtures of captivity and utopia developed in these works produce widely divergent visions of the interaction between Enlightenment and non-European cultures. Each novel includes an early episode of African captivity that leads to a European protagonist's discovery or formation of a perfect polity. Each novel, moreover, frames this narrative structure through a rhetoric of paradox, treating captivity as a metonym for a personal discipline of self-restraint that enables psychological and political perfection. But if these novels celebrate similar versions of the personal enlightenment conferred by captivity, they develop very different visions of the relationship between enlightenment and colonialism. Paltock's protagonist uses what his novel represents as African ideals in order to build an idealized colony on a fictional south seas island, involving a total material and intellectual transformation of the colonized to British cultural ideals. The other two works set enlightened utopias south of the Sahara in order to develop a critique of British culture and politics that extends even to the point of imagining an "African" colonial project in Europe. In each case the satiric theme of an African influence on European culture extends a broader paradoxical potential that is always inherent in the captivity plot.

This intensive experimentation within British fictions of colonial captivity reflects not only the varied settings and approaches of British colonialism nor only the various attitudes of metropolitan Britons to the activities of their colonial counterparts. The variation within British captivity fictions also represents an imaginative outgrowth of the unstable, contradictory, and hybrid character of the factual captivity genre. For the captivity narrative was a genre that based its protagonist's status as author and hero on an experience of alienation and abjection, and it reinforced the captive's unstable authority through an aggressive, and somewhat chaotic, assimilation of materials from other genres. We can gain a better understanding of the captivity genre's flexibility, ambiguity, and ideological impact by moving beyond restrictive definitions built on notions of American experience and identity, by tracing the British captivity tradition through all of its settings and back to its earliest single-text exemplars, and by exploring the rhetorical and ideological variation that marks the genre from its inception. Through this broader focus, we can develop a more effective analysis of the fundamental tensions within the captivity genre, produced as their authors tried to harness a particularized experience of abjection for ethnographic and nationalist purposes. As these tensions reveal, the captivity narrative is more properly conceived as a genre that belongs to the troubled emergence of a particular political disposition, liberal individualism, and a particular intellectual disposition, philosophical modernism, than as a genre that belongs to any particular nation of origin. For British readers and writers of the seventeenth and eighteenth centuries, the captive provided an early and vivid model for the modern individual, freely born yet self-actualizing, subject to an alien-seeming society and perhaps made abject by it, yet capable of mastering its complexities through the modern intellectual schema of science, and capable of turning an alienated experience of cultural abjection to personal and national triumph.

PART I

Narratives of Fact

ONE

Travel, Travail, and the British Captivity Tradition

In 1567, according to the narrative that bears his name, Job Hortop's quiet life as a powder maker ended when English seamen pressed him to join what would later become known as one of the great Elizabethan voyages of trade and plunder, led by John Hawkins and Francis Drake. The 1590 text that records Hortop's experiences follows the voyage from Africa to America, as the Englishmen weather storms, seize the ships of other European powers, pursue trade and slavery in Africa, and finally raid some strongholds on the Spanish main. But this account of English glory comes to an end when a difficult battle isolates Hawkins's ship and leaves the crew hungry, forcing him to strand Hortop and nearly one hundred other volunteers on the Mexican shore. After a brief, violent encounter with some Amerindians, the stranded Englishmen reach a Spanish settlement, where they receive food and lodging but are later forced "to carde wooll among the Indian slaves, which drudgery [they] disdained, and concluded to beat [their] maisters."[1] Thus begins for Hortop a series of subjugations, accommodations, and rebellions among a variety of Spanish authorities. First he spends two years in a Mexican prison. Then, on a transport ship back to Europe, he briefly inspires the captain's favor before an escape attempt lands him in the stockades. In Seville he spends one year in prison before escaping, but after recapture he spends another year moldering in an inquisitorial prison, then twelve years rowing a Spanish galley, and finally four years wearing a "cote with S. Andrews crosse" in the "everlasting prison remedilesse" (28–30). He eludes this final pit of extreme degradation through three years' service as a "drudge" for a Spanish official, and the increased liberty of this service enables him to sneak aboard a Dutch ship and return home to England.

This highly varied and highly ambiguous text foregrounds a number of important problems affecting our recognition of the first English captivity narratives. The most obvious problem is that scholars have sometimes erroneously identified this text as the first account of an Englishman in American captivity, apparently through an interpretive inflation of what Hortop describes as the crew's "robbery" at the hands of native Mexicans.[2] If the dedication intimates that Hortop and the other volunteers "were constrained to be set on shore . . . amongst the wilde Indians" (A2r), the text makes clear that the force behind this constraint was not the Indians, but the ship's empty larder and Hawkins's decision to abandon his men. Although the natives kill some of the stranded Englishmen and steal their clothing, this narrative sequence includes no details or even intimations of forced detention. Far from capturing the Englishmen, the natives give them directions to the nearest Spanish settlement. Once the Englishmen meet the Spanish, however, Hortop documents his experience as an extended captivity narrative, a sequence of events dominated by images of bodily suffering, occasional instances of comfort or accommodation, and constant efforts to escape. His experiences in a variety of Spanish prisons include many motifs that will later stand as hallmarks of the captivity narrative, whether British or American. He must resist efforts in proselytism, endure the humiliating ritual of an inquisitorial auto da fe, and suffer the rigors of forced labor in what Europeans regarded as one of its most terrible instances, rowing a galley. This portion of his narrative pays especially close attention to details of close quarters, poor clothing and bedding, "hunger, thirst, cold, and stripes" (29). Contact with the Spanish, far more readily than contact with Native Americans, furnished the material of the captivity narrative at this early stage of its development.

But if the label of captivity narrative seems appropriate for some portions of Hortop's work, the text as a whole is framed according to very different generic formulae, those of the travail narrative. Typical of much travel writing in the early modern period, but especially important in popular chapbooks such as the Hortop narrative, these formulae sit somewhere between our modern conceptions of the separate genres of travel narrative and captivity narrative. Both the generic imprint and the generic ambiguity of the travail narrative are evident in Hortop's title: *The Trauailes of an English Man, Containing His Svndrie Calamities Indured by the Space of Twentie and Odd Yeres in His Absence from His Natiue Countrie; Wherein Is Truly Decyphered the Sundrie Shapes of Wilde Beasts, Birds, Fishes, Foules, Rootes, Plants, &C. With the Description of a Man That Appeared in the Sea, and*

Also of a Huge Giant Brought from China to the King of Spaine. As the primary generic signal, the word "travail" carried a double meaning, suggesting both the painful labor and the curious adventure of journeys far from home. The word neatly encapsulates the tension that lies at the heart of this particular narrative, as it simultaneously promotes national pride and commiseration in the traveler's experiences. On the one hand, in keeping with the title's promises, the text includes much detailed description of alien flora, fauna, and cultural items within its autobiographical framework. To the eyes of twentieth-century readers, these descriptions range from the familiar to the fanciful, from plantains to sea monsters. Advertising itself partially on the basis of such curiosities, organized as autobiographical proof that an Englishman had experienced them, and set within the context of English maritime expansion, the text promotes national pride in the experiential capacities of a single English seaman.

But within this narrative, as in the "travail" narrative more generally, the explicit appeal and implicit pride of the traveler's experience extend from his discoveries to his tribulations. Hortop opens his narrative by framing his experiences as proof of the fallen, miserable state of humanity, "that man beeing borne of a woman, living but a short time, is replenished with many miseries," a theological position that he learned to accept "by experience in myselfe, as this present Treatise insuing shall shew" (A3r). Illustrating this proposition throughout this tersely phrased narrative, Hortop's positivist identifications of charming curiosities alternate with positivist descriptions of abjection and confinement. Within a single sentence, for example, he describes two years of imprisonment in Mexico and a giant skeleton sent as a gift from China to Spain (23). If the text introduces the wonders observed by Hortop rather haphazardly within its loose autobiographical structure, it turns to more formal documentary strategies in treating his imprisonments. His narrative closes with a schematic "Computation of my imprisonment," a chart tallying the years he spent in various prisons (30–31). Hortop's text thus seeks a high ranking in the scale of travail literature by formalizing its narrative "account" of an overwhelmingly lengthy and far-flung series of captive "travails." Within this tally of imprisonments, Hortop's encounter with the Native Americans does merit inclusion, but only under the heading of "robbery." Even so, the radically inclusive drive of the travail narrative easily assimilates a violent encounter with Native Americans amidst its vision of global misfortunes and curiosities. The English narrative of American captivity, to the extent that it can be described as a separate genre at all, initially emerges as a curious addition within a narrative system focused on Mediterranean travails.

As the Hortop narrative reveals in a particularly telling manner, the quest for a uniquely American captivity narrative has led scholars to obscure the global range of settings evident within the earliest British captivity narratives. But the Hortop narrative is also important for highlighting other important features of the captivity narrative that scholarship on the American tradition has tended to obscure, most notably the genre's wide-ranging mixture of rhetorical conventions. On the rare occasions when scholars have discussed accounts of captivity published primarily or exclusively in Britain, they have tended to assimilate such material to what is often described as a fundamental structural unity within the American genre, typified by such famous accounts as Mary Rowlandson's. In order to reverse this tendency, the current and following chapters focus on the fundamental variety of the previously established British tradition, interpreting the American material as a branch, rather than the central root, within this tradition. Part of this effort involves locating the captivity narrative's roots in generic features, such as titling conventions, that were originally established in the British press. Instead of replacing an American unity with a British one, these chapters will locate the genre's roots in a broad range of rhetorical strategies for negotiating an oppositional experience in any foreign land. Thus these chapters will resist the notion of an American captivity genre not only by turning to captivity narratives set in a broader geographical context, but also by arguing that this context calls for a more flexible definition of the captivity genre. As we shall see, the genre's varied rhetorical strategies often mingled in uneasy juxtaposition rather than in perfect harmony. At bottom, the captivity narrative incorporated a number of discursive conflicts reflecting its involvement in several large-scale, gradual, discordant transformations in the early modern intellectual climate, including the rise of liberal individualism, the creation of a scientific ethnography, and Western Europe's increased intervention into the affairs of foreign peoples. As the current chapter will show, the most important of these conflicts involved a mismatch between the captive's personal narration of abject experience and his intellectual mastery of an alien culture.

The captivity genre places a premium on empirical inclusiveness, on capturing a broad range of experience, everything that the captive can remember, everything he or she witnessed or heard reported from other captives, and further, on shaping that material as the full truth about an alien, allegedly archaic people. From the late medieval period through the eighteenth century, captivity narratives provided increasingly detailed and influential sources for Western knowledge of alien cultures. From the late sixteenth to the early eighteenth century, with the steady expansion of British colonialism, captivity narratives attained a prominent place in English writing on the foreign. Such narratives offer a crucial point for understanding enlightenment strategies of representing the allegedly savage on the eve of their systematic implementation within the burgeoning science of anthropology. Many of these narratives employed the lists, hierarchies, and other discursive schema of travel description, and these schema enabled the development of detailed portraits of alien cultures as tyrannical, barbaric, and superstitious foils for the modernity of Western civilization.

In these early efforts to develop systematic forms of cultural description and evaluation, however, British captivity narratives ultimately prove far more ambivalent than systematic, revealing fundamental instabilities within enlightenment strategies for documenting the alien. Published from the early years of British expansion, such narratives offer an early and particularly vivid register of the fundamental conflicts of articulation and authority that Homi K. Bhabha has associated with colonialist discourse in general.[3] The captivity genre's most basic epistemological conflict stems from its claim to mount a generalized cultural description on the experience of a single captive. Even if a captive does not explicitly undermine this epistemological equation by suggesting that his experience ran counter to the ethnographic norm, the extreme violence and strangeness of the captivity experience tends to weaken its potential for dispassionate empiricism. Within the advertising and presentational frameworks of titles and prefatory material, captivity narratives often stress the uniqueness of the captive's experience and its general ethnographic utility in the same breath. As a result of such conflicts, many narratives resort to complex mechanisms of extratextual authority, such as certifications of the captive's truthfulness, carefully documented editorial frameworks, and citations of parallel reports from competing ethnographic accounts.

Including reports from other witnesses forms one element within a broader pattern of restless inclusiveness that marks the captivity narrative's anxious struggles for sales and cultural authority. If we examine captivity narratives set across the globe, the genre reveals both the multiple generic borrowings and the multiple narrative voices that Bakhtin has associated with the novel. As a recent overview of the American narratives has acknowledged, "more often than not the individual captivity narrative constitutes an amalgamation of voices and input, each with its own agenda and design."[4] Even more extravagantly inclusive than the American texts, English narratives set in other locations often turn to the generic formulae of the sea journal, the spiritual autobiography, political history, and even, in one case, the picaresque novel. Although some texts rely on first-person narration exclusively, others turn to omnibus narrative structures incorporating multiple autobiographical voices, plural first-person voices, and shifts between first- and third-person narration. The captivity genre's claims to ethnographic truth thus sit within an uneasy juxtaposition of multiple voices and multiple discursive modes, which blur the boundaries between fact and fiction, and between general and personal accounts of experience.

In tracing the formal outlines and naming conventions of the captivity genre, we must begin with texts produced before the expansion of European colonial power, even before Columbus's journey to America. Before the westernmost European cultures produced narratives of captivity in foreign lands, the genre's earliest exemplars came from the pens of central Europeans. These narratives, moreover, resulted not from European colonial expansion but from the early modern spread of Islamic power within eastern Europe, an advance that culminated with the first siege of Vienna in 1529. A particularly early and widely distributed account was that of the Bavarian Johan Schiltberger, whose 1396 capture led to twenty years of travel in Europe, Asia, and Africa before his return produced a narrative that crossed the face of Europe in a dozen editions and countless manuscripts during the fifteenth and sixteenth centuries.[5] Another international best-seller was the account of Bartholomew Georgijevic, first published in 1544 and republished in eighteen subsequent editions, including translations into German, French, Dutch, Polish, and English.[6] In addition to these central Europeans, Italians, Frenchmen, and Englishmen began to produce accounts of Islamic captivity with the increased power of the Turkish navy and the Mediterranean corsairs throughout the sixteenth and seventeenth centuries.

The early continental narratives employed a variety of naming conventions, but from the sixteenth century they increasingly relied on terms such as "captive," "slavery," and "customs." While the generic imprint of Schiltberger's title was carried by the keyword *Reisen*, or travels, Georgijevic's account appeared in English as *The Ofspring of the House of Ottomanno, . . . Whereunto is added Bartholomeus Georgieuiz Epitome, of the Customes, Rytes, Ceremonies, and Religion of the Turkes: with the Miserbale Affliction of those Christians, whiche Liue vnder their Captiuitie and Bondage.* A similarly generalized ethnographic focus was also paramount in such titles as George of Hungary's *Tractatus de Moribus Turcorum*, which resulted from his 1438 capture, and in G.A. Menavino's *Trattato de Costume et Vita di Turchi*, printed in 1548.[7] On the other hand, the experience of captivity itself dominated the title of Alfonso de Dominici's *Trattato della miserie, che patiscono I fideli christiani shiavi de' Barbari . . .* (Rome, 1647), and the experience of a particular captive came to the fore in the anonymous *L'Esclave religieux et ses avantures* (Paris, 1690). As the shifting patterns of these titles suggest, the early modern era witnessed both a long-standing tendency to exploit the captive's knowledge of alien cultures and a steadily increasing interest in the experience of captivity itself, culminating with the production of an individuated title at the end of the century.

During the same period, a similarly gradual movement from generalized accounts of captivity to the perspective of a single captive is also evident in another important element within the captivity tradition: a genre recording the experiences of inquisitorial martyrs and captives. Such narratives played a prominent role in Protestant propaganda directed against the various Catholic courts of inquisition from the sixteenth through the nineteenth century. Out of the very different courts operating in various eras and cultures of southern Europe, Protestant polemic imagined a monolithic Inquisition as the ultimate seat of European tyranny, injustice, and torture, the product of a Popish master plot designed to impose a tyrannical ecclesiastic authority on the states and consciousnesses of Europe.[8] In promoting this myth, British propagandists relied at first on translation and plagiarism of continental histories and martyrologies focused on continental victims. From the mid seventeenth to the late eighteenth century, however, Anglo-American propaganda increasingly relied on lengthy, particularized narratives focused exclusively on the experiences of individual, isolated Britons, such as Katharine Evans and Sarah Chevers (1662), Isaac Martin (1724), and John Coustos (1746). Each of their texts builds an extensive personal narrative from experiences of capture, interrogation, and torture within an inquisitorial court, represented as an alien space, illustrative of a broader cultural division between Britain and southern Europe. This kind of tension between general truth and individual experience, as we shall see, posed a problem for the British captivity tradition from its inception.

Drawing primarily on Middle Eastern and inquisitorial settings, the first flurry of factual English captivity narratives initially developed, at the close of the sixteenth century, in the form of particularly telling episodes within longer travail narratives such as Hortop's. Organized primarily as a travail narrative, the first factual English captivity narrative, produced by an English author and focused exclusively on the experiences of Englishmen held captive in a foreign land, concerned not America but the Barbary Coast. First published in 1587, this twenty-four page chapbook introduced autobiographical and ethnographic data primarily in order to document a generalized experience of travel misery, as indicated by the title: *A True Discription and Breefe Discourse, of a Most Lamentable Voiage, Made Latelie to Tripolie in Barbarie, in a Ship Named the Iesus: VVherin Is Not Onely Shevved the*

Great Miserie, That Then Happened the Aucthor Hereof and His Whole Companie, Aswell the Marchants as the Marriners in That Voiage, According to the Curssed Custome of Those Barbarous and Cruell Tyrants, in Their Terrible Vsage of Christian Captiues: But Also, the Great Vnfaithfulnesse of Those Heathnish Infidels, in Not Regarding Their Promise. Together, with the Most Wonderfull Iudgement of God, vpon the King of Tripolie and His Sonne, and a Great Number of His People, Being All the Tormentors of Those English Captiues. Set Foorth by Thomas Saunders, One of Those Captiues There at the Same Time. Although the title initially places the work within the genre of voyage narrative, the repetition of "captive" rather clearly marks the importance of captivity to the publication's conception, purpose, and advertising.

Despite the title's promise of eyewitness testimony, Saunders himself seems largely absent from the text, which concentrates on the sufferings of the crew in general and on the key historical figures whose actions lead to the drama of captivity. The text begins according to the framework of a voyage narrative, with an account of the ship's financing and construction, its departure from Portsmouth, and its journey to Tripoli. Once there, an English trader incites the wrath of a local monarch, who offers a reward to his slaves for taking the ship and thus ultimately inspires a Spanish captive to capture the Englishmen. When the Spaniard's reward evaporates and the king returns him to prison, the narrative cites these events as evidence for cultural opposition, as details "whereby may appeare the regard that a Turke or Infidell hath of his word."[9] In describing the suffering of Saunders and several companions as galley slaves, the narrative initiates what will soon become a standard pattern within the captivity genre. Like many of its successors, the Saunders text provides details of sordid accommodations, paltry food, abject labor, and harsh punishments for trivial offenses, although in this case these details concern several sufferers rather than a singular, isolated protagonist. The narrative closes with the galley's capture by European ships, and with examples of providential punishments meted out to the king in particular and to Tripoli in general. Through its generalized narrative perspective, the captivity genre's earliest exemplar thus initiated several rhetorical patterns that would remain important for its successors. In addition to devoting careful attention to the details of captive abjection, the Saunders text also took care to organize its material as evidence for a general contest, sanctioned by providence, between Western and Oriental cultures.

During the century following the *Iesus* text, the English narrative of factual captivity was a London publishing phenomenon, focused on merchants and seamen who traveled to Mediterranean and Oriental settings, and advertised by titles that oscillated among the closely associated concepts of adventure, travail, captivity, and slavery. The Saunders narrative preceded a handful of similar chapbooks, including the Hortop account and other works set within the context of Mediterranean shipping. In 1614, for example, appeared *A Trve Relation of the Travailes and Most Miserable Captiuitie of William Dauies,* a work exhibiting not only a particularly early use of "captivity" within the generic imprimatur of the main-title, but also a close equation between the abstract concepts "travaile" and "captivity." It is difficult to assess the cultural impact of such early chapbook captivities, and we cannot know how many chapbook editions and titles have disappeared into the dustbin of history. Still, chapbook narratives such as Hortop's often achieved wide cultural distribution through reprinting in the massive and enormously influential anthologies of travel writing published by Richard Hakluyt in 1589 and Samuel Purchas in 1613.[10] Other early English captivity narratives appeared as brief episodes within longer texts focused on travel or history. Six years after John Smith's *Generall Historie of Virginia* portrayed his now famous American captivity and rescue by Pocahontas, his 1630 *True Travels* included a section focused on *How He Was Taken Prisoner by the Turks, Sold For a Slave.* The title of Smith's "Oriental" work advertised the experience of captivity whereas the title of the American text, often cited by scholars for its early captivity episode, did not mention the subject.

Thus the titling convention of the English captivity narrative emerged within the London press around the turn of the seventeenth century. Not only did the early modern captivity texts rely on title keywords such as "captive" and "captivity," but they also established the convention of highlighting the specific, named identity of the captive, as well as his tie to the English nation and even to a local region. The importance of nation is evident in Hortop's main title, *The Trauailes of an English man,* as well as in a 1590 main title, *The Rare and Most VVonderfull Things vvhich Edvv. VVebbe an Englishman Borne, hath Seene and Passed in his Troublesome Trauailes.* An emphasis on local identity is evident in the 1595 title, *Strange and Wonderfull Things. Happened to Richard Hasleton, Borne at Braintree in Essex, in His Ten Yeares Trauailes in Many Forraine Countries.* Such individuated titles rather clearly promoted pride in the experiences of ordinary, representative Englishmen. The name or national identity of the individual captive quickly became so important for the genre's titling convention as to help separate it from other kinds of travel narrative. Whereas the titles of travel narratives more generally tended to focus on the identity of the observed land, captivity titles gave equal if not greater weight to the national and individual identity of the isolated captive-observer. The cumulative effect of this convention can be measured in the parlance of scholars who work on the American narratives, which are usually distinguished by the captives' last names.[11]

After the titling conventions of the captivity narrative took root in the London press over the course of the seventeenth century, the American press did not initially recognize these conventions when it began printing texts focused on local experiences of captivity at the end of the century. Instead American printers adopted titles invoking sectarian theology; thus the Rowlandson account, in its first Boston edition, appeared under the main title, *The Soveraignty & Goodness of God*. When British publishers printed versions of narratives that had previously appeared in America, they chose titles that more clearly placed the texts within the genre of captivity. The most famous instance of such adaptation was the Rowlandson account, which in its first London printing carried the title *A True History of the Captivity & Restoration*. When American printers began to reprint this narrative in the last quarter of the eighteenth century, they returned to the titling convention established in the British press.[12] The various titles of Elizabeth Hanson's account underwent a similar evolution. Whereas the original 1728 and 1754 American editions were named *God's Mercy Surmounting Man's Cruelty*, a different version of her experience appeared in several British editions beginning in 1760, under the main title, *An Account of the Captivity*. In this latter version and with this latter title, Hanson's narrative gained its widest distribution in an American anthology of the nineteenth century, entering the canon of American literature after a generic reformulation in the British press. That we now describe the Rowlandson and Hanson texts as captivity narratives indicates that we have come to accept the generic assessment of the British publishers, who recognized the affinity of these accounts with a previously established genre focused on captivities in other lands.

But the British captivity tradition's precedence over the American one is not simply a matter of titling conventions. Compared to early modern captivity texts set in North America, British captivity narratives set in other lands commanded not only greater priority but also greater length, broader production and distribution, a more consistent generic identity, and a larger impact on metropolitan culture. In the middle decades of the seventeenth century, just prior to the publication of the Rowlandson narrative in 1682, the British captivity narrative began to grow beyond the confines of the episode and the chapbook, reaching lengths that enabled the genre to stand on its own, separated from other kinds of narrative within a text focused exclusively on one person's single experience of captivity in a foreign land. In 1640 appeared Francis Knight's fifty-six page *Relation of Seaven Yeares Slaverie under the Turkes of Argeire, suffered by an English Captive Merchant*. . . .

Over 250 pages were needed for the 1670 printing of *The Adventures of (Mr T.S.) an English Merchant, Taken Prisoner by the Turks of Argiers,* while William Okeley's narrative of Algerian slavery, which borrowed several conventions from spiritual autobiography, carried over one hundred pages in its 1675 and 1676 printings. Another high-water mark was reached with Robert Knox's *An Historical Relation of the Island Ceylon,* based on the author's twenty years of captivity in that island. Published in 1681, the year before the Rowlandson narrative, Knox's work exceeded two hundred folio pages, and it stands as the longest and, as we shall see, the most ethnographically ambitious captivity narrative of the seventeenth century. During the century from 1640 to 1740, captivity narratives produced in Britain greatly expanded in length and complexity, while texts produced in America generally lagged behind in terms of detail, structural refinement, and subjective exploration. Only in the mid eighteenth century did the American narratives surpass their British counterparts in terms of quantity, and only in the nineteenth century did the Americans match the British in terms of length and complexity. Until then, no American narrative matched the length of the narratives by Joseph Pitts (283 pages on Algeria in 1738), Thomas Pellow (396 pages on Morocco in 1739), and Robert Drury (480 pages on Madagascar in 1729).[13] Until well into the eighteenth century, British readers would have regarded American captivity narratives as faint, distant echoes of more substantial pronouncements from British authors concerning other lands.

It might be objected that the variety of British captivity texts does not constitute a coherent tradition or genre but rather a collection of disparate threads within the larger generic cloth of travel narratives. This objection, however, applies equally to American captivity texts, at least prior to the war for independence. Scholars of the American genre often trace its tradition back even to the early days of Spanish exploration and settlement, but the American captivity narrative did not acquire its own generic identity until after independence. From that period the American press saw a fairly regular stream of reprints and new compositions, and from that period a set of narrative conventions driven by expansionist ideology and heightened editorial supervision streamlined the production of individual texts, especially through the medium of anthologies. Before the war for independence, however, American captivity narratives, just like their British predecessors, entered the press in a random, piecemeal, and inconsistent manner. Some American narratives appeared as anecdotes within sermons or jeremiads, while others, such as John Smith's famous account of captivity and rescue by Pocahontas, appeared within general histories, travel narratives, and autobiographies. Only a few, like the Rowlandson account, appeared as individual texts, with a specific generic identity, and even her text, in its initial printing, was combined with a sermon by her husband. Some captivity narratives set in America appeared in the British press but not in the American, while others entered the American press but not the British, and still others appeared on both shores. In gathering these disparate narrative strands under a single rubric, scholars sometimes throw early Spanish and French texts into the mix.[14] If scholars prove willing to grant the genre an international linguistic framework as long as the setting is America, they prove unwilling to acknowledge the global framework of settings that the evidence demands. In reality, the varied strands that compose the colonial American genre of the captivity narrative fail to match the consistency of earlier captivity texts published in Britain.

Several factors have prevented us from recognizing the British predecessors and parallels to the American captivity narratives. One factor is simply that scholars have put more effort into separating American captivity narratives from larger generic categories such as travel narrative. As a subset of this larger category, however, American narratives were no more prominent than British narratives until the nineteenth century. The study that scholars use as the standard bibliography of colonial American captivities, R.W.G. Vail's *Voice of the Old Frontier*, actually documents only a smattering of them amidst a much larger number of travel narratives set in America and published on both sides of the Atlantic. The ratio of captivity narratives to travel narratives is perhaps somewhat larger in the American publishing world than in the British, but in both cases the percentage is so low as to make the difference negligible. The work of separating British captivity narratives from other genres is no more difficult than that needed for the American texts. In both contexts, short accounts of captivity sometimes appeared within longer texts framed according to very different agendas, such as Cotton Mather's *Magnalia Christiana* or Adam Elliot's *Modest Vindication of Titus Oates*. Even when publishing texts focused exclusively on captivity, authors and editors in both contexts sometimes chose main titles invoking frameworks other than captivity, such as Mary Rowlandson's *Soveraignty & Goodness of God* or Robert Drury's *Madagascar*. Since these issues arise with both publishing traditions, it is less intrinsic difficulties than scholarly priorities that keep us from recognizing the British texts as captivity narratives.

Another factor blocking scholarly recognition of the British captivity tradition is a scholarly penchant for exaggerating the impact within the British press of captivity accounts originally published in the thirteen colonies, especially the Rowlandson narrative. Exaggerated descriptions of avid British readership create the impression that American captivity offered Britons something that they could not find in texts treating other colonial lands. In a fairly typical case of such exaggeration, Nancy Armstrong and Leonard Tennenhouse have described Rowlandson's text as "without question one of the most popular captivity narratives on both sides of the Atlantic."[15] In reality, however, her narrative's only entry into the British press before the twentieth century was the London edition of 1682, and the most thorough study of her early editions interprets this fact as evidence that the reading public "apparently was not overly receptive in England."[16] Many American bestsellers of the eighteenth century, moreover, such as John Williams's narrative and the Manheim anthology, never interested the British press at all.

Rather than import texts previously published in America, the British press, when it turned to the topic of American captivity, tended to concentrate on producing its own, original, domestic narratives. Not only did these narratives usually reflect the American experience of protagonists resident in Britain at the time of publication, but they also often reflected a British social, political, and conceptual perspective. Because of this perspective, narratives that originally appeared in Britain tended to interest American printers, if at all, only after the war for independence. The autobiographical perspective of Henry Grace's *History of the Life and Sufferings,* for example, earned two printings in Reading during 1764 and 1765 but never reached the American press until Garland's 1977 series of facsimiles. Instead of flowing from America to Britain, some of the most popular captivities with American settings originated in the British press and then migrated to America. Of the three narratives that Vail calls the "most popular stories of Indian captivity," two produced sensations in the British press long before they inspired American printings.[17] From a British perspective, the domestic best-seller of American captivity was Peter Williamson's narrative, first published in 1757 under the title *French and Indian Cruelty.* Assessed by Vail as "the most popular of all Indian captivities," with a grand total of forty-one printings, this narrative earned a dozen British printings and plagiarisms during the eighteenth century, before American printers quietly joined the flood of British reprints at the turn of the nineteenth century.[18] Williamson framed his text largely within the contexts of local Scottish politics, British law, and the cross-Atlantic concerns of an Anglo-American empire. Despite his British frame and publishing success, American editors and scholars have often plagiarized his narrative, trimmed it, retold it, and placed it under the rubric of the American captivity genre, so that it seems to stand as a record of American experience.[19] The Williamson text is a particularly telling example of how the broad rubric of "American captivity" hampers our recognition of the British captivity tradition by reframing texts that initially reflected a British metropolitan perspective so that they reflect the crucible of American experience.

While concentrating on domestically framed accounts of American captivity, the British press only rarely turned to accounts first published in America. The most prominent exceptions, the Quaker narratives of Elizabeth Hanson and Jonathan Dickinson, only prove the rule of broader separation. While the former was reprinted in four British pamphlets from 1760 to 1791, the latter was the true cross-Atlantic best-seller of American captivity during the eighteenth century, with nearly a dozen British printings and retellings beginning in 1699. But the frequent appearance of both texts in the British press reflects a broader mobility within the cross-Atlantic world of Quaker publishing more than the particular mobility of individual captivity texts. With only such occasional exceptions, then, the American and British presses produced separate threads within the weave of captivity narratives set in America. Even the publishing record of the "American captivity narrative" militates against its definition as an American genre and instead reveals its emergence as a cross-Atlantic publishing phenomenon.

By the time of the Rowlandson publication in 1682, the British press had already established the generic identity of the captivity narrative. The genre's conventions emerged not through the influence of a particular foundational text, whether of British or American origin, but rather through an evolutionary process in which a wide range of texts borrowed, isolated, and transformed key elements from earlier genres. In the Anglophone print world of the 1670s, the captivity experience no longer simply added lively episodes to general histories, travel narratives, and martyrologies. Instead British printers and pundits saw great potential in isolating the experience of captivity in a foreign land as the central focus of a text, and they signaled this focus through title keywords that highlighted confinement and identified the names of individual protagonists and foreign lands. But if this unification around the experience of captivity provides a baseline for defining the captivity genre, we should not make this unification overly restrictive by insisting on a definition of the genre in terms of a single protagonist held captive within a single foreign land. Such a definition cannot encompass Job Hortop's narrative, which achieves closure by gathering his captivities in a variety of settings within a unifying tally. Such a definition also fails for the Saunders narrative, which focuses on the experience of a group in captivity. These early chapbook narratives, moreover, do not represent final moments of multiplication within a genre that was afterwards uniformly individuated. Despite a marked tendency towards individuated narrative, the basic notion of the captivity narrative permitted a wide latitude for including not only a variety of foreign lands, but also a multiplicity of captive voices, speaking in a variety of rhetorical modes.

Recognition of the broader generic context underlying the Anglophone captivity narrative requires abandoning one of the central tenets of the literary scholarship that has evolved in relation to the "American captivity narrative." In claiming an American center for the genre, literary scholars have created an exaggerated impression of its structural unity, centered on the experience of Anglo-American settlers. As early as 1943, Phillips D. Carleton's first self-consciously literary treatment of the American texts insisted that they carried an essential "uniformity" of style and structure, based especially on several standard events: an Amerindian attack on an English settlement, a capture, a journey away from the settlement, an escape or release, and finally a return to the settlement. In an explicit response to Carleton, Roy Harvey Pearce declared only a few years later that the genre carried several "significances" that varied widely according to the time and purpose of publication.[20] Despite Pearce's caveat, and sometimes explicitly rejecting it, the most influential treatments of the genre have continued to stress its structural unity. One of the most influential has been a mythic reading of the genre, initiated by Richard VanDerBeets and developed most thoroughly by Richard Slotkin, whose *Regeneration through Violence* interprets the unified structure as an archetypal expression of heroic transformation with peculiar significance for American identity. More recently, in Kathryn Derounian-Stodola and James Levernier's 1993 study of the genre, although the authors cover an unusual variety of textual examples, they still agree with Carleton that, "not only did the content of captivity narratives provide unity, but their standard formal elements of attack, capture, and escape or return also gave them coherence and definition as a group."[21]

Scholarly insistence on the unity of the American texts helps to transform the captivity narrative into an American literary genre, with an American consistency, a precise origin in a particular text and a particular cultural moment, and a unique place in the global literary archive. Defining the genre in terms of the standard formal elements of attack, capture, and return is a way of insisting on the preeminence of the Rowlandson narrative, female captives in general, and the American pattern of large-scale agricultural settlement. The American settlement pattern, much more than other early colonial ventures, provoked sudden, random raids on colonial households, and thus contributed to the narrative formulation of these attacks as the sudden incursion of a random external savagery into the ordered interior frame of domesticity. An impression of sudden external violation is particularly marked in the vivid opening lines of the Rowlandson account: "On the tenth of February 1675 came the Indians with great numbers upon Lancaster. Their first coming was about sunrising. Hearing the noise of guns, we looked out; several houses were burning and the smoke ascending to heaven. There were five persons taken in one house; the father and the mother and a suckling child they knocked on the head; the other two they took and carried away alive."[22] Quoted repeatedly from one study of American captivity to another, these terse, compelling lines have come to define the initial context of the captivity plot in terms of a native attack. More broadly, the continued critical and popular appeal of the Rowlandson text lies partially in its relative unity vis-à-vis other captivity narratives, as it concentrates more tersely, rigorously, and exclusively on her personal suffering.

In defining the captivity narrative's structural unity, scholars tend to treat the early Puritan accounts, especially that of Rowlandson, as models of aesthetic or generic purity from which the vast panoply of disunified American followers has degenerated. A fairly standard chronology of the American texts appears in Richard VanDerBeets's introduction to his anthology of them, where he describes "an all-important sense of authentically human experience that characterizes the earlier, genuine captivities," before the increasing sensationalism and propaganda of late eighteenth-century accounts led to excessive "stylistic embellishment," an "infusion of melodrama and sensibility," and the production of sentimental fiction, a development that "culminates . . . in the travesty of the penny dreadful."[23] In this view as in many others, the humanistic literary potential of the American texts is most fully represented in their original, Puritan exemplars, while the discursive variety of the later accounts is dismissed as alien to the genre's defining qualities, even if such variety eventually becomes predominant.

Because such assessments often take Rowlandson as their standard, the textual power and authorial context of her account have in many ways distorted the broader literary history of the captivity narrative. In many literary histories, her narrative engrosses a chapter of interpretation that establishes the core features and standards of the captivity genre, so that the more briefly handled narratives written by later authors come to stand as digressions, degradations, and failures. Moreover, because her narrative builds an impression of unity through rigorous application of a providential interpretive framework, this framework can seem to provide the conceptual ground on which the genre rests. Conceived in this way, the captivity genre can offer material even for a historian of religion, Gary Ebersole, whose recent book on the genre treats it as a secular dilution of an initial sacred impulse housed most purely and transparently in Rowlandson.[24] If we consider captivity narratives from a global range of settings, we can observe not only that many narratives invoke the providential interpretive framework of British Protestantism, but also that the genre emerges amidst the competition between this framework and a variety of secular impulses, as my next chapter will demonstrate. Exploring the global range of captivity settings also permits us to observe the competition between a terse style and a more florid style, as well as multiple possibilities for plotting the captivity experience.

The captivity genre's supposedly unified, American structure, based on standard elements of attack, capture, and return, holds neither for captivity narratives set in other lands, which British settlers did not invade on a large scale until the nineteenth century, nor even for some of the most famous American narratives. With nearly every captivity text first published in Britain, whether set in Asia, Africa, America, or Europe, the initial frame narrative involves a voyage of trade with an alien people, a journey outward from a seat of British civilization, most often in the British Isles. With a voyage outward at the beginning and a voyage home at the close, a circular structure often informs the British captivity tradition from late sixteenth-century chapbooks such as those of Hortop and Saunders to the longer accounts produced through the eighteenth century and set in Barbary, Madagascar, Ceylon, or Malaysia. Most of these narratives came from the pens of traders and seamen rather than settlers, and their efforts to address a domestic British audience found a natural shape in the circular structure of the voyage narrative, a much more prominent genre. The frame of the voyage narrative also structures the accounts of Jonathan Dickinson and Peter Williamson, the two American captivities most frequently printed in Britain before American independence. Dickinson organizes his account as a sea journal, a daily log of nautical minutiae beginning with his departure from Port Royal in Jamaica and closing with his party's long-delayed arrival at their original destination, Philadelphia.[25] Similarly, Williamson precedes his captivity experience with a fairly long discussion of his childhood in Aberdeen and his youth in American indenture, and many editions close with his attempts to seek economic security in Scotland. Many later American accounts employ a structure beginning with an adventurer's penetration of an unknown wilderness rather than with a native attack on the seat of domesticity. John Filson's popular and influential account of Daniel Boone's captivity, for example, entered the press as an appendix to a historic account of *The Discovery, Settlement and Present State of Kentucke* (1784).

The frame of the voyage narrative was one of many strategies that captivity writers borrowed from other genres, along with elements of spiritual autobiography, ethnography, and martial and political history. Most captivity narratives juxtapose these variable narrative structures within an uneasy tension instead of sticking closely to a single paradigm or archetypal structure. The generality of American narratives, even an early account such as that of Puritan minister John Williams (1707), incorporate multiple discursive forms and styles. After opening with a native attack and a forced journey, Williams draws from spiritual autobiography in documenting his personal experience but soon shifts to a more inclusive framework, recording the experiences of other captives and especially the struggles of his family and congregation against Catholic proselytism after they reach Canada. Williams adds not only some of his own poetry but also several long letters between himself and a son, including one letter allegedly forged by the French. There is also much casuistic assessment of French successes in conversion, and Williams closes with an account of French colonial difficulties at Detroit.[26] A similar inclusiveness marks Peter Williamson's best-seller of American captivity, as he documents not only his personal detention but also several others that he witnessed or simply heard reported, as well as his experiences as a kidnapped servant, a frontier planter, a colonial soldier, and a litigant in a Scottish court. Amidst a welter of anti-French and anti-Indian propaganda, he assembles a collection of travel descriptions, schematically organized ethnographic material, and proposals for colonial military strategy. Far more distended than unified, these accounts do not represent a departure from a simpler structure lying at the heart of the captivity genre so much as a return to the developmental problems that mark their British predecessors.

Working against the earlier scholarly emphasis on the generic unity of the "American captivity narrative," more recent scholarship has explored discursive tensions within the accounts of Rowlandson and other female captives, especially as they develop perspectives that conflict with the Puritan, authoritarian, and colonial ideologies of their culture.[27] That such discursive conflicts characterize the captivity genre as a whole and not merely its greatest exemplar or the narratives of female captives becomes clearer if we expand the critical frame. Reaching beyond American shores forces us to recognize that the central discursive conflicts of the captivity genre stem from broad-based cultural developments affecting all English-speaking peoples and not simply from the specific cultural tensions of the Puritan community or even of American settlers more generally. When we attend to the many captivity narratives published in Britain from the earliest days of its colonial expansion, we can recognize that the genre's instabilities stem not only from the secularization of the Christian worldview represented by the notion of providence but also from the interrelated developments of increasing cultural contact, increasing British power overseas, and increasingly scientific standards for ethnographic discourse.

The varied rhetorical strategies and purposes indicated by the continental titles of the Renaissance continue to mark those of the first English captivity narratives. Since the long titles of early modern publishing served the same purposes as the advertisements, prefaces, and dust jacket blurbs of our own publishing world, they illustrate the conflicting agendas of the travail narrative with especial clarity. Titles suggest that the travail narrative carried a particularly early and a particularly strong pitch towards the documentary strategies that Michael McKeon has labeled "naïve empiricism" in describing their place in the seventeenth-century epistemological conflicts underlying the rise of the novel.[28] For McKeon the period's increased emphasis on direct experience emerged in tandem with an increased skepticism towards documentary strategies. The documentary impulses of the seventeenth-century travail narrative developed as writers anticipated their readers' potential skepticism towards the foreign, the exotic, and the extreme, categories of experience that were most clearly instanced within these texts by the situation of captivity itself. Rather typical of the documentary impulse was the Hortop narrative, whose title promised a text *Wherein Is Truly Decyphered the exotic features of alien lands, including a Man That Appeared in the Sea, and Also . . . a Huge Giant Brought from China.* Other titles also resorted to claims of transparent presentation and direct experience in support of their efforts to document the fabulous truths of the world outside of Europe. We have already noted the 1595 text *Strange and wonderfull things. Happened to Richard Hasleton, borne at Braintree in Essex, in His Ten Yeares Trauailes in Many Forraine Countries.* The main title promises its readers a direct apprehension of wonders and guarantees their veracity through the strategies of naive empiricism, emphasizing direct experience and even a locally established identity. The narrative itself, however, stretches plausibility by asking readers to believe that its protagonist endured three consecutive captivities, first in an Algerian galley, then in a Genoan galley, and finally in the Inquisition. Whereas Hortop's narrative included other categories of the exotic, this text's primary instance of strangeness is the experience of captivity itself.

Captivity experiences provided particularly significant instances of travail because, in comparison with ordinary travel experiences, they involved a much greater emphasis on both the abject miseries of subjugation and the possibility of intimate access to the curiosities of alien cultures. The ambiguous potential of captivity is especially evident in a 1614 account titled *A True*

Relation of the Travailes and Most Miserable Captiuitie of William Dauies, Barber-Surgion of London, Vnder the Duke of Florence. Wherein Is Truly Set Downe the Manner of His Taking, the Long Time of His Slauerie, and Meanes of His Deliuerie, After Eighte Yeeres, and Ten Moneths Captiuitie in the Gallies. Discouering Many Mayne Landes, Ilandes, Riuers, Cities, and Townes, of the Christians and Infidels. . . . Although the title initially concentrates on the abject details of Davies's captivity, the opening of this brief pamphlet works in support of the title's promise to retail documentary information, by supplying a four-page list of towns visited by its errant narrator. The list promotes a sense of the potential for English accomplishment overseas, a potential evident in the breadth of knowledge shown by this ordinary London citizen, in the textual schema he employs, and in his ability to survive so many potentially hostile lands. After opening with this unabashed pride in Davies's experiences, the bulk of the text focuses on ethnographic description of towns such as Algiers and Tunis. But the matter-of-fact tone that accompanies Davies's peaceful visits to these towns ends when he enters galley slavery in Florence. This section of his narrative concentrates on captive debasement, especially when he contemplates the expected punishments for an attempted revolt: "we should presently have lost our nose and eares, and received a hundred blowes on our bare backe, and a hundred on our belly with a double rope."[29] But this section also claims to document the nature of an alien people, as Davies declares the Florentines a "very decietfull people . . . yet they are very cowards being naturall Italians: their women are altogether wicked and lewde."[30] The disposition to rest general truth claims on the experience of a single captive remains constant even as the ease and pride of peaceful travel decays into the debasement and hostility of captivity.

Even when a protagonist suffers abject subjugation, the travail narrative often evokes pride in the exoticism of such an experience. A sharp emphasis on documenting the exotic appears in the main title of Edward Webbe's account, published three times beginning in 1590: *The Rare and Most VVonderfull Things VVhich Edvv. VVebbe an Englishman Borne, Hath Seene and Passed in His Troublesome Trauailes, in the Cities of Ierusalem, Damasko, Bethlehem and Galely and in the Landes of Iewrie, Egypt, Gracia, Russia, and Prester Iohn, VVherein Is Set Forth His Extreame Slauery Sustained Many Yeeres Together in the Gallies and Warres of the Great Turke, Against the Lands of Persia, Tartaria, Spaine, and Portugale.*[31] After the title's initial promise to convey a direct apprehension of strange things, it then appeals to eyewitness testimony as a guarantee of the knowledge it provides. The documentary impulse continues in the list of fabulous lands that extends even

after the protagonist's slavery would seem to vitiate the appeal of the fabulous. Within the text itself, the impulse to document the exotic leads to the
inclusion of short sections of pure description, focused on geography, fauna,
and culture rather than autobiographical events, and covering topics from
Turkish government to unicorns. The exotic can incorporate both an emphasis on cultural alienation (the Turks "doe wonderfull thinges, as going upon
Ropes, and thrusting their swords in their naked flesh") and an emphasis on
the hideous details of Webbe's torture ("fine Lawne or Callico [was] thrust
down my throat and pluckt up againe ready to pluck my hart out of my
belly").[32] Both as a miserable experience and as an opportunity to delineate
the strange customs of foreign peoples, captivity thus constitutes the ultimate fulfillment, rather than the termination, of an exploratory "travail."

In their titles and the varied impulses of their contents, early travel narratives carry an implicit tension between the enormous personal success of
the traveler's multiplicitous experience and the potential for abject slavery
that travel always seems to entail. This tension finds concrete expression in
John Lithgow's enormously lengthy and popular travel narrative. After the
early editions of his narrative had brought him international fame as the
author of a constantly expanding record of his peregrinations across Europe
and the Middle East, a later edition of 1632 introduced an account of his
capture, interrogation, and torture at the hands of the Spanish Inquisition.
In Lithgow's self-portrait, he vents a sudden burst of euphuistic speech, apparently addressing his captors after they have shackled him to the ground:
"remarke in me the just Judgements of God; and loe how the Heavens have
reduited me to this meritorious reward, and truely deserved; for I have dearely
and truly bought it; that I whose legges and feete the whole Universe could
scarcely contayne, now these bolts and irons keepe them fast, in a body length,
of a stone-paved Floore. O foolish pride, O suppressing ambition! and va-
porous curiosity! woe worth the fury of your aspiring vanities; you have taken
mee over the face of the earth, and now left me in a Dungeon hole."[33] As this
outburst reveals, captivity provides an instance of travel that throws its central tensions into sharp relief. On the one hand, captivity here seems to offer
an inevitable end and the most fitting punishment for the sinful pride of
traveling overseas and desiring to know alien cultures, and thus it stands as
an imaginative reversal of the momentum that had propelled both Lithgow's
travels and the narration built upon them, halting and even invalidating the
narrative accumulation of foreign experience that constitutes the bulk of his
text. But on the other hand, captivity still provides one of the most successful
means for coming to know foreign cultures, even when that knowledge con-

cerns a disposition for tyranny and torture, and it still provides a source of national pride, represented at the very least by the captive's power to endure.

The conflicting impulses of the travail narrative became more fully developed over the course of the seventeenth century, as long, individualized, separately published accounts of captivity drew closer to the unified, narrowly focused structure that we find in female-centered American accounts such as Rowlandson's. In the English travel writing of this period, shipwreck and captivity came to stand apart from other experiences of travail as the most terrible fates that could possibly befall the traveler, fates worthy of treatment in separately published accounts. The most prominent form of captivity narrative no longer strung together a loose series of subjugations but instead focused extensively on a single experience in captivity, permitting both a more substantial exploration of captive psychology and a more substantial documentation of a single foreign culture. Because of these two competing impulses, captivity narratives throughout the seventeenth and eighteenth centuries continued to reflect the central tension of the travail narrative, posing abject miseries against wondrous curiosities. Proud declaration of isolated wonders gradually transformed into long, systematic, and comprehensive descriptions of alien cultures, with a calm tone of skeptical distance and standardized discursive schema serving as guarantees for the veracity of strange data. At the same time, the rhetoric of wondrous admiration for the strange gradually transformed into a rhetoric of scorn for the alleged inferiority of the alien. As a result of these transformations, the central tension of the captivity narrative no longer resulted from the gap between the abjection of captivity and the pride of the traveler's experience, but rather from the conflict between the captive's personal narrative of abjection and the generalized, triumphant discourse of systematic ethnography.

Increased length afforded increased scope for an intensive focus on the protagonist's degradation and his conflict with the religion of his captors. The potential for developing these themes brought the captivity narrative in line with spiritual autobiography, that most crucial of seventeenth-century genres, centered on the spiritual degradation, psychological conflicts, and final redemption of a self-reflective protagonist. In comparison to the Puritan and Quaker captivity narratives of America, the British captivity tradition tends to downplay elements of spiritual autobiography, but one important exception, William Okeley's 1675 narrative, may have provided a model for the production of the Rowlandson account, published in 1681. Okeley's title is unique in British captivity literature in carrying the initial generic imprint of spiritual autobiography: *Eben-ezer: or, a Small Monument of Great Mercy Appearing in the Miraculous Deliverance of William Okeley . . . from the*

Miserable Slavery of Algiers. . . . The main title's invocation of a biblical
identity marks the work as a spiritual autobiography, as does also the subsequent move to interpret the captive's release as a providential blessing.

Okeley's text displays a number of parallels to the Puritan captivity narratives and the spiritual autobiography more generally. First, Okeley often
cites biblical texts that match his experience in captivity, and he shares a
favorite comparison with the Puritan captives and many other spiritual auto-
biographers: the Israelite captivity in Babylon. Second, Okeley's text projects
an image of his interiority by documenting inward debates, minutely rehearsed
cases of conscience, which in his case center on the problem of conducting
himself as a Christian while in the power of Moslems. One prominent case
of conscience, for example, results from his forced service on a pirate vessel
whose primary prey will be his fellow Christians.[34] Another results from his
difficult choice between two unpleasant options, either working for his Moslem masters or resisting them by surrendering to laziness.[35] Third, like the
spiritual autobiography more generally, Okeley's text creates a sense of spiritual progress through stages of doubt and inner turmoil, but in his case the
internal struggle climaxes in distinctly secular terms. After he finds that he
can maintain a circumspect Christian practice while in Moslem slavery, his
central problem becomes the possibility of growing accustomed to slavery,
of losing a desire for liberty. Conquest of this lethargy provides the climax of
his narrative, along with his successful organization of an escape project. As
Okeley's narrative suggests, the British captivity narrative, even when framed
as a spiritual autobiography, does not embrace the Puritan strategy of interpreting the protagonist's captivity as a sign of personal or collective sinful-
ness. Instead, as the next chapter will show more thoroughly, the British
narrative of Islamic captivity typically defines Christian freedom of conscience
against the alleged oppressiveness of Islamic governments.

While showing less interest in spiritual autobiography than its American counterpart, the British captivity tradition tends to show more interest in the
genre's ethnographic potential. The scholarly tendency to research the captivity narrative as an American genre has downplayed, if not completely ob-
scured, its heavy reliance on the discursive strategies of ethnography. Although
scholars of American captivity narratives have occasionally described them
as important sources of ethnographic information, critical discussion of this
information has primarily involved documentation of specific categories of
images, such as images of native women or images of native religion, rather
than analysis of the rhetorical strategies that organize the information.[36] This
obfuscation of ethnographic method partly results from the heavy emphasis

Turks taking the English.   Selling slaves in Algiers

Execution with A batoone.   Turks burning of A Frier er

Divers Cruelties   Makeing the boat & their Escape to Mayork

Torture is the primary sales pitch in William Okeley's frontispiece graphy and the heroic rationalism of escape. (This item is repro- *Marino, California.*)

EBEN-EZER:

OR, A SMALL

MONUMENT

OF GREAT

MERCY,

APPEARING IN THE

Miraculous Deliverance

O F

William Okeley, ⎱ John Anthony,
William Adams, ⎰ John Jephs,
John —— Carpenter,

From the Miserable Slavery of *ALGIERS*,
with the wonderful Means of their Escape *in
a Boat of Canvas*; the great Distress, and utmost Extremities which they endured at Sea for Six Days and
Nights; their safe Arrival at *Mayork*: With several
Matters of Remarque during their long Captivity,
and the following Providences of God which brought
them safe to *ENGLAND.*

By me *William Okeley.*

*Bless the Lord, O my Soul, and forget not all his Benefits,
who Redeemeth thy Life from Destruction, who Crowneth
thee with Loving Kindness, and tender Mercies,* Psal.
103. 2. 4.

London, Printed for *Nat. Ponder*, at the Peacock in
Chancery-Lane, near *Fleet-street.* 1675.

even though his text concentrates on spiritual autobio-
duced by permission of *The Huntington Library, San*

on the early Puritan accounts as generic exemplars. Unlike their British counterparts of the seventeenth century, the Puritan captivities only occasionally included ethnographic details while organizing their texts within a framework of providential interpretation based on personal and communal struggles of sin and salvation. But this framework largely receded as ethnographic strategies of documentation became increasingly prominent within American accounts of the late eighteenth and early nineteenth centuries. Within some later American accounts as within many of their earlier British counterparts, the ethnographic impulse is so strong as to overwhelm narration of the captive's personal experiences, which are organized in some cases as appendices or prefaces to scientifically framed documents. As captivity narrators from many times and many places attempt to apply the self-consciously scientific standards of ethnographic discourse to the captivity experience, their variable methods of application and the fundamental epistemological tensions raised by these methods reveal that ethnography played a central and recurring role within the captivity narrative's process of generic formulation.

For early modern European readers, knowledge of alien cultures was often closely tied to the experience of captivity. Former captives or Europeans working to release captives produced some of the most fully documented and influential accounts of Islamic lands. Fra Diego Haedo, a former prisoner at Algiers, produced a body of work that a recent historian of the region has described as "fundamental to all subsequent western histories of Algiers."[37] With a broader territorial sweep, a former Moroccan slave, Luis del Marmol-Carvajal, produced a geographical and historical *Description General de Affrica* in 1573. Another influential early modern account, the *Histoire de Barbarie et ses Corsairs* (1637), came from Père Pierre Dan, superior in the convent of the St. Trinity and Redemption of Captives at Fontainebleau. Ethnographically sophisticated narratives by former British captives joined these continental predecessors from the late seventeenth century, often reaching a level of documentary plenitude that inspired respectful citation. Although Robert Knox's account of his Ceylonese captivity inspired only one printing in 1681, its ethnographic portrait of the island gained such notoriety that John Locke could cite it ten years later as an easily accessible instance of tyranny.[38] Furthermore, as a bibliographer of Western writings on Ceylon has attested, Knox's work was regularly "pillaged" for its ethnographic information during the nineteenth century.[39] Another ethnographically influential account was that of the former Algerian captive Joseph Pitts, which, after its 1704 publication, stood for many years as the only firsthand English description of Mecca. The influence of this text alone has led one scholar to describe Pitts as "the Englishman who contributed most to the popularisation of the themes of slavery and piracy."[40] A similar assessment applies to Robert Drury's 1729 narrative of captivity in Madagascar. Judging the ethnographic influence of this text, a late Victorian historian of that island observed that "not a single work on Madagascar has been published since which does not quote, one way or another, largely from Drury's observations."[41]

Captivity narratives not only influenced the production of European ethnographic knowledge, but, as their titles suggest, ethnographic knowledge played an important role in understanding, organizing, and selling the captivity experience. Titles often advertise captivity as an effective means of intellectual access to alien cultures. Although the Drury narrative observes a strict autobiographical chronology, his title initially promises an ethnographic account: *Madagascar; or, Robert Drury's Journal, during Fifteen Years' Captivity on that Island.* After the main title proclaims that the text has captured and epitomized Madagascar as a fixed essence, the subtitle suggests that the experience of captivity is fully adequate to providing knowledge of that essence. Even more confident than Drury in the sweeping ethnographic authority conferred by captivity, Joseph Pitts records his experiences as an Algerian captive under the title *True and Faithful Account of the Religion and Manners of the Mohammetans.* A similar title advertises an ethnographic narrative edited by the Orientalist Simon Ockley in 1713: *An Account of South-West Barbary Containing What Is Most Remarkable in the Territories of the King of Fez and Morocco. Written by a Person Who had been a Slave.* What makes this text particularly remarkable is that it contains no section of autobiographical captivity, but only a standard Orientalist ethnography, at the close of which Ockley explains that his anonymous manuscript source expressed an unfulfilled intention to append a narrative of his or her personal experiences. The mere idea of a personal captivity experience, then, could authenticate an ethnographic text even when that experience itself remained undocumented. Captivity narratives continued to carry ethnographic titles in nineteenth-century America, as evidenced by two very popular and influential works, Alexander Henry's *Travels and Adventures in Canada and the Indian Territories* (1809) and John Dunn Hunter's *Manners and Customs of Several Indian Tribes Located West of the Mississippi* (1823). In the very frameworks of their self-presentation, captivity narratives from many lands carried an implicit claim that the captive could offer a unified, complete, and accurate vision of an alien culture because of the nature of the captivity experience itself.

To fulfill such promises of ethnographic documentation, captivity narratives over the course of the seventeenth and eighteenth centuries often turned to the discursive strategies recommended by Western intellectuals who wished to formulate an objective standard for characterizing alien cultures. In the seventeenth and eighteenth centuries, European writers began producing longer, more detailed, and more systematically organized accounts of alien cultures than ever before, and European theorists often matched this evolving practice by developing explicit guidelines designed to help travelers systematize their observations. Such guidelines came to occupy an especially influential position under the auspices of the Royal Society, the general academy of science given a royal charter in 1662 and treated to a considerable vogue in the Restoration decades. The society published an intermittent series of guidelines for travelers in its periodical *Philosophical Transactions,* beginning with the first volume of 1665 and 1666, which included a three-page section of "Directions for Seamen, bound for Far Voyages."[42] The society published such directions because it considered the observations of travelers to hold crucial importance for the development of a national repository of scientific information concerning the entire world, including all of its inhabitants and their customs. The directions were expanded and reprinted by later authors, most notably by the Churchills in the "Introductory Discourse" to their 1704 *Collection of Voyages and Travels,* one of the most popular exemplars of one of the period's most popular genres.[43] Frequent resort to these directions testifies to the society's influence in teaching British intellectuals to associate travelers' reports with the progress of a global, systematic, and objective ethnography.

One of the central features of the society's advice for travelers concerned systematic organization of observations within a set of standard headings. For example, one of the society's most famous luminaries, Robert Boyle, published a set of "General Heads for a Natural History of a Countrey, Great or Small" in the first volume of the *Transactions.* Aspiring to the kind of systematic rigor that would later produce biological nomenclature and the periodic table, Boyle's plan outlines a standard framework of broader headings and narrower subheadings. Beginning at an abstract level, apparently dictated by the order of nature itself, Boyle identifies three "*General* heads of Inquiry," the "*Air,* the *Water,* or the *Earth,*" before turning to narrower, "*Subordinate* subjects" within those broader headings.[44] Ethnographic observations fall under the category of earthly products, and Boyle further divides them into several subcategories: "there must be a careful account given of the Inhabitants themselves, both Natives and Strangers, that have been long settled there: And in particular, their Stature, Shape, Colour, Features, Strength, Agility, Beauty (or want of it), Complexions, Hair, Dyet, Inclinations, and Customs."[45] A similar set of headings forms a key element within the expanded guidelines for travelers developed within the Churchill collection: "The principal Heads by which to regulate their Observations are these, the Climate, Government, Power, Places of Strength, Cities of note, Religions, Language, Coins, Trade, Manufactures, Wealth. . . ."[46] The goal of such headings, rather clearly, was to establish a standard, objective system for organizing the disparate experiences of individual travelers so as to avoid the vagaries of personal style and inclination. For the Royal Society, a set of standard headings would ease the formation of a national repository of scientific information. The society's program, moreover, exerted direct influence on the practice of late seventeenth-century travelers, as R.W. Frantz has demonstrated.[47] Although the travel narrative did not metamorphose into a fully scientific document overnight, or ever, still the Royal Society's program represents an emergent intellectual understanding of a broad but never complete shift in the practice of travel writing from the fabulous to the scientific.

As travel writers, with former captives among them, tried to adhere to the expectations of the Royal Society and of readers in general, they tended to include in their works increasingly ample sections of formal description, usually organized by the kind of headings recommended by the society. During the late seventeenth and early eighteenth centuries, formal travel description became an increasingly common discursive strategy, turning up in novels and political histories as well as in texts that openly advertised themselves as travel or ethnographic literature. Within the space of a travel description, the past tense and personal references that normally mark such genres are all temporarily suspended, as the narrator turns to a series of descriptive sentences in the present tense, mostly simple, declarative sentences, and mostly beginning with abstract or plural nouns, which serve to mark headings. The description is clearly separated from the normal flow of narration, if not by an introductory heading or spacing, then by an introductory sentence that identifies the name of a town, island, or some other discrete and manageable unit of geography. The sentences that follow mostly begin with some variant of the vague reference, "they" ("They have . . .."; "Their religion is . . .."). Depending on context, this broadly inclusive reference might cover the most important property owners, a dominant ethnic group, or all of a region's inhabitants. Within the flow of such generalizations appear several sentences that mark transitions from one important component of culture to another, as indicated by abstract nouns: "Their religion is . . .."; "Their government is . . .."; "Their women are. . . ." Although the particular selection and arrangement of these abstract cultural categories vary from text to text, the steady repetition of practice across an enormous number of texts meant that readers could expect a travel description to contain certain generally established categories of cultural analysis, especially geographic situation, physical appearance, religion, government, military defenses, and economic patterns. At the close of a particular section of travel description, the next paragraph or section begins with the name of a new location, indicating a new description, or with a resumption of the past tense, indicating a return to personal narration. Thus within a longer narrative, a travel description stands as a hermetically sealed unit of scientific practice, purporting to capture the timeless essence of a particular locality by divorcing it from the temporality and contingency of narration. With the problems of temporality carefully concealed, the plain style of travel description, with its plodding repetition of simple declaratives and its clearly signaled topical transitions, creates an impression that a rigorous method has captured a foreign culture in all its plenitude and strangeness.

That such discursive practices influenced the authors of captivity narratives can be measured in the anxiety they sometimes expressed concerning their adherence to the generic expectations of ethnography. In his 1729 account of Madagascar, Robert Drury echoes the Royal Society's agenda for ethnographic discourse in declaring his "purpose, which is to give all the account [he] can of the different customs and manners of this island as may be useful to traders and navigators" (230). But Drury also reveals considerable anxiety about his failure to meet the society's ethnographic standards: "If my observations are not so many, or so just and good as they should be, they must not be looked on to come from a man, but a boy; for as I grew in years, it will appear, I grew in knowledge and courage, was capable of making more proper remarks" (47). That Drury imagined such an apology necessary suggests that by 1729 the captivity narrative had developed enough generic uniformity that audiences could expect a modicum of ethnographic rigor. A similar apology appears in the preface to the fourth edition (1738) of Joseph Pitts's highly successful and ethnographically influential account of Algiers. Although Pitts boasts that he has heard his book called "the best Account of the Mahometan Religion we have extant in our Language," his preface also includes a modest disclaimer of ethnographic rigor: "I do not pretend to give an exact and methodical Account of what I have observ'd."[48] Especially when we recognize that travel description structures the bulk of Pitts's narrative, the combination of modesty and pride here suggests an anxious attempt to match a difficult, widely accepted, and highly valued standard of scientific discourse.

Some explanation for the anxiety of Pitts and Drury lies in the difficulties of forcing the often agonistic material of captivity into an objective framework. One method of handling this central tension of the captivity genre was to bifurcate the experience of captivity into two sections, one focused on personal suffering and the other on ethnographic description. In employing such a division, captivity narratives paralleled what Gordon M. Sayre has described as the central discursive strategy of colonial French explorers in Canada, who routinely divided their texts into two sections, one for an autobiographical narrative of exploration and the other for a schematically organized ethnography.[49] Nineteenth-century American captivity texts continued to employ this strategy; John Dunn Hunter's 1823 narrative, for example, offered an autobiographical narrative as a lengthy preface to the ethnographic description advertised in its title, *Manners and Customs of Several Indian Tribes.* This practice embraced not only the high cultural sanction of French travel literature but also the more direct precedent set by British accounts of captivity in various Oriental lands. Francis Knight's 1640 account was the first English captivity narrative to attempt such a bifurcation, developing two separate but equal sections, as indicated in the title. His experiences in captivity come to the forefront in the main title, *A Relation of Seaven Yeares Slaverie under the Turkes of Argeire, suffered by an English Captive Merchant. . . .* The subtitle, however, indicates that a second book contains an ethnographic *Discription of Argeire, with its Originall, manner of Government, Increase, and present flourishing Estate.* In keeping with his two-part title, Knight's text devotes roughly equal sections of twenty-seven pages to each of its goals, first a narration of captivity experience and then an ethnographic description. A similar split structures Robert Knox's 1681 narrative, titled *An Historical Relation of the Island Ceylon, in the East-Indies: Together, With an Account of the Detaining in Captivity the Author and divers other Englishmen now Living there, and of the Author's Miraculous Escape. . . .* This text strives to fulfill its main title's promise to represent the plenitude of an alien land, which it organizes into a rigid hierarchical framework. Parts 1 to 3 divide Ceylon into sections concerning geography, political organization, and social customs. Part 4 adds the author's experiences in captivity as a seeming afterthought, apparently divorced from the hard facts of Ceylon itself.

In both texts, however, the rigidly imposed dyadic structure breaks down. Knight begins by fulfilling his main title's promise to record his personal experience of Algerian slavery, adopting an autobiographical framework, with a strict chronological sequence, until he enters galley slavery. Thereafter he mixes occasional personal details with a more developed history of political events that occurred in Algiers during his captivity. At the end of this ostensibly personal section, he explains why general history has subsumed his personal experience: "I have recorded a plenary memoriall of my seven yeares bondage, but not the severall accidents of my indurances; there wanting in me the abilitie to devulge them" (28). The pain that underlies this incapacity seems particularly acute in the case of Knight's galley slavery. At the end of this first part (ostensibly personal and chronological) and just before the start of the second part (ostensibly timeless and generalized), Knight provides a lengthy, detailed, and horrifying description of galley slavery (29). Organized as a discussion of Christian slaves in general and thus ostensibly divorced from his own experience, this account nevertheless seems an impersonal reflection of the personal "accidents" that Knight could not narrate on his own behalf. Knight seems capable of describing the horrors of his personal suffering only by generalizing them into an ethnographic framework of national oppositions, involving Christian slaves and Algerian despots in general. What cannot be narrated at a personal level thus seems to reemerge at the ethnographic level, even to provide a transition to the text's ethnographic section, an initial ground for understanding Algerian culture. Whereas a macrocosmic framework of national history constantly subsumes the avowedly personal section, the avowedly scientific section seems haunted by a personal experience of agony and hatred.

Epistemological conflicts emerge even in Knox's account, the most carefully bifurcated and the most scientifically rigorous of captivity narratives. As the text's prefatory material proclaims, Knox's memories reached the public through an exacting editorial process designed to render them through the objectifying standards of the Royal Society. In Knox's 1681 captivity narrative as much as in any other text in travel literature, the Royal Society exerted a direct influence in the process of textual production. The opening pages include official imprimaturs from a functionary of the East India Company and from Christopher Wren, then president of the society, followed by two dedications from Knox to the East India Company and a preface by Robert Hooke, another of the society's luminaries. Hooke's preface adopts the Royal Society's standard line concerning travel writings, lamenting the imperfection of ethnographic knowledge that results from its publication in small, ephemeral tracts (such as travail narratives) and from the lack of sufficient standards for travel writing (such as the subheadings printed by Boyle). More specifically, Hooke laments the "want of fit Persons both to Promote and Disperse such Instructions" to travelers, and suggests that socially responsible experts can help "by examining the [travelers] more at large upon those and other Particulars. And by separating what is pertinent from what is not so, and to be Rejected" ([a]2v). That Knox required such expertise and indeed received it becomes evident in an autobiographical manuscript, where he wrote that the book needed the "assistance of my Cousen John Strype a Minister who Composed it into heads & Chapters for my papers were promiscuous and out of forme woth several inlargements one such heads as I

Cap.t Robert Knox.

In the frontispiece of Robert Knox's narrative, the author poses triumphant above a map representing the land of his former captivity. (This
item is reproduced by permission of *The Huntington Library, San
Marino, California*.)

had but touched briefly which then my memory was fit to doe haveing the very Idea or representation of what I wrote so perfectly in my mind, by my longe detainment and Conversation thare as if they had bin visible to my sight."[50] Hooke's preface similarly proclaims that the former captive had "Transport[ed] the whole Kingdom of *Cande Uda* in his Head" ([a]3r), but even if captivity placed transparent knowledge into the mind of the captive, Hooke clearly regarded some level of institutional intervention as necessary in helping the captive avoid the pitfalls of earlier captivity texts.

With the inspection, official sanction, and editorial assistance of such august institutions as the Royal Society, the East India Company, and the Anglican church, Knox's personal experience in captivity reached print through the mediation of several self-consciously modern conceptual systems, confident in their ability to render knowledge of an alien culture in a transparent text. At one level this complex editorial framework suggests the production of an authoritative text within a unified institutional setting, stressing the concepts and values of science, various forms of religious dissent, and the middle-class professionalism of clergymen, scientists, merchants, and publishers. But at another level, the mixture of institutions suggests a mixture of motives, as the Royal Society's claim to an interest in objective knowledge seems attuned to the colonial interest of the East India Company and the evangelical interest of the Anglican church. And at another level still, the vast institutional effort needed to translate Knox's allegedly perfect knowledge into print suggests some anxiety about the reliability of captive knowledge.

In Knox's second dedication to the East India Company, he attributes his production of the text to his friends' inquiries concerning his ethnographic knowledge, and their request that he "digest it into a Discourse" ([b]1r). In response to this request for systematic organization, Knox indicates, he devoted much effort to developing a "Method," and finally settled on digesting his experience of Ceylon into four parts: "The first concerning the Countrey and Products of it. The second concerning the King and his Government. The third concerning the Inhabitants, and their Religion and Customs," and the last concerning his captivity ([b]1v). Not only does Knox adhere to this plan, but he divides each part into smaller chapters, and each chapter with several subheadings. A list of these "contents" requires nine folio pages, and the term "contents" seems peculiarly fitting in this case, as the majority of the subheadings are nominal, at least in the first three parts, so that a nominal standard comes to dominate the headings, creating impressions of permanence and particularity. Part 3, for example, contains eleven chapters, including the following: "CHAP. VII. Of their Lodging, Bedding, Whoredome,

Marriages, Children," "CHAP. VIII. Of their Employments and Recreations," "CHAP. IX. Of their Lawes and Language." Knox gives chapter 6, concerning domestic routine, twenty-three subheadings, beginning with the following: "Their *Houses* mean. No Chimneys. The *Houses* of the *better sort*. Their *Furniture*. How they eat. How the great Men eat. Discouraged from nourishing *Cattel*." Even when a subheading is not couched as a nominal phrase, the italic type emphasizes the nominal standard. The subheadings do not establish an air of systematic rigor merely within the initial table of contents, but they are also retained as marginal notations within the body of the text itself, so that Knox's textual practice foregrounds its adherence to an initially determined system of nominal identification.

Although Knox's text is much more stable and thorough than Knight's in its separation of personal narrative from ethnographic account, the two divisions still tend to confirm each other and to reveal their common origin in an experience of captivity. At one level both sections seem to confirm Western possession of a modern system of knowledge formation capable of documenting the obsolescence of Ceylonese society while asserting the captive-knower's distance from this society, and thus his objectivity and modernity. The ethnographic section describes the people as given to "windy protestations" and "customary lying," "in design subtil and crafty, in discourse courteous but full of Flatteries" (64–65, 106). The captivity section confirms this assessment when the natives use the "craft" of deceptive diplomatic messages in order to capture the English (118–19). Furthermore, the ethnographic section labels the people "very proud and self-conceited" and "Ambitious of their Titles, having but little else that they can boast in" (64, 95). Knox's captivity narrative reinforces this account when he blames the capture of the English on their failure to treat the haughty monarch with "sutable State" (120). Another key tenet of the ethnographic section finds "Nothing so common as whoredom," and the text illustrates this tenet through detailed description of "The Womens craft to compass and conceal their Debauchery" (91–92). This description receives further support from the captivity section's account of Knox's resistance to cohabitation with Ceylonese women. Even as the captivity section provides concrete examples for the generalizations of Knox's ethnographic sections, the generalizations create a heightened impression of personal danger for his captivity section. Despite this mutual reinforcement at the level of details and events, the autobiography ultimately undermines the epistemological authority of the ethnographic sections. Although they posit an unchanging Ceylon, apparently captured and epitomized for all time through the rigors of scientific method, the final captivity section locates the imputed features of this culture within the limits of one person's experience, within a sequence of contingent and perhaps isolated events. The personal hostilities revealed within the captivity section suggest that a former captive may not make the most objective of reporters.

As captivity narrators continued to apply ethnographic standards to foreign lands over the course of the eighteenth century, their efforts continued to produce distinctly ungainly and unsettling moments. In 1714 appeared Walter Vaughan's *The Adventures of Five Englishmen from Pulo Condoro . . . Who were Shipwreckt upon the little Kingdom of Jehore . . . and detain'd for some Months . . . Together with an Account of the Mannors and Customs of the Inhabitants. . . .* Following the strict format and careful dating of a sea journal, Vaughan narrates his personal experience of shipwreck, several short journeys, and a series of captivities in various petty Islamic states. In an extremely terse style, he records even the most uninteresting of personal minutiae in a relentlessly inclusive manner, apparently eschewing criteria of selection and organization in his zeal for narrative plenitude. Near the end of his narrative, however, Vaughan suddenly turns to minor sections of travel description for Pulo Condoro and Jehore, fulfilling his title's ethnographic promise with schematically organized assessments of native geography, flora, fauna, people, economy, and military forces. Rather than include these descriptions as an initial preface or background to his experience, Vaughan appends them as a seeming afterthought, so that these city-states seem to exist in some timeless realm completely separate from his own experience, as if he were a captive somewhere else, not in the places so carefully codified in his hermetically sealed descriptions.

Ethnographic schema begin to penetrate the American narratives, often in an equally ungainly manner, beginning in the middle of the eighteenth century. The first inclusion of ethnographic sections within an American captivity text, as Gordon M. Sayre has pointed out, occurred with John Gyles's 1736 account.[51] Although Gyles organizes his narrative according to an autobiographical line, he suspends personal narration near its midpoint in order to include several haphazard chapters of ethnographic description. As marked by its headings, the organization of this section first treats native "powwowing," then "An Instance of the Devil's Frightening the Indians," "Two Indian Fables," and several local animals such as the beaver, before he turns to native feasts, mourning, and marriage, back to feasts again, and finally to "Their Extraordinary Ways of Getting Fire and Boiling their Food." Simultaneously pulled towards the disparate appeals of wondrous curiosities and the scientific schema of ethnography, this middle section seems distinctly disorganized both internally and with respect to the text's larger autobiographical framework. Randomly intruded scientific schema also seem an important appeal to readers, as well as a source of textual disorder, within the best-selling account of Peter Williamson. The first edition includes standard travel descriptions for Philadelphia, New York, and Boston, a catalogue of friendly American tribes, footnotes explaining such alien cultural features as the wigwam, the tomahawk, and scalping, and finally a lengthy, inset description of native dress, cookery, and military strategy. Later editions advertise improvements such as a series of travel descriptions for the principal American states and a geographic plan for invading native territories. Williamson's drive towards ethnographic inclusion is so strong that he applies ethnographic schema to the cultures of both the colonized and the colonists. His continuous revisions, moreover, thwart the captivity narrative's generic claim to offer a unified and completed vision of an alien culture, and the variable discursive schema that equip the revisions sit within an uneasy and haphazard juxtaposition, especially as the timeless present of Williamson's travel descriptions encounters both the many phases of his past and his various proposals for the future of British colonialism.

The captivity genre's restless and random inclusivity produced a number of inconsistencies that threatened to undermine the ethnographic authority of a unified captivity experience. One important set of complications resulted from the captives' claim to a plain, objective, scientific style, a transparent medium capable of capturing their personal experiences, and even the truth of an alien culture, and rendering them pristinely on the printed page. The plain style occupied an increasingly important place in rhetorical theory and practice over the course of the seventeenth century, especially under the auspices of the Royal Society. Thomas Sprat's official *History of the Royal Society* developed probably the most influential formulation of plain style theory, praising the society for making their writings adhere to plain matter of fact: "They have exacted from all their members, a close, naked, natural way of speaking; positive expressions; clear sense; a native easiness: bringing all things as near the Mathematical plainness, as they can."[52] Like a number of English writers from Bacon to Locke, Sprat defined an objective standard of plain discourse against the pitfalls of personal inclination, contentious wrangling, superstitious fables, and rhetorical figuration.[53] Advocacy for a plain style became particularly pronounced in the case of travel writing because of its notorious mixture of the factual and the fabulous. Endorsements of a plain style for travelers often appeared in the guidelines that the Royal Society intermittently published in the *Transactions*. In the volume for 1676–1677, the society praised "Some late Travellers, who have made more accurate and faithful reports of the Countries they have travelled . . . than formerly was done," before asserting that "in our designed Natural History we have more need of severe, full and puntual Truth, than of Romances or Panegyricks."[54] Juxtaposing rigor and plenitude against fiction and bias, the passage recommends empiricism as a suppression of the subjective.

Throughout the Anglophone captivity tradition of the seventeenth century, a prefatory apology for a "plain" style or a "plain" author functioned as a shorthand declaration of scientific rigor. When merchants, seamen, and American settlers apologized for a style that suited their humble social positions, their ostensible humility acted as a claim to empirical truth, a promise to follow widely recognized standards for the scientific project of documenting alien cultures. While these apologies appeared occasionally in American narratives such as Williamson's, they provided a standard topos in Barbary narratives. For example, Thomas Phelps concludes a 1685 narrative of an Algerian captivity with an apology for the "rough and unpolish'd" style of a "blunt Seaman, acquainted with nothing so much as Dangers and Storms, yet I do profess I have Penn'd this Narrative with all the sincerity and truth, that becomes a plain-dealing English-man."[55] Plain speech thus comes to reside both in the experience of maritime travel and in the seemingly natural truth of the English people, suggesting that even, and perhaps especially, the plebeian Englishman possesses a natural aptitude for documenting the alien. The plain style thus offers an important point for selling captivity as an experience that confers an authority to evaluate cultures, no matter what the status or education of the author. That the former captives largely succeeded in producing a plain style is often evident in the praise of literary critics. For Pearce and especially for Richard VanDerBeets, the American captivity narratives of the late eighteenth century corrupted the initially pure and simple style of earlier captivity narratives with rhetorical flourishes and sentimental excesses. George Starr offers similar praise for the plain style of seventeenth-century narratives of Barbary captivity, linking the calm tone in which the narrators describe horrific events to the prose style of Defoe.[56]

But if an unadorned style is effective in establishing an ethos of calm objectivity, it can also drive readers to maximal impressions of horror, shock, and alienation. Even in sections narrating first-person suffering, the captives often describe their tortures, humiliations, labors, and other forms of abjection in a laconic manner. A particularly telling example appears in the narrative of John Coustos (1746), describing his tortures at the hands of Portuguese inquisitors:

> First, they put round my Neck an Iron Collar, which was fastened to the Scaffold; they then fix'd a Ring to each Foot; and this being done, they

stretched my Limbs with all their Might. They next wound two Ropes round each Arm, and two round each Thigh, which Ropes pass'd under the Scaffold, through Holes made for that Purpose; and were drawn tight, at the same time, by four Men, upon a Signal made for this Purpose.

The Reader will believe that my Pains must be intolerable, when I solemnly declare, that these Ropes, which were of the Size of one's little Finger, pierc'd through my Flesh quite to the Bone; making the Blood gush out at the eight different Places that were thus bound.[57]

Plain by any standard, the passage consists largely of single-syllable words and gives especial attention to details of size, number, and material. The logical process of the torture method is explained through a carefully organized series of additive clauses, signaled primarily through the transition, "then." In the only rhetorical maneuver with any prominence, the paragraph break briefly engages the reader's empathy and the problem of veracity only to return to the direct simplicity of the previous description. Plain style thus seems to guarantee ethnographic veracity even as it maximizes the horror produced by the naked facts of bodily suffering. With its potential for both maximal objectivity and maximal subjectivity, the plain style can invoke its readers' revulsion for extreme suffering as a seemingly necessary response to the ethnographic truth that is ascribed to cultures where inquisitorial courts flourish.

Despite their claims to the plain style and their relative success with it, captivity narrators cannot maintain it uniformly, and sometimes they foreground its limits and failures. Several pages after Coustos describes his tortures, he glances back at this section as a "very imperfect, though faithful Narrative," suggesting both the constant struggle for empirical rigor and the peculiar difficulties of empiricism in circumstances of extreme pain.[58] In many narratives, moreover, sections of terse autobiography and ethnographic dryness alternate with passages of astonished indignation and rhetorical bombast. While Puritan writers wax passionate over the fate of God's people, British captivity writers celebrate the virtues of English liberties with heightened patriotic fervor. The possibility for a dispassionate, rational assessment of an alien culture often seems overwhelmed by the captives' open acknowledgment of the powerful emotions that result from recollection of personal subjugation or that drive particular argumentative goals. Knight's preface evokes powerful emotions for both author and readers in framing his captivity narrative as a "Treatise, expressing my ardent affection for the inlargement of the Multitude of my poore Country-men, groaning under the mercilesses yoake of Turkish thraldome" (A3r). Even so methodical an account as that of

Robert Knox stresses, at one point, "that grief and sorrow I had undergone by being so long detained from my Native Countrey," a time when "I scarcely enjoyed my self. For my heart was always absent from my body" (151). With its simple yet vivid metaphor, this passage momentarily reveals Knox as a victim of chronic psychological pain rather than as the unflappable and objective reporter required by the tenets of the Royal Society, described in Robert Hooke's preface, and modeled in the book's ethnographic section.

Adherence to a plain style further collapses as captivity narratives from all over the world express astonished indignation at the cultural practices of the peoples they describe, or simply stress their extraordinary nature and the strangeness of the captivity experience, phenomena that sometimes seem to exceed the power of language to provide a transparent mediation of the real. Against the impulse to dominate alien cultures by rendering them known runs a contrary impulse to render them strange, and this impulse produces a rhetoric of excess that sometimes overwhelms the plain style. Because the early travail narratives organize themselves as catalogues of wonders, they often treat foreigners as fabulous rather than intelligible. Even when later narratives turn more rigorously to the plain schema of ethnography, they still sometimes pause to insist on the strangeness of the material that their schema encompass. Although Francis Knight displays knowledge of Algerian character elsewhere in his text, he also attests that his captors are "a people unknowne, monsters more like than men" (2). That the Algerians lie beyond knowledge forces Knight into bald paradox. An equally virulent portrait of ethnic alienation appears in Robert Knox's account of his first days in Ceylonese captivity. Although at first he finds comfort in the company of his fellow English captives, eventually "it came to pass that we must be separated and placed asunder, one in a Village, where we could have none to confer withall or look upon, but the horrible black faces of our heathen enemies, and not understand one word of their Language neither" (121). Memory of this isolation completely overwhelms the normally calm distance and unflappable demeanor of Knox's narrative voice, suggesting a cultural gap so terrible as to preclude ethnographic objectivity.

Because the world outside England could attain levels of strangeness that seemed to exceed the powers of the plain style, captivity narratives often resorted to extratextual methods of documentation as a means of reinforcing the authority of the unitary captive voice. But a tension arose with the introduction of multiple and even conflicting perspectives as editors played a prominent role in respelling, revising, and even reshaping the narratives recounted by the captives themselves. In some cases the former captives lacked the skills of professional rhetoric if they could write at all, and prominent professional writers, especially clergymen, often composed literate versions of narratives as told by illiterate captives. The input of editors and ghostwriters probably contributed to some level of generic uniformity but also produced internal conflicts within many narratives. As we have seen, even the early travail narratives often advertised themselves in the manner of Richard Hasleton's 1595 account, *Penned as he deliuered it from his owne mouth*, but their early editors could not prevent themselves from spicing the bland reports of the captives with anecdotes and prints retailing fabulous beasts, monsters, and the wonders of the East. A penchant for bland facticity in Edward Webbe's 1590 narrative suggests that an actual experience underlay the title's loud promise to document wonders with eyewitness testimony, but the text also includes a section describing the mythical kingdom of Prester John. This section, moreover, contains several extremely brief references to fabulous details, such as a unicorn, an elephant, and a hairy "wild man," apparently as justification for including some of the standard illustrations in Renaissance publishing. As this evidence suggests, an editor enhanced Webbe's narrative by adding the Prester John section and several narrative details that could justify inclusion of a readily available set of images for documenting the fabulous.

More overt but still problematic editorial frameworks often produced epistemological tensions in later and more substantial captivity narratives. As studies of early American captivity narratives have long recognized, Puritan clergymen such as Cotton Mather played a central role in editing written accounts, writing verbal accounts, and generally shaping the production of personal experience towards the goals of strengthening the Puritan community.[59] Scholars studying these narratives have conducted a long-standing and lively debate over the extent and effects of such editorial revision. Rowlandson's account, for example, has produced widely varying critical assessments of her relationship with Puritan culture, ranging from claims that her narrative subverted Puritan ideology to claims that Puritan culture offered a religious framework that her narrative readily embraced.[60] Other scholars have pointed to the fundamental conflict entailed in Cotton Mather's multiple attempts to subjoin Hannah Dustan's captivity experience to a Puritan framework of communal sin and salvation. Rather than submit to the divine will or interpret her captivity as a sign of divine anger, Dustan escaped by killing her captors and then scalped them in order to collect a bounty from the colonial government. The violence of her actions has produced a tradition of troubled retellings by American men, beginning with Mather and continuing with Hawthorne, Thoreau, and Leslie Fiedler.[61] Because the

ſhoulders, and all ouer their bodies they haue wonderfull long haire, they are chained faſt by the necke, and will ſpéedely deuour any man that commeth in their reach.

There is a beaſt in the court of Preſter John, called Arians, hauing foure heades, they are in ſhape like a wilde Cat, and are of the heigth of a Maſtie Curre.

In his court alſo there is Fowles called Pharoes fowles, whoſe fethers are verie bewtifull to be wozne, theſe fowles are

Standard illustrations of a unicorn and a "wild man" give an captivities. (By permission of the British Library. G.6931.)

are as big as a Turkey, their flesh is verie sweet, and their feathers are of all maner of colours.

There is Swannes in that place, which are as large againe as the Swans of England, and their feathers are as blew as any blew cloth.

exotic flavor to Edward Webbe's series of abject

captivity experience verges on the extreme, the disturbing, and the implausible, it often seems to demand the editorial intervention if not the ideological reformulation of cultural pundits.

Editorial intervention remained a factor even when late-seventeenth- and eighteenth-century narratives came to advertise themselves as ethnographic documents based on the eyewitness testimony of the captive. Like many of the travail narratives, the 1670 account of T. Smith was *fitted for the Publick View* by an editor, whose contribution suggests the insufficiency of the captive's personal observations, methodical organization, or prose style. A much more prominent editorial hand is evident in Robert Drury's narrative, especially when his terse review of autobiographical facts suddenly shifts to speculations in comparative theology and political theory. In the editor's prefatory defense of his intervention, he declares that, "in all those Places where religion is touched on, or the Original of Government, [he] is only answerable for putting some Reflections in the Author's Mouth." The editor defends his additions by insisting that "he could not pass such remarkable and agreeable topics without making proper Applications, and taking useful Instructions from them" (31). To these "Applications" we can attribute the text's shifts in conceptual register and the erroneous scholarly speculations that Drury's entire captivity experience sprang entirely from Defoe's imagination; in this case intensive editorial intervention has continued to undermine the text's veracity over two centuries after its publication.[62] An even more overtly problematic editorial framework encompasses Thomas Pellow's 1739 Barbary captivity narrative. Pellow's editor includes many footnotes confirming the captive's authority and extending his descriptions, providing, for example, a description of Sallee when the author fails to give one. Against Pellow's description of the palace of Sherres, the editor juxtaposes a parallel description from a contemporary competitor, and this text runs for several pages beneath that of Pellow, overwhelming his in its length and detail. When Pellow documents an emperor's cruelty, the editor feels compelled to support his author with a footnote. After the note recognizes that "these most shocking Accounts of Cruelty appear incredible, as seeming too barbarous and inhuman for any Man to commit," it then adds one of many citations of parallel authorities confirming the author's testimony.[63] The longest excursus from Pellow's authority involves thirty pages of extracts from the contemporary publication of an English ambassador. While such persistent and multiform editorial incursions certainly provide some parallel support for Pellow's authority, they also call attention to the need for such support, to the potential contingencies of his experience, and to the limitations of any single perspective.

That believability represents a problem within these narratives is evident especially when the captives themselves appeal to extratextual authorities. Near the beginning of William Davies's 1614 narrative, he lists names of ship captains and surgeons who relieved him during his sufferings, and who can thus supply further "proof of what I have herein written, concerning my slauery and thraldome."[64] One hundred years later, Drury's account of captivity in Madagascar opens with a standard affidavit, this time from the captain who brought him home: "This is to Certify, That Robert Drury, Fifteen Years a Slave in Madagascar, now living in London, was redeem'd from thence and brought into England, his native Country, by Myself" (28). Drury's editor, moreover, admits in a preface that he initially doubted the captive's story but then details a series of meetings with witnesses who verified his testimony (29–30). At the text's close, finally, Drury promises further verification of any particulars that a reader might question: "I am every day to be spoken with at Old Tom's Coffee-house in Birchin Lane, where I shall be ready to gratify any gentleman with a further account of anything herein contained, to stand the strictest examination, or to confirm those things which to some may seem doubtful" (313). Such anticipations of skeptical reactions on the part of English readers suggest that the single voice of plain documentation cannot encompass the extraordinary demands of captive experience.

Inquisition narratives rely on similar kinds of extratextual authority. Isaac Martin's 1724 account ends with an affidavit from several divines, who verify that the narrator lived in Portugal and suffered confinement in the local Inquisition. A similar affidavit appears just prior to Coustos's main narrative, as several physicians declare that they have examined his bodily scars in order to confirm that they resulted from violent injury. A much more developed documentary framework encompasses the 1662 account of Katherine Evans and Sarah Chevers, two Quaker women detained by the Maltan Inquisition on their journey to preach in Jerusalem. In addition to their separate accounts of personal captivity, their editor includes "A Copy of a Writing from their hands" sent to a local friar; a letter written from Evans to an inquisitor; precisely dated letters from the captives to their relatives at home; and letters the editor exchanged with the captives during his efforts to secure their other writings. To these documents, moreover, he adds a personal narrative of his own difficulties with various Catholic authorities, recounting, for example, his troubles obtaining and copying some of the letters.[65] His perplexed efforts to obtain such personal testimony create a sense of its preciousness and precariousness, enhancing the value of multiple voices. Within all of these narratives, multiple witnesses, as well as multiple forms of evidence, seem to speak more powerfully than the single voice of plain documentation.

Another type of multiplicity occurs as individual narratives from many lands document the sufferings of multiple captives or shift perspective from one captive to another. Scholarship on the American narratives, whether based in a religious, feminist, or mythopoeic perspective, has tended to stress an isolated narrator as a crucial feature of the genre, and this stress is certainly warranted by the rhetorical strategies of narrators such as Knox and Rowlandson, as well as by the generic emphasis of titles and prefaces on the unitary authority of the single captive voice. Not all narratives stress isolation, however, and many develop a rhetoric of common struggle among a group of captives, positing captivity as a collective or national rather than an individual experience. The title of William Okeley's 1675 narrative of Algerian captivity, for example, includes the names of several other captives, *William Adams, John Anthony, John Jephs, John Carpenter,* in addition to the author himself. In Walter Vaughan's 1714 narrative of Malaysian captivity, the English captives unite in a struggle against Islamic conversion: "We endeavored to confirm one another in unmoveable Resolutions to see undauntedly Death's Frightful Face for the Sake of the Christian Religion."[66] In other narratives, a national or communal perspective sometimes overtakes the most fundamental grounds of narration, so that most sentences begin with "we" rather than "I." An extremely impersonal mode of narration marks the first English captivity narrative, recording the capture of the *Jesus* in Tripoli. Although the text advertises itself as written by one of the escaped captives, Thomas Saunders, its initial perspective focuses on the ship's owners, its financing, and the crew in general, and it recounts the experiences of the English captives less as separate individuals than as a group. On the one occasion when the text records the peculiar experiences of a single captive, the incident does not concern Saunders himself, but another captive who suffers forcible proselytism and circumcision. Narrative closure results from the release of the entire crew through the intervention of European ships, and the text reinforces this nationalist climax with examples of providential punishments meted out to the king and people of Tripoli.[67] The captivity tradition in English, then, starts from a perspective of religio-political community rather than individualist isolation.

A partly nationalist but more palpably religious community grounds the multiple narrative voices within the 1662 inquisitorial narrative of Evans and Chevers. As their editor describes his efforts to visit them in prison, promote their release, and obtain their writings, he offers a third voice of individual experience in addition to the personal voices of the Quaker women. Beyond these three individual voices, the personal account of Evans sometimes shifts to a first-person plural voice in recounting experiences that she shared with

Chevers. An image of the unity underlying their separate voices enters the narrative itself when the inquisitors place the women in separate prisons and try "to entangle us in our talk," to catch the separately interrogated women in a contradiction; Evans, however, declares that "we were guided by one spirit, and spoke one and the same thing."[68] With its multiple voices seemingly grounded in the spirit of Quaker belief, this text envisions captivity as a common struggle for unity in multiplicity rather than an experience of absolute abandonment and isolation.

A similarly multiplied perspective characterizes another Quaker captivity narrative, the popular account of Jonathan Dickinson, which ranked second, among texts with American settings, in terms of its impact on the eighteenth-century British press.[69] Like the Saunders account, Dickinson's strictly adheres to the format of a sea journal as it recounts the fate of an entire crew. Throughout their shipwreck, their multiple captivities, and their struggles to reach a British port, Dickinson relies on the pronouns "we" and "us," even when describing conflicts within the group. A particularly frequent and puzzling locution is the phrase "some of us," used especially to describe the reliance of some captives on providence while others proved less pious. Dickinson's plural narration grows most confusing when the castaways divide into groups that travel separately. On one occasion, he explains, "The rest of our company had left us, expecting not to see some of us again."[70] The narration grows most individuated when he uses the third person to describe the experiences of captives other than himself, such as a crew member temporarily separated from the group, or his own wife, the only Englishwoman among the captives. Constant shifts from an immediate yet plural perspective to distanced reflections on the experiences of other captives create a mobile subjectivity defined through the variation within the party's experiences.

Even when an autobiographical rather than a plural perspective formed the primary ground of narration, captive narrators often introduced the perspectives of captives other than themselves. The Saunders narrative initiated one of the central strategies of the captivity genre, the grisly account of another captive's victimization, abjection, or torture as witnessed by a narrator who faced the threat of similar treatment. This strategy is central to Francis Brooks's 1693 narrative of captivity in Morocco, *Barbarian Cruelty*. Although Brooks details no personal experiences of torture or proselytism, he offers many anecdotal accounts of other captives, including third-person descriptions of a male slave tortured to death because "he would not turn Moor," and of a female slave who finally surrendered to conversion and concubinage after several pages of tortures and deprivations.[71] Brooks's strategy for organizing a catalogue of torture scenes within a loose autobiographical framework inspired several later American narratives, beginning with Peter Williamson's similarly titled *French and Indian Cruelty* in 1757. In addition to his own torture, Williamson fills his text with scenes of carnage and maltreatment, culminating with a full page of emotive description triggered by his discovery of a female captive, "Her lovely tender Body, and delicate Limbs, cut, bruis'd, and torn with Stones and Boughs of Trees as she had been dragg'd along, and all besmear'd with Blood!" This tableau not only furnished material for readers to speculate about the untold horrors of the woman's experience, but also enabled Williamson to interpolate his own subjective depths as pained witness and memorialist: "The very rememberance of this Sight, has at this Instant such an Effect upon me, that I almost want Words to go on."[72] The doubled perspective that results from such narration simultaneously represents both variation within the experience of different captives (in this case, variation along gendered lines) and a commonality within Anglo-American identity that overrides such variation.

The captivity narrative identifies its protagonist with other captives not only through scenes of witnessed suffering, but also through scenes of consolatory reunion that permit an exchange of stories and a sense of communal struggle. In a device common to narratives set in many lands, the narrator meets a compatriot, and the two exchange personal histories and sympathy. When Robert Drury describes a meeting with another isolated Englishman after a decade of captivity in Madagascar, he devotes a page to detailing the other's experiences and notes the extraordinary pleasure of meeting even an unknown countryman: "we were more glad to see each other than relations who live at a distance" (273). American accounts often similarly explored the experiences of a range of captives. The settlers usually entered captivity in groups, as Amerindian tribes abducted whole families and towns before separating the captives among their own families. Accounts such as Rowlandson's portray anxious inquiries into the fates of neighbors and family members, fear of their permanent cultural transformation, and moments of consolatory reunion. A vision of anxiously retained community is particularly evident in the narrative of John Williams. From the perspective of a Puritan minister, Williams recounts his persistent efforts to speak with his captive congregants despite the constant observation and interference of French authorities. As Williams includes multiple conversations with his flock, summaries of their varied experience, anecdotes of his efforts to meet them, and letters between himself and his proselytized son, he creates an impression of a community strained by isolation yet unified by a common struggle. That the captivity genre could support such a collective vision enabled leading

Puritans such as Cotton Mather to adapt it for sermons and writings designed to fortify the Puritan community, especially through a connection between the subjugation of a singular captive and the community's collective captivity to sin.[73] Thus even the captivity genre's potential for supporting the communal perspective of Puritanism reflects the crucible of a peculiarly American experience no more than the mobility of the rhetorical methods developed within the earlier tradition of British captivity narratives.

As the British tradition of captivity narratives developed from the late sixteenth to the late seventeenth century, the genre began to take as one of its most basic grounds of self-presentation the claim that the experience of a single captive, when organized according to the standards of scientific ethnography, provided a unified and complete understanding of an alien culture. But at the heart of this claim lay a pair of basic contradictions: first, between an individual experience of extreme strangeness and the general, normalized content of ethnography, and second, between an individual experience of rapid transitions and a cultural content represented as unchanging. While captivity narratives marshaled a wide array of rhetorical strategies in an effort to resolve these contradictions, many of these strategies, such as spiritual autobiography and schematic travel description, or the plain style and ethnic vituperation, undermined each other in their very juxtaposition. Often, moreover, the variable and contingent patterns of captivity experience forced narrators to acknowledge exceptions to their ethnographic generalizations. In their variable methods of plotting the captivity experience, as we shall see in the next chapter, many authors departed from what literary scholars have sometimes taken as the genre's defining organizational device, an opposition between the captive as isolated, civilized, passive reporter and a faceless mass of alien, uncivilized, aggressive captors.

TWO

The Captive as Hero

Just as the generic signals and formal structures of the Anglophone captivity narrative took their primary shape in the London print marketplace before migrating to American shores, many of the genre's common patterns of characterization emerged initially within the global context of British colonial travel before reaching their most prominent development within American settings. When defined through its earliest American exemplars, the captivity narrative often seems a genre particularly given to exploiting a binaristic rhetoric of "self" and "other," where "self" refers to the radically individuated subject of Western discursive authority, while "other" refers to those objectified within that writing as foils for the ideal qualities of the self. This model of the genre's cultural dynamics works especially well for the early Puritan texts, which place heavy emphasis on the captive's spiritual trials in cultural isolation, sequestered from the Puritan community amidst an extremely alien people.[1] Although studies focused more broadly on the American texts sometimes reduce them to similar formulae, the most recent studies recognize that the genre ranges from virulently racist propaganda to deeply troubled accounts of extensive transculturation.[2] Considering captivity narratives set all over the world, the current chapter will place their efforts to build a stable opposition between a Western self and an alien other within a broader context of multiple and ambiguous relationships among British captives and their foreign captors.

As former captives reconstructed their experiences in alien cultures for homeland audiences, they developed a variety of patterns for portraying cultural interaction, from colonial heroism to cultural conversion. The basic situation of captivity in an alien land suggested for British readers a national struggle, with the captive acting as a representative of the homeland, and his or her captors acting as representatives, not only of a particular alien culture, but of alien cultures in general. Although the Anglophone captivity tradition involved some variation in content as a result of the enormous differences among captive-taking cultures, it also tended to rely on a set of cultural stereotypes that originated in the early modern struggles between Islam, Protestantism, and Catholicism. At one level every English captivity narrative at least implied the narrating subject's potential mastery over the foreign even if this implication did not crystallize into an aggressive colonialist agenda. Because a captivity narrative recorded a Briton's subjugation at the hands of a supposedly inferior culture, it created a sense of cultural imbalance, a violation of the imagined national hierarchy that placed Western above non-Western cultures, northern European cultures over southern European cultures. But in the very fact of its publication, a captivity narrative marked the restoration of this imbalance by implying both the happy ending of the captive's release and the possibility of knowing and recording the captive-taking culture.[3] Many narratives developed this implicit cultural victory at more explicit levels, celebrating a captive's capacity not only to endure whatever an alien culture could impose, but also to turn such impositions to advantage, whether of increased knowledge, economic benefit, colonial endeavor, or simply escape. Thus one of the genre's most basic strategies involves transforming the situation of captivity into a basis for a heroism of resistance and reversal. In the British narratives, this pattern of heroism emerged as early as the late sixteenth century and continued to develop over the course of the seventeenth century, although it did not become important in the American context until the mid eighteenth century.

The heroism of captivity often takes shape through sharp reversals of the basic situation of detention in an alien land. The captive gains liberation after confinement, actively escapes after forced passivity, returns to the seat of civilization after experiencing the "savage" or the "barbaric," and achieves mastery over the culture that had formerly enslaved him. But the terms of these oppositions permit extended struggles as well as abrupt reversals. While captivity narratives set in many lands and times organize whole texts or small portions of narrative around such nationalist oppositions, many individual narrators also distinguish variable personalities among their captors, isolating particular tyrants from their more genial subjects, observing ethnic variations, or praising some natives while blaming others. Captivity narratives, furthermore, do not all establish the consistent oppositions between a civilized self and a savage other, or between a passive self and an aggressive other, that studies built around the Rowlandson account might imply.[4] Instead conflicts between captive agency and abject passivity develop across and even within specific accounts of captivity, and some accounts even undermine the opposition between European civilization and non-European savagery. As a genre, then, the captivity narrative opens multiple possibilities for constructing relationships between a subjugated self and an overruling other.

In its inception as a central motif within the travail narrative, captivity did not stand as an experience that marked a particular relationship between two racial groups, Amerindians and Euramericans, on a particular frontier, in the eastern seaboard of North America, but rather as an experience that marked the nature of travel in any ocean, as one of the many travails that could result from voyages of colonial exploration, trade, and plunder on any coast. In the early stages of the British captivity tradition, no stable relationship developed between a consistently captive-taking culture and a consistently captured culture, and no consistent pattern of blame attached to any particular people. Instead every people, even the English, seemed intent on taking captives within a framework of global competition. Not only did the notion of a "just war" authorize British enslavement or sale of captured enemies, but the travail narrative often gave voice to Britons whose subordinate status in their own community led to the kind of experiences that we associate with the captivity genre. In a pattern that recurred with several later Anglophone captivity narratives, both factual and fictional, Job Hortop's 1590 travail narrative opened with his capture by fellow Englishmen, who pressed him into maritime service on one of Sir John Hawkins's voyages of semiprivate plunder.

Other travail narratives of the early modern era likewise undermined what might seem the standard cultural oppositions of the captivity genre, those between civilized, unjustly captured Europeans and savage, tyrannical non-European cultures. The previous chapter has already noted the role of inquisitorial captivity in narratives such as Hortop's, one of several travail narratives that portrayed captivity in southern Europe's religious or even secular institutions. In the early modern Mediterranean, Christians as well as Moslems filled their galleys with captives of other faiths, and Protestant travelers feared the galleys of the Catholic powers as much as those of the Islamic corsairs. In the 1614 account of William Davies, for example, after he peacefully visits Algiers and Tunis, he meets capture and galley slavery with the Duke of Florence's navy.[5] Similarly, Edward Webbe's 1590 narrative records his youthful capture by "Tartarians" while traveling through Russia, his subsequent years as a court slave, and his entry into a "greater slavery" in a Turkish galley, before he suffers a final captivity when accused as a spy in Naples.[6] In a 1595 narrative, Richard Hasleton exposes the ironic potential of such plotting after he suffers a series of captivities, first in an Algerian galley, then in a Genoan galley, and finally in the Inquisition. In the midst of an inquisitorial interrogation, he indignantly denounces his persecutors, declaring "that when God by his mercifull providence, had thorow many dangers, set me in a Christian countrie, and delivered me from the cruelty of the Turkes, when I thought to finde such favour as one Christian oweth to another, I found them now more cruell than the Turkes."[7] A similar overthrow of the opposition between Christians and Muslims occurs in William Lithgow's account of inquisitorial captivity, as throughout his confinement he gains food and encouragement from a Turkish slave and an African slave, and at one point expresses the hope that an Islamic invasion would destroy the power of his captors.[8] With their variable forms of cultural opposition and alliance, early British captivity narratives often reversed what would later emerge as the genre's definitive cultural binaries.

Later captivity narratives, even to the end of the eighteenth century, also occasionally blurred the conceptual boundaries between Western captives and non-Western captors. In the 1704 narrative of Joseph Pitts, immediately after he returns home from a lengthy sojourn in Algiers, he meets imprisonment at the hands of an English press gang. In Peter Williamson's 1757 narrative, his journey into Native American captivity begins with his kidnapping and sale into indentured service as a child in Aberdeen.[9] Other reversals of what were becoming the captivity genre's standard cultural oppositions resulted from military contests between European powers in colonial lands, especially in the northern forests of America. Stimulated by the various colonial wars between the British and the French, anti-Gallic propaganda reached an apex in the captivity narratives of Williamson and Robert Eastburn (1756), both of whom blamed native captures on the instigation of their colonial competitors. As they foment native violence, Williamson avers, the French "render themselves as obnoxious, cruel, and barbarous, to a human Mind, as the very Savages themselves" (26–27). During and after the war for American independence, however, the target of propaganda shifted from the French to the British, especially in texts that blamed native captures on British instigation, such as the anonymous *Narrative of the Capture of Certain Americans at Westmoreland* (1780) or *A Narrative of the Capture and Treatment of John Dodge* (1779). In the latter text, republished that same year in a British periodical, Dodge endures both native capture and

British prison, and he labels some British officers "barbarians" while citing several Amerindians who resisted the extremities of British violence.[10]

   If the captivity genre permitted such reversals of British assumptions about ethnic hierarchies, the evolution of the genre over the course of the seventeenth and eighteenth centuries meant that these reversals represented increasingly rare occurrences within an increasingly Eurocentric and nationalist regimen. An explicit rhetoric of reversal characterizes Williamson's equation of Frenchman and Indian, as he expresses horror at the violation of what seems a natural boundary between civilized and savage. By the middle of the eighteenth century, captivity authors assumed that the Christian cultures of northwestern Europe shared common bonds of civility that separated them fundamentally from non-European cultures. Although captivity narratives sometimes observed differences between non-European peoples, they relied on a common repertoire of images, rhetorical patterns, and narrative structures in describing the "savage" natives of America, the "barbarous" natives of the Middle East, and the "tyrannical" institutions of southern Europe.

   Within a variety of settings, the captivity genre leant itself to nationalist agendas. Scholars have long recognized the nationalistic drive of the many American captivities that served as propaganda during the Anglo-Gallic struggle for North America, during the war for American independence, and finally during the later wars of American territorial expansion.[11] Scholars have sometimes described this nationalist impulse as an unfortunate addition to the psychological and religious purity of the seventeenth-century's originary American texts, but from a British perspective, expansionist propaganda surfaced within the earliest accounts of Islamic captivity at the end of the sixteenth century. Often these accounts frame the captivity experience in terms of the protagonist's identification with the English state. Edward Webbe, for example, opens his 1590 narrative with a dedication to Elizabeth, declaring that memory of her happy rule comforted him "even in the middest of my greevous thraldome in Turkey"; his preface, moreover, frames his text as an act of political homage and subjection: "I do in all humbleness prostrate myself, and this plaine discourse of my travels to your most excellent Majestie."[12] The captivity narrative's prefatory materials, however, celebrate monarchy less often than ordinary British citizenship. When Thomas Phelps dedicates his 1685 narrative to naval secretary and diarist Samuel Pepys, the captive subscribes himself as "a poor, yet honest Sea-man, who have devoted my Life to the Service of His Sacred majesty and my Country, who have been a Slave, but now have attained my freedom, which I prize so much the more, in that I can with Heart and Hand subscribe my self . . . Your most Obliged and Humble Servant."[13] As captivity narratives celebrate the relative freedoms of subjection within the British state, they often promote pride in the national contributions of the state's humbler subjects. Pride in the contributions of laboring men verges on class consciousness in the dedication of John Rawlins's 1622 escape narrative, addressed to the Lord High Admiral of England. Speaking as a representative of his fellow seamen, Rawlins celebrates their contribution to the English state: "for by such men, as my selfe, your Honour must be served, and England made the happiest of all Nations. For though you have greater persons, and more braving spirits to lie over our heads, and hold inferiours in subjection; yet we are the men that must pull the ropes, weigh up the anchors, toil in the night."[14] Within such dedications and prefaces, the captivity experience seems to authorize the claims of the lowborn for a prominent position within the English nation.

The most common nationalist argument developed within Islamic captivity narratives draws a lesson of appreciation for the benefits of life in the British state. Such an argument provides a frame for T. Smith's 1670 narrative of Algerian captivity, as he begins by blaming his capture on a Crusoe-like "vain-glory of being named a traveler" before captivity teaches him the value of his homeland's liberties: "Liberty was sweet to me that was taken as a Slave."[15] Barbary captives promoted their accounts not only as records of their own education in appreciating English liberty but also as a means to convince their neighbors to share their appreciation, by forcing them to contemplate the absolute authority, partial justice, and intolerable subjugation attributed to alien political systems. In the preface to William Okeley's 1675 narrative of Algerian captivity, the former captive intones, "Let the Reader Learn from our Slavery, to prize and improve his own Liberty."[16] Published ten years later, Phelps's preface similarly enforces the value of British subjectivity, both in emotional and political terms. As he insists, his "Countrymen . . . of all the Nations of the Earth are possessors of the greatest Liberty, but least sensible of the happiness." Although he himself may have once lacked such sensibility, his experience in captivity has prodded its development: "now that I enjoy the immunities and freedoms of my Native Country, and the Privileges of a Subject of England, altho' my circumstances otherwise are but indifferent, yet I find I am affected with extraordinary emotions, and singular transports of joy; now I know what Liberty is, and can put a value and make a just estimate of that happiness, which before I never well understood. . . . Liberty and Freedom are the happiness only valuable by a Reflection on Captivity and Slavery."[17] As the introductory framework of the preface suggests, Phelps hoped that his captivity narrative would help his readers to interpolate the subjective depths of nationalist identification, sympathy, and pleasure capable of ameliorating a subordinate position within the English polity.

That captivity narratives did help their readers conceive the nature of liberal subjection is especially evident in the most important early modern exposition of liberal theory, John Locke's *Two Treatises of Government.* Written from 1680 to 1682 but first published in 1689–1690, and thereafter exerting an enormous influence on liberal political thinkers from Rousseau to Jefferson, this work develops its argument through a partial reliance on examples of European captives in Eastern lands. Mediterranean slavery first enters the more important second treatise at its very opening, where Locke outlines the analytical grounds of his argument. After the first treatise has finished attacking the theory of divinely ordained monarchy, the second treatise begins by suggesting "that the Power of a *Magistrate* over a Subject, may be distinguished from that of a *Father* over his Children, a *Master* over his Servant, a *Husband* over his Wife, and a *Lord* over his Slave," and that, consequently, "it may help us to distinguish these Powers one from another, and shew the difference betwixt a Ruler of a Common-wealth, a Father of a Family, and a Captain of a Galley."[18] Here and throughout the treatise, Locke's references to "slavery" suggest less the American context of plantation slavery than the Mediterranean context of galley slavery, a context that would assist his argument the more because he addressed its potential victims.

Captivity is central to Locke's argument. The figure of the captive or slave, subject to an arbitrary power as spoils of war, helps to define the rights of the ordinary citizen, subject to a sovereign power only by his own consent, through an unwritten social compact: "*Captives,* taken in a just and lawful War, and such only, are *subject to a Despotical Power,* which as it arises not from Compact, so neither is it capable of any, but is the state of War continued. For what Compact can be made with a Man that is not Master of his own Life? What Condition can he perform? And if he be once allowed to be Master of his own Life, the *Despotical, Arbitrary Power* of his Master ceases. He that is Master of himself, and his own Life, has a right too to the means of preserving it, so that *as soon as Compact enters, Slavery ceases,* and he so far quits his Absolute Power, and puts an end to the state of War, who enters into Conditions with his Captive" (383).[19] Throughout Locke's text, the contrast of the captive, the person owned by another, helps to define the liberal subject by setting the very grounds of political identity in terms of property, including both the pursuit of private goods and the possession of the self.

These definitions acquire further particularity through Locke's descriptions of arbitrary governments, often supported by examples that he expected his audience would immediately understand as cultures given to the taking of captives, such as Middle Eastern cultures. Locke defines a proper government, like that of Britain, as one subject to law, whereas a despotic governor respects no guide but his own arbitrary will, as instanced especially by summary execution and seizure of private property. Throughout the *Second Treatise* Oriental governments provide examples of tyranny that can be denoted without gloss. Insisting on a people's right to depose an alien government of occupation, Locke asks rhetorically, "Who doubts but the Grecian Christians descendants of the ancient possessors of that Country may justly cast off the Turkish yoke which they have so long groaned under when ever they have a power to do it?" (394). In a chapter defining "Civil or Political Society," Locke's argument that "*Absolute Monarchy* . . . is indeed *inconsistent with Civil Society*" resorts to the abrupt and undetailed example of the "*Grand Signior*," ruler of the Turkish empire (326). Both with this example and with another that soon follows it, Locke assumes his readers' ready familiarity with the stereotype of "Oriental" tyranny. In order to produce a rapid invocation of the concept of monarchical tyranny, without the burden of definition or description, Locke relies on a brief citation of an Oriental captivity narrative: "For what the *Protection of Absolute Monarchy* is, what kind of Fathers of their Countries it makes Princes to be, and to what a degree of Happiness and Security it carries Civil Society, where this sort of Government is grown to perfection, he that will look into the late Relation of *Ceylon*, may easily see" (327). Locke feels no need to include his own description of what he regards as a perfect example of tyranny because he expected his readers to accept and to recall the ethnographic production of this example within Robert Knox's *An Historical Relation of the Island Ceylon*. In the year of its publication (1681), this was the longest and most ethnographically detailed captivity narrative in the English language. Locke expected his readers to accept its ethnographic documentation as enormously powerful evidence, fully adequate, through the vaguest of citations, to defining absolute monarchy against a moderate, civil government such as Britain's.

Oriental captivity surfaces again, finally, at the transition between Locke's penultimate chapter, "Of Tyranny," and his ultimate chapter, "Of the Dissolution of Government," where he argues for the rights of subjects to depose unjust authorities. The final, transitional paragraph of the penultimate chapter consists of a single rhetorical question, designed to invoke a chain of circumstances denoting a progressive movement from just government to tyranny and demanding the ordinary subject's recognition of the need for rebellion: "how can a Man any more hinder himself from being perswaded in his own Mind, which way things are going; or from casting about how to save himself, than he could from believing the captain of the Ship he was in, was carrying him, and the rest of the Company to *Algiers,* when he found him always steering that Course, through cross Winds" and a host of other physical obstacles? Although a modern editor must gloss this passage for twentieth-century readers by explaining that *Algiers* referred to a "slave market," Locke contents himself with a bare reference to the city's name, assuming his readers' readiness to accept the city as a self-evidently appropriate background for imagining a natural, laudable compulsion to resist unjust tyranny (405). Ideas of captivity in a variety of Eastern lands, then, lie at the basis of some of the most influential Western definitions of despotism, slavery, and the rights and freedoms of the liberal subject.

The nationalist drive of the Barbary captivity narrative continued in the eighteenth century, adapted to the patriotic language of liberty, property, and law that reigned after the revolution of 1688 and the publication of Locke's *Two Treatises.*[20] In a preface to Thomas Pellow's 1739 account, his editor declares that "Here . . . the Reader will have a true and lively Picture of the vast Miseries which those who are subject to an Arbitrary Government, continually groan under; and will, by that Means, have a higher and more delightful Relish of the exceeding Happiness he enjoys, in living under an English Government, where his Life and Property is always secure, where he is subject to the Laws only, and where he cannot be violated by Arbitrary Power."[21] As so often in eighteenth-century British political discourse, insistence on the arbitrary power of Oriental potentates helps to define and celebrate the British constitution as a moderate balance of national and private interests. Spurred by the examples of texts such as Pellow's, Barbary captivity narratives, whether factual, novelistic, or dramatic, became popular in the fledgling United States shortly after independence. As the new nation sought to assert itself as a nation, it turned to a narrative pattern that had already helped to enforce British nationalism, during a time when the British themselves found this pattern less appealing.[22]

Drawing from an equally prominent topos of British political discourse, eighteenth-century narratives of inquisitorial captivity often adopted a framework that juxtaposed the moderate subjection of the British constitution against images of Catholic absolutism. Dedicating his 1724 narrative to George I, Isaac Martin thanks the king's intercession for his "Deliverance from the House of Bondage," and declares that his publication aims to give "those of Your Majesty's Subjects, who have not been Abroad and seen the cruel Effects of Popish Tyranny, a just Abhorrence for the Spirit of Bigotry and Persecution" evident in the Inquisition, and an appreciation for the "inestimable Blessings they enjoy under Your Majesty's auspicious Reign."[23] In John

Coustos's account, published a year after the 1745 Jacobite rebellion, the nationalist implications of inquisitorial captivity relate directly to domestic politics, as the narrator's preface upbraids the rebels as misguided subjects: "I only wish that those mistaken Britons, whose hearts may be alienated from His Majesty . . . had seen the Inquisition."[24] An even more explicit connection between the domestic, "Catholic" uprising and the experience of an inquisitorial victim appears in a second preface, written by Coustos's editor, "On Occasion of the Present Rebellion." The editor offers a broad assessment of the captivity genre in terms of its potential contributions to Protestant propaganda and liberal ideology: "every new Treatise of this kind, is an Addition of Strength to the Protestant Cause; as such open more and more the Eyes of Mankind with Regard to their natural Rights."[25] Authors and publishers produced such narratives because they believed that individuated experiences of captivity in alien lands would grant readers a direct apprehension of a contrast between liberty and tyranny, Britain and southern Europe, Protestantism and Catholicism.

Framed by the interpretive guidance of such prefaces and dedications, British captives in many lands came to stand as representatives not only of their nation but also of modern peoples in general, and individuated experiences of captivity often stood as proof of a colossal struggle between allegedly modern peoples, who embraced the laws of nations and liberties, and allegedly archaic peoples, whose practices flouted such concepts. The contrast between the captives' modernity and the archaism of captive-taking peoples resulted both from the deployment of implicitly modern ethnographic schema and from a standard repertoire of cultural oppositions. Within neatly schematized ethnographic sections or within offhand comments interrupting chronological sections, captive narrators treated a variety of cultures with the same set of cultural stereotypes, centered especially on the topics of government and religion. These stereotypes emerged with especial force and priority in early captivity narratives describing the Middle East before later captivity narratives applied them to points all over the compass.

According with the general tendency of early modern ethnography, captivity narratives set in many lands build a consistent opposition between a highly cultivated British civilization and the archaic, degraded, or less cultivated counterparts represented by captive-taking cultures. Many narrators portrayed the Middle East as a fallen civilization, corrupted by a false religion and the oppression of tyrannical governments. T. Smith's 1670 narrative, for example, declares of the Algerians that "Arts and Sciences are almost extinct among them" (146). Narratives set across the globe create a sense of the captors' cultural inferiority through a common strategy of ethnographic description, the reductive equation, in which a native custom or technology is described as an inferior version of a recognizable feature of British life. Recalling his life as a Ceylonese captive, Robert Knox's 1681 narrative scoffs that a cot and a mat "in their Account is an extraordinary Lodging."[26] Similarly, John Gyles's 1736 American narrative briefly mentions "Indian barns, i.e., holes in the ground lined and covered with bark and then with dirt."[27] At one level this strategy renders the strange familiar, but it does so by transforming a lacuna in the reader's experience into a cultural opposition, an instance of one culture's superiority to another. Despite occasional admiration for alien customs, captive narrators generally describe them in reductive terms.

One common point for ethnographic censure is religion. While early American narratives tend to concentrate on the captives' spiritual affliction and offer few observations on foreign religions, their British counterparts give less weight to exploring the private religious experience of the captives and more to documenting the religions of the captors as debased foils for Protestant Christianity. Despite immense variation in Islamic, Native American, and Catholic religions, British captives rather consistently describe them in opposition to the implied modernity and rationality of Protestantism, as archaic systems of superstition built on native dispositions for subjection to material impositions. T. Smith links his captors' superstition to powerful priestly impositions, insisting that the Algerians "listen very much to the Reports and Whimsies of their Soothsayers," who "make a great advantage of the Peoples Folly" (146). Within many portraits of alien religions, superstition comes to stand as a failed approximation of Christianity. Thus Peter Williamson's 1757 narrative describes Native American religion: "Although they have but a very faint idea of a Deity, yet they are very superstitious, in their way" (104). The topic of Ceylonese religion requires three chapters and fourteen folio pages within the long ethnographic analysis that forms the bulk of Robert Knox's 1681 text. When first introducing the topic, he abruptly declares, "The Religion of the Countrey is Idolatry" (72), as if such phrasing involves a bald statement of fact. Portraying the Ceylonese as "subjected to the Devil," Knox represents their religion as fomenting a loss of mastery over self and world, so that its adherents become "possest" and "run mad" (77). He anticipates many other captives in viewing superstition as a subjection to the contingency of the material, declaring that his captors "are very superstitious in making Observations of any little Accidents, as Omens portending good to them or evil" (64). Within the Protestant self-promotion that undergirds many captivity narratives, the religions of captive-taking cultures often stand accused of conflating the sacred and the ordinary. Captives such as Knox often scorn a native interest in connecting material minutiae to a broader framework of the sacred while failing to recognize the parallels to their own interest in the particular signs of providence.

Even more than alien religions, alien governments provided a frequent site for cultural opposition. When ethnographic sections turned to the topic of government, they described what seemed inevitable systems of despotism against the implicit standard of the self-consciously modern political system of Britain. Captivity narratives set across the globe relied on a standard assortment of images, including a corrupt political hierarchy, a luxurious but ineffectual court, a despotic but unproductive monarch, and fawning upstart ministers, all given to cruelty, intrigue, hypocrisy, and rapine. By linking the political tyranny they described to a false epistemology and a misuse of language, captivity narratives defined the British constitution, parliament, and legal system as modern and rational. These images and oppositions developed with especial vehemence in accounts of Islamic captivity before later captivity narratives applied them with less facility to the political milieus of other lands.

The widespread European image of the Orient as a land of seemingly inevitable despotism, enforced by an ancient set of type characters from the Bible, heroic romance, and political history, surely must have influenced the captives' portraits of the social and political environments in which they had found themselves enslaved.[28] A hoary language of Orientalist vituperation surfaces in Thomas Phelps's 1685 description of a Moroccan emperor as a "Monster of Africk, a composition of Gore and Dust, whom nothing can attone but humane Sacrifices," and whose "Tyrannical humour" makes "him Butcher many thousands with his own hands," while even an "inconsiderable circumstance, will raise such a caprice in the Emperours Noddle, without any other provocation, as to endanger all the Heads before him." Like the superstition attributed to captive-taking peoples, such despotism seems based on an improper evaluation of the ordinary and the significant, whereas the epistemological reassessment performed by modern, Western systems of law seems to have properly divided capital from trivial crimes. The archaic epistemology of tyranny receives further emphasis when Phelps describes the emperor's ambassador as "a great Master in the art of Dissimulation and Flattery, a qualification, which seems very requisite in a Courtier of such a Barbarous Bloody Tyrant as his Master is." The danger of this antiquated manipulation of language is illustrated when the ambassador travels to England: "by his fineness and Moorish subtilty, he stole into the Inclinations of the well-meaning and good natur'd English," and this "deep dissimulation" assisted his abuse of English slaves in Barbary.[29] The alleged tyranny, subtlety, and irrationality of Oriental government help to define, by implicit contrast, the liberty, honesty, and rationality of the English people, especially as represented by the former captive himself, whose preface takes pride in his "plain-dealing." In the accounts of former captives, not only does the Orient's archaic epistemology buttress its tyranny, but its tyranny in turn stifles the progress of civilization and economy. According to T. Smith's account of Algeria, "the great swallow the little ones, as Fishes; they feed upon them, and from their Labours derive a maintenance to their idle Bodies: a sad encouragement to Laziness and Vice, and the grand Cause of the Disorders of [the] Nation" (46). From the perspective of this captive merchant, the Orient carries a seemingly natural disposition for trade-stifling tyranny.

The standard patterns for describing Middle Eastern states also found ready application in captivity narratives describing points further east and south. Applying the standard portrait of Orientalist despotism to Malaysia, Walter Vaughan's 1714 narrative focuses on the arbitrary justice of local governments, especially on the possibility of death at "but a Word of the King's."[30] When Robert Knox's ethnographic account of Ceylon turns to the topic of politics, he shifts the motifs of Orientalist despotism from the Islamic Mideast to a Hindu-Buddhist island. Like Smith, Knox attributes the low state of the civilization he describes to its despotic government. He finds the "People discouraged from Industry by the Tyranny they are under," especially as the king wastes their labor in vast ornamental projects, so "that he may inure them to Slavery" (32, 44). As in many other early modern descriptions of Islamic states, the implicit standard of modern British law underscores this portrait of native political despotism: "here are no Laws, but the Will of the King, and whatsoever proceeds out of his mouth is an immutable Law" (101). Knox handles the king with the standard Orientalist vocabulary for describing despotism, calling him immeasurably proud, "crafty, cautious, a great dissembler," "naturally disposed to Cruelty," even though his people "give him divine worship" (38–39). In this typically Orientalist account, the concentrated power of despotism does not produce effective government, and the king represents an antitype of an ideal Western monarch and Western standards of order: "So far is he from regarding the good of his Countrey, that he rather endeavors the Destruction thereof" (45). Knox, furthermore, describes the king as "most pleased with high and windy Titles" (38), and this foolish predilection weakens his power, allowing the sycophantic and manipulative Dutch to gain a foothold in Ceylon. As in portraits of Oriental governments more generally, corruption spills from the leader down through the hierarchy of his underlings, so that Ceylonese soldiers employ "Craft, more than . . . Courage," while "Inferior Officers commonly get their Places by Bribery," and the state constantly suffers because of conspiracies and mutual incriminations among subordinate officials (52–56).

In contrast with captivity accounts from Asia and Africa, American narratives generally failed to distinguish a developed political system among the Amerindians, reflecting the contemporary European tendency to reduce Native American social structures to an anarchic state of extreme liberty. American captives found it easier to invoke the language of tyranny when describing the French Canadians, drawing on a long-standing British tendency to associate the French with absolute monarchy, military aggression, and papal authority.[31] Within John Williams's 1707 narrative, the duplicitous proselytism of various captors confirms a more general portrait of the French as naturally proud, "boasting, triumphant"; one Frenchman speaks in a "lofty manner of great things to be done by them and having the world . . . in subjection to them" (Vaughan and Clark, 192). As anti-French propaganda increased with the wars of the mid eighteenth century, captivity narratives such as Peter Williamson's could attribute American captivities to a combination of "French Chicanery and Savage Cruelty," ultimately caused by "Schemes for gratifying the Ambition of a tyrannic Monarch[, Louis XV, and by] the weak Contrivances and indolent Measures, of blundering Ministers" (10, 77). With a strong emphasis on trickery, sycophancy, and a corrupt hierarchy, the stereotypical vision of the French polity allowed American captivity narratives to deploy the same images that previous captivity narratives had drawn from early modern Orientalism.

Inquisition narratives produced similar portraits of the judiciary methods of Catholic tribunals. Prefaces and editorial comments often directly attacked Catholic absolutism and championed the British political system, citing the experience of the individual captive as an instance of judiciary practices that allegedly pervaded southern Europe, and thus furnishing an interpretive framework for the events of the captivity experience. Within many of these narratives, the primary method of documenting the judicial depravity of the Inquisition involves long, schematically organized dialogues, in which the inquisitors, apparently hoping to force the captives into confession or conversion, drill them with a series of seemingly random, absurd, and pointless questions and accusations. Such dialogues provide a circumstantial dramatization of Protestant and Enlightenment attacks on the improprieties of inquisitorial method. A particularly vivid example occurs in the 1724 narrative of Isaac Martin, which devotes over three quarters of its length to inquisitorial dialogues. As Martin handles himself with an air of scornful confidence and forceful honesty, these dialogues portray inquisitorial language and knowledge as a system of fundamental irrationality, especially in contrast with the self-evident proof that Protestant inspiration or enlightened argument seems to grant the captive. Martin scoffs at his persecutors' technique of asking questions to which they already know the answers, such as questions about his name and background. When the inquisitors ask questions about the fundamental tenets of Protestant belief, such as whether he worships the Virgin Mary, his simple responses to these questions give this Protestant exemplar an air of natural candor and uncomplicated truth while the inquisitors seem conniving and disingenuous.[32]

Whether set in an inquisitorial court, an Islamic state, or the American wilderness, a captivity narrative's most precise register of alien tyranny was its detailed documentation of torture. Throughout the seventeenth and eighteenth centuries, torture occupied a crucial place in the distinction that European intellectuals increasingly drew between Europe's enlightened modernity and its barbarous past. In the same period, moreover, Englishmen took particular pride in the absence of torture within the common law tradition.[33] Within Anglophone captivity narratives set across the globe, torture helped both to augment the ethnographic evidence for the depravity of archaic, captive-taking cultures and to establish the character of the captive protagonist, as one capable of withstanding the threat or the actuality of physical coercion. As the previous chapter has shown, many narratives took care to document torture through personal testimony in the plain style. Some narratives, moreover, were organized as catalogues of individuated torture scenes even if the captive narrator did not suffer personal victimization. In Francis Brooks's aptly named *Barbarian Cruelty* (1693), for example, documentation of torture provides the central rhetorical impulse, leading to the inclusion of several particularized narratives of the tortures undergone by other captives. Torture scenes also command a prominent place among the engravings in such narratives. Francis Knight's 1640 narrative of Algiers, for example, opens with a particularly gruesome frontispiece. The first edition of John Coustos's 1746 inquisitorial narrative includes only three plates, all depicting tortures that he documents in five and a half pages of personal, closely detailed, and schematically organized narration. Although neither Robert Knox nor his fellow captives suffered torture in Ceylon, three of the plates that illustrate his ethnography display gory images of native techniques for punishing malefactors, such as crushing them under elephants' feet and full-body impalement on a vertical pole.[34] Thus, even in narratives where

The torturers in this image from John Coustos's inquisitorial narrative seem both animated by innate, passionate cruelty and guided by the impassive oversight of authority. (By permission of the British Library. 501.d.5)

torture does not provide a title, framing principle, or autobiographical incident, the threat of torture always looms over the captivity experience, helping to document alien cultures as debased opposites for the modernity of the British polity.

The rhetorical strategies for documenting torture as a feature of alien cultures migrated from British captivity narratives to American ones in the mid eighteenth century. In the midst of John Gyles's 1736 narrative, after he documents one method of torture as practiced on another captive, he suspends narration in order to list five other methods (Vaughan and Clark, 101). According to Gyles, torture was an inevitable feature of Amerindian culture: "A captive among the Indians is exposed to all manners of abuse and to the utmost tortures unless his master or some of his master's relations lay down a ransom" (Vaughan and Clark, 100). Torture is central to the most frequently published American captivity narrative, Peter Williamson's *French and In-*

An Execution by an Eliphant.

"Execution by an Elephant" occupies a much larger place among the graphic images accompanying Knox's text than it does amidst his own description. (This item is reproduced by permission of *The Huntington Library, San Marino, California.*)

dian Cruelty, which followed not only the format but also the naming convention of Francis Brooks's 1693 *Barbarian Cruelty.*[35] Williamson's text fulfills the promise of its title not only by documenting his own torture in a first-person voice, but also by including a host of particularized third-person scenes that he purportedly witnessed both before and during his captivity. In a typically gory and ethnographically reductive example, he describes how the Indians "not only scalped [one victim], but immediately roasted him, before he was dead; then like Canibals, for want of other Food, eat his whole Body, and of his Head, made what they call'd, an Indian Pudding" (21). After Williamson's precedent, American narratives were often organized as catalogues of torture, which came to stand as a definitive feature both of Native American culture and the American captivity experience. Williamson's text was not the only American torture catalogue to imitate the titling conventions used by British predecessors, and the quick migration of these conventions suggests the enormous advertising and ideological weight that torture carried on both sides of the Atlantic. Two American reprints of Coustos's Inquisition narrative carried the main title, *Horrid Tortures* (1798 and 1800), while a similarly phrased title, *Horrid Indian Cruelties,* headed a 1799 printing of a particularly gruesome American catalogue of tortures, the Manheim anthology. Even today, torture dominates popular understanding of the captivity experience, furnishing one of the most common visual images of American cultural contact, that of an aboriginal death dance around a burning European.

As the global context of English captivity narratives reveals, the genre constantly resorted to a set of cultural stereotypes that created a narrative dynamic centered on the forced imposition of an allegedly inferior culture on the representative of an allegedly superior culture. The most important areas for cultural scorn, government and religion, were precisely those that most directly affected the captive's sense of cultural identity. Captives in many lands encountered compulsory proselytism, and their descriptions of alien religions portrayed systems of coercion, deception, and submission to the material. Nearly all narrators, moreover, resented their captivities as unjust subjugations, and they often matched their resentment with portraits of native governments as systems of insatiable tyranny and abject slavery. At one level these stereotypes represent foils for the qualities that the British wished to see in themselves, modernism, rationalism, and liberty. But at another level they represent a harsh reaction to the fundamental crisis of identity produced by the situation of captivity, by the captive's subjugation and participation within an allegedly inferior culture. The next section will consider the genre's variable methods for handling this crisis through narrative structures that produced variable patterns of captive agency and even of captive heroism.

Captivity narratives set across the globe celebrate the liberties and Protestantism of Britain against the cultural systems of captive-taking peoples, portrayed as naturally prone to the machinations of despots, priestly charlatans, and physical impositions, and therefore necessarily reduced to forcible methods of conversion when faced with the seemingly natural freedom and rationality of a captured Briton. Against native systems of governance and belief that seem fundamentally lacking in ideals of personal mastery, captivity narratives often develop a heroism of resistance, insularity, and self-control. But this represents one among many varieties of captive heroism. Instead of leading automatically to a single, consistent model of the persecuted self, the captivity experience raises fundamental crises of identity by dramatizing a series of personal transformations. After an initial agon results from the captive's transformation from the status of free Briton to the degraded position of slave, commodity, or object, the protagonist undergoes further internal struggles, perhaps in reconciling such abjection with the doctrine of providence, perhaps in fortifying the self against external compulsions, or perhaps in marshaling the scattered resources of effective action. Often these struggles coalesce in various forms of heroic aggression, ranging from escape to warfare and economic activity, and often these behaviors resemble the activities of British colonists, whether settlers, soldiers, or traders. In its global context, the captivity genre does not reveal a persistent opposition between the protagonist as passive, disembodied observer and the captor as active force of nature; instead a tension between abject passivity and the potential for heroic action arises as a basic condition of the captivity experience.

The heroism of passive resistance developed as early as the first English captivity narrative, the 1587 account of the *Jesus'* detention in Tripoli. After the capture of the ship's crew, a local tyrant commands his subordinates to impose forcible conversion on one of the English captives, "to make him Turke, and they did so, and circumcised him, and would have had him speake the words that thereunto belonged, but he answered them stoutlie that he would not: and although they had put on him the habit of a Turke, yet said he, Christian I was borne, and so I will remaine, though you force me to do otherwise."[36] This pattern of stalwart resistance to physical coercion soon became a standard pattern within the captivity genre. Many narratives developed an opposition between the forced imposition of outward cultural forms, such as clothing, speech, and gesture, and an inner personal essence that remained true to its cultural origins despite outward alterations. Other narratives simply defined the inner strength of a Christian soul against the coercion and torture of the body. In the 1595 travail narrative of Richard Hasleton, for example, an inquisitor threatens the captive protagonist with death if he does not embrace Catholicism, but he retorts, "you cannot prevaile though I be now in your hands, where you have power over my body, yet have you no power over my soule."[37] Similarly, Edward Webbe's 1590 narrative records his efforts to resist his captors' Islamic proselytism, "though by them greevouslie beaten naked for my labour, and reviled in most detestable sorte . . . but I give God thankes he gave me strength to abide with patience these crosses." Webbe fortifies himself by recollecting Scripture, a "comfort" that makes him inwardly "resolute" and capable of resisting outward temptation. As his preface boasts and his narrative illustrates, he might have lived in "prosperitie" if he had embraced Islam or served the Spanish.[38] The heroism of resistance encompasses both a struggle against forcible conversion and a struggle against the material temptations offered by systems of government and religion whose seeming archaism dooms them to such expedients.

Later Islamic captivity narratives extended this model of heroism through increasingly detailed episodes and more overtly political oppositions between the cultures of captive and captor. When Francis Knight declared in 1640 that he and his fellow Algerian slaves felt a "resolution to attaine libertie or death," he provided an early formulation of what was to become a constant refrain in the literature of Barbary captivity.[39] Smith's 1670 narrative details a variety of sexual and monetary temptations offered by his Algerian captors in their efforts to convert him, but he manages "to prefer the Life of a Slave with Honour, and my Religion before the greatest Riches and the most pleasant Life" (216). A particularly lengthy (twenty-page) account of heroic resistance to apostasy surfaces in Vaughan's 1714 narrative of captivity among the Moslems of Malaysia. Constantly tempted, cajoled, and ordered to embrace Islam and "turn Malaya's," Vaughan and his companions resist offers of wealth, power, and wives, but suffer particularly from threats of circumcision, punishment, and death: "if the Case were so that we must either die, or yield to their wicked Impositions, we had all resolved upon Death."[40] Although his companions relent somewhat, Vaughan continues to resist even when his captors threaten to "bind me Hand and Foot, and Cut or Circumcise me by Force," but he declares that while his inner "Resolutions remain'd firm and unshaken it would avail nothing."[41] As with other captive-narrators, Vaughan's account of suffering and resistance enhances his heroism by separating him from other British captives who could not match the fullness of his resistance.

American captivity narratives also celebrated their protagonists' heroic resistance to the material impositions of seemingly archaic religions, especially when, as in the account of John Williams (1707), the captives reach the settlements of Catholic Canada. Like many other French settlers and French-influenced Indians portrayed in these narratives, Williams's native master tries to impose a material conversion on his captive, forcing him to cross himself and attend mass. There the Puritan minister sees "a great confusion instead of gospel order," and later he derides a procession as given to "great pomp, carrying (as they said) as an holy relic one of the bones of St. Paul" (Vaughan and Clark, 185, 193). In addition to superstition, ceremony, and disorder, Williams also associates his "popish captivity" with the "subtlety," "wiles," and "witty stratagems" of the many "cunning crafty enemies" who try to convert his fellow English captives (Vaughan and Clark, 205, 208). An extended narrative example of these strategies involves a complex hoax by the French, who claim that Williams's children and neighbors have converted and produce a fake letter from his son as corroboration (Vaughan and Clark, 204–8). While French religion thus seems a chaos of deceptive appearances and superstitious attachments to the material, Williams's resistance to such forms defines a heroism of orderly self-fortification and rigid adherence to the intangible.

Beyond a passive adherence to British culture, the heroism of resistance often develops as a struggle to embrace more active efforts to reverse the impositions and abject conditions of captivity. Michelle Burnham has analyzed the tension between passivity and activity in several American captivity narratives as a function of gender, resulting especially when female captives adopt aggressive behaviors in violation of cultural prescriptions for female passivity.[42] Another kind of tension results when narrators describe their passivity under abject conditions, a passivity that seems to violate the self-direction, or at least the self-possession, that readers expect from an author, especially when the author is an overseas traveler and a male. Captive narrators often adopt a voice of anguish in exaggerating the conditions of captivity through such techniques as likening themselves to animals. When Robert Drury and his companions are shipwrecked and detained in Madagascar, they must remain passive in their captivity because they lack the weapons and numbers for resistance, and "it galled us to the quick, to think how we were forced up the country at the pleasure of heathenish negroes, like a flock of sheep, without power to make terms for ourselves like men."[43] As suggested by such images of animality, the passivity that results from captivity seems tantamount to a loss of civilization and manhood.

Images of animality often arise at the moment of sale, as the captive narrators bitterly lament their transformation into commodities. In James Wadsworth's 1629 account of captivity in Sallee, he describes how he and his companions were "crammed like Capons, that we might grow fatter and better for sale."[44] Sale in a public market place is a standard motif within Barbary captivity narratives, and the abject commodification of a captive can raise considerable tension even within accounts of captivity in America, where regular slave markets never developed. John Gyles, for example, mourns his sale from an Amerindian to a Frenchman, declaring, "The word *sold* . . . almost broke my heart!" (Vaughan and Clark, 125). Another troubled motif of passive abjection within the American accounts is the running of the gauntlet, as former captives painfully describe their entry into a tribe or village through two rows of Amerindians who reviled and beat them, although sometimes in only a perfunctory manner.[45] A similar custom often surfaces in accounts of Islamic captivity. In Adam Elliot's 1682 account of his arrival in Sallee, the captives "were forct like a drove of Sheep, through the several streets, the people crouding to gaze upon us and curse us."[46] Like the American gauntlet, this custom provokes moments of distinct tension within the captivity genre, recorded in a highly emotive language that suggests not only cultural animosity but also the fearful recognition that the subordination and passivity imposed by the captivity experience permit total absorption and debasement within an alien culture.[47]

As a narrator plots his experiences in captivity, its abject conditions can seem to threaten permanent damage to the active drive that many texts presuppose as a grounding feature of British character. After a lengthy captivity in Algiers, William Okeley comments that, even though he and some fellow captives had achieved a moderate livelihood as traders, still "the Truth is, in time we were so habituated to Bondage, that we almost forgot Liberty, and grew stupid, and sensless of our Slavery . . . like those Israelites in Babylon, who being once settled, forgot Canaan." In this case economic adaptation to an alien land seems to threaten the captive's attachment to his native soil and to his concomitant liberty. As Okeley struggles to regain his active drive for liberty and homeland, he describes himself as forced to muster "those few Wits Captivity had left me."[48] Although he manages to overcome the lassitude entailed by captivity, this happy outcome closes a lengthy, detailed examination of the psychological damage inflicted by passive subjugation.

A similarly detailed account of the unnerving effects of captivity appears in Adam Elliot's 1682 account of his captivity in Sallee. While still aboard ship, he and his companions are tied to a mast and whipped, then put below decks, where their captors indulge themselves in beatings, "insulting most intolerably over us, lifting up our dejected heads and spitting upon our Faces, not vouchsafing us any other Name than Dogs. I must confess this inhumane usage was very hard to digest at first, but a little time and the discipline of our skillful Tutors, easily reconcil'd us to it." Here and elsewhere, Elliot's rhetoric anticipates perplexed or skeptical reactions and tries to forestall them by evoking sympathy for his suffering or contempt for his captors. Once the captives reach shore, they undergo a forced march through a desert and become so weak and hungry that "our condition of life must appear very pitiful, seeing we long'd for the place of our Captivity, and panted after our Afflictions." When subsequently locked in a particularly noisome prison, Elliot even looks forward to his sale. After this sale, when his new owner regularly beats him, forces him to labor for a "black-moor," and assigns him "harsher and severer tasks" on a daily basis, the resulting "lassitude" threatens to undo his will to escape.[49] Although he eventually rouses the active faculties of hero- ism and manages a solitary escape, his narrative progress through abject rec- onciliation to defiant self-preservation builds on an implicit contrast with the alternative represented by the majority of captives, who could not match his heroic progress or return home to tell their stories, who apparently became inured by harsh treatment to subordination and alterity.

Despite the always present threat of abjection, captivity protagonists exhibit a variety of heroic activities. Beyond the effort devoted to escape, one particularly surprising form of heroic action, given the abased condi- tions of captivity, involves economic success. In a famous instance of such success, Mary Rowlandson manages to support herself occasionally by sell- ing her sewing skills among the tribe who captured her; several feminist readings have contrasted this relative economic "independence" with her economic coverture under Puritan patriarchy.[50] A somewhat different vision of captive entrepreneurial skill appears in William Okeley's Algerian narra- tive. After his master forces him to adapt to the labor of a seaman and a weaver, he arrives at economic independence as a trader in tobacco and wine. His success fulfills an implicit nationalist and colonial agenda, suggesting that even subjugated Britons can display a seemingly natural economic acu- men within environments that seem ripe for its application. A captive's eco- nomic progress often stands as a reversal of the abject conditions of captivity, as in William Vaughan's Malaysian narrative. At the court of a petty poten- tate, Vaughan first finds a means of supporting himself by entertaining the natives with a common "trick of cutting a String in Two." After a brief period of service as a court clown, he eventually arrives at the more impressive social standing of a doctor and finds himself "mightily in Favour, enjoying as much Freedom in the whole Compound as if I had been at Home with my Relations."[51] Thus develops a plot in which an improperly subjugated cap- tive seems to demonstrate Western superiority, as he obtains a limited freedom within captivity through the seemingly natural effects of European knowledge, registered from the depths of clowning to the heights of medicine.

In one of the fullest visions of a captive's economic success, Knox's Ceylonese narrative establishes a sharp contrast between his commercial activity and a stagnated native economy. At various points in his ethnographic section, he declares that "the Chingulays are Naturally, a people given to sloth and laziness," that "their Manufactures are few," and that "their Learning is but small" (32, 96, 109). In contrast with this alleged failure to turn the native environment to productive use, Knox and his fellow captives rise to rapid capitalist success. They begin on the small scale of knitting and selling caps but soon progress to lending corn, trading other goods, and buying land. Eventually the author and a partner amass so much profit that their neighbors must come "to beg or borrow" (149). On a small scale Knox comes to emulate the patterns of economic colonialism, beginning in the typically British manner of selling cloth manufactures before securing the economic dependence of his former trading partners. His text rationalizes this success, moreover, through various tenets of colonial ideology. On the one hand he attributes his success to a divine sanction of his people, one that raises the English above other foreign peoples resident in Ceylon: "by the blessing of God our Nation hath lived and still doth, in as good fashion as any other People or Nation whatsoever" (146). On the other hand, he recognizes that the success of the English also depends on their "having the Language, and being acquainted with the Manners and Customs of the People" (140). Since an extended captivity enforces such a developed acquaintance, the acculturated captive comes to seem an ideal colonist.

As the Knox text vividly illustrates, the captive was a figure who offered Britons particularly salient possibilities for imagining the nature of their colonial activity, its origins, its prospects, its potential problems and dangers. At the level of origins, captivity raised questions about who initiated cultural aggression. Many a captivity narrative opened with a voice of innocence, positing the protagonist as a traveler interested only in fair exchange, before the capture itself signaled an inherent disposition for aggression among the captive-taking people, evidence for an inherent tyranny that seemed to make them an appropriate vehicle for European oversight. When the captive subsequently moved from subjugation and passivity to liberty and economic success, his transformation seemed to mark colonial aggression as justified revenge in a manner that carried historic implications. Especially in the case of seventeenth-century narratives set on the Barbary Coast, the movement from subjugation to aggression not only replicated the historical situation of Christian Britain with regard to the Islamic states of Barbary but suggested the possibility of further British advance in an area of great British interest. But the very nature of foreign subjugation always carried a surplus sense of terror and transgression that competed with the national pride evoked by the captive's accomplishments. The captive provided a vivid, concrete formulation of a paradoxical yet crucial tenet of colonial ideology: that the seeds of colonial power lay in the abjection of the isolated adventurer.

Throughout the period covered by this study, the nature of British colonialism led both its practitioners and the metropolitan populace to view the project less with a sense of the colonists' systematic cultural domination of other peoples than with a sense of the colonists' dependence, vulnerability, and transformation when surrounded by alien cultures. The situation of the early modern colonist, paradoxically, was something like that of the foreign captive. The initial phase of European colonialism, notwithstanding the highly visible exception of the Spanish conquests, largely involved the creation of isolated trading outposts in foreign lands. Throughout the sixteenth century, most British voyages to America focused on trade and exploration rather than conquest and conversion. Even though the east coast of North America would soon see the most extensive European settlement in the Americas, the groundwork for this settlement developed through sixteenth-century trade, in which British interlopers depended on the material and intellectual aid of Amerindian rulers and adapted to their prescriptions for the processes of trade.[52] Even after the coastal settlement, frontier encounters between Amerindians and Britons still occurred in terms partially dictated by the natives, who tried with some success to control European access to their resources. Rapidly waning but still extensive Amerindian cultures posed real threats to frontier communities, and the isolation of these communities occupied an inordinately large place in the colonial imagination.[53] Beyond the American captivity narratives themselves, images of intransigent, energetic, and hostile Amerindians are central to a widespread Puritan theme comparing the New England settlements to the Israelite captivity in Egypt. Images of a besieged, potentially backsliding Puritan community carried much influence outside the Puritan colonies and even after the Puritan decline, as American settlers continued to interpret their expansion in Puritan terms. Even as late as 1782, with the highly successful publication of Crèvecoeur's *Letters from an American Farmer,* American settlers could imagine themselves as isolated interlopers, housed in scattered outposts, surrounded by a still extensive, even robust native culture, with much appeal for uneasy settlers.

Outside of the thirteen colonies, the image of the surrounded, dependent, and corruptible colonist was tied especially to the figures of the economic diplomat and the colonial trader. The European colonial trader of the early modern era was a self-supporting military agent and sometimes a privateer. When sailing far from home, he and his men faced a constant threat of capture either from non-European natives or from European competitors. In order to trade in alien lands, he depended on the conciliation of alien rulers, always facing the possibility of capture, detainment, and execution. Colonial trade, even the African slave trade, centered on "factories," fortresses tolerated only to the extent that they provided personal benefits to native rulers. In the various lands of the "Orient," from the Barbary States to Japan, European traders and ambassadors encountered highly successful autocrats, who usually forced them into closely watched enclaves. The writings of British diplomats and traders often complain of the indignities to which they submitted in complying with the forms demanded by "Oriental despotism." Historians who study the earliest British settlers in the East highlight their insularity from the alien cultures that surrounded them and the psychological pain of extreme cultural isolation.[54] It was the colonist's maneuvers within a position of subservience and alienation, however, that ultimately produced the political and economic footholds underlying later administrative power. Encounters between powerful native patrons and colonizing clients led to increased European power, as British ships began to supplant and eventually to suppress native ships, and as the very process of colonial trade redirected native patterns of production and exchange to satisfy an increasing dependence on European goods and capital. Nevertheless, the conditions of early colonial trade could easily lead Europeans to imagine the first colonists as relatively powerless figures, surrounded by hostile alien cultures, dependent on powerful governments, and in many ways analogous to captives.

Within the captivity narratives themselves, the advancement of protagonists within foreign societies often entails dangers as well as rewards, producing a tense vision of the captive as a masterfully effective yet dangerously subordinate subject. When captives achieve success within Oriental societies, colonial heroism can take the form of a wily management within the strictures of a debased government, as the captives limit their advancement out of fear that it will expose them to the tumults and punishments associated with Oriental politics. Among his Algerian captors, Joseph Pitts easily masters the "Turkish character beyond their Expectation" but then prudently limits his linguistic mastery in order to prevent promotion within the government (*True and Faithful Account* [1738], 225). Similarly, after Knox's Ceylonese successes, he receives a summons to the king's service but avoids the call, not only because he fears it will interfere with his plans for escape, but also because he believes that it will lead inevitably to the king's disfavor and to summary execution, "as happens to all that serve him" (151). In these accounts, the captive virtues that can afford pride to British readers, such as a prudent mastery of personal inclinations, an intellectual grasp of alien cultures, and an overwhelming drive for liberty, combine to enable both the protagonists' successful mastery of alien cultures and their recognition of the safe limits of personal advancement within such cultures. This recognition raises ambiguities within a success that might seem capable of offering an unalloyed source of national pride, but that is ultimately revealed as a degraded victory within a degraded, tyrannical culture.

For a captive colonist such as Knox, success amidst an alien culture requires avoiding native systems of advancement and concentrating one's energies on the road home. In the early stages of his captivity, he finds little prospect for escape because Ceylon lacks a modern road system, "here being no great High-ways that run thro the Land, but a multitude of little Paths" (153). However, Knox and partner come to know this chaotic and alien system, as a result of their economic practice, better than the natives themselves. Eight or nine years of itinerant trading enable the protagonists to grasp the labyrinthine intricacies of the roads as their trade enables them to penetrate further away from the center of Chingalay society and nearer its borders. Not only does their geographical knowledge contribute to their economic success, but this success further combines with this knowledge to enable their escape. As Knox recalls, "every Voyage we gathered more experience" and "grew acquainted both with the People and the Paths" (154). Their economic activity provides a cover for their inquiries about the lay of the land and eventually for their escape, as the natives believe "we had made these inquiries for the sake of our Trade, but our selves had other designs in them" (153). Thus the captivity and escape of Knox and partner offer yet another analogue for the activity of colonial traders, as they patiently wait and plan for delayed rewards, as they exceed the natives in their knowledge of the land, and as their easy economic success confirms the alleged laziness of the natives. Like colonial traders, moreover, Knox and partner must balance conflicting drives towards penetration of alien intricacies and a return to the British homeland.

Beyond the implicit equation between captive and colonist entailed by common patterns of economic mastery, captivity narratives often more literally transform their protagonists into figures of colonial conquest, figures who turn the tables of domination at both a personal and a national level. Near the close of Francis Knight's narrative, he outlines a plan for colonial intervention in Algiers, proposing the establishment of an English factory and declaring that Algerian wealth "is sufficient to answere the charge of that Navie and Armie that shall be sent to Conquer her." Knight recommends both his colonial plan and his ethnographic knowledge through a contrast with recent English efforts in diplomacy, which failed because the negotiators "wanted experience in the Country." The former captive's ardent desire to enlist his experience in a national project to conquer Algiers becomes further evident in his text's peroration: "Oh that I might live to be an actour in a Marshall way, to see her Conquest, they feare none so much as our English Nation."[55] Because the narrative closes by dramatizing Knight's escape, this personal transition from captivity to freedom provides an implicit analogue for the English nation's relationship with Algiers, as one of past violation authorizing future conquest. Within accounts such as Knight's, the former captive's personal experience of subjugation, conferring both a comprehensive cultural knowledge and the motive of revenge, seems to authorize his rise to colonial leadership, just as, on a national level, the allegedly "barbarian" tactic of capture creates an imperative for British territorial intervention.

Some narratives offer more literal equations between British conquest of alien cultures and the intellectual mastery conferred by captive experience. When a captivity narrative concludes by showing how a captive's personal knowledge can contribute to British naval power and trade, this closure offers a literal apotheosis of the ethnographic mastery demonstrated in the text's portions of travel description. In the 1685 account of Thomas Phelps, after the narrator escapes from a Moroccan port and meets an English warship, he boldly proposes a plan to guide the English into port so that they can fire the local navy, and his text expresses keen satisfaction at the fulfillment of his plan. The intellectual mastery gained through the captive's personal experience rectifies the seeming national imbalance entailed by the situation of captivity, as the plot moves the British protagonist from a seemingly unnatural position of enslavement among an uncivilized people to a seemingly more natural position of colonial aggression. Similarly, after Knox escapes from Ceylon, his vast expertise on the kingdom of Cande leads the Dutch to consult his knowledge of the king's political strength. Even more tellingly, after Robert Drury's escape from Madagascar, he guides an English ship in a slaving tour of his former home, dresses in Malagasy costume, and draws on his extensive personal experience as a slave when negotiating with local slave dealers. Here even the slave status of the captive contributes to his experiential mastery over an alien culture. The view from the bottom of an alien system of despotism, it seems, grants the captive a particularly strong understanding of that system and an ability to manipulate it for European ends. Through experiential mastery of an alien environment, the captive becomes a leading participant in the colonial mastery of this environment, whether through conquest, trade, or slavery.

Overt textual applications of captive knowledge to colonial situations became important in the Anglo-American context during the second half of the eighteenth century, with the aggressive propaganda that marks such narratives as Peter Williamson's *French and Indian Cruelties* (1757). After Williamson's return from captivity, the authority conferred by his experience receives official sanction when the governor of Pennsylvania "examined me very particularly, as to all Incidents relating to my Captivity," and this testimony is put into writing, sworn to, and deposited among the state's public papers (36–37). Not satisfied without personal retaliation, however, Williamson soon joins a local militia "with the greatest Alacrity and most determined Resolution, to exert the utmost of my Power, in being revenged on the hellish Authors of my Ruin" (38). After enlisting, he finds himself chosen for an expedition to rescue a female captive from the Amerindians, "as I had been so long among them, and pretty well acquainted with their Manners and Customs, and particularly their skulking Places in the Woods" (43). The captive's ethnographic knowledge grants him an authority within the settlers' program for exploration, rescue, and revenge. Later editions of Williamson's narrative tried to raise further capital on his military expertise by including, as his title advertised, a *Description of the most convenient Roads for the British Forces to invade Canada in three Divisions, and make themselves Masters of it.*[56] When a former captive such as Williamson documents the potential colonial efficacy of a personal knowledge gained through an experience of subjugation, this documentation reinforces the genre's dramatic narrative structure, its heroic reversal of the captivity experience's violation of assumed cultural hierarchies.

As the heroism of resistance fuses with various concrete forms of action, it sometimes extends to a colonial violence that ruptures the captivity genre's opposition between "alien" systems of aggressive despotism and the captive as a representative of civilization and liberty. Within Williamson's narrative, for example, the standard oppositional rhetoric of British civilization and American savagery collapses with his zealous description of the results of his scouting expedition. When the expedition slaughters some natives, he reports that "our Men were busily employed in cutting, hacking, and scalping the dead Indians," so that the British seem thoroughly capable of the "Cruelties" that the title ascribes to the French and Indians (46). Williamson's rhetoric does not acknowledge this tension, but more overt moments of moral confusion sometimes surface within other narratives. Soon after the capture of Robert Drury in Madagascar, his fellow British captives seize a local monarch and demand a ransom; recounting these actions, the narrator worries that readers might regard them as somewhat "criminal."[57] Although he quickly resolves this moral dilemma, the incident allows a brief explication of what usually remains an implicit problem within captivity narratives: that captives regularly and sometimes gloatingly resort to the violence and aggression that they cite as the hallmark of captive-taking cultures.

The aggressive heroism of individual action entails further conflict with another of the captivity genre's central strategies, the discourse of providence. In some scholarly accounts, a providential interpretive framework often seems to stand as a unifying feature of the captivity genre, especially as studies of the American narratives often begin with a focus on the Puritans, who often interpreted the passivity enforced by the captivity experience as a sign of the need for Christian reliance on God.[58] But the providential interpretive framework provides not so much a universal formula for understanding the captivity experience as a set of variable strategies for conceiving relationships between God, nations, individuals, and the contingency of events. On the one hand, as studies of the American narratives have repeatedly emphasized, the early Puritan texts framed the personal experience of captivity as an exemplum of the Christian life. In the Puritan vision, captivity among the heathen corresponds to the Christian's captivity to sin and to the world, and the captive must learn that reliance on worldly satisfactions leads to inevitable disappointment, while reliance on God's providence furnishes internal peace.[59] Like the bulk of early American accounts, narratives set in other lands sometimes frame the captivity experience in terms of providential interpretation. Vaughan's account of Malaysia includes a heavy emphasis on the captives' efforts to resign themselves to providence, their "Hope that God will give us his Grace, and so strong a Faith, as not to fear Dying for him." When an English trader arrives and works to obtain the captives' release, they "could not but think it an extraordinary Providence of God in sending so worthy-minded a Friend to our Relief."[60] For Vaughan and his companions, as for many early American captives, reliance on the dispositions of providence seems concomitant with a passive acceptance of contingency and captivity.

Other captives, however, harness the providential interpretive framework in support of various heroisms of action, at both an individual and a national level. Many narratives with Middle Eastern settings, especially, develop the kind of secular application of providential discourse that marks the material progress of Defoe's protagonists, provoking a conflict among literary critics as to the relative weight of religious and materialist perspectives within his novels.[61] Both material and spiritual impulses, both pride in personal achievement and a tendency to displace personal agency, mark the use of providential discourse in captivity narratives such as Knox's Ceylonese account. His dedication to the East India Company insists that his goal in entering the press is "chiefly that I might Publish and Declare the great Mercy of God to me, and Commemorate before all Men my singular Deliverance," which manifests "so many notable Footsteps of his signal Providence" ([b]1r).[62] That such blessings manifest themselves within the success of individual actions becomes apparent at the close of his narrative, when he congratulates providence for his escape after a lengthy, tension-filled account of an arduous overland journey. Although this account highlights his personal fortitude, ingenuity, and resourcefulness, he declares "the whole Business . . . a miraculous Providence . . . the hand of God did eminently appear to me, as it did of old to his People of Israel in the like circumstances, in leading and conducting me thro this dreadful Wilderness" (169). That such blessings manifest themselves at the levels of nations and economies becomes apparent when Knox boasts that the entrepreneurial success of the English captives had forced their Ceylonese neighbors to "confess that Almighty God had dealt far more bountifully with us than with them, in that we had a far greater plenty" (149). In serving a nationalist and colonialist agenda, the discourse of providence can support an ideological justification for aggressive material action by displacing the responsibility for such action onto God.

Other captives likewise frame their colonial success in providential terms. After the escape of Thomas Phelps, when he contributes to the destruction of the very ship that had taken him captive, this personal success leads him to "admire the wonderful providence of God, to whom alone Vengeance belongeth, in vindicating my cause, and making me an unwitting instrument of revenge."[63] Providence seems to support the captives even if its workings seem mysterious or ambiguous, as with Francis Knight's variable assessments of the wellsprings of his personal heroism. At the conclusion of a section where he emerges as the resourceful leader of a successful escape, he attributes his achievement entirely to God, who "has done this great worke for me in delivering me from such an inextrecable labarinth of misery." An earlier comment, however, cites providence as an ingredient in a recipe for action rather than passivity, suggesting that God's power works through individual actions: "I account every Christian oblieged to use all possible attempts for the effecting his libertie; for a man doth not onely discover a pusilanimous heart, and indocible disposition in neglecting the least opportunitie, but also commit a sinne against God, who hath not given us wings to outflie our enemies, but reason to devise strategems and hands to execute them."[64] As a force that seems always to side with Christian captives against their pagan captors, providence can motivate a rhetoric of active resistance as easily as a rhetoric of passive endurance.

From ethnographic vituperation to providential interpretation, the captivity genre develops several rhetorics of generalization that often stand in conflict with each other or with the contingent events of individual experience. Depending on the events of a captive's experience, a narrative might develop a plot that offers an analogue for aggressive colonialism or a model for passive dependence on providence, or the narrator might try to unite the two perspectives. Individual captors might encourage initiative on the part of their servants, carefully limit their movements, or force them to undergo torture, proselytism, hard labor, or abject squalor. Furthermore, the harsh conditions of subjugation might reduce the captive to psychological turpitude or stimulate an active drive for escape, revenge, or success. Through all of these variable conditions runs a fundamental tension between passivity and action that stems from the debasement and subordination of the captivity experience and the difficulties of narrating it for a domestic audience. Within that tension lies a potential for transforming the debased, subordinate, and passive captive into a figure of aggressive, nationalist heroism, but the heroism of the captive is always ambiguous. Although the captive's escape and colonial activity reverse the terms of subjugation imposed by the captivity experience, such activity often depends on the captive's successful participation and accommodation within an alien culture. All of these tensions, as we shall see in the next chapter, become more pronounced with the situation of transculturation, especially when narrators describe their conversion and success within alien cultures.

THREE

The Perils and the Powers of Cultural Conversion

If the captivity narrative is a genre particularly disposed towards a binary rhetoric opposing self and other, this rhetoric always overwrites an experience of necessary intimacy between captive and captor, or at least between the captive and the alien culture of the captor. Many British captives entered systems of household servitude rather than gang labor, systems encouraging familial intimacy rather than hierarchical distance. Even if a narrative does not acknowledge such distinctions, the captive's situation as a household servant often produces moments of cultural intimacy that sit somewhat uneasily amidst a rhetorical frame stressing liberty and oppression. Even when a captive had joined an ethnically divided system of gang labor, his retrospective account would always raise the question of cultural conversion because of his enforced separation from British culture and his participation, whether willing or unwilling, in another culture.[1] Captive participation in alien cultures runs the gamut from eating foreign foods to embracing alien religions. The varied experiences of captivity necessarily "expose the captive and her readers to the alternative cultural paradigms of her captors," as Michelle Burnham has argued in discussing narratives focused on American women; because of this exposure, such narratives "traverse those very cultural, national, and racial boundaries that they seem so indelibly to inscribe."[2] But with culture-crossing as with other captivity themes, the American captivity tradition tended to follow the ambivalent patterns established by its British counterpart. The fullest and richest accounts of American transculturation emerged from the nineteenth-century press, whereas the British press produced extensive accounts of transculturation in other lands during the first half of the eighteenth century. Within the British captivity tradition, the texts that most intensively engaged the problems of culture-crossing still struggled to embrace the textual strategies of ethnography, colonial heroism, and the early novel, and their struggle throws into sharp relief the ambivalent place of transculturation within the captivity genre as a whole.

The ambivalence of the captive's culture-crossing lay primarily in that it often seemed to confer enormous empirical authority but also tended to undermine the oppositional grounds of ethnographic knowledge. In promoting the captive's ethnographic authority, some texts aggressively exploited the ambiguities of his identity. In the preface to Thomas Pellow's 1739 account of captivity in Morocco, for example, his editor insists that other visitors to the region had lacked "sufficient Opportunities of Observation: Whereas, the Writer of this History, by his long Abode in the Country for the Space of 23 Years, and by his outward embracing of the Mahometan Faith, and becoming, as it were, one of the Natives, had repeated Opportunities of knowing and noting every Thing worthy Observation, or which would give him a thorough Knowledge of the Nature and Temper of the Inhabitants; and still the more so, as he was so long employed in the Palace about the Emperor's Person, and afterward so much concerned in all their bloody Wars."[3] Here it seems that Pellow's deep involvement in Moroccan culture, his penetration of its most intimate recesses, and even the transformation of his cultural identity all serve to buttress his ethnographic authority. That a hybrid cultural identity could carry appeals as well as anxieties for English readers is further evident in the title of James Wadsworth's 1629 account of his imprisonments first at a Spanish Jesuit school and then in a Salleean galley. Despite its heavy doses of anti-Catholic diatribe, this narrative carries the main title *The English Spanish Pilgrime,* advertising Wadsworth's experiences in captivity through a hybrid identity that strengthens his authority to speak against the Jesuits at the cost of highlighting the malleability of English identity.

As a result of such fundamental ambiguities, even the most systematically ethnographic of captivity narratives register significant tensions in their efforts to develop a stable opposition between Western observer and alien culture. Even the most insular and resistant of captive-narrators record moments when they failed to resist their captors' efforts in cultural conversion, moments of personal crisis that rupture the smooth veneer of ethnographic description. On the other hand, narrators who admit to conversion during their captivity reveal especially anxious attempts to prove renewed attachments to Christianity and to Britain now that they are home. Captive-narrators who achieved positions of relative comfort within alien cultures often shift between a tone of satisfaction at their achievements and hostility towards the alien means of their advancement. Cultural participation can raise problems at the most fundamental levels of language, such as when the former convert Joseph Pitts describes his pilgrimage to Mecca, shifting uncomfortably back and forth among the pronouns "I," "we," and "they," as if unable to establish a grounded subjective position from which to narrate this alien experience.[4] Such tensions result because Pitts is torn by multiple forms of identification in the very process of recording his participation in an alien culture for an English audience. He uses "we" to identify himself as a participant in shared Islamic customs, and thus as a beneficiary of the augmented cultural authority conferred through transculturation, but he turns to "they" in conforming to the oppositional demands of travel description. "I" helps to separate him from the culture he describes, especially when he wants to convince his British readers that his religious observance was formal rather than genuine. This divided narrating subject provides a particularly clear instance of the epistemological conflicts that occur when narratives of extensive cultural participation struggle to engage the captivity genre's framework of ethnography and cultural insularity.

The importance of transculturation narratives within the captivity tradition can be gauged by their popularity and influence. Along with the Barbary narratives of Pitts and Pellow, the 1729 narrative of Robert Drury's captivity in Madagascar dominated the market for captivity narratives in the first half of the eighteenth century, before the explosion of American accounts in the second half of the century. At the time of their publication, these three accounts of extensive transculturation among African peoples were the longest and most ethnographically detailed captivity narratives in the English language, and the fullness of their ethnographic information made them standard references for Western discussions of these cultures until well into the nineteenth century. These early eighteenth-century narratives, moreover, acted as direct precursors for the most successful and influential American captivities of the nineteenth century, those of Alexander Henry, John Dunn Hunter, and Mary Jemison, which recorded extensive transculturation among Native Americans, won fame for their authors on both sides of the Atlantic, and influenced the developing American myth of cross-cultural brotherhood.[5] As attested by the length, influence, and popularity of these texts, whether set in America, Africa, or the Orient, the possibility of cultural conversion was a definitive point of interest for Anglophone documentation and consumption of the captivity experience.

In an effort to understand the enormous yet ambiguous appeal of captive conversion, this chapter will briefly consider the question of culture-crossing within the captivity genre as a whole, before concentrating on an extended reading of the Drury and Pellow texts. Despite external evidence for the factuality of these texts, twentieth-century scholars have sometimes taken them for novels, and certainly both show strong signs of editorial intervention and even of outright fabrication. As the mixture of fact and fiction within these texts suggests, accounts of cultural conversion not only disturbed and excited British readers but also provided an effective means for experimenting with novelistic patterns of subjectivity, for playing with the boundaries and internal conflicts of national identity. Narratives of extensive culture-crossing, then, in addition to helping us understand the captivity genre as a whole, provide a good starting point for investigating the genre's relationship with the novel.

Of all the tensions that mark the captivity genre, the sharpest stem from the possibility of transculturation that sits uneasily at its heart. Every returned captive faced an audience suspicious of and yet intrigued by the possibility that the author had gone native, forced by the very situation of captivity to participate in the alleged depravities of an uncivilized culture if not to redefine himself or herself as a member of that culture. Far from straightforward, untroubled records of cultural opposition, many captivity narratives inscribe anxious struggles to prove that their protagonists' attachments to Britain and to Christianity never lapsed. Although captivity narratives often exploit their protagonists' extensive participation in alien cultures as a source of ethnographic authority, nationalist pride, and colonial success, they also take care to forestall any impression that such participation might have climaxed with a complete cultural transformation.

These struggles are especially marked in the case of Islamic captives such as Pitts and Pellow. In the most thoroughly researched study of English literature on the Islamic world, Samuel Chew has suggested that returned captives often exaggerated their captors' efforts in cultural conversion: "The general impression in England that Moslems practised forcible conversion was probably founded upon the reports of escaped or ransomed captives who hid under the pleas of compulsion their voluntary lapse from Christianity."[6] On the rare occasions when captives admitted to conversion, their narratives reveal sharp anxieties about their audience's reactions to this transformation. Thomas Pellow's 1739 account, for example, abruptly departs from calm autobiographical retrospection when he describes his first assumption of Moroccan dress, his first "appearing like a Mahometan; and I make no Doubt but some ill-natured People think me so even to this Day" (16).

Even when captives did not convert, they faced suspicion and accusations after their return to their natal culture. Adam Elliott produced his 1682 captivity narrative as the opening salvo of a text designed to vindicate himself from a slew of charges made by Titus Oates. According to this former captive, the infamous fabricator of the Popish plot had labeled him "a Jesuit who is no Christian but a Turk," and a "Mahumetan [who] had been thereupon Circumcised"; through such labels, Elliot charged, Oates had rendered him "unworthy of credit or reputation, uncapable of the advantages of converse amongst Christians."[7] To defeat a charge of a hybrid identity that would seem to disbar him from the benefits of Christian civility, Elliot offers a straightforward account of his sufferings and escape in order to show that he faced no efforts in conversion.

Even when a captivity narrative does not explicitly register a former captive's anxieties about his reception within English culture, the tense possibilities of cultural conversion enter the narrative in other forms. One source of tension is the narrators' concern with the conversion of other captives, especially among Islamic captors. Former Islamic captives who had themselves converted or faced accusations of conversion would understandably tend to exaggerate the number of other European converts. In many narratives, emphasis on the powerful temptation, prevalence, and efficacy of conversion helps to constitute the heroism of resistance *as* a heroism, an arduous deviation from a normal failure to resist. Introducing his narrative of heroic escape from Algiers, Francis Knight comments in his preface, "I have knowne many who through the extremitie of their sufferings hath renounced their Saviour, and imbraced the Mahomitan and diabolicall Imposture."[8] The conversion of other captives provides an opening framework against which Knight defines his own experience of heroic resistance. Similarly, William Okeley's 1675 Algerian narrative, which devotes much attention to the psychological tensions of the captivity experience, also cites the conversion of others as a direct counterpoint to his own temptation: "We were under a perpetual temptation to deny the Lord that bought us, to make our Souls Slaves, that our Bodies might Recover Liberty. . . . How many have made Ship-wreck of Faith, that they might not be Chained to the Galleys?"[9] Constantly repeated across many captivity narratives and confirmed by other travel descriptions of Islamic states, such comments sought to convince British readers that Islamic captives were completely encompassed by proselytizers and converts.[10]

Another source of tension results when former Islamic captives record the results of conversion for those "renegadoes" who become accustomed to alien identities and even achieve high social positions with the relatively open hierarchies of Islam. In adopting Islam, a renegado can seem to have adopted the full ethnic identity, even the allegedly natural disposition, of a Middle Eastern people, such as when T. Smith's 1670 Algerian narrative identifies a Cornish convert with the hoary stereotype "Deceitful Turk."[11] In some accounts of Barbary captivity, renegadoes seem entirely infected with the imputed violence and passion of the East, more Oriental than the natives themselves. Smith describes a Spanish renegado as "animated with a strange fury and desire of revenge," passions so strong that he cuts off and eats a piece of a captive's cheek (22). Similarly, when Pellow describes an "Exeter man" turned Moroccan executioner, he details the convert's considerable pride and dexterity in mastering the cruelties so often ascribed to Barbary cultures (102). If cultural conversion sometimes seems to result in extreme mania or violence, captive narrators more frequently attest to the power of renegadoes within Islamic cultures. Smith cites their power to support a claim for the low state of Islamic civilization, insisting that they "are most skillful because they are acquainted with the Affairs of Europe, and better able to manage the Publick Business relating to that part of the World, and to give Orders" (68). While such a comment enforces an impression of European superiority, it also portrays conversion as an experience that enables a managerial success such as budding colonists might want to emulate. The material success of renegadoes raises other kinds of tension within Joseph Pitts's 1704 account of Algiers: "these Renegadoes have a greater Blessing than the natural Turks, for they commonly become great Men and bear sway" (107). Nationalistic pride in the success of renegadoes here extends to the possibility that providence may have rewarded Christians for their apostasy. Another kind of tension arises when Pitts includes a reversed captivity episode, the tale of an Irish renegado captured at a young age and raised as a Muslim, but then recaptured and enslaved in Christian galleys. Pitts's report on the Islamic perspective of this Christian captive directly parallels the language commonly used to describe the plight of Christian captives in Islam: "he passionately told me, that God had delivered him out of Hell upon Earth" (153). The reversed application of a phrase so frequently used to describe the Barbary states creates one of the strongest moments of reversed perspective in all of captivity literature.

Besides the tension produced by the third-person figure of the full convert, other moments of textual disturbance arise through first-person narration of willing or unwilling accession to various aspects of an alien culture. Although many captive narrators portray their captors as an undifferentiated mass of tyrants, others offer praise for exceptional governments or portray exceptional figures, beneficent masters, and exemplary leaders. Positive masters often entail significant ideological confusion. Within Okeley's 1675 account of his Algerian captivity, his final master proves so friendly that the text fills two pages with the captive's internal debates about the propriety of escape, before the logic of natural rights and consent finally determines his path.[12] Positive masters sometimes invoke the noble savage tradition of primitive exemplars offering an implicit satire of the civilized. In his 1729 narrative of captivity in Madagascar, Robert Drury praises one tribal leader whose example can teach Christian princes "to be in reality so truly just, honourable, and good as this gallant black prince was in all his actions; and yet I question not but he must be called an illiterate heathen."[13] The palpable goodness of this native exemplar throws the narrator into doubt, ironically expressed as certainty, as to the general English usage for labeling a culture such as that of Madagascar.

When captives find happy relationships with their masters or with other friendly natives, they sometimes introduce a language of familial relationships that suggests a particularly intimate level of cultural participation. After Joseph Pitts's first masters torture him and force his conversion, he finds a sympathetic final master, who raises him above his slave status and buys him a slave of his own. As Pitts recalls, this final master "seldom called me anything but Son," and "I had a great Love for him, even as a Father" (224–25). Similarly, William Vaughan's 1714 Malaysian narrative is filled with suffering for the captive protagonist until his adoption by a powerful native couple, who ask him to "call them Father and Mother, as they did me Child." This familial bond creates an impression of lingering tenderness when, at Vaughan's departure, his "*Syam* Mother" asks if he will remember his adoptive parents.[14] Likewise, near the end of Robert Drury's sojourn in Madagascar, he finds a mistress whom he learns to call "my mother" and a master who "spake as tender things to me as my own father could" (197, 282). Especially when complemented by intimations of emotional attachment, terms of familial address suggest a happy adaptation to a transformed cultural identity. A similar attention to the practice of cross-cultural adoption, likewise heightened by familial terms of address, later became a prominent feature of the American captivity narrative, especially when, in the early nineteenth century, the popular and influential accounts of Alexander Henry, Mary Jemison, and John Tanner offered positive views of lengthy adoptions into Native American families.[15]

If some captivity narratives portray captives who occupied positions of familial identification within alien cultures, every captivity narrative entails an implicit yet pervasive sense of the protagonist's accommodation with a culture treated as inferior. Coupled with prefatory claims of experiential authority, the narratives' consistent devaluation of the foreign creates an ambivalent vision of the protagonists' subjection to inferior cultures. While a captive's scorn suggests a successful maintenance of British cultural standards during the period of captivity, the narrative occasion for such scorn is often the captive's personal experience of the very objects of derision. Thus the most ethnographic of captivity texts, Robert Knox's 1681 account of Ceylon, expresses harsh scorn for native bedding at the point in his narrative where he must first adapt to its regular use.[16] In a text published fifty-five years later, the American captive John Gyles scoffs that "Indian barns" are mere "holes in the ground" while describing native agriculture from the perspective of a participant, with the plural pronoun "we."[17] Even when a captive scorns a native custom without an overt indication that it formed an element within his personal cultural transformation, the possibility and even the necessity that it did so always remains implicit within the narrative's epistemological framework, which grants the captive the authority to scorn an alien culture on the basis of his forced experience of it. Within the broader structure of a captivity narrative, scorn for a wigwam, for example, always rests on an implicit understanding that the captive must have slept in one for days, months, or even years.

Many objects of cultural scorn also entail an implicit pride in the breadth, variety, and exoticism of the personal experience that encompasses such objects. A particularly concrete topos of mixed scorn and accommodation is native foodstuffs. Captives held across the globe complain of hunger, criticize native food production, and attribute their deprivation to the mismanagement of uncivilized peoples. Remembering his Ceylonese sojourn, Knox scoffs that a primarily vegetarian diet is "with them accounted Good Cheer," and records his terrible suffering at a time when general sickness revealed the scanty capacity of native food stores.[18] Adopting a similar perspective in describing Madagascar, Robert Drury finds the local fare inadequate and blames widespread hunger on the constant warfare of petty tyrants. However, he also reports, "I began after a while to reconcile myself to their manner of eating, seeing no better was to be had" (79). A more enthusiastic culinary adaptation surfaces in Pellow's account of Moroccan couscous, as he declares himself as "really so far of the Moors Opinion, as that I cannot but in every Respect allow it truly deserving of their so very high Esteem" (31). Pellow relishes the dish even after his escape, illustrating the wide-ranging possibilities of cultural adaptation even in a case where the captive presents most of his experience as a struggle against native culture.

American accounts are famous for the captives' commentary on the deprivation imposed by native food preparation or times of scarcity, especially during harsh New England winters. In some narratives both captives and captors starve for days at a time, and the captives blame their hunger on the natives' level of civilization. As Elizabeth Hanson's 1728 narrative observes, her captors possessed "no other way to depend on [meat] but hunting" (Vaughan and Clark, 235). Like many an early European commentator on American alimentary customs, she describes the natives' winter eating habits as a foolish mismanagement: "for these kind of people when they have plenty spend it as freely as they get it, spending in gluttony and drunkenness in two days' time as much as with prudent management might serve a week" (Vaughan and Clark, 237). American captivity narratives, however, are equally famous for their protagonists' adaptation to what they portray as the wretched fruits of native culinary practice, such as bear meat, deer fetus, beaver skin, tree bark, and horse entrails. The locus classicus here is Rowlandson, who like Hanson, deplores the "wast" of a native feast and describes native food as fit for animals, although she too eventually finds it satisfying: "The first week of my being among them, I hardly ate any thing; the second week, I found my stomach grow very faint for want of something; and yet it was very hard to get down their filthy trash: but the third week, though I could think how formerly my stomach would turn against this or that, and I could starve and dy before I could eat such things, yet they were sweet and savoury to my taste" (Vaughan and Clark, 44).[19] This passage records the most telling moment within a lengthy process of psychological adaptation to native foodstuffs. Similar processes of adaptation within many captivity narratives hint that European captives can overcome the most palpable of cultural aversions.

A rather different case of a captive's proud adaptation to the very customs he scorns appears in T. Smith's 1670 account of Algerian sexuality. Like many narratives of Islamic captivity, Smith's portrays the Orient as a sexual snare, but one whose rampant, polymorphous perversity raises titillating possibilities of cultural accommodation. According to Smith, the confinement of the seraglio leads Oriental women to become "furiously debauch'd" adherents of a "wandering" sexuality that takes "pleasure in variety" (205–6). Other allegedly Oriental forms of sexuality also earn the merchant's scorn. Observing a vaguely described statue of a "bestial" sex act, he cites it as evidence for the proposition that "it is necessary that the Moors should have such signal Tokens of Gods Displeasure always before their Eyes; for they are enraged to commit such filthy Actions more frequently than other Nations" (240). The seemingly rampant sexuality of the Orient affects the merchant personally as he resists a variety of sexual advances, especially since he fears "that all addresses that were made to me of that nature were but Designes to ensnare me, and oblige me to Apostacie" (204). At one level such forward sexuality supports a heroism of resistance in the form of sexual restraint, especially when one woman pursues him with such "tricks and inventions" as are "not to be imagined," while Smith retains "constancy enough, and was sufficiently wary, to frustrate all of her undertakings" (206, 219). On the other hand, Smith also takes pride in his adaptation to the alleged forwardness of Algerian women. After narrating his seduction by the wife of the Algerian king, Smith turns to his purchase by the wife of another older man, and the sexual interest of this new mistress grants the merchant a merely nominal captivity, so that he "only wore a Chain out of Formality" (40). This enterprising captive gains freedom and a secure place in the ranks of Algerian society through an accommodation with its alleged sexual freedom. Although these incidents promote a national pride in the captive Englishman's transition to sexual mastery, they also represent, within the broader rhetorical framework of Smith's comments on Oriental sexuality, a moment of accommodation with what he represents as a degrading feature of an alien culture.

Although many narratives contrast the outward imposition of alien cultural forms with the captives' inward adherence to Christianity, liberty, and Britain, such outward forms also sometimes effect powerful changes in cultural identity, and these changes sometimes endure, like Pellow's taste for couscous, even after the captive returns among Europeans. In one motif that surfaces in captivity narratives set across the globe, the physical appearance of the returned captive, as a result of sartorial transformation or bodily abjection, leads his fellow Europeans to mistake the European identity he wishes to assert. In Peter Williamson's 1757 American narrative, after escaping his captors, he meets a European who takes him for an Indian.[20] A similar case of mistaken identity threatens to undo the climactic resolution of Thomas Pellow's narrative. After he escapes Morocco and reaches Gibraltar, British guardsmen refuse him entry into the garrison, insisting "that till they had Orders for my so doing, they would not suffer any Moor to land" (376). Such skepticism about the captive's cultural identity often arises soon after his or her escape, transforming a long-hoped-for moment of cultural reunion into a moment of isolation, dislocation, and cultural confusion.

A similar experience of cultural dislocation occurs after the climactic escape in Robert Knox's 1681 narrative of Ceylonese captivity, even though his European rescuers immediately recognize him as a European. After he and another escapee join the garrison of a Dutch governor, Knox recalls with some perplexity, "we seemed not fit to eat with his Servants, no nor his Slaves," and "it seemed not a little strange to us, who had dwelt so long in Straw Cottages among the Black Heathen, and used to sit on the Ground and eat our Meat on Leaves, now to sit on Chairs and eat out of China Dishes at Table." Because their poverty prevented their assumption of European clothing, "all the Soldiers came staring at us, wondring [sic] to see White-men in Chingalay Habit."[21] Here the captives' psychological adaptation to an uncivilized culture seems to match their assumption of uncivilized clothing, and both seem to hold them separate from the European culture that they have ardently wished to rejoin. As these various incidents suggest the permanent efficacy of native clothing in shaping perceptions of cultural identity, they emphasize the malleability of cultural identity, especially under the conditions of forced adaptation entailed by captivity.

While isolated moments of heightened cultural malleability mark the experiences of even the most insular and resistant of captives, other captives offer texts that document extensive processes of cultural transformation. Especially exciting and troubling for English readers, it seems, were narratives of captives taken at a young age, narratives recording conversion to Islam, and narratives documenting the creation of a successful lifestyle within an alien culture. These themes are especially prominent in the three most prominent Anglophone captivity narratives of the early eighteenth century, the accounts of Pitts, Drury, and Pellow. First published in 1704 and revised in three other editions until 1738, Pitts's narrative records a lengthy enslavement in Algeria, a conversion to Islam, and even a pilgrimage to Mecca. Twenty-five years later, in 1729, appeared the first of four eighteenth-century printings for Robert Drury's *Madagascar,* which followed its author's successive enslavements and cultural adaptations among a variety of tribes on that island. The 1739 edition was the first of four printings of Thomas Pellow's aptly titled *Long Captivity and Adventures,* which detailed his twenty-three years' captivity in the Barbary States, his conversion, and his military leadership in the service of several tyrants. All three of these narrators experienced nearly complete cultural transformations among peoples that contemporary English readers would have associated with extreme barbarism, and yet all three texts not only acknowledged their successful adaptation to these cultures but even recorded with some pride their advancement from positions of abject enslavement to moderate prosperity. All three texts, furthermore, reveal distinct problems in constructing a relationship between autobiographical voice and alien world. These problems result from their juxtaposition of conflicting discursive modes, such as the documentary schema of ethnography, the rhetoric of British nationalism and colonial expansion, and personal accounts of cultural conversion and accomplishment.

For Pitts, the need to explain and justify cultural conversion creates sharp tensions within his narrative structure and strategies of authentication. After beginning his account in autobiographical fashion and then recording his capture and sale, he quickly abandons this linear structure and turns to a series of travel descriptions, starting with Algiers, moving through Egypt, and culminating with Mecca. But it is not until after he completes his description of Mecca, three-quarters of the way through his text, that he provides "An account of the Author's turning Mahometan." This personal account, moreover, begins defensively: "The Reader, I suppose, will expect an Account, how I became qualified to write such an History as this . . . and how I was let into the Secrets of the Mahometan Religion, so as to be able to give such an exact Description of it, and particularly of their Pilgrimage to Mecca" (180). This offhand, accommodating tone backfires, however, because its defensiveness foregrounds the chronological incongruity involved in placing the early conversion experience after an ethnographic description of places visited much later in the author's experience. If Pitts had placed his conversion narrative before his travel descriptions, it would have enhanced his ethnographic authority. But removed from its proper place in a strict chronological rendering, the conversion seems self-consciously buried and self-consciously exposed, advertising itself as a secret and a problem. Similar ambiguities occur as he justifies his conversion. Like many captives, Pitts attributes his conversion to torture, but like no other captive, he insists that the Algerians rarely used such means for conversion: "it was my hard Lot to be so unmercifully dealt with: They do not use to force any Christian to renounce his Religion" (181). This account of conversion renders him an isolated case, a unique instance, the only Westerner who could boast such an extensive knowledge as could grant a legitimate claim to sell such a text. But there is something equivocal in Pitts's uniqueness, because his experience departs from the very ethnographic norm that he wishes to allege. His careful, defensive handling of the conversion material suggests the high ideological stakes that it raises as a potential source of both the writer's authority and the reader's suspicion, as a sign both of the heroic breadth of the author's experience and his difficult accommodation within an allegedly inferior culture.

Even greater confusions in structure and voice attend the highly edited narrative of Thomas Pellow, especially as it records his steady advancement through a political system that he routinely attacks in the standard Orientalist idiom for vituperating despotism. After his capture at the age of eleven, his sojourn in Morocco includes some of the most widely varied experiences in captivity literature, from his upbringing in the household of a tyrannical emperor to a standard account of personal torture, from his leadership in the Moroccan military to his picaresque wanderings as a medical charlatan. Though the text narrates Pellow's religious conversion in terms of a heroic but unavailing resistance, it records his subsequent cultural accommodations with little overt impression of psychological disturbance and with much implicit pride in the vast accumulation of his varied experience. His accommodations with Moroccan culture, moreover, are so thorough and so successful that he arrives at a position of relative power in what he represents as a barbaric system of political despotism. In attempting to position Pellow as simultaneously superior to and part of this despotism, the text becomes tangled both with the conflicting generic effects of its varied sections and with basic confusions in narrative subject and tense.

Whereas Pitts struggles to maintain the organizational structure of a travel narrative, Pellow and his editor develop one of the most ungainly, distended, and disorganized captivity narratives in the English language. After beginning in an autobiographical format, the text often shifts randomly between personal narration and general schemes of documentation. Part of this confusion seems to reflect the extreme length of Pellow's captivity. Captured in his youth and writing over twenty years later, he produced an account whose level of personal detail expands exponentially as he ages. Perhaps because of the paucity of detail documenting his youth, his editor's footnotes and insertions seem particularly extensive and intrusive in the early stages of the narrative. The text attributed to Pellow includes some sections of travel description but also sometimes refuses to employ such discursive schema at moments when they seem appropriate. In recalling his first voyage, he disclaims the strict format of a sea journal because of his youth and inexperience. Later, recalling his arrival at Morocco, he observes that "it may be expected that I should give a particular Description, and an Account of all its Curiosities; which I could readily, and would as willingly do, did I not think it altogether inconsistent with my main Point, and would enlarge my History to very little Purpose" (94). Pellow's purpose here seems curiously inconsistent with that avowed by his editor's preface, which proclaims the ethnographic authority of the converted captive. The text moves closer to the editor's purposes soon after this point, breaking from personal narration for a historical account of a tyrant's reign, and thereafter mixing general political history with Pellow's autobiography.

Thus Pellow's narration seems expedient rather than rigorous, following the trail of his memory and inclinations rather than the strict documentary framework that the editor sometimes tries to interpose. A particularly disjointed section begins with the promise to provide an account of "My Wonderful Escape and Happy Return," but in its place either Pellow or his editor inserts a section giving "some further Account of the strange Customs and Manners of the Moors" (244). Immediately after this long, rambling, and stereotypical ethnography, the climactic escape section finally arrives, but it resembles a narrative of captive heroism less than a picaresque novel. The most painstakingly detailed and most overtly fictionalized section in the text documents Pellow's wanderings through Barbary as a medical charlatan during a period of political chaos, as he preys on the natives' putative credulity but also suffers multiple beatings and hunger. In typical picaresque fashion, the narrative devotes particular care to his efforts to secure food, his gruesome abuse of gullible patients, and his avoidance of any political authorities who might force him back into military service.

Amidst this disparate array of discursive strategies, Pellow's retrospective voice both vituperates the tyranny that he ascribes to Morocco and portrays his active participation in that tyranny. On the one hand, his text relies heavily on a standard Orientalist framework of political, economic, and religious oppositions. In the midst of a section recording his experiences during several ruthlessly repressed rebellions, the narrative pauses for a standard opposition between British government and Oriental despotism: "Here we may see the dangerous Consequences of ARBITRARY POWER, and thank GOD that we are governed by such wholesome Laws, as are those of this happy Nation; whereby every one is allowed fair Tryal in Matters of Life and Death, as well as like Equity in the Recovering and keeping their own" (103). This standard oppositional pattern continues for several pages, as Pellow or his editor adds a contrast between the economy of Morocco, where tyrants plunder their own people and destroy trade, and the prosperous economy of Britain (104–5). In some ways, Pellow's text represents the nationalist capstone of the Oriental captivity tradition, developing detailed descriptions of the political and economic institutions of Oriental lands in order to support a rhapsodic celebration of British institutions.

This generalized rhetoric of tyranny and freedom finds a concrete narrative parallel in the description of Pellow's conversion. Given to an emperor's son who tries forcible conversion, Pellow suffers close confinement, shackling, and "bastinading" (15). In recording the moment of his surrender, the text invokes a standard oppositional framework of bodily subjugation and inner freedom: "My tortures were now exceedingly encreased, burning my Flesh off my Bones by Fire; which the Tyrant did, by frequent Repetitions, after a most cruel Manner; insomuch, that through my so very acute Pains, I was at last constrained to submit, calling upon GOD to forgive me, who knows that I never gave the Consent of the Heart, though I seemingly yielded, by holding up my Finger" (15–16). Once the captive accepts what here seems a merely physical adherence to Islam, other material forms of cultural adaptation seem to follow in course. Although at first he suffers imprisonment for "refusing to put on the Moorish Habit," he later comes to regard this refusal as "a very foolish Obstinacy, since it was a Thing indifferent in its own Nature" (16). After the early conversion scene, the subsequent narrative evokes much less concern for Pellow's adaptations to what the ethnographic portions cite as the defining features of Moroccan culture.

As a whole, the narrative depicts a captive's gradual, precarious, and voluntary rise through the ranks of a society ruled by tyrants, a progress that involves acceptance of and adaptation to the norms of subjugation and violence that he attributes to this society. As a child he fills the difficult position of servant to the Moroccan empress, who subsequently recommends him "to the Emperor's good Liking as a careful and diligent Servant, and as indeed I really was, so far as I thought might be consistent with my Advantage and Safety" (26). For all this wary self-interest, Pellow attains a life of relative comfort primarily by adapting to positions of subjugation. Elsewhere he records his conformity to the degrading physical formalities that Orientalism often cited as a hallmark of despotism, gestures such as "bowing twice, falling to the Ground, and kissing it, and after that the Emperor's Foot, (which is the Custom of those who desire to be heard[)]" (71). Serving the emperor also requires the captive's habituation to the violence associated with Oriental despotism, as his master "used, on any slight Occasion, to knock his People on the Head, as I had several Times the Pleasure of beholding; for in short (although I did not know how soon it might have been my own Fate) I did not care how soon they were all dead" (27). In this compressed, ambiguous, and perhaps ironic phrasing, Pellow seems to have adopted the disregard for life that Orientalism in general, Barbary captivity narratives in particular, and even this passage itself all ascribed to Oriental rulers.

Pellow's accommodation with the violence that he depicts as the hallmark of Moroccan culture forms a central element within his narrative's largest pattern of ambiguous adaptation, as he achieves a position of authority within the emperor's tyrannical regime. When not suppressing various rebellions, Pellow enjoys a life of genteel leisure as an officer within the emperor's military establishment and system of collecting tribute, among an elite that "spen[t] the best Part of our Time in shooting and hunting in the Woods" (106). Despite this rise to power and leisure, he still regards himself as a subaltern, "always obliged to follow the Emperor's Pleasure" (98). As master and servant, given both to exploitative leisure and to degrading service, Pellow stands as an Englishman who has accommodated himself to one of the most thoroughly vituperated stereotypes in eighteenth-century Orientalism: the tyrant's lackey, the tyrannized functionary who becomes a tyrant in his own turn.

Pellow's position as tyrannical lackey enhances the authority of his ethnography, by giving him ample opportunity to travel and to observe instances of despotism, but it also raises fundamental problems in narrative voice. In collecting tribute and subduing rebels, he works to support the tyranny that he ascribes to various potentates. Throughout much of a long section documenting this career, Pellow's narration vacillates among a personal voice of cultural distance, a personal voice of proud success, and a plural voice of cultural participation. While personal phrases such as "my garrisons" and "my troops" suggest pride in his personal power, plural phrases such as "I and my comrades" firmly situate the narrator as a congenial participant within a culture that he elsewhere repudiates as alien (83). More tellingly, Pellow often distances himself from governmental tyranny by expressing sympathy for the plight and valor of various rebels, but he also frequently adopts the plural perspective of governmental organization, even when describing the cruelties used to subdue the rebels, cruelties that he elsewhere cites in order to separate himself, and the British in general, from the peoples of Barbary. In recounting one revolt against a particular emperor, he praises the rebels as a people "resolved to deliver their Country from his Tyranny, or perish with it," a people who "fought us to the last with a noble Resolution" (194). This passage closely follows another, however, where he describes "our cruel Treatment of those we took alive, as unmercifully cutting some to Pieces, and hanging others up alive by the Heels, till they were dead thro' Anguish and Hunger" (193). Here and elsewhere a doubled perspective results from Pellow's use of the first-person plural voice to describe the cruelties of the government he served. At another point he describes his regiment as "ravaging and plundering the Country all Round us of their Corn, Fruit, Cattle, &c after a most shocking Manner" (199). The narrator is both part of and distanced from such plunder, simultaneously recalling his participation in it and marking its repugnant alterity.

Pellow often adopts the organizational perspective of his tyrant-masters as a simple result of his efforts to assist English readers in understanding the alien geographic and political context of particular rebellions. Despite his sympathy for various rebels, he also repeatedly labels them "Malecontents." In describing how one set of insurgents sued for peace after a bloody struggle, he avers that they "were very reasonably answered" with a refusal, and he implies that such rebels could hold no bargaining position (115). As the narration adopts the perspective of Moroccan government, this perspective sometimes coalesces, quite ambiguously, with the documentary schema of travel description. At one point Pellow interrupts his narration with a list documenting the tribute paid to a particular emperor. Elsewhere he organizes an account of a long journey, undertaken to quell yet another rebellion, as a catalogue of towns that provided garrisons for his troops. The catalogue presents each town in terms of its political allegiance, with one town ruled by a leader "in very high Esteem with the Emperor," with a second "very friendly to us," and with a third governed by "one of the Emperor's Sons" (110). At one level Pellow's position within the Moroccan government augments the ethnographic authority of his documentary schema, whether they list towns or demonstrate tyranny, but the conflation of such schema and the organizational perspective of the government ultimately destabilizes the captivity narrative's generic opposition between Western intellectual modernity and Oriental political archaism. In place of this opposition, Pellow's narrative suggests that systematic ethnography benefits from participation in political tyranny. More generally, his impulse to portray tyranny as a keynote of Moroccan culture leads to confusions in narrative voice when he records his participation in such tyranny.

Another cultural dislocation in narrative voice occurs because of Pellow's constant shifts between past and present tense. Many paragraphs open in the present tense, with the word "now" providing an introductory signal, as if the former captive, in the act of composition, has relocated himself within a past that seems tangibly present in his memories. When he describes a besieging army, for example, he writes, "Now am I one in the above Number before Old Fez" (165). When applied in the second person, moreover, this narrative device thrusts the reader into the timeless present of the narrator's memories: "Now might you hear, even in all Places, the Blacks threatening" (226). After such present-tense openings, Pellow's paragraphs quickly shift to the past tense and hold it for their duration, but these shifts often occur with chaotic abruptness. Contemplating his escape, he recalls, "Now am I soon about to encounter with this so hazardous and painful Undertaking; and at the End of the eighth Day . . . I set out" (289). In foregrounding the process of memory, these shifts also foreground the singularity of Pellow's perspective, and thus they overthrow the captivity narrative's structural opposition between the pristine, timeless world of ethnography and the troubled chronology of captive experience.

The text's troubled chronology reflects deeper conflicts in the representation of Pellow's cultural identity. A particularly odd sentence describes the maneuvers of his army: "We are now . . . 3206 on the Road, all well mounted, the Men of fine Horse; which, as they are so famous for Goodness, it will not be improper to say something of the Moors Method of managing them.— The Moors take a great deal of Pride in their Horses, and order them after a very different Manner from us" (79). Pellow begins the recollection with his subjective position firmly imbedded in the timeless recall of the present tense and firmly wedded to that of the Moors, who are marked by a curiously precise number. But then he, or perhaps his editor, breaks the timeless unity of recollection in order to explain the differences between cultural forms, and he does so in a manner that entails some confusion as to the precise identity of "us" and "they." In this sentence the present tense of Pellow's recollection briefly fuses with the timeless present of ethnography; more generally, the constant use of the present tense throughout his personal narration produces a troubled equation between his singular, contingent experience and the timeless truths that his ethnographic sections purport to have captured. This equation places the supposedly distant observer within the same epistemological realm as the material he describes, constantly pushing him into the frame of his timeless snapshots of Moroccan culture, highlighting his participation within that culture.

Pellow participates not only in the tyranny that he attributes to Moroccan culture but also in its superstition, especially when he manipulates the superstition of others for his own benefit, much like the priestly charlatans so often cited in European ethnography. After he flees the Moroccan military, the text metamorphoses into picaresque. A lengthy section recounts his meeting with two Spanish mountebanks, who support themselves by "deceiving the credulous Inhabitants with their Quack Medicines" and who encourage him to develop a similar practice, "the better to conceal my Intentions in my Travels thro' the Country" (290–91). Even as this section celebrates Pellow's rational mastery over native superstition, his success results from a descent to what seems a native level of chicanery, as if he has come to emulate the impositions of the seers, magicians, and quacks that he elsewhere vituperates as much as any Orientalist. Not only does Pellow manipulate some native beliefs for his own benefit, but he also arrives at a full acceptance of other native beliefs. Despite his initial scorn for the "Fopperies" of soothsaying, the text portrays a gradual conversion to wholehearted belief in some local superstitions, especially after he hears some accurate predictions and sees some impressive magical performances (243). His confidence in soothsaying palpably augments with the dream interpretation of a black conjure-woman, whose predictions of an eventual escape overwhelm his initial skepticism: "Notwithstanding my present State, and no hopes of a Vessel at that Time, yet did my Mind daily tell me that my Captivity was running out apace, and my nocturnal Imaginations were sufficiently stuff'd with foolish Fancies and Dreams about it" (325). The narrative's slight tone of ironic distance from these beliefs does little to weaken their force within the plot as a whole, especially when his dreams finally reach fruition with the aid of an English captain who transports him to Gibraltar and whom he recognizes as the centerpiece of a particularly prognostic dream. In this narrative the structural climax of the captivity plot seems to depend more on the efficacy of native belief systems than on the dispositions of providence or the rational heroism of the captive.

Pellow remains a figure of ambiguous cultural standing even after he rejoins his countrymen, when his position as knowing captive makes him a potent but highly ambiguous colonial figure. Before he finally reaches Gibraltar, he aids some English vessels on the Moroccan coast, acting as a linguist and expert on the imputed dispositions of the inhabitants. He earns the good will of the captain who finally transports him to Gibraltar by helping him avoid several attempts to steal his cargo. These skills in cultural negotiation earn high praise from the captain after they leave Barbary, when, as Pellow boasts, this newfound patron admits that "had he not very accidentally and most opportunely happened to meet me there, he should not in all likelihood have been permitted to come from hence himself" (375). Again the former captive gains an ethnographic knowledge that transforms him into a paradigmatic agent of colonial trade, a mediator capable of keeping British merchants from falling into captivity themselves. But Pellow's knowledge grows precisely out of the split in his identity. As part of his Moroccan negotiations, he manipulates a recalcitrant official by suggesting that his obstinance might provoke the retaliation of his superior, Muley Abdallah; the official recognizes Pellow's suggestion as "very likely to be true, for that as I had been brought up with Muley Abdallah from a Child, I therefore knew his Temper" (358). Here the colonial expertise of the captive seems to penetrate the deepest recesses of the Islamic state, but that expertise results from a conversion so thorough as to engage a familial level of intimacy.

Both Pellow's heroism and the glaring inconsistencies of his text stem from his potential definition as a member of two seemingly opposed cultures. The text's internal inconsistencies suggest an attempt, whether performed by authorial retrospection or editorial intervention, to smooth over the anxieties raised by a narrative depicting an extensive, thorough, and even heroic process of cultural accommodation. Pellow's potential apotheosis as a colonial expert and hero stems from the vast knowledge granted to a captive who not only joined the family of a Moroccan emperor, but climbed the ladder of success within the Moroccan military. An attempt to soften the appeal or the anxieties raised by this heroism of conversion seems to lie behind the text's shifts in mood and voice, such as the sudden intrusion of pain and indignation at the moment of Pellow's religious conversion, or the vacillation between nationalist vituperation and calm acceptance of tyranny in the account of his military leadership. But the heroism of conversion is more severely undercut by the sections showing the most glaring signs of editorial intervention, such as the travel descriptions that the editor lifts from other texts, or the picaresque plot, with its patent absurdities. Because the ethnographic sections clothe Morocco in the standard motifs for portraying Oriental governments, Pellow's heroism sometimes stands as a degrading submission, if not a selfish accession, to a culture of tyranny. And by imposing the picaresque plot in the text's later sections, the editor overwrites the heroism of conversion with a heroism of roguery and alienation. As the Pellow narrative reveals in a particularly telling manner, metropolitan culture needed to fix the captivity experience, to reshape and even fictionalize its disturbing materials in a manner that harnessed but also suppressed its potential for exploring interior conflicts and the boundaries of cultural identity.

Although a question of cultural identity also lies at the heart of Robert Drury's narrative, it does not surface through the manifest disturbances in voice, chronology, and structure that mark the narratives of Pitts and Pellow. Compared to the accounts of the former Islamic converts, the Drury narrative holds more successfully to an autobiographical framework, so successfully, indeed, as to produce a sustained debate over the possibility that the work represents one of Defoe's fictions. The debate began when John Moore developed two extensive arguments, based primarily on internal evidence, for Defoe's authorship.[22] Arthur Secord, however, much more convincingly demonstrated that Drury had indeed suffered a lengthy captivity in Madagascar, and that he provided at least an oral version of his story to an editor, most likely Defoe, who added substantial commentary in fitting the narrative for the press.[23] The text does resemble a Defoean bildungsroman in a number of ways. Although somewhat plodding and repetitive in its detail, it plots an organic vision of personal conflicts, growth, and adaptation to a complex social structure. The Drury text also exhibits the subtle conflicts between retrospective voice, narrated experience, and ethical position that scholars have located at the center of Defoe's contribution to the early development of novelistic interiority. Whether produced by Defoe's revision of Drury's narrative or by Drury's revision of his own experience, such conflicts are especially marked in this text because its drama of character formation is set amidst the tribal society of Madagascar. If the Drury narrative does not exhibit the same overt conflict between editor and captive that marks the Pellow narrative, the two texts share similar patterns of ambivalence towards their protagonists' adaptation as subordinates within alien systems of governments.

The tensions of the Drury narrative result especially from its portrait of a successful adaptation to Malagasy society, an utterly alien one for English readers, and from the conflicts of allegiance, ethics, and cultural evaluation that this adaptation entailed. Within a rigid autobiographical structure, the text subjoins a barrage of ethnographic commentary as suggested by the sequence of individual events, and this commentary oscillates from high praise for particular customs and individuals to the standard European idiom for cultural vituperation. At times the protagonist's cultural adaptation seems to have taught him a cultural relativism, but at other times the narrative voice adopts a position of aggressive hostility towards Malagasy culture, and this position finally subsumes the narrative's closure, when Drury the escaped captive leads a British slaving expedition to his former home. Although the text molds a complex vision of personal identity around the problems of transculturation, its vision of cross-cultural identity finally splits when the captive subordinates his adoptive people, and his adopted identity, to the pecuniary impulses that rule his natal culture.

Ambiguities surround the construction of Drury's identity even when the textual commentary is most negative and distanced from Malagasy culture, in its descriptions of native religion. On the one hand, the text dismisses native religion, in one summation, as "indeed, but little" (173), and describes widespread superstition and quackery. But in interpreting the people's credulity, the text offers multiple and somewhat conflicting explanations. On one occasion, as Drury recalls the natives' veneration for a local spirit, the retrospective voice scornfully rejects their justification of their belief, declaring, "I think my reader may arrive at a more satisfactory knowledge of the native disposition of the people in morals and religion from such instances and occurrences, than from any set and formal description which I can make" (178). Here a single anecdote stands equal to the generalizing and oppositional demands of ethnography. Elsewhere, however, the text attributes the credulity observed by its protagonist to distinctions of class rather than culture. Observing the practice of a Umossee, or holy man, the text insists that this "wonder-working prophet" finds his prey especially among the "vulgar" (246). The skeptical narrative voice even speculates that some native leaders, "who are men of sense, keep one of the Umossees out of policy only to amuse the common people, who here, as well as in other places, must be humoured in their bigotry, and captivated by such artifices which politic governors know very well" (246). This effort to understand the logic of native rule creates a common bond of rational mastery, available both to native leaders and to British readers, who can equally recognize the superstition of others as a means of subordinating them to a system of personal power.

Sharper ambiguities result from the text's presentation of native government.[24] Much in the manner of Defoe's fictions and political tracts, the Drury narrative blends a liberal discourse of rights, freedoms, and slavery with a patriarchal discourse that contemplates ideal rule.[25] Within Drury's account of Malagasy society, the tyranny of particular men destroys a cultural system that seems not only moderately serviceable but also potentially instructive for the British. The narrative depicts a land of natural abundance, easy labor, "good-natured" people who share resources in common, and a workable system of oral law. Not only does Drury praise "the general usage of the princes here to converse very familiarly with everybody," but overhearing one such political discussion makes "the Parliament in Great Britain run strangely in my head" (144, 127). In the speculations of Drury or perhaps of Defoe, the government of Madagascar offers evidence both for the antiquity of parliaments and the character of government "in the state of nature, and the beginning of men joining in societies" (128–29). If the government of Madagascar represents a precursor for the British, it is not a savage state marking an antiquated opposite for British progress but rather an original and seemingly natural government offering a model for British reform.

For all the primal soundness of Madagascar's governmental institutions, Drury maintains that "the epidemical evil of this island is their frequent quarrels with one another," especially those caused by cattle raids and petty tyrants "addicted to this kind of thievery" (111–12). In their constant raiding, these leaders often "follow the dictates of a blind passion, . . . scolding at one another, like women," and "always regard[ing] each other with jealous and watchful eyes" (114, 119). Throughout the narrative, the captive protagonist meets individual exemplars of this pervasive tyranny. One particular king, because "glory was his chief aim," repeatedly indulges an inclination "to show that he could act according to his own will" and thus often orders his subjects "to immediate execution for very trivial, and sometimes no faults," leading to the most "abject slavery" on the island (274–76). As so often in captivity narratives, execution without trial provides a defining instance of uncivilized lawlessness. Occasionally the narrative explains such tyranny as a result of the people's natural disposition. When one king suddenly orders the captive's immediate execution, he observes "the people idly lamenting my hard misfortune, instead of turning on the monster and delivering themselves from his tyranny" (287). The abject failure of the natives to resist tyranny seems to stem from a natural disposition implicitly contrasted with the inborn freedom of the Briton forced to rely on them.

Despite Drury's frequent scorn for the natives' political behavior, his narrative structure, like Pellow's, portrays captivity as a gradual process of political accommodation. This process, however, creates an impression less of systematic cultural tyranny than of a journey through a series of masters who occupy various positions along a psychological spectrum of tyranny, generosity, and paternalism. After Drury blames his initial slave status and abject labor on the particular cruelty of the tribe that first captured him, his narrative documents a lengthy quest for an ideal patron. In a constantly iterated pattern, he escapes from one tyrannical master and seeks the protection of another, who initially woos him with fair treatment, a comfortable livelihood, and wives, but who then betrays signs of an oppressive disposition. Chafing under stricter oversight, Drury then undertakes a new search.

As the text follows a variety of permutations on this basic pattern, its discourse of freedom, tyranny, and patriarchy mixes with Malagasy political patterns in highly ambiguous ways. Drury's new or prospective masters sometimes become spokesmen for natural rights, especially when they criticize his old ones in an effort to gain his allegiance. One declares that it was inappropriate "to keep free men against their will in a strange country," and another that "it was natural for a man to fly for his life who was every day in fear of it, and used like a brute" (194–95). Furthermore, many of these masters undermine the text's general comments on the selfish tyranny of native rulers. In declaring one master "generous and humane, of great authority, and therefore an able protector," the text hints at the kind of deferential appreciation that subordinates such as Colonel Jack express for good masters (229). Drury's final master, moreover, treats him so well that, even after he has escaped captivity and returned to Madagascar as a prosperous trader, he retains a filial regard for this native, whose "former most generous and humane behaviour to me made me esteem him as my father" (312). Although the captive rises steadily to positions of relative power and respect, as a military scout and even "captain of my master's guard" (264), he remains a dependent within a traditional system of patronage and servitude. The retrospective voice sometimes handles this system in patriarchal language but also sometimes tries to force it into a language of tyranny, freedom, and rights.

Because these varying perspectives emerge from a voice of personal narration, their intermixture suggests a sustained interior conflict between independence and service, British nationalism and cultural accommodation. In contemplating his captive adolescence, the autobiographical Drury is sometimes proud of his service under idealized masters and sometimes outraged by their subjugation of him. This conflict within the narrative voice, moreover, seems to reflect a psychological conflict at the heart of Drury's experience in captivity. Like the plot of a bildungsroman, Drury's captivity experience involves an internal struggle over social accommodation, ending in liberation, but the text itself gives so much weight to the gradual improvement in Drury's relationships with his masters that the narrative seems, rather paradoxically, to plot a progress towards an ideal servitude. The text builds as much towards Drury's happy servitude under his final master as it does towards the final escape. Within this text, a native of Britain, presumed seat of modernity and freedom, grows into liberation and adulthood through a process of accommodation within an alien system of patriarchal servitude.

Much of the ambivalence surrounding Drury's cultural adaptation attaches to a native custom in which underlings show respect for their masters by crawling on the ground to meet them and licking their feet or knees. Within the narrative, this custom acts both as a particularly concrete illustration of tyranny and as a particularly troubled locus of Drury's cultural accommodation. When his first master demands an initial performance of the custom, the text verges towards a heroism of resistance, as the captive refuses to kneel before his master, "thinking it an adoration that I ought to pay to none but God" (84). But when his master grows violent, Drury accedes to the ceremony, and after repeated performances he grows accustomed to it. During his long search for an ideal master, the narrative highlights his careful manipulation of the custom, as he uses it to charm potential masters with reputations for benevolence or to appease angry masters whom he has offended.

That Drury the protagonist succeeds within native culture by mastering such subordinate behavior constantly undermines the text's assumption of cultural superiority. He embraces the custom not only as a subordinate but also as a master, taking an apparent delight in receiving this homage from his wives. His final performances of this ritual, moreover, create moments of particular tension in the text. In describing his departure from one potentate, he attests, "I licked his feet, and took my leave of him, and of this custom too; for this was the last time I licked a black man's feet" (293). Unadorned yet highly emotive, the phrasing simultaneously evokes triumph and repugnance, relief and lingering hostility. The captive returns to this custom, furthermore, even after his rescue by a British ship and his assumption of western costume, when his favorite master does not recognize him until Drury jogs his memory by licking his knee (295). Since Drury accedes to the custom out of affection rather than force, the narrative's final image of this form of abjection concerns an Englishman's eager acceptance of it.

During Drury's servitude, he manages a slow but steady economic career, much like the protagonists of other factual captivity narratives or of Defoe's *Moll Flanders* and *Colonel Jack*. But in Drury's case more than in Defoe's fictions, economic progress depends on cultural adaptation. In an episode that smacks of Defoe, Drury's economic progress begins when his superiority to native laborers greatly impresses his first master, who boasts to his fellows, "Look on that white slave; for looking after cattle, digging of wild yams, and improving of honey, there is not the fellow of him" (164). If Drury

Robert Drury was a child at the time of his capture, but his
fellow Britons, who were all adults, seem equally childlike and
passive in this image from the early portion of his text. Drury's
face presents a clear image of unhappiness, and his posture is
clearly opposed to that of his captors. (This item is reproduced by permission of *The Huntington Library, San Marino,
California*.)

By page 345 of the narrative, Drury has spent years in
captivity, and this image portrays him as one of the Malagasy,
at home among them, now closer to them in skin color, and
almost as faceless as they are presented. (This item is
reproduced by permission of *The Huntington Library, San
Marino, California*.)

surpasses native slaves, this accomplishment amounts to successful adaptation within a position of physical servitude. But the captive soon demonstrates intellectual as well as physical preeminence. As a trader in honey, Drury gains as much wealth as any other slave, eventually owning a slave of his own. Much of his initial rise to economic success, however, stems from his manipulation of native superstition. Though he scorns a charm supposed to protect bee hives from theft, he nevertheless learns the charm, pretends to apply it to his own hives, and reaps much financial benefit because it prevents native competitors from molesting his produce. Even more lucrative is his manipulation of what he calls a "silly custom" stipulating that only the son of a king can butcher meat (289). Because the natives believe that a ship captain fathered Drury and that a captaincy is equivalent to monarchy, they permit him to occupy this lucrative office. In explaining his initial motives for accepting the office, however, Drury seems ashamed of its status, if not also of his means of acquiring it: "whatever mean thoughts I might have as to the honour of it, I had too great an opinion of its value" (143). Although at one level the captive's successful manipulation of Malagasy superstitions suggests an intellectual triumph, the language here remains guilty, even apologetic. Far from converting the natives away from superstition, this captive profited from it, much like the harshly scorned Umossees. Within the text's larger framework of scorn for native superstition, the captive's economic career stands partially as a degrading accommodation to native culture.

Less heroic aspects of Drury's cultural adaptation turn up less often within the text but evoke unusual emotional intensity. By the end of the narrative, the captive has undergone such a complete transformation that the grounds of British identity seem slippery and malleable rather than stable. After many years in captivity, he eventually forgets the English language, so that it "seemed like unintelligible sounds of a strange language, which I could not form to my own tongue to imitate, insomuch that I was in fear I should never be able to speak my mother-tongue again" (233). As a result of similar cultural losses, his reconnection with his native culture raises sharp anxieties about the extent of his transculturation. When he meets a Dutchman and some Europeanized Africans, they laugh at his adherence to such native customs as hiding by himself to eat his meat. Here the grounds of cultural identity are doubly destabilized, as native Africans adopt a position of European cultural superiority in their mockery of a native Englishman's assumption of African customs. The text summarizes his behavior on this occasion with the comment, "I found myself here a perfect negro in my way and manner" (232). The bizarre phrasing suggests a crisis of self-division imposed by the experience of captivity, as if the captive Drury had unconsciously redefined himself as a native of Madagascar until his contact with European customs suddenly forced him back into his natal perspective, so that he perceives his transculturation as a mysteriously completed fact but not as a process.

As the narrative charts the progress of Drury's cultural transformation, the text often reverses the ethnographic perspective typical of English travel description, as if the former captive has learned to judge Eurocentrism from a non-European perspective. In its praise for particular individuals or cultural traits among the Malagasy or in its criticism of British cultural traits, the text destabilizes common assumptions about British cultural superiority, the progress of civilization, and the goals of colonialism. For example, Drury's attempt to teach the natives the Ten Commandments leads to his discovery that "they have the purport and meaning of all of them by nature," and so do not require his proselytism (151). An even greater repudiation of colonial goals, and an even sharper reversal of cultural perspective, occurs with Drury's observation that "the behaviour of English pirates, and others too, who are not willing to be called so, has been very barbarous," so much so that among certain tribes, who "have no experimental knowledge to distinguish that wicked men are the production of every land[,] every white man is looked on as not less a monster than we think a cannibal" (205). Here the text resorts to the supposedly objective standards of "experimental" science in order to combat the effects of a reversed cultural perspective whose very empirical weight seems to compel its inclusion among Drury's observations.

The narrative's sharpest reversals of ethnographic perspective occur in relation to Drury's fullest accommodation with native culture, his marriage. To placate his wife's hostile mother, he tells her that, "though I was not a black man, I had as tender a heart as any black man whatever" (170). The text returns to this comment a few pages later, when its praise of native women leads into a broad-ranging critique of European racism:

> as to their fidelity, behaviour to their husbands, good-natured dispositions and agreeable conversation, so far as their little knowledge extends, I think the Europeans must not compare with them. We white people have a very contemptible and mean opinion of these blacks, and a great one of ourselves. They also have a great opinion of us, and think we excel them vastly in knowledge, arts, and sciences. So far they are right, but if an impartial comparison was to be made of their virtue, I think the negro heathens will excel the white Christians. It will be remarked, I dare say, that the best character I could give myself to my wife's mother was, that I had as tender a heart as a black; for they certainly treat one another with

> more humanity than we do. Here is no one miserable, if it is in the power
> of his neighbours to help him. Here is love, tenderness, and generosity
> which might shame us; and moral honesty too. (172–73)

After reversing standard European stereotypes about African women, the
text shifts immediately to a general critique of European cultural pride, before recalling Drury's personal, practical need to assert an African identity.
Within the context of this praise for the Malagasy and this criticism for Europeans, the repetition of the words with which Drury recommended himself
to a native wife suggests a moment of particular pride in his identification
with the alien.

The fullness of Drury's cultural transformation seems an especially positive outcome towards the close of the narrative. Just before his departure for
England, he explains, he had attained a life of such material comfort that
"had it not been for the hopes of seeing my father and mother, I don't know
whether I should have taken much pains to have come to England" (284).
Other moments suggesting positive transformation occur with the text's efforts to capture the perspectives of natives. One Malagasy leader tells Drury,
for example, that he had changed so thoroughly that "I had none of that
barbarous disposition which some white men have; for he looked on me as a
native black man, I having accustomed myself to the manners of the country" (244). Here the narrator seems not only willing to adopt the reversed
cultural perspective of a Malagasy ruler but even proud that his cultural transformation made him acceptable within that perspective. Elsewhere the
captive's cultural identity seems capable of controlled movement in either
direction, oscillating from natal to adoptive culture and vice versa. When he
first meets the Britons who help him to leave Madagascar, his rescuers at
first "took me for a wild man" (293). But he quickly doffs this wildness as his
rescuers clothe him in the western costume that prevents his favorite master
from recognizing him. When he licks his master's knee, the former captive
seems capable of establishing an identity within either culture, either as British
traveler or as African dependent, through voluntary manipulation of cultural
forms. Within the framework of the captive's psychological growth, cultural
malleability, after initially posing a threat to his identity, finally becomes a
source of cultural power, enabling him to perform variable cultural identities as occasions arise.

But the impression of a complete and happy cultural transformation finally ruptures with the narrative's closure, after Drury escapes from Madagascar and returns as an active participant in the colonial system, revisiting
the land of his former captivity as an ethnographic expert, guiding a slave

ship. As he explains, "my business was to assist in the trade which my knowledge of the language and customs of the country had qualified me for" (304). To perform this function effectively, he adopts native dress and matches this appearance of cross-cultural identity with manipulation of cross-cultural knowledge. When a native demands a high price for a slave, Drury "soon let him understand that I knew the country, and that if they had none to sell us I knew where to go" (307). Here the most aggressive depths of colonial rapacity benefit directly from the experience of transculturation and the cultural knowledge that it confers. Drury's hard progress in acquiring a malleable cultural identity now seems to find its climax in its direct applicability to his hopes for an economic independence that depends on reversing the terms of his former captivity, making slaves of a people who had formerly enslaved him. This final vision of cross-cultural identity marks a final, particularly resonant, and particularly ugly moment of contradiction within the broader kaleidoscope of the text's conflicting views of the adopted captive and his adoptive people. At one level this text expresses a measure of sympathy and praise for the adoptive people, as well as a pride in the captive's identification with them, that no other captivity narrative would match until the early nineteenth-century American accounts of John Dunn Hunter and Mary Jemison. But Drury's transformation within native culture produces moments of shame as well as pride, moments of abject compliance as well as successful mastery, moments when he guiltily admits to deceiving his adoptive people as well as moments when he triumphs in his ability to enslave them effectively.

As the narratives of Pitts, Pellow, and Drury reveal in a particularly telling manner, the captivity genre is a highly unstable, scabrous, messy genre, one that permitted wide variation in exploring the dynamics of cultural identity. These narratives of extended transculturation are particularly suggestive of the struggles over identity that underlie the genre as a whole, with former captives and their editors always striving to organize the strange and enormously varied experiences of captivity according to structures of plot and rhetoric that might prove acceptable to curious but also skeptical, and even hostile, audiences. That audiences turned to such narratives with especial excitement is attested by their relative popularity and influence compared to other captivity narratives. After the initial success of transculturation narratives within an eighteenth-century British context, their popularity, fictionalization, and cultural impact became even more important within the American context of the nineteenth century.

The transculturation narratives of Drury and Pellow are two of the longest, most complex, and most problematic captivity narratives in the English language, and it is not surprising that scholars have mistaken both for novels. Produced during such crucial years for the novel's evolution, carefully revised by editors who may have written novels themselves, and probably padded with fictional episodes, these narratives straddled the thin line that divided fictional and factual narratives during the period. In their length and complexity, moreover, these two narratives reveal with particular depth and clarity that the captivity genre faced the same problems and harnessed the same tensions as the novel in its early evolution, offering a parallel if not a model for its development. Like the novel, the captivity narrative struggled to reconcile general and particular versions of truth, and the doctrine of providence with various heroisms of individual action. Captivity narrative and novel also shared interests in the new and exotic, in the juxtaposition of the ordinary against the extreme, and this juxtaposition itself increased the power of both genres to represent character in terms of interior conflict. While the fluidity of both genres permitted wide-ranging exploration, broad inclusiveness, and troubling ambivalences, both also tended to ground their multiplicity in a common narrative structure pitting a persecuted yet autonomous individual against an oppressive and alien social fabric. Like the novel, the captivity genre succeeded because its manifold juxtapositions of cultures, ideologies, and discursive forms permitted an extended, thick, and unresolvable exposition of the problematics of identity.

PART 2

Narratives of Fiction

FOUR

Mastering Captivity

Published in 1729 and 1739, respectively, the lightly fictionalized narratives of Drury and Pellow entered the English press at the close of a period that witnessed the rise of the captivity plot in English fiction. The first important group of English captivity fictions, whether set in domestic or foreign locations, appeared during the 1720s, with a sudden burst of novels based wholly or partly on Oriental captivity. In this crucial period of expansion and consolidation for both the British nation and the English novel, Penelope Aubin and William Rufus Chetwood combined to create a set of highly popular fictions that directly incorporated, intensified, and recast the individualistic heroism and colonialist agenda of factual captivity accounts. These novels of colonial subjugation and individualist triumph achieved such prominence that they inspired a pair of partly parodic versions from Eliza Haywood in 1727. As these three writers transformed the ethnographic motifs and methodology of the factual captivity genre, they developed more elaborate versions of the captive protagonist, producing a range of character types, whether male or female, mercantile or noble, who personified Western freedom, self-assertion, and ingenuity, or in Haywood's works, a glaring absence of these qualities. In the broad potential of its character structure for celebrating or denigrating individualistic and colonialist ideologies, the Oriental captivity plot provides an early and significant point for investigating the connections among the captivity genre, colonial ideology, and patterns of identity formation that were crucial to the early evolution of the English novel.

Scholars have occasionally explored the generic connection between captivity narrative and novel, but the predominance of the American critical perspective has limited their insights. In arguing that the captivity genre constitutes something like the "American Origins of the English Novel," Nancy Armstrong and Leonard Tennenhouse have suggested that the Rowlandson narrative represents an important precedent for *Pamela,* since both texts confirm the textual authority of an isolated, nonaristocratic, English-writing female in opposition to an alien and threatening environment.[1] More recently, Michelle Burnham has extended this connection by suggesting that the captivity genre's transgressive models of female agency, especially as embodied in Hannah Dustan, reflect a larger parallel between the captivity narrative and the sentimental novel as genres built on transgressive self-fashioning and culture-crossing.[2] Each of these arguments overstates the significance of a particular female captive, either Rowlandson or Dustan, but even if we look at the American captivity tradition as a whole, it ultimately contributed much less to the early development of English fiction than did the prior tradition of British captivity narratives set in the Middle East.

Until more than a decade after the 1740 publication of *Pamela,* readers in metropolitan London would have associated the captivity narrative with Oriental settings more than American ones. By the 1720s at least a dozen Oriental narratives had appeared in print, so that Oriental settings, especially the Barbary Coast, had come to dominate the factual captivity genre and to establish the generic features that would prove most amenable to fiction. Factual accounts of captivity in Barbary employed what would soon become a central feature of novelistic authority, as G.A. Starr has suggested, in that they developed a persistent type of "narrator-hero," who recounts his efforts to escape with an even-handed tone, a wealth of circumstantial detail, and reflections on past experience in the manner of spiritual autobiography.[3] At the same time, the mercantile and artisanal captives of the Oriental narratives greatly outdistanced their American counterparts in providing models for one of early eighteenth-century fiction's favorite character types, the self-reliant capitalist hero.[4] As the captives master the alien circumstances of the Orient for their own advantage, whether for escape or profit, they simultaneously develop powers of self-control, self-preservation, and self-reliance, and their texts confirm this narrative expression of progressive ideology through explicit comments supporting economic and political individualism. Finally, the basic situation of Islamic captivity acts as a continual source of psychological tension, as the captives detail their efforts to maintain an insular integrity, an adherence to Christianity, and a secret agenda of escape, despite the threats of despair and discovery and despite the putative corruptions of Oriental institutions.

Compared to their American successors, moreover, factual narratives of Oriental captivity much more explicitly engaged the imperatives of British colonial expansion. Usually told by merchants and seamen rather than Puritan goodwives or divines, Oriental captivity narratives included earlier and more frequent portraits of captive protagonists as colonists in their own right, and they produced earlier and more frequent assessments of captive-taking cultures as enemies to trade and progress. Additionally, as previous chapters have shown, the Oriental genre, much more than its American counterpart, developed both an explicit rhetoric of native "English liberties" and a systematic representation of the captive-taking culture as debased and despotic. Because the Oriental captivity narrative relied more heavily on the totalizing ethnographic framework of travel description, it created a sharper opposition between the liberated Western knower and the alien culture as a debased object of knowledge. In depicting the captives' personal mastery of the Orient, the factual narratives connected the alien-dominating subject of Orientalist observation with the free, enterprising, and self-distanced subject of political and economic individualism, and this connection provided a crucial site of elaboration and parody within the fictional adaptations. Both the debased Oriental setting and the plot of subjugation and escape enforced an expansionist ideology by suggesting that autonomous and self-reliant Western captives possessed a natural right and a natural ability to control the alien cultures that had enslaved them.

The most precise way to compare the relative impact of the two captivity settings on the English novel is to consider their relative importance within the eighteenth century's marketplace for suppositional narratives. Over the course of the eighteenth century, as chapter 5 will show, the American captivity genre inspired a scattering of brief novelistic episodes, with only one significant example appearing before 1767. These episodes, moreover, generally appeared in minor, relatively unpopular works, and they veered away from the factual genre's primary focus on spiritual affliction. On the other hand, the Oriental genre led to earlier, more extensive, and more popular fictional imitations, some directly imitative and others quite elaborate in their experimentation. After an early episode in *The English Rogue* (1665), and the widely read episodes in *Robinson Crusoe* (1719) and *Don Quixote* (translated 1700–1703), the Oriental plot reached center stage with the fictions of Aubin and Chetwood. Oriental captivity furnished the main narrative thread for three of Aubin's popular novels, beginning in 1721, as well as lengthy episodes in two others. Oriental captivity thus furnished one of the central plot lines animating a body of fiction that scholars have described as an important precursor for Richardson's novels and a crucial element in English fiction's shift from amatory plots towards piety, "virtue," and psychological interiority.[5] In addition, captivity in Algiers provided the primary plot line for Chetwood's *Adventures of Robert Boyle* (1726), which at twenty-three printings represents one of the century's most successful fictions of colonial adventure, certainly its most popular narrative of captivity under a foreign people. Chetwood also included shorter episodes of Oriental captivity in three less popular novels, published from 1720 to 1743. Additionally, minor episodes appeared in two popular fictional collections of the1720s, by Jane Barker and Elizabeth Singer Rowe.[6] In that decade the Oriental captivity narrative furnished one of English literature's most prominent plot formulae of extended subjugation and individualist triumph, amidst a fictional landscape dominated by the picaresque and love intrigues. In that decade the captivity plot acquired enough prominence to inspire a sharp rejoinder from Haywood, in the form of three fictional episodes that radically undercut its aggressive individualism. Later in the century, as chapter 6 demonstrates, Simon Berington and George Cumberland used the Oriental captivity plot as a framing device for utopias focused on problems of liberty and self-control. In addition, writers as diverse as John Shebbeare and Ann Yearsley occasionally spiced their novels with minor episodes of Oriental captivity, while Robert Bage once again centered a novel on the theme in 1787. At the end of the century, during a comparable period of nation- and literature-building across the Atlantic, American publishers began to print Barbary narratives with American protagonists, and these texts, along with reprints of Aubin's and Chetwood's novels, inspired Royall Tyler's *Algerine Captive* (1797) and other fictional imitations.

In an effort to gauge how these fictions adapt and transform the Oriental captivity plot, this chapter will briefly survey a few factual accounts and some early fictional episodes before concentrating on the early fictional versions of Aubin, Chetwood, and Haywood. Continuing in the path of the earliest fictional episodes, Chetwood intensifies and concretizes the captivity plot's ideology of masterful individualism and colonial expansion, by celebrating the transformative self-assertion of protagonists whose captivity teaches them to know and dominate alien lands. On the other hand, Aubin introduces a broader range of captive protagonists, especially women, aristocrats, and priests, who embody the ideology of colonial individualism in a more subdued, less transparent form. Her transformation of the captivity plot enables not only a vision of moderate female self-assertion but also a critical departure from the aggressive individualism of the captive hero, especially in her depiction of captive males as weak, passive, or at least pacific, in many ways commensurate to her female captives. Haywood further complicates and even ridicules the captivity plot's common patterns of heroism, particularly by subjecting heroic male captives to the extreme violence of castration. Through grim comedies centered on the figure of a castrated captive, her narratives enact a caustic critique of both the aggressive masculinity and the sexually victimized femininity that characterize the captives of Chetwood and Aubin. Thus, within a single decade, the figure of the Oriental captive as masterful proto-colonist inspired a variety of fictional enhancements, adaptations, and revisions, and the close development and interaction of these varied character types indicate the pervasive cultural force, imaginative potential, and ideological import of the Oriental captivity plot during this crucial moment in the novel's evolution.

Despite the wide variation in these writers' ideological strategies, all three capitalize on the captivity genre's opposition between a persecuted Western self and an alien, debased, and despotic setting. All three writers mix the captivity plot with elements of romance, defining idealized Western sexual subjects through images of Oriental lust and dramas of besieged chastity that anticipate Richardson's novels in their emphasis on the sexual constitution of identity and on individual freedom to choose a marriage partner. All three writers also anticipate Richardson in complicating the subjective depths of their captives through a sharpened focus on the psychological tensions, conflicts, and transgressions produced by the situation of captivity in an alien land. Thus these fictions of Oriental captivity produce early versions of several crucial patterns of character development within subsequent English fiction, precisely through a complication of the factual genre's basic narrative pattern of an individual's exposure to, isolation within, and resistance to an alien and oppressive environment. With further extensions, complications, and revisions, this pattern continues to animate the English novel, whether we consider Pamela's confinement in the various houses of Mr. B., the London peregrinations of David Simple or the Man of Feeling, Evelina's experiences in the fashionable world, or Emily St. Aubert's confinement at Udolpho. In sum, a significant moment in the development of English fiction occurred when the popular fictions of Aubin, Chetwood, and Haywood adapted the colonialist discursive strategies of the Oriental captivity narrative for male and female versions of the persecuted, autonomous, and internally divided protagonist.

Models of divided Western identity could emerge so forcefully within the Oriental captivity plot because it developed them at least partially within the already well-established yet highly ambivalent framework of Orientalism. In Edward Said's influential formulation, Orientalism depends heavily on a totalizing ethnographic framework, which implies the intellectual mastery of the Western travel-writer, but it also creates an impression that the imputed pleasures, vices, and excesses of the Orient can undermine the traveler's rational stability.[7] While Said's analysis originally focused on academic and literary discourses of the nineteenth century, he also traced Orientalism's roots in the centuries-long struggle between Islam and Christianity, and certainly the seventeenth and eighteenth centuries witnessed increasingly elaborate strategies of discursive domination parallel to the West's increasing economic and political intervention in various Eastern lands. British scholars devoted extensive study to Near Eastern lands and languages well before the rise of Indology at the end of the eighteenth century.[8] Although the totalizing concept of "the Orient" belongs more properly to the nineteenth century, British writers of the seventeenth and eighteenth centuries employed Orientalism's hierarchical framework and many of its standard stereotypes in describing broad sections of Islamic territory, including the North African coast, Turkey, Persia, and parts of India. Throughout the early modern period, images of excessively passionate, ineffectual, and despotic Muslims helped to define and elaborate the Western self as a stable, rational, and free political subject. At the same time, early modern writers also began to portray Oriental cultures as exotically incommensurate to the West, capable of offering Westerners alien pleasures, such as illicit forms of sexuality, but also capable of overwhelming them with irrational excesses. Within early modern travel descriptions of Oriental lands, such portraits often established an opposition between, on the one hand, the rational mastery of self and alien world revealed in the traveler's knowledge about and resistance to the Orient, and, on the other hand, the imputed features of the Orient and Orientals, traits that seemed to disqualify them for such mastery.[9] By suggesting that the autonomous Western subject possessed a natural aptitude for knowing and ruling lands seemingly racked by political injustice, ineptitude, and extravagance, these proto-Orientalist accounts created a justification and even an imperative for Western colonial expansion.

The Orientalist vision of the Islamic world helped to shape the ideological structure of the Barbary captivity narrative even as this genre provided in its turn crucial illustrations for some of the most prominent Orientalist stereotypes. The British saw the Coast as a bewildering chaos of petty states and tribal powers, all more or less dependent on the Ottoman Empire, and full of a bewildering variety of peoples: Arabs, Berbers, Moors, Turks, Jews, African and Balkan slaves, even a number of "renegadoes," or Western converts to Islam. British travel writers tended to lump these peoples together under the broad headings "Turk" and "Moor," portraying them as altogether given to tyranny, cruelty, lust, chicanery, immoderate passion, and superstition.[10] This negative outlook at least partially developed in response to the capture and enslavement of Europeans in Turkey and Barbary. By the early eighteenth century, tens of thousands of Britons had entered Islamic slavery, mostly in North African ports such as Sallee, Algiers, and Tunis. In these city-states British captives sometimes gained freedom through ransom, but more often they faced lengthy servitude and occasionally even galley slavery, torture, coercive proselytism, or confinement in a seraglio.[11] As chapter 1 has shown, early modern descriptions of the Middle East and North Africa often came from the pens of captives or ambassadors working to secure the release of captives. Thus reports by and about enslaved Britons contributed to the characterization of North Africa as a land of despotism, religious zeal, and sexual predation.

For the British as for other Western trading nations, the Barbary corsairs represented a particular threat to the spread of colonial commerce. Until the mid nineteenth century, when the Western powers divided North Africa into directly controlled imperial territories, British activity in the Middle East depended on small-scale colonies, trade factories or coastal strongholds, designed to open or protect the lines of Levantine trade, which returned immense profits for British traders and simultaneously rendered local polities dependent on British finance. Even as British trade and power in the region grew steadily from the late sixteenth through the eighteenth centuries, the corsairs grew increasingly independent of the Ottoman Turks, while internal troubles reduced the extent and power of an empire that had once terrified the West. Despite British treaties with Constantinople or with the Barbary states themselves, the corsairs frequently interrupted the Levantine trade and even harried Britain's crucial oceanic route through the Atlantic islands to the American colonies, the African slaving districts, and the Indian factories. Although the British, like other Western trading nations, still sometimes sold captured Muslims in Mediterranean slave markets, they tended to downplay their own predations while describing the peoples of Barbary as devoted to slavery and plunder, inherently hostile to trade. Again like the other Western colonial powers, Britain sent several punitive expeditions to the Barbary Coast and managed occasionally to control strategic ports, such as Tangier from 1662 to 1683 and Gibraltar from 1704. By the 1720s the British and French had attained a nearly complete naval domination over the Mediterranean and perceived the corsairs as pesky vestiges of an empire now superseded by modern Western trading powers.

In that decade, as the early fictions of Oriental captivity began to imitate the factual genre, the powerful colonial imperatives associated with the

Mediterranean basin led them to retain the aggressively antagonistic and totalizing epistemological framework of Orientalism. Like the factual accounts, the early fictions conflate Turks with Moors, Arabs with Egyptians, and they produce detailed specifications of Oriental customs, behaviors, and inclinations, representing these cultures as inverted models or parodies of Western civilization. The fictional versions also sometimes borrow the hierarchical framework and authenticating devices of travel description. Interrupting Chetwood's fictional *Adventures of Robert Boyle* is a long portion of pure travel description, which analyzes Morocco through a catalogue of towns and sections on religion, government, and physical appearance. When his *Adventures of William Vaughan* (1736) turns to an episode of captivity in Tunis, it includes several footnotes explaining details of Tunisian geography, economy, religion, and dress. Even novels lacking the formal apparatus of travel description often interrupt their narratives with minor ethnographic details, such as a favorite food or superstition. Because a protagonist often introduces such cultural traits only to scorn them, their presence in the narrative underscores his or her cultural insularity. Traits such as superstition and inebriation, adduced as typically Oriental, often assist a protagonist's escape, further highlighting his or her rational superiority.

The epistemological framework of Orientalism provided one of several means by which both factual and fictional narratives asserted the captives' potential mastery over captive-taking cultures. Like their factual predecessors, the fictional versions of Aubin and Chetwood routinely celebrate a heroism of resistance to the imputed depravities of native culture. Whereas the factual accounts occasionally literalize the captives' mastery over alien cultures by showing that their knowledge contributes to British naval power and trade, Aubin and Chetwood produce fantastic visions of former captives turned into successful colonists. Furthermore, their novels develop a variety of motifs, such as exotic jewels or happily converted natives, that for the next two centuries would animate the fantastic colonial landscape of adventure fiction.[12] Thus their works provide a crucial point for investigating not only the generic connection between captivity narrative and novel, but also the place of colonialism in the early development of English fiction.

Within the factual accounts, the situation of slavery within a degraded Orientalist environment seems to demand both the captives' assumption of individualistic behaviors and overt textual reinforcement of such behaviors. As the captives try to escape Oriental slavery, the texts bolster their efforts with explicit endorsements of the British systems of limited monarchy and mercantile capitalism, which are themselves reinforced by explicit condemnations of the political and socioeconomic practices of the Orient. The narrators often complain of their slavery in the language of economic individualism, especially as they express a desire to keep the earnings of their labor. In the 1622 escape narrative of John Rawlins, for example, the hero resorts to such language in order to persuade his companions to resist their captors: "Oh hellish slavery to bee thus subject to dogs! to labour thus to inrich infidels, and maintaine their pleasures, to be our selves slaves, and worse then the out-cast of the world: is there no way of releasement? no devise to free us from this bondage? no exploit, no action of worth to bee put in execution, to make us renowned in the world, and famous to posteritie?"[13] Built partially on an opposition between Western industry and Oriental luxury, the passage enforces the value of individual "labour" and the need to seek opportunities for personal renown.

Moreover, as the captives recount the hardships of their slavery and their efforts to escape, they construct themselves as abducted from their native environment but still maintaining its rationalism and intellectual dexterity. Portrayed as alien to Oriental cultures, these principles appear all the more positive, necessary, and natural for Western sojourners in Barbary. In their efforts to escape, the captives exhibit what Starr describes as a pattern of enterprise and mental "improvisation," a dexterous manipulation of alien circumstances.[14] Under the various pressures of slavery, the captives often mask hidden motives and attitudes towards their captors, adapt local objects for useful ends, and even achieve some entrepreneurial success. When the captives hide their internal intentions, secretly contrive escape plans, and deceive their captors with elaborate subterfuges, the narratives depict guile and dissimulation as positive Western traits, often contrasted with portraits of Oriental captors as easily deceived dupes. Constant emphasis on the captives' efforts to maintain false appearances and inner resolves creates an impression of psychological tensions and difficulties, suggesting a complex world of Western consciousness, juxtaposed against a seemingly simple Orient, easily known and mastered.

A particularly early and particularly clear case of active, improvisational heroism appears in the Rawlins account, as this heroic ship's pilot leads his fellow captives to freedom even before their captors' ship reaches port at Algiers. Rawlins introduces the narrative with a dedication celebrating the improvisational skills of the artisan, "ready for all impositions," as an important contribution to the English nation (A3r). In its celebration of his exploits, the plot creates a sharp contrast between Western ingenuity and Oriental luxury, sloth, and shortsightedness. The text repeatedly describes Rawlins's careful deliberation and restless watchfulness as he waits for an opportunity to escape. Finally he notes the utility of several crowbars that might prove useful in locking the Algerian leaders in their cabins (C2v). When the Algerians search their captives' cabins for potential instruments of rebellion, they ignore the ostensibly harmless "crowes," which thus help to construct an opposition between Oriental misrecognition and European prescience in recognizing the utility of ordinary objects. Connecting such misrecognition to the Orientalist stereotype of superstition, the text carefully documents a series of "foolish rites," especially a system for adjusting sails, based on the directions of a "conjurer" and the position of two arrows on a pillow. As the narrator scornfully notes, children, "Lunaticks and changelings" might randomly alter the arrangement behind the back of the credulous conjurer (C2r). Such credulity makes Rawlins's captors easy dupes for his ability to improvise a deceptive facade. In order to escape, he pretends to join the interest of his Algerian captain and argues that they'll find good pirating near the European coast, ultimately hoping to draw the ships beyond the reach of possible reinforcements (D1r). More generally, his improvisational skills succeed because his captors exhibit opposite tendencies, sloth and superstition in place of his activity and perspicacity.

Published eighteen years later and also focused on Algerian captivity, Francis Knight's narrative develops an equally concrete image of a national heroism built around the virtues of careful observation, adaptation, perseverance, and leadership. After the failure of a first escape attempt, the English protagonist remains patient while his partner reveals a "French fury, which my English resolution cared not for; its not the ill event of an action that can disanimate a good Spirit, the weake faint with every succeeding trouble, but the good heart recollects a double courage."[15] This animated resolution raises Knight to a position of leadership among a group of English slaves, first as "treasurer" of their pooled finances and then as director of their joint efforts to build an escape boat.[16] He further aids his countrymen by projecting a false demeanor of complacency under bondage. When this demeanor earns the trust of his guardian, Knight receives better treatment and enough freedom and responsibility that he can free other European slaves when his guardian embarks on a long voyage. After releasing the slaves, the quick-thinking Knight deceives their gaoler by arranging a set of opened locks so that they appear closed. The gaoler returns from a debauch, "well fudled or well drunke, whereby no search was made to our Fetters," so that the captives can easily escape.[17] In a pattern that will continue to animate the fictional adaptations of the captivity plot, the English protagonist carefully calculates opportunities and manipulates the appearances of the material, whereas his captors seem susceptible both to the power of the material and to the deceptive images that he creates.

An even more developed portrait of the English captive as dexterous mercantile hero appears in William Okeley's 1675 narrative, again as the protagonist's individualistic drive and subjective complexity emerge in sharp contrast to opposing tendencies in his Algerian captors. Okeley attributes a hypocritical self-indulgence to his captors, dismissing the custom of fasting as a mask for an inner compulsion to "Riot," "Lust," and gluttony.[18] While he thus depicts Orientals as superstitious and unable to control bodily impulses, he characterizes himself as a rational and resourceful Englishman, who adapts to varied occupations in Algiers, first as a seaman and then as a weaver. Later he transforms himself into a successful trader in tobacco and wine, arriving at such a pitch of entrepreneurial acumen that he can advise another English slave about methods of earning a living. Within this portrait of captive self-reliance, the circumstances of Barbary captivity and the urge to escape create a complex world of enterprising, improvisational thought. A complaint about the economic circumstances of slavery leads directly to careful deliberation on modes of escape: "it was difficult to raise increase out of no stock, and to pay Interest out of no Principal; but there was no contending: It cost me much Debate with my self, and I turn'd my thoughts into all forms and shapes" (17). Deprived of favorable economic conditions, the merchant becomes an escape artist, whose enterprise involves a complex process of mental adaptation to a wide variety of alien situations. Through such ingenuity, Okeley, like Rawlins and Knight, attains a leadership role among a group of English captives. First he forms a "rude draught, and general Model" for an escape plan (43), and then he persuades his cohorts to constructive action when they prove reluctant. Like Rawlins, he relies on individualistic ideology in order to move his companions to action, as he argues that captivity compels two alternatives, either active self-assertion or a contemptible acceptance of "Bondage" under an Oriental master: "Let us be up and doing, and God would be with us. To begin is one half of our work: Let us make an Essay, and Answer particular Objections as they Offer'd themselves, and as we met with them in our work" (50). Okeley rejects his companions' passivity with a manifesto of improvisation, depicting "work" as a largely unplanned process of adaptation to fit varying circumstances. When he pursues this method in the construction of a boat, he makes oars out of "pipe-staves" (57), and the boat's construction and transportation engross over ten per cent of the text. Far from mere filler, this mechanical activity provides a crux of dramatic tension and heroic triumph. Moreover, such resourcefulness, with its mastery of the external circumstances of an alien culture, appears as a natural and inevitable response to the circumstances of captivity.

In addition to his resourcefulness, other complexities of Okeley's personality also take shape against the seemingly uncomplicated threat of the alien Orient, especially as he struggles to conceal his escape plan and to create a deceptive facade for his captors. On one occasion, when the observation of a spy forces him to dissemble his efforts to escape, he recognizes the difficulty of masking his internal design, and wonders, "how boldly could I hold up my Head to this Spie [?] . . . . The Reflection of my Conscience was enough to write Guilt in my Countenance . . . and this had betray'd me, had I not suddenly pluckt up my Spirits" (58). Here, as in the captivity narrative more generally, many opportunities for development of an opposition between external "Countenance" and internal "Conscience" result from the dramatic tensions of captivity, the need for dissembling, and the threat of discovery. Such dissembling often results from the captives' adherence to Christianity in the face of proselytism and persecution. As chapter 2 has shown, Okeley draws heavily from the psychological profile of spiritual autobiography: although his "whole outward man is in Bondage," he finds comfort in the thought that slaves can still "enjoy the freedom of their own Consciences" (14). This constant play with oppositions between liberty and slavery, internal consciousness and external appearance, contributes depth to Okeley's construction of a narrated self. With its concern for liberty, economic individualism, and the foil of the Oriental, his narrative, like other Barbary captivity narratives of the seventeenth century, offered readers a complex, nationalist model of English identity, opening an ample field for experimentation within fictional adaptations.

Oriental captivity first entered English fiction in the form of brief episodes. Although these episodes generally followed the narrative pattern established in the factual captivity genre, their subscription within larger narrative structures often transformed captivity into something of a colonial apprenticeship for a picaro or mercantile hero. In *The English Rogue*, in Defoe's *Robinson Crusoe* and *Captain Singleton*, and most thoroughly in Chetwood's *Robert Boyle*, the traveling hero first encounters the world beyond Europe through the threat of capture and slavery in Turkey or Barbary. In some cases the hero enters Islamic slavery even in the act of escaping what seems a more threatening form of confinement, such as a British jail, and the subsequent facility of his escape from the Orient suggests that its seemingly degraded institutions cannot contain the energy and ingenuity of a heroic

Briton. Often these narratives portray the easily mastered situation of Oriental captivity as an initial provocation and test of the hero's colonial individualism. After the Orient draws out his colonial skills, he quickly applies them to what seem wilder, more dangerous, and more profitable colonial lands further away from Europe.

The first instance of this pattern occurs in the first English fictionalization of the Oriental captivity plot, in the first volume of Richard Head's popular *English Rogue.* Here Turkish captivity serves as a crucial transition in the narrator's roguish movement to colonial mastery. Towards the end of the first volume's lengthy series of trickster episodes, Latroon finds himself in prison and on his way to an American transportation. But after his domestic rogueries thus reach a limit imposed by what seems a fairly successful system of British justice, he escapes the rigors of American servitude through an accidental shift to Oriental slavery, with the wreck of his transport ship and his eventual capture by Turkish galleys. In recounting his protagonist's Turkish slavery, Head draws several proto-Orientalist motifs from his factual predecessors, including paltry food, abject labor, and cruel beatings.[19] Latroon obtains release from this abuse and degradation through a characteristic roguery, by feigning a desire for suicide so that a particularly cruel master sells him to one less cruel. Though the Oriental system of slavery temporarily debases the roguish hero, it proves incapable of permanently confining his aggressive self-assertion, ingenuity, and mobility. Eventually slavery opens a broader field of opportunities for the rogue, when his new master starts him on a colonial career through the East Indies.

This colonial world offers Latroon ample space not only for roguery but also for exercise of another set of skills more transparently connected to colonialism. After the brief episode of Turkish captivity, several chapters adopt the framework of travel description for detailed specifications of Malabar, Ceylon, Siam, and Bantam. This schematically organized section includes several exorbitantly tall tales and several harshly racist stereotypes, focused especially on the rampant sexuality of native women. In Bantam Latroon finds a guileless culture seemingly suited to his roguish disposition, as he cheats a native man of some jewels before having him killed, and then marries a native woman whose wealth permits him to set up in trade. This movement into colonial trade marks a climax for the rogue's career, at least within the text's first volume. When his talents have reached the limits of their applicability in England, he discovers a new field of application in a seemingly homogenous Orient, as the degrading but easily outmaneuvered world of Islamic slavery provides a gateway to the East, granting him access to a seemingly limitless and easily mastered field of colonial opportunities, where he can reach economic independence through the apparently interconnected colonial skills of careful observation and ruthless trickery.

A similar pattern develops in the most famous English fictionalization of Oriental captivity, the *Robinson Crusoe* episode, and to a lesser extent in *Captain Singleton* (1720). In the latter novel the hero begins his colonial career with a few journeys to Newfoundland before briefly falling into the hands of Algerine pirates; his subsequent rescue by the Portuguese moves him beyond the sphere of British influence into a broader colonial world of fabulous wealth and piracy. Crusoe's captivity in Sallee similarly occurs after an initial voyage on an English ship and similarly removes him from the sphere of British influence. During his captivity, Crusoe emulates the captive escape artists of the factual accounts. Like Okeley, the captive Crusoe seems to possess inborn skills in mercantile adaptation, and these skills first lift him out of degrading bondage and then enable his escape. After a Sallee rover takes him, he avoids hard labor by proving "nimble" for the Captain's "Business," and later his fishing skills gain such a high reputation that his master allows him access to a boat without supervision.[20] Seizing this opportunity, Crusoe attempts to improvise an escape plan, and, as with the factual narratives, the text devotes much attention to the captive's patient cogitations as he searches for expedients: "I meditated nothing but my Escape; and what Method I might take to effect it, but found no Way that had the least Probability in it: Nothing presented to make the Supposition of it rational . . . so that for two Years, tho' I often pleased my self with the Imagination, yet I never had the least encouraging Prospect of putting it in Practice" (19). Oriental captivity thus impels two years of heroic rational introspection at the opening of the most important rational career in English fiction. Finally the cogitating Crusoe benefits from the "odd Circumstance" of a canceled fishing excursion (19), recognizing its utility despite its apparent insignificance. The text devotes nearly a page to his efforts to supply an escape boat, noting such minutiae as a "Lump of Bees-wax" and "a Parcel of Twine," items "which were of great Use to us afterwards" (22). As in the Rawlins narrative, the improvisational captive recognizes potential utility in commonplace objects.

Crusoe resembles both the factual captives and the roguish Latroon in his ability to fabricate hoaxes that easily fool his captors. As he prepares his escape vessel, his "first Contrivance" involves stocking the boat with extra supplies on the pretense that he and his Salleean companion must not eat their master's food (21). Next Crusoe gains powder and shot when "Another Trick" also fools his "innocent" companion (22). Finally, after Crusoe gains control of the boat, he steers towards Africa rather than towards Europe, "as indeed any one that had been in their Wits must ha' been supposed to do" (23), in order to send any pursuers in the wrong direction. Crusoe's performance of this archetypal adventure ploy involves a careful assessment of rational and irrational behavior, as well as a careful manipulation of appearances, and these skills seem to place him in a superior position of mental dexterity, beyond the gullible simplicity of his captors.

These seemingly interrelated colonial skills of adaptation, planning, and deception, first revealed during Crusoe's captivity in Barbary, find further narrative fulfillment on his island. As Defoe's language itself attests, the isolation and deprivation of the island create a more extreme version of "captivity,"[21] providing greater scope for development of the improvisational skills that Crusoe first manifests during his captivity in Barbary. When the hero later finds his island filled with other peoples, both natives and potential colonial competitors, he asserts his colonial governance through a roguish game worthy of Latroon, remaining hidden while his underlings build a myth around his power. As in *The English Rogue*, the easily mastered Orient lays the groundwork for a more substantial drama of isolated subjectivity and mastery of the alien.

Within these late-seventeenth- and early-eighteenth-century fictions, the British hero's brief subjugation and escape in the Orient performed a trio of complex ideological functions. The first involved a quick replay of recent imperial history. The Briton's momentary subjugation, occurring at the start of his colonial career, rehearsed Europe's sixteenth-century weakness in the face of the Ottoman Empire. Then his quick and facile triumph over the Orient, as a seeming initiation into a broader colonial career, suggested that Barbary and Turkey no longer represented a legitimate empire, but had yielded to new imperial powers. The early placement of this Oriental triumph in the colonial hero's career suggested that reducing Islamic power over the West represented a precondition for Western expansion, just as, throughout the seventeenth century, suppression of Oriental shipping had broadened Western naval power and Western potential for territorial conquest. The second ideological function of this narrative pattern was to provide a model for the skills of colonial heroism. For English readers of the period, an Oriental captivity episode dramatized the hero's mastery of skills in improvisation and dissimulation within the well-traveled setting of the Orient, according to patterns already made familiar by the popular factual accounts, before he graduated to more exotic and more profitable locations such as a deserted Caribbean island. The third ideological function of the Oriental captivity episode was to help legitimize the trickery or, in its more mystified form, the intellectual dexterity of the colonial hero. When the hero's colonial journey began with an episode of Oriental captivity, this most familiar form of captivity among an alien people provided English readers with an early reminder of the threat faced by colonists in any alien environment, whether from natives or from European competitors for colonial power. Just as Oriental captivity taught the hero to suspect alien cultures and to trick them before they had a chance to capture him, it taught English readers to respect antagonistic wariness and anticipatory guile on the part of the idealized colonist.

The clearest instance of this ideological agenda appears in the most popular and faithful of the fictional adaptations: Chetwood's *Robert Boyle*.[22] After an early and largely undistinguished episode of Barbary captivity in Chetwood's first novel, *The Voyages of Captain Richard Falconer* (1720), this second novel develops an extended captivity narrative as its central plot line. Not only does the novel intensify the Orientalist materials of its factual predecessors, but it also creates a captive protagonist with a complicated subjective life and a pronounced individualist drive. Far from an experience of abjection, captivity transforms the young Boyle into a masterful colonialist hero, especially as prior to his capture he appears an unprepossessing, somewhat inept youth. He first leaves England when a wicked uncle sells him into American indentured service, and he enters Barbary captivity after falling overboard during his transport ship's successful repulse of a Sallee rover. At first this abject entry into captivity deprives him even of national companions in suffering, but the novel soon transforms his isolated capture into an opportunity for heroic self-assertion, with Boyle deciding that Oriental slavery offers greater chances for a return home than a more distant servitude in America. As in *The English Rogue*, this shift from American servitude to a seemingly less threatening and less final captivity in Algiers suggests that the Orient provides a more easily handled field of opportunities for the enterprising young captive or colonist in the making.

Boyle's servitude, moreover, involves no recital of squalid accommodations and hard labor but rather opportunities to assume mastery over the alien, as Chetwood sharpens the Oriental captivity narrative's opposition between the protagonist's mechanical skills and the luxurious decadence of his captors. Since the novel borrows its hero's name from a famous Restoration scientist and since it further identifies its hero as a former watchmaker and the orphan son of a West Indian merchant-captain, its representative Englishman emerges as a figure with a natural disposition for science, mechanics, and colonialism, possessing inborn skills for mastering the alien circumstances of Barbary captivity. His first task in servitude involves restoration of an "indifferently kept" garden, as his master laments the "want of a Gardiner," and Boyle confidently offers to adapt himself to the position despite his lack of experience (27). The text devotes several pages to his "Plans" for improvement and repair, including his direction of his master's Moorish servants, his importation of "European Seeds and Roots," and his restoration of a fountain with statues drawn from Greek mythology (28–29). After the garden's transformation, both the incapable master and his superstitious "Workmen were astonish'd to see with what Expedition I had compleated it, and imagin'd I had dealt with the Devil" (29, 43). In presenting this restoration of the garden to its original European splendor, the text projects an image of the decay of Western design under Oriental caretaking. Moreover, the incident suggests that captivity can call forth an Englishman's seemingly natural, interrelated skills in adapting himself to an alien environment, managing mechanical projects, ruling Oriental servants, and reshaping Oriental land.

While Boyle himself appears as a rational and enterprising captive hero, the novel constructs an intricate foil for him in his master, Hamet, a far more complex villain than the tyrannical captors of the factual accounts. As an Irish renegado, Hamet represents an alternative version of the Western self, a Briton thoroughly saturated by the imputed vices of the Orient, made weak, credulous, and rapacious by contact with the corrupting influence of institutions such as slavery and the seraglio. In contrast with the self-reliant Boyle, Hamet is surrounded by ineffectual servants, both natives and other renegadoes, who share his superstition, gullibility, and inability to control bodily impulses. Whereas the renegado's subscription within native culture seems to render him unfit for management of his servants, Boyle's oppositional insularity seems to enable his mastery over the natives and thus to suggest that resistance to native culture represents a precondition for British colonial mastery of the Orient.

The novel most sharply opposes Boyle's masterful subjective depths and Hamet's limiting acculturation through the introduction of a romance plot, which involves the captive's passion for a English slave, Mrs. Villars, confined in the renegado's harem. By adding a female slave to the captivity plot, the novel suggests that Oriental slavery can call forth not only the Englishman's colonial aptitude but also his sexual energies. Prior to his capture, he "never . . . had the least Regard to any of the Female Sex," but after Hamet's servants confine Boyle in order to keep him from the harem, an accidental glimpse of Mrs. Villars in a "Turkish Undress" produces love in the formerly aloof hero (30–31). This transformative initiation into sexual desire occurs partially through the circumstances of captivity, through the confined position of the desiring protagonist, through his outrage at the thought of a countrywoman's sexual confinement, and through invocation of the Orientalist vision of the seraglio as a site of heightened yet perverse sexuality, of both predation and promiscuity. The novel further heightens the sexual tension through its image of Mrs. Villars in the seductive attire that marks her captivity, creating, as in Defoe's *Roxanna*, a paradoxically exotic and reassuringly familiar sexual object by placing an Englishwoman in Turkish costume, described as an "Undress," a tantalizing antithesis to Western covering.

But if such Orientalist details seem to induce Boyle's desire, the plot of sexual confinement also contributes to the novel's contrast between his rationality and the depravity of his captors. After an initial moment of lover's despair, Boyle struggles to "think with Reason" and to "manage my Passion. I began to reflect the Moors were jealous of their Women even to a Degree, and did not in the least doubt but my *Irish Renegado* had learnt that part of their Manners" (31–32). Boyle's efforts to manage his passion first take concrete form with his recollection of an Orientalist stereotype and his efforts to manipulate this imputed feature of Oriental culture. The romance plot provides Chetwood with many opportunities to celebrate Boyle's dexterous manipulation of alien circumstances. Confined away from the seraglio, he must first find peepholes to observe his love, then contrive a system for passing notes to her, and finally engineer her escape by intoxicating her guardian eunuchs. In contrast with Hamet's rapacity, Boyle demonstrates sexual restraint in his own relations with Mrs. Villars, struggling to suppress his desire even when they share a bedroom after their successful escape. Thus the novel celebrates a rational sexual mastery in its Western hero by imagining a Western villain corrupted by Oriental sexuality, whereas the hero feels its allures but manages to control its effects.

As in the romance plot, the novel also more generally opposes Boyle's rational mastery of self and world to contrary tendencies in his captors, who appear vulnerable to the physical, unable to preserve a subjective insularity against its appeals, and thus unable to properly assess and control it. The novel portrays them as fond of and vulnerable to wine, despite "hypocritical" laws proscribing it, as Boyle repeatedly inebriates Hamet's servants in order to gain their confidence and reduce their watchfulness during key moments of his escape. He also benefits from his captors' superstition, especially when the scraps of a note to Mrs. Villars fall into the hands of a eunuch. Observing his captors' general veneration for small scraps of paper, Boyle "ask'd the Reason of all this Bustle, about a Thing we Europeans put to the most servile Uses." When he learns that the Moslems believe that the paper will help them "get to their Prophet" on judgment day, his contempt for this "whimsi-

cal Story" relies on a standard Western opposition between Oriental superstition and scientific or mercantile evaluation of the "servile Uses" appropriate to ordinary objects (42). Superstition apparently prevents the eunuch
from recognizing the material resources of the Western captive. Through
this portrait of the captor's superstition, and of his appetites for flesh and
wine, the text constructs the Oriental as a subject susceptible to the power of
objects, so that he provides a sharp contrast for the Western subject's mastery over objects.

Another key contrast between the masterful captive and his susceptible
captors involves management of narrative resources, a crucial concern for
Richardson, Fielding, and many other eighteenth-century novelists.[23]
Chetwood transforms the Oriental captivity narrative's interest in dissembling into an elaborate plot of masterful storytelling. From the moment that
Boyle falls into the corsairs' hands, he manipulates Hamet with flattery and
lies. The false assertion that Boyle *chose* to join the corsairs in order to escape American servitude earns him their sympathy, ultimately enabling his
relative freedom of movement and the more elaborate deceptions that lead
to his escape. His dissembling continues with an effort to conceal his passion
for Mrs. Villars behind a feigned "Detestation of all Females" (32). This veil
of misogyny, buttressed by "several extravagant Tales of my own Invention,"
helps him to fool a eunuch into sharing information about Mrs. Villars and
into granting Boyle a free run of Hamet's compound (33–34). But Boyle
cannot always manage such complicated chicanery with facility and confidence, and throughout the text the threat of discovery underscores the tenuous opposition between his carefully calculated exterior image and the interior
truth of his passions for liberty and Mrs. Villars. His heroic efforts in "Dissimulation" require enormous mental labor, as he spends a "whole Night in
thinking of a thousand Expedients to forward my Designs, till I had thought
of so many that they were all confus'd like a Skein of Silk pull'd the wrong
way" (34). Thus dissembling provides the captive hero with an intricate and
difficult interior life, especially in contrast with his dangerous yet easily understood and manipulated captors.

The power of Western storytelling emerges most concretely with the
realization of Boyle's escape plan and his final transformation from slavery to
mastery. He escapes through an elaborate sham "project," which occupies
most of his time and energy in captivity, and which plays on Hamet's superstition and lust for Mrs. Villars, by promising him a love potion based on
putatively scientific "Experiment" rather than Oriental "Witchcraft" (49). To
sell this project, Boyle improvises a *senex amans* tale that illustrates the power
of this "wonderful Arcanum" (50) and emphasizes its rarity, secrecy, and su-

pernaturalism. Blinded by passion and superstition, the renegado foolishly agrees to absent himself for the duration of Boyle's project, granting him enough time, money, and freedom to bring it to fruition. Boyle applies the time to scouting out escape routes and applies the money to Moorish disguises and other tools of escape. As the escape plan emphasizes both the complexity of his intelligence and the gullible superstition of his captors, the internal depths of the masterful Western subject take shape against the apparent inferiority of the deceived Orientals.

Boyle's discursive mastery of the Orient enters a new, institutionally sanctioned phase after he completes his escape and becomes a practicing Orientalist. When a French ambassador recognizes in him a "Capacity fit" for collecting "some Observations of the Customs and Manners" of this land (116–17), the novel suddenly metamorphoses into an Orientalist travel description, as he documents the people, customs, government, and religion of Morocco. The travel description relies on a standard scientific methodology, schematically dividing Morocco into sections for different cities and customs, as the fictional captive fulfills the guidelines for travel description published by his famous scientific namesake. With this sudden assumption of an Orientalist framework, the text seems quite literally to restore the West's imagined hierarchy of nations, as the former English slave achieves a scientific mastery over an Oriental environment that had formerly subjected him, but now lies subject to his scrutiny. Through this transformation of both text and character, the novel literalizes the captivity genre's more subdued connection between Western intellectual mastery of the Orient and the physical mastery of the Orient that enables the captive's escape. In highlighting Boyle's capacity to document the alien, Chetwood suggests an alliance of mercantile or entrepreneurial capacity, observational or scientific capacity, and diplomatic or political capacity, all based on skills of adaptation and observation.

Like his Algerian captivity narrative, Boyle's travel description generally presents Moroccan behavior as an irrational, impassioned, and excessive contrast to what is described as the normal rational subjectivity of the Westerner. After a detailed list of Moroccan cities establishes a tone of scientific rigor and documentary fullness, he shifts suddenly to a tone of ethnographic vituperation: "As to the nature of the Inhabitants, they are most of a tawny Complexion, of a lazy, idle Disposition, and curs'd with all the Vices of Mankind; mistrustful to the last Degree, false, jealous, and the very Picture of Ignorance" (120). Boyle's travel description repeats many standard Orientalist stereotypes, insisting on Moroccan cowardice, superstition, and disposition for bodily indulgence. When he asserts that the women are "very amorous" (125) and that the natives follow their religion "only like Children . . . because they are order'd" (127), such imputed features of Oriental peoples stand in implicit opposition to the heroic religious and sexual self-possession of Boyle and Mrs. Villars. Several customs inspire explicit contrasts with Western rationality, such as when Boyle observes some Moroccans stripping naked and sitting on their clothes during a rainstorm: "If a Man were to do so in England, he would be counted a Madman, or a Fool" (127). On another occasion, typically Orientalist in its citation of extreme brutality as representing the truth of the Orient, Boyle describes an innocent workman's arbitrary punishment at the hands of the Moroccan emperor, who repeatedly strikes the servant with a dart as he compliantly returns the weapon after each blow. Imagining himself in the servant's place, Boyle declares that he would have killed the emperor and accepted his own death as punishment rather than tolerate such repeated abuse. Again Chetwood builds an image of Western self-assertion by juxtaposing it with images of Oriental servility.

Given concrete intellectual form in Boyle's travelogue, his colonial aptitude enables worldwide travel and economic mastery when he resumes his autobiographical narrative. As with Crusoe, the hero's early experience as a Barbary captive seems to provide an education in the colonial skills that he later applies to other alien lands. Boyle's Barbary experiences, moreover, seem to offer a more explicit justification for his colonial drive. After his escape and sojourn in Morocco, he becomes captain of a trading vessel and immediately "long'd for an opportunity to be reveng'd on the Moors," especially after hearing a false report of Mrs. Villars's recapture by Hamet and subsequent suicide (153). When Boyle finds an opportunity for revenge through a chance encounter with Hamet's vessel, the resulting struggle, climaxed by the renegado's death and capture of his booty, both rectifies the seeming national imbalance of the hero's captivity and serves as his first lucrative colonial transaction. Next, as he undertakes a longer colonial voyage, he remains haunted by the memory of Mrs. Villars and even names a ship after her, so that the radical colonial drive of the Western male seems grounded in his radical devotion to a woman lost to Oriental captivity. As the plot follows his career around the coast of South America, he offers a series of travel descriptions emphasizing the natural resources and military defenses of various colonial ports. The observational skills and colonial imperative evident in these schematic descriptions find a parallel at the level of plot in Boyle's Defoe-like itinerary, with its illicit trade and privateering among the Spanish and Portuguese and its battles against Native Americans, which produce huge spoils and loyal slaves. Throughout these transactions Boyle relies on the skills in dissimulation and assessment of alien peoples that he had initially honed in Barbary captivity, and he reveals generosity in treating prisoners and in sharing wealth with his multinational subordinates. His skill in managing an enormous range of colonial peoples for an immense profit creates an image of an exemplary colonial master born in the crucible of Barbary captivity. In fictionalizing the Barbary captivity narrative, Chetwood transforms the defensively assertive captive into a radically aggressive and enormously successful proto-colonist, through an intensification of the genre's latent opposition between Western colonial skills and an Oriental culture that provides the initial provocation for development of these skills.

In his final extended venture with this genre, Chetwood recoded the colonial formula of the captivity plot in somewhat different sexual terms. A lengthy interpolated tale in *The Adventures of William Owen Gwin Vaughan* (1736) recounts the experiences of the protagonist's brother Jonathan, a former captive in Tunis. Although the novel links the Vaughan family with genteel pretensions, the captive Jonathan follows the pattern of mercantile heroism developed in Okeley and Boyle, achieving a marked success in the business his master assigns him while carefully concocting and concealing an escape plan. His ordeal, however, resembles the captivity of Boyle less than the captivity of Mrs. Villars, especially when he becomes the sexual prey of his "luxurious, idle" master. When his master appears "possess'd with the most hateful Passion Man can be guilty of," Vaughan enforces his refusal in the standard eighteenth-century language of heroic sexual self-defense: "I let him know, I would rather suffer Death, than comply with his infamous Desires."[24] What appears in Chetwood's fiction as the polymorphous perversity of the Orient allows, then, for variations in the construction of the English subject. Here a masculine subject adopts a feminine pattern of self-definition and self-preservation. After the novel plays with the threat of sexual violation to the Western male, it restores an impression of his mastery over the Orient in overtly sexual and covertly colonial terms, as the sister of Vaughan's Tunisian master also reveals a passion for this appealing Western captive. To provide Western sanctions for their transcultural romance, Chetwood contrives her conversion to Christianity and emphasizes her subjugated position within the predatory sexual system described by Orientalism. Intent on controlling his sister's sexuality as well as that of his slaves, the despotic brother plans to force her marriage to a friend. Despite the episode's sympathy for the plight of a Tunisian female, its plot ultimately hinges on defining a debased and predatory Oriental master as a foil for its devoted hero. After Jonathan escapes from Tunis, his well-armed return enables the sister's escape and the death of the despotic master who had variously persecuted this cross-cultural couple. In its seemingly manifold despotism, the Orient not only helps to define the Western male's heroic devotion to women but also helps to justify both religious conversion and military force. In the Vaughan narrative as in the Boyle narrative, such despotism compels variable forms of self-definition and self-assertion, constant only in their insistence on the force of British liberty, self-reliance, and colonial aptitude.

Further variations on this pattern characterize Penelope Aubin's adaptations of the Oriental captivity plot, although her works, when compared to Chetwood's, exhibit a less pronounced colonial agenda. In place of aggressively mercantile English heroes, she focuses on continental captives, especially passive noblemen, proselytizing priests, and women, character types that are essentially absent from factual accounts of Barbary captivity. This shift in character types would seem to offer infertile ground for individualistic or colonial ideology, especially since it seems consistent with Aubin's position as a woman and a Catholic, doubly removed from the circles of British mercantile expansion. Nevertheless, her novels link even these character types with tempered versions of the captivity plot's individualistic and colonialist motifs. Here I will focus particularly on her captive heroines, characters who demonstrate the captivity plot's broad potential for developing varied images of the Western subject's mastery of self and world.

Aubin's characterization of the female captive ranges from virtuous passivity to transgressive activity, but she shares, along with the male captives of the factual accounts, common features of insularity, self-assertion, and self-control, defined through the threats of subjugation and debasement in Oriental settings. With her many female captives, as with Chetwood's Mrs. Villars, threats of Oriental lust, bodily constraint, seduction, rape, and forced marriage all help to reinforce the Western female subject's preservation of sexual virtue, which represents, as it were, Western integrity and self-possession. Such dramas of besieged virtue, situated within the Orient, provide the primary narrative drive for Aubin's first novel, *The Count de Vinevil* (three printings, first 1721), for her most popular novel, *The Noble Slaves* (six printings, first 1722), and for her final novel, *The Life and Adventures of the Young Count Albertus* (one printing, 1728). Oriental captivity also figures prominently in *The Life and Amorous Adventures of Lucinda* (one printing, 1722) and in *The Life of Charlotta Du Pont* (four printings, first 1723). In these works the stereotypical dangers of the Orient often force female captives to improvise a variety of self-reliant, aggressive, and even mercantile behaviors, including many of those exhibited by Boyle and the heroes of the factual accounts. As the self-preservation of Aubin's heroines involved transgression of gender roles in male disguise, a choice of active self-defense over passivity, and even participation in a limited colonial economy, the circumstances of Oriental slavery provided English readers with an imaginative liberation from the period's increasingly domestic guidelines for female behavior.

Aubin's echoes of the Oriental captivity tradition are especially pronounced in the preface to *The Noble Slaves,* where she situates her plot of female chastity and transgressive self-fashioning within a framework of Orientalist and specifically nationalist oppositions. The preface offers a series of generalizations about Oriental government, economy, and sexuality, all emphasizing their departure from Western standards of political and economic individualism: "In our nation, where the Subjects are born free, where Liberty and Property is so preserv'd to us by laws, that no Prince can enslave us, the Notion of Slavery is a perfect Stranger. We cannot think without Horror, of the Miseries that attend those, who, in Countries where the Monarchs are absolute, and standing armies awe the People, are made Slaves to others. The Turks and Moors have been ever famous for these Cruelties."[25] Aubin further echoes the factual narratives of Oriental captivity in suggesting that, whereas the English "Constitution will always keep us rich and free," Oriental government, or "Turkish Policy," centers on a despot who "beggar[s] his People" and "fills his own Coffers with their Wealth" (x). The preface develops a specifically feminine role within this nationalistic and individualistic ideology through its assertion that Oriental custom allows the tyrant sexual power over many female slaves, including Western women: "There the Monarch gives a loose to his Passions, and thinks it no Crime to keep as many Women for his Use, as his lustful Appetite excites him to like" (x). Within the preface's framework of oppositions between Oriental despotism and the free-born English subject, chastity assumes national importance as a field in which a limited female autonomy can be defined against images of Oriental predation.

Although Aubin's plots place sexually predacious men all over the planet, the longstanding Orientalist motifs of despotism and ferocious sexuality provide imaginative resources to which she repeatedly turns, whether she locates the captivity plot in Barbary, Turkey, or Persia.[26] Her novels multiply episodes of besieged chastity and captive integrity through a complex, interlaced structure of interpolated tales, as a variety of captives arrive briefly on the scene to announce their personal subjugations, resistance to sexual predation, and efforts to escape. Slight variations in the basic pattern, assisted by common Orientalist stereotypes, build an image of the Orient as a world of polymorphous, uncontrollable, and predacious sexuality. To explain the aggressive desires of a Moroccan prince, Aubin declares in *The Noble Slaves* that "the Moorish Nobility, and indeed the Whole Nation, are much inclin'd to Love, very amorous and gallant" (107). In the same work a male captive narrates his sexual coercion at the hands of an old female master, and another male recounts a Tunisian governor's efforts to seduce him to "a use the Mahometans often keep young Men for" (139). More often female characters narrate various masculine attempts at sexual constraint, whether performed by a luxurious despot, an animalistic slave, or a vicious renegado, whether enacted through rape, seduction, or simply imprisonment within a seraglio. The most common pattern, involving a stereotypical potentate, recurs so insistently that it borders on the inevitable. As one captive husband predicts to his wife, immediately following their capture by Algerian pirates, "you will be ravished from me by some powerful Infidel, who will adore your Charms" (42). Within Aubin's fiction, the potentate often develops an institutional system of sexual predation; one of her heroines finds herself bought by the Bey of Tunis as part of his systematic purchase of "handsome European Virgins" at the local slave market.[27] In its seeming inevitability and connection to an underlying cultural system, this recurring narrative pattern imagines Oriental rulers as necessarily despotic, predatory, and particularly interested in Western women.

Aubin combines this vision of the Orient with other aspects of the captivity plot in order to celebrate heroines whose piety and chastity stand equal to the extremes of power, wealth, and depravity described by Orientalism. Her works often define the heroic virtue of Western women against images of the already fallen women of the seraglio, as powerful Oriental men repeatedly abandon their jealous and beautiful countrywomen for Western slaves.[28] Often the potentate, far from buying the Western heroine in a simple economic transaction, sees in her a noble beauty commensurate to his power. His failed efforts to seduce her with offers of freedom, extreme wealth, and even political influence reinforce her heroic maintenance of chastity, which itself often staggers him, increasing his passion but also sometimes ennobling and reforming him, even forcing him to grant her freedom. When the potentate resorts to violence, the Oriental setting exacerbates the plot of besieged chastity, as the heroine's distance from her homeland helps to emphasize her lack of any recourse to law, money, or family, while explicit comments on Oriental despotism highlight her powerless subjugation. Within the seraglio, the master, like Lovelace, often enlists the aid of his sexually experienced concubines to help his rape or seduction. Like Pamela or Clarissa, the female captive sometimes contemplates suicide and frequently threatens or even performs violence against herself in defense of her sexual virtue. Aubin's texts often voice Orientalist stereotypes to reinforce their heroines' proto-Richardsonian defense of chastity. In *The Noble Slaves* the enslaved Emilia swears, "I will die rather than live a Vassal to a vile Mahommetan's unlawful lust" (42). Like many similar vows in Aubin's fiction, this declaration compresses the drama of besieged chastity with the Orientalist vision of the East as a place without the protection of laws, where absolute tyranny can exercise political power over vassals and sexual power over virgins. Ultimately, however, the potentate's continual desire for and failure to subdue the Western heroine portrays the Orient, even in the very heights of its power, as abject and impotent when faced with the seemingly inexorable appeal and incorruptible resolve of Western self-possession.

However, these dramas of chastity and fidelity, far from defining the female subject entirely in terms of resistance to sexual assaults, also grant her a limited autonomy by depicting assertive behavior as demanded by the situation of Oriental captivity. Often Aubin's heroines must assert themselves because their male companions prove inadequate in dealing with Oriental potentates, who easily isolate the women from any possible assistance from their nominal protectors, sometimes even forcing the latter into degrading bondage. In *The Noble Slaves*, for example, Emilia's male companions try to prevent an Algerian potentate from separating male from female captives, but his soldiers immediately reduce the men to passivity and debilitating confinement. Such separations and confinements often contribute to the romance motif of heroic male devotion to women, especially when the despots punish Western men out of jealousy or when they suffer continued debasement in the Orient while waiting for the escape of their inamoratas. Whereas Aubin generally depicts female slaves as surrounded by luxury, she often describes the bondage of Western men according to a pattern well established in the factual captivity narratives, with a wealth of particular details concerning locks and chains, humiliating drudgery, wretched food and bedding. A captive nobleman in *Charlotta Du Pont*, for example, laments his condition as a slave forced to "draw Water, dig, and labour hard all Day, at Night chain'd like a Dog in a Hole," and eventually reduced by labor and poor food to such "Fever" and "Weakness" that his escape depends entirely on the help of his master's daughter (109–10). When Aubin does include more active Western males, they are hermits and priests such as Count Albertus, men who master the Orient quietly rather than spectacularly, secretly gaining a small livelihood, converting natives, and collecting escaped slaves for return to Europe.

Because the Oriental captivity plot can render Western men abject, ineffectual, or mild, it allows Aubin to imagine situations that demand a modicum of female self-assertion. Deprived of male protection, her female captives assume some of the autonomous, improvisational, and transgressive activities of the escaping captive hero. In *Charlotta Du Pont*, for example, the brief interpolated tale of Angelina highlights a resourcefulness and "Wit, which exceeded her Sex (tho Women ever were esteem'd more quick and subtile than Mankind at cunning Plots and quick Contrivances)" (105). With pointed irony, Aubin adduces a misogynist stereotype as justification for creating a heroine with the dexterous ingenuity of the captive hero. After Angelina's capture by Algerian corsairs and sale to a lustful Tunisian ruler, she shows a "heroick Spirit and consummate Virtue" as she "bravely resolv'd to die, rather than submit to a Mahometan; and thus determin'd, began to consider what to do to deliver her self" (101). The text moves immediately from a standard vow of chastity to the careful deliberation of the Barbary captive. Her planning showcases her observational skills, as she immediately discovers the keys to her prison in the hands of a "Moorish slave," and then carefully notes the advantage that her master's absence gives her. The escape plot hinges on a series of problems that she easily overcomes, first climbing out her window with some bed sheets, next breaking into a closet to secure Turkish clothes, and finally fashioning these clothes into Oriental disguises. To obtain the all-important key from the slave, Angelina plans to "stab him with a Penknife I have hid about me" (145). However, this carefully contained violence, so important for Clarissa as for many other eighteenth-century heroines, does not become necessary for Angelina, who steals the key from her drunken captors. The text justifies this contingency with a stereotype concerning hypocrisy and alcohol: "Altho their Prophet does forbid it them; . . . few Mussulmen refuse it in Private" (105). In sum, this escape parallels those of the factual accounts in several ways: in the captive's careful deliberation on method, in her ability to recognize favorable circumstances and the utility of ordinary objects, and in her ability to capitalize on the stereotypical weaknesses of Orientals. By placing a triumphant female protagonist in an Oriental captivity plot, Aubin creates a transgressive heroine who can approach male adventurers in their resourcefulness, observational skills, and mastery of the alien.

Within Aubin's fictions, transgressive female mastery of the Orient extends even to colonialist motifs, although her heroines' modest and carefully contained financial successes fall somewhat short of the masterful colonialist aptitude registered in Okeley or Boyle. After Angelina escapes, she builds a nascent colony on the Tunisian coast, along with a noble Spanish couple, also escaped captives. Like many characters in Aubin's Oriental fictions, the husband pursues a Crusoe-like existence as a self-reliant castaway, growing "well acquainted with the Country" and adapting to its alien circumstances, even building a home, complete with a fireplace, out of an abandoned mosque (114). He obtains a more secure refuge in a manner typical of Aubin's male

Instead of portraying capture and torture, the frontispiece to
Aubin's most popular novel seems to invoke the Crusoe-like
survivial of some escaped captives in an abandoned mosque. (By
permission of the British Library. 12511.CC.14.)

escapees. Taking advantage of supposed Oriental superstition, he masquerades as a dervish and convinces a local fisher-couple to give their own home to these budding Western colonists. These peasants eventually convert to Christianity, prove "very serviceable" to the Europeans, and secure their escape on a Spanish vessel (116). Within this episode, quick-thinking deception and more general skills in adaptation enable the former captives to fulfill, at a microcosmic level, the colonial agenda of converting native peoples, gaining their support, and appropriating their resources. Despite continual fear of recapture, the colonists also achieve some economic success. While in captivity the noble husband had adapted to the labor of making straw hats and baskets, and after his escape these skills blossom into a cottage industry, as he teaches the women to make such products "with great dexterity," sells them in town, and receives "enow to supply them with Bread and Meat in way of exchange" (116). Thus isolation within an unknown and threatening environment compels the noble trio to alter themselves according to its demands, as they transgress boundaries of gender and status while drawing on the resourceful skills of the mercantile hero. Under the guidance of a Western male, the female escapees make what seem properly limited, even domestic contributions to this mini-factory of colonial mercantilism.

Another important female economic contribution results from the sale of jewels that the women had fortuitously discovered and prudently confiscated during their escape. Throughout Aubin's novels, female captives gain wealth from their Oriental masters through such accidents; several heroines obtain hordes of jewels from the luxurious costumes their masters had forced them to wear. In the case of Angelina, when she examines her stolen disguises, she discovers that, "instead of being mean, such as Slaves wear," they contain a fortune in "Cloth of Gold," "Rubies," "Emeralds," "Diamonds, Pearl, and other Jewels" (148). Thus Aubin grants her heroines one of the common motifs associated with the adventurous hero of colonial fiction, translating colonial appropriation of resources into images of fabulous booty gained through accident rather than planning, as a chance by-product of the radical self-assertion demanded by the circumstances of subjugation under a putatively tyrannical and inferior people.

Within Aubin's fictions, subjugation within a dangerous Oriental setting can force female characters to extremes of violent self-assertion from which later fiction, with its focus on domesticity and sensibility, would tend to dissociate its heroines. In *The Noble Slaves*, the Spanish slave Maria tears out her eyes in order to thwart the lust of a Persian emperor, who, cowed by this extreme defense of her sexual virtue, grants her freedom (33). Aubin's heroines more often direct their violence against their aggressors. When an Algerian overlord threatens to rape Emilia, she kills him with a ritualized declamatory vaunt like those that accompany male violence in epic or heroic romance: "Villain, I fear you not, I'll sacrifice you to preserve my Vertue; die Infidel, and tell your blasphemous Prophet, when you come to Hell, a Christian spilt your Blood" (48). Next she kills a renegado in order to escape, but the novel also tries to control the effects of all this carnage by highlighting the heroine's mental disturbance, which appears in a "look that spoke the Terrors of her Mind, and the strange Deed she had done" (48). While these "Terrors" suggest a partial shift towards the ideology of female passivity and sensibility, Aubin's fictions nevertheless repeatedly depict the "strange" actions of female violence as justified resistance to the subjugation of Oriental slavery. One of her heroines, after threatening to kill her lustful Turkish captor, escapes by setting fire to his seraglio, and thus inspires another Western woman, who had accepted concubinage, to reproach herself for lacking the heroism of resistance.[29] The contrast between the two characters creates a justification for female violence under such extreme conditions as those which seem to characterize the Orient.

Aubin's Oriental settings demand other transgressive forms of female behavior, signaled most concretely in their dexterous manipulation of disguises. Like the heroes of the factual captivity narratives, her heroines achieve and maintain their freedom by projecting false selves to deceive their captors, sometimes through the resourceful dissembling associated with male captives, but more often through elaborate and carefully planned costumes. Within her works, almost every iteration of the captivity plot involves the female captive's adoption of native dress, sometimes because her master insists that she wear the finery of "Turkish" costume, but more often because she needs to disguise herself in order to escape. Whereas Chetwood employs Turkish costume as a sign of danger for his hero's inamorata, Aubin celebrates her heroines' Roxana-like control over alien costume. Thus the Oriental captivity plot helps her to develop a crucial motif in heroic romance and in novels by Englishwomen from Behn to Inchbald, where female manipulation of costume marks an ideological fantasy or protest about female power within the limits imposed by domesticity and consumerism.[30]

Aubin's use of disguise intensifies the captivity plot's emphasis on the dexterous self-mastery and subjective depths of the captive, especially as contrasted with images of an exotic yet inferior Orient, easily understood, resisted, imitated, and deceived. When masters force Turkish costumes on their female slaves, the novels describe this clothing with a wealth of descriptive detail and luxurious epithet, creating an air of exotic sexuality. Despite the temptation of this luxurious and provocative clothing, the women remain uncomfortable with its imposition and indifferent to its allures, so that their seemingly incorruptible essence of chaste purity resists redefinition within an alien culture that seems to exist at the level of surface rather than depth. An even greater sense of Western female mastery over Oriental culture results when the captives choose Turkish costumes themselves. In the tale of Angelina, for example, the heroine carefully deliberates over her choice of a eunuch's costume and then switches to that of an Oriental lady, finally reaching a perfect disguise with a darkened face. Through this skillful assumption and alteration of disguises, such a narrative highlights the captive's careful observation of her environment and her ability to adapt herself to its demands. The narrative tension surrounding disguise continues after escape, especially with the threat that any passing Oriental male will penetrate the Western fugitive's seemingly unnatural disguise, seeing through outer appearance and behavior to the inner female subject in all her sexual vulnerability. Thus disguise helps to interpolate the depths of Western female consciousness, constructed in terms of a division between an inward essence and an outward image, so that the outward image can provide the basis for a skillful and temporary play with boundaries of race, gender, and status, while the inward essence retains its inborn, "natural" integrity. While Aubin's clever Western females easily master the details of Oriental costume and behavior, her Oriental characters remain forever fixed in such costumes as in the putative attributes of their culture.

When the circumstances of Oriental captivity require Aubin's heroines to assume masculine disguise, this motif contributes to a heroism of transgressive self-fashioning and masterful adaptation, most fully realized in *Lucinda.* Throughout her sojourn in the Orient, the eponymous heroine wears male attire in order to protect herself against various threats associated with Eastern lands. Her assumption of masculine disguise both endangers and transforms her, placing her in situations that threaten her chastity, but also allowing her to abandon passivity for an array of cross-gendered resources. As she explains, "The garb, I fancy, had inspired me with manly Resolutions; I had no timorous Thoughts . . . and applied my self diligently to attain their Airs."[31] This heroic process of adaptation reaches an apotheosis when she easily adapts to combat with a Barbary rover: "no one who had been a witness of my Behavior, would have suspected me for any other than a finished hero" (228–29). Once she enters Turkish slavery and confronts the putative sexuality of the Orient, her disguise produces a set of problems that she handles with the improvisational skills of the resourceful captive. When her Turkish master places this seeming male slave in charge of his personal apartment, including his attire, much dramatic tension arises from the discrepancy between an inward female essence defined by chastity and the cross-gendered sexual possibilities of her outward appearance, behavior, and situation. Another test of her skills in impersonation arises after a chance meeting with her long lost but still favorite suitor, now a fellow slave reduced to passive weakness and abject bondage but still strangely attracted to this masculine simulation of his lady love. A final complication plays on Orientalist sexual stereotypes, as the disguised Lucinda excites a "fruitless Passion" in a "young Turkish Lady" and consequently fears the "Fury of her Desires," especially as "the Women of that Country were not framed of the coldest Mould" (244–45). To preserve both her masculine disguise and her feminine "virtue," Lucinda blinds all of these potential discoverers of her identity by fabricating histories of a masculine past, and thus her impressive storytelling skills, like those of Boyle, signal a Western ability to adapt and dissemble as they allow her to maintain her chaste essence against the dangers associated with Oriental slavery. While the romance device of a masculine disguise helps to create a transgressive female subject and a concomitant liberation from feminine social constraints, her most extreme moments of transgressive and emancipatory self-fashioning result precisely from the extreme duress of Turkish captivity. The dangerous and alien setting of the Orient enables and even demands female assumption of a masculine heroism along with a masculine disguise, and thus the placement of the female subject within a narrative pattern of Western self-preservation aligns her self-assertion to that of the heroic captive male, similarly defining her rational mastery of self and alien environment against the seemingly irrational excesses of that environment.

To an even greater extent than Aubin, Eliza Haywood used the Oriental captivity plot to create visions of male passivity and female aggression, as part of an even more disruptive transformation of the plot's customary patterns of character and incident. Haywood's first effort in this genre, a brief episode in *Idalia* (1723), develops a straightforward reversal of audience expectations about Oriental despots and degrading bondage, while subsequent episodes in *The Fruitless Enquiry* and *Philidore and Placentia* (both 1727) offer a pointed response to the captivity fictions of Aubin and especially of Chetwood. Published a year after Chetwood's *Robert Boyle* and at the height of Aubin's popularity, Haywood's 1727 episodes enact parodic reversals of her predecessors' plot lines, severely undercutting their celebration of aggressive colonialism, masculine individualism, and female chastity. While Haywood absolutely rejects the captivity plot's standard vision of European men and women, she largely retains its vision of the Orient. In the Orientalist vision of the East as a land of extreme despotism, slavery, and lust, Haywood finds a setting that enables vivid emplotments of Western social problems, particularly the multiple and conflicting connections between sexuality and power.

Idalia resists the prevailing model of Oriental captivity by transforming it into a positive experience, as the heroine discovers friendship among her captors rather than despotism and sexual subjugation. Although at first she fears the threat of slavery under an "uncivilized" people, her captivity leads to a rapprochement with the alien when she finds herself captured, not by a depraved and lustful tyrant, but by a mannered and genteel Oriental couple.[32] The heroine's happy captivity, moreover, follows an earlier series of subjugations, including kidnapping and rape, at the hands of European men, so that her chaste and gentle Oriental captors provide an ironic counterpoint to European sexual predation. Moreover, the novel grants this couple the subjective depths of romance protagonists by presenting their history in an interpolated tale, full of divided loyalties, arranged marriages, and the imprisonments that result from a despotism still seemingly inherent to the Orient. As this tale engages the heroine's empathy, she grows to respect and admire her Oriental captors, and she even laments their loss by shipwreck, despite her consequent release from a merely nominal captivity. Thus Haywood replaces the standard plot of female subjugation and Oriental depravity with a vision of Orientals as exotic but subjectively commensurate to Europeans.

On the other hand, both *The Fruitless Enquiry* and *Philidore and Placentia* retain standard stereotypes about Oriental peoples but employ them in a manner that radically undercuts the captivity plot's colonialist drive and celebration of masculine self-assertion. Each novel includes an episode that transfers the Orientalist motifs of piracy, despotism, and vindictive passion to locations east of the Ottoman territories and less familiar to British readers. Set in the Maldive islands but probably indebted to Robert Knox's account of Ceylon, the captivity episode in *The Fruitless Enquiry* connects a local governor with pomp and despotism, asserts that he is "worshipped as a god," and describes the "savage inhabitants" as "wholly uncivilized."[33] Haywood attributes the natives' practice of taking captives to a sadistic "delight in triumphing over and detaining them," and she blames the natives' refusal to exchange their captives on a general economic turpitude (69). Playing on another set of Orientalist stereotypes in its portrait of Persia, *Philidore and Placentia* insists on the natives' "luxury," their "haughty disposition," and their devotion to "self-satisfaction."[34] This latter trait, for Haywood, seems connected with cool deliberation and duplicity; one European slave warns another to beware the general "disposition of the persons of this country. If they show you any favour, 'tis to please themselves" (198). But if Haywood attributes the putative despotism of the Orient to a native disposition for excessive self-indulgence and even for sadism, her exotic settings ultimately serve to reveal in peculiarly stark terms her vision of cross-cultural connections between power and pleasure.

This vision develops partially through a parodic reformulation of the heroic male captive. Whereas Barbary captivity narratives generally employ Orientalist stereotypes to depict the East as a land easily understood and mastered, just waiting for colonization, Haywood employs the same stereotypes to depict the East as monstrous and unmanageable, a threat that Englishmen should avoid. Instead of focusing on captive merchants, artisans, or priests, she follows the journeys of gallants forced unwillingly to visit the Orient by the vagaries of courtship and economic dependence. In Chetwood's vision of the East, the experience of captivity seems to call forth the sexual, entrepreneurial, and colonial powers of the formerly feckless Boyle, but Haywood's captives remain pathetically and even comically inept at handling the circumstances of alien lands. She dwells on the abject details of their slavery, and her captivity episodes climax not with their triumphant escape but with their castration as a result of entanglements with beautiful women of the harem. In connecting the harem to the castration of Western men, Haywood suggests the impotence of Europeans in the face of institutions that appear irrevocably despotic and barbaric.

At the same time, the castration narrative allows Haywood to flout increasingly rigid British notions of domestic gender roles through a parodic reformulation of the captivity plot's vision of the Orient as a sexual threat to Europeans. Whereas Aubin and Chetwood employ the Orientalist vision of the seraglio in order to characterize European females as chaste, autonomous, and free, Haywood imagines the seraglio as a site of female sexual power and male victimization. In *The Fruitless Enquiry,* the enslaved male suffers castration when he refuses the sexual advances of his master's wife, Elphania, a European woman who has risen from Oriental slavery to despotic power through marriage to a local potentate. Thus the European woman in the seraglio appears not as a suffering protagonist, not as a determined captive fighting for her chastity and national integrity, but as a figure of illicit carnality and despotism, corrupted and empowered by a dangerous sexual system. In *Philidore and Placentia,* the interpolated tale of a "Christian Eunuch" recounts this former captive's efforts to penetrate his master's seraglio in order to pursue an affair with one of his wives, only to meet discovery and the punishment of castration. Whereas for Aubin and Chetwood the seraglio represents the Orient's despotic but usually conquerable threat to a European female's chastity, Haywood's vision of the seraglio focuses on the associated image of the eunuch and its potential for ironically treating European issues of male and female power.

Haywood's vision of the Orient as a land where pleasure and power reveal their interdependence allows her to imagine castration as an ironic analogue for rape, as a violent sexual subjugation that defines the male as a patriarchal victim. In *The Fruitless Enquiry*, as Elphania announces her punishment for her recalcitrant slave, she declares that "since he is no man for me, he shall not for another," and the novel later describes the castrato as "deprived for ever of the dear names of father and husband; robbed of his sex, and doomed to an eternal sterility" (73, 75). The novel posits potency as a male sexual essence, roughly equivalent to female "virtue" in that it defines men as the objects of a female sexual competition and locates their position within a patriarchal lineage. On the other hand, although *Philidore and Placentia* also defines the essence of manhood at the moment of castration, it does so by focusing on male sexual competition, as the castrato narrates how the potentate's servants "deprived me of all power of ever injuring their lord . . . and left me nothing but the name of man" (206). In both cases Haywood links the Orientalist vision of sexual predation to male rather than female victims, and thus she parodies the images of male activity, female victimization, and chaste virtue that characterized both contemporary captivity plots and the general movement of eighteenth-century fiction.

Haywood's revision of captive heroism also involves ridicule of the romance fantasy of radical male devotion to women.[35] Whereas the captivity plot allowed Chetwood and Aubin to celebrate their heroes' devotion to women in spite of the extreme separations caused by captivity, Haywood mocks the ideal of male devotion by subjecting maximally devoted men to a violence that radically undercuts their devotion. In each of Haywood's castration episodes, the violation of the male slave results from his radical devotion to a woman, so that castration represents not only Oriental despotism but also male subjugation within the empire of love. In *The Fruitless Enquiry*, the enslaved Montrano refuses the addresses of the despotic Elphania out of devotion to his own wife, while the "Christian Eunuch" enters the forbidden ground of the harem because he so strongly loves one of its women. When Haywood's Oriental despots castrate her devoted male lovers, their victimization indicates the extremity of their subjugation to women, and Oriental despotism seems correlated with the power of the devotee over the devoted. Although at one level these images support a fantasy of female sexual power and maximized male devotion, this fantasy ultimately undoes itself in the very extremity of its violence.

At bottom, this aborted fantasy comprises a grim parody of British gender relations as idealized in contemporary captivity fictions. In Haywood's episodes of Oriental captivity, maximally devoted male characters finally prove incapable of satisfying women or of handling the world's violent political, economic, and social structures. This vision of masculine failure occurs as each novel expressly reverses several of the captivity plot's central motifs within an interpolated tale that reworks the larger themes of the main plot line, especially those of sexuality, potency, subjugation, and dependence. In *The Fruitless Enquiry*, the castration narrative is told by Iseria, the unhappy wife of the castrato, and appears within a series of tales strung together by a loosely organized frame narrative, which follows a central heroine as she listens to the tales in her "Fruitless Enquiry" for a truly contented female. Illustrating the unhappiness of a woman with a devoted but "fruitless" husband, Iseria's tale begins with a focus on unhappy courtship, as the young lovers marry despite her poverty and despite his dependence on an uncle, who, outraged by his choice, kidnaps and exiles him to Ceylon. Eventually Montrano finds himself shipwrecked in the Maldives, sold in a slave market to a local potentate, and finally castrated, so that his mutilation signals a broader incapacity and the unhappiness of a wife forced to depend on a feckless man.

This portrait of Montrano's multiple incapacities enacts one of several parodic reversals of the Oriental captivity plot's heroic patterns of self-fashioning. Unlike Chetwood, Haywood begins this captivity narrative by placing emphasis on the abject conditions of her captive's life as "a slave amongst the most barbarous people in the world, condemned to offices with which he was no way acquainted," repeatedly punished "by stripes," and further tortured by "the belief, that his service was eternal" (61). Montrano rises above such abject labor not through his own active exertions but through his passive physical appeal to the aggressive Elphania. Further reversals of the heroic captivity plot result from the characterization of this European female antagonist, who, we learn, originally entered the Maldives as a criminal punished by transportation to an "eternal slavery," before her marriage makes her the "greatest woman in the island" (62–63). Here a roguish female rather than a picaro or merchant-adventurer finds opportunities for success in transportation and Oriental slavery. After the female rogue rises to power through sexual means, she rather than her husband fills the role of sexual tyrant. Whereas Haywood's Oriental potentate earns mild approval for generously raising a slave to monarchy, Elphania seems to have mastered an alien system of sexual predation in her aggressive pursuit of the enslaved Montrano. In describing her abuse of him, Haywood compares this female antagonist to the stereotypical Oriental potentate: "the humour of the mistress he now served, was more perplexing to him than the tyranny of his former masters; nor had he less to expect from her revenge, . . . than from the most inhuman of his own sex" (66). When Montrano's punishment fulfills this suggestion that Western men have more to fear from angry Western women than from the terrible despots of the Orientalist imagination, Haywood employs the Orientalist image of castration to develop a fantastically exaggerated and ultimately ironic vision of retributive female power, a vision that intimates both the potential violence of female anger and the difficulties of acting on it in Western society.

Montrano's castration not only signifies his failure to satisfy women but also corresponds to a complete failure to develop the active, self-assertive virtues of the captive or colonialist hero. Before his castration, he spends a whole year in a manner typical of the captive hero, searching for "contrivances" of escape, but he finds escape impossible because of native watchfulness and the threat of "the most cruel punishments imaginable" (68–69). In a manner typical of the captive heroine, he tries to avoid despotic sexual advances with a series of dissimulations, first "affecting a satisfaction" with Elphania's desires (65), next alleging a two-year vow of celibacy that would prevent their fulfillment. But these and other deceptions backfire. He supports his next ruse, feigned sickness, to the point of undergoing a native cure, which involves "shoot[ing] arrows into many parts of the patient's body" (70). Thus native custom and the captive's meager skills in self-preservation combine for a grim exercise in bodily subjugation rather than a triumphant escape. As a final ruse, he feigns madness, but Elphania easily sees through this ploy and condemns him to abject punishment. Further failures to imitate the virtues of the captive hero occur after his castration. He obtains release not through his own exertions but because a repentant Elphania gives him freedom and money. On his way home, he loses the money to thieves and suffers a debilitating wound, which weakens him so much that he "appeared more like a ghost than a living man" (77). As Montrano's castration corresponds to a more general pattern of ineptitude, weakness, and dependence, the plot suggests that fully realized male devotion would incapacitate a man for negotiating alien lands and power structures. Within this novel, then, Haywood's reformulation of the Oriental captivity plot amounts to an attack on its related ideologies of radical male self-assertion and radical male devotion to women.

Castration likewise connects to larger issues of gender, power, and dependence in *Philidore and Placentia; or L'Amour trop Delicat*. In this novel as in *The Fruitless Enquiry*, the Oriental castration episode provides an ironic counterpoint to a frame tale set in the West. In the frame tale, the gallant but impecunious Philidore falls in love with the wealthy Placentia and, in order to be near her, joins her household as a servant. Linking the subjugation of his devotion to the subjugation of Oriental slavery, the novel explicitly labels him a "slave" and has him disguise his complexion to suit the "Egyptian breed" (159, 166). Once his devotion earns Placentia's affection, he refuses to take advantage of her wealth and forward sexuality, and this "too delicate" love of the subtitle forces him to flee to Persia, where he plans to acquire a competency with a merchant uncle. Within this protagonist, Haywood unites the themes of genteel destitution, masculine sexual forbearance, and the degraded status of an Oriental slave, so that the heroine's economic and sexual powers seem to correlate to the absolute powers that Orientalism linked to the monarchs of the East. Once again Haywood's connection between the Orient and female power involves a playful irony that ultimately underscores the unlikelihood that women might wield such power in the West.[36]

As in *The Fruitless Enquiry,* the Orient appears a difficult and dangerous environment for such an unwilling and delicate colonist as Philidore, who, like Montrano, encounters a series of disasters that reverse the standard motifs of colonial domination. Captured by pirates and marooned in Persia, he and his companions suffer acute feelings of ignorance and incapacity, and ultimately they must throw themselves on the mercy of the inhabitants (185). When they ask a local potentate for aid, they "fell prostrate on their faces, as is the custom in all the Eastern parts to do before the ruler" (186). In its alterity and despotism, Persia appears as a land formed for highlighting the weaknesses of Westerners. In this landscape of abjection, Philidore's amatory misery produces a disregard for life that, somewhat paradoxically, strengthens him and allows him to assume a leadership role among his companions. Here, ironically, it is the abjection of the protagonist rather than his intellectual dexterity that seems to fit him for travel through the Orient.

As developed within the main plot line, Philidore's colonial abjection correlates with the sexual status of the "Christian eunuch," whose interpolated tale engrosses a third of the novel and climaxes its vision of male abjection and Oriental despotism. The correlation between Philidore and the eunuch begins from the moment they meet, when the former rescues the latter from a battle with some Persians, and then feels an overwhelming curiosity to fathom the mystery of this "lovely stranger" in Persian costume (189). Philidore's desire augments with a pair of discoveries. First he learns that the stranger also loves a woman, a "belief, more uniting him to him by a kind of sympathy of soul" (191). Next Philidore learns that "This beauteous person had been deprived of his manhood," a discovery that renders the listener's "curiosity doubled" (192). Some explanation for this multiple doubling and sympathy of souls appears at the end of the novel, when we learn that the eunuch is actually the Baron Bellamont, Placentia's brother. Through this final narrative twist and through the plotting of the Baron's castration tale, the novel ultimately subsumes its oblique intimations of same-sex attraction within a formula that employs the eunuch first as an extremely illustrative analogue for Philidore's "too delicate" love and then as a means for restoring masculine sexual prerogative.

From the opening of the Baron's tale, Haywood introduces several reversals of the captivity plot's standard patterns of characterization. After "Persian privateers" interrupt his youthful travels, the Baron finds himself sold to a genteel bashaw rather than to a stereotypical tyrant, and "treated with a kindness which left me nothing but the name of slave. All the others he was master of were ordered to serve and obey me" (197). After this transformation from abject slavery to an exotically absolute mastery, further reversals of the standard captivity plot result when the Baron falls in love with his master's wife, Arithea. As he explains, his desire renders him foolhardy and opens the possibility of extreme physical subjugation: "to be more her slave, I ran hazards which madness only could have led me into," especially when he enters the seraglio in disguise, an action punishable by "the worst of tortures" (199). In order to attack the romance celebration of male devotion and its language of mastery and slavery, Haywood imagines the Orient as an environment where the language of devotion reaches an ironically concrete fulfillment. The bashaw quickly discovers the Baron's penetration of the seraglio and then confines him to a "dungeon," limits him to "bread and water," and lashes him three times "with iron whips a hundred strokes on my naked back" (202). Once again Haywood capitalizes on the motifs of Oriental captivity in order to create a fantastically vivid, farcically exaggerated image of masculine devotion to woman as sexual object.

The Baron's inordinate devotion entails a further reversal of the typical pattern of captive psychology, by destroying both the desire and the capacity for escape. As he "abandon[s] all thoughts of . . . religion, kindred, friends, country, and freedom," he even rejects the bashaw's offer of liberty: "I threw myself at his feet and conjured him not to discharge me from his service, assuring him that I thought it greater honor to be his slave than to command in any other place" (201). Whereas Boyle carefully controls his own behavior and watches for signs of his captors' suspicion, the captive Baron "neglect[s] everything" and appears before the bashaw "with so wild and confused an air, made answers to what he said which were so little to the purpose and behaved in everything so unlike myself, or as I ought to have done, that he imagined my brain was in good earnest disordered" (201). As a result of this failure in self-control, the bashaw strengthens the watch on the motions of this distracted slave. Whereas Boyle's rationally managed passion contrasts sharply with the debasing passion of Hamet, the Baron's hysterical passion contrasts sharply with his master's cool deliberation. As the Baron looks back on his behavior, he judges himself against an idealized equation between mastery, manhood, and the virtues of the captive hero: "Had I been the master of the least share of soul or spirit, or had [I] been possessed of any part of that fortitude and resolution which every man ought to have, I should have . . . ventured everything for my escape rather than have tarried in a place where I was doubly a slave" (203). But he finds the "shadowy joys" of occasionally seeing his mistress "preferable to the real ones of liberty" (203). These passages explicitly pose the Baron's lack of the usual captive virtues ("fortitude," "resolution," "liberty") as a problem of gender, in terms of his departure from the substance of masculine norms and his devotion to womanly "shadows."

Castration climaxes this descent into sexual slavery, abjection, and unmanliness. The bashaw's servants discover the Baron in the seraglio at the moment of sexual intercourse, so that his loss of manhood interrupts a common Orientalist fantasy about the Western male's final penetration of the East's sexual secrets. Afterwards forced to attend the seraglio as a eunuch, the Baron loses what seem associated desires for women, freedom, and homeland: "as I had no longer the power of enjoying, [I] had very little of the wish remaining. Slavery also seemed a less misfortune to me than it had been. I quit all thoughts of ever returning to my country" (206). Even when he decides to return home out of Christian devotion, he proves an ineffectual escape artist. Not only does his departure depend on Arithea's financial support, but he even lacks "foresight enough to have changed my habit"; his "badge of servitude," moreover, enables the bashaw's servants almost immediately to track him down before Philidore finally rescues him (208). As with Montrano, castration signals a character defined in terms of sexual devotion, abjection, and incapacity to handle the alien.

As in *The Fruitless Enquiry*, the connection between the castration episode and the main plot line turns on problems of male and female power. The captive Baron's castration through devotion to an Oriental woman doubles Philidore's "enslavement" at the hands of Placentia, so that the Orient again seems connected to a dangerous, exciting, and ultimately ironic form of female power. However, in this case a final captivity episode rectifies the problem of male impotence, at least within the main plot line, through a restoration of Western male prerogative over both Western women and the Orient. When the death of Philidore's uncle leads to a huge inheritance, this sudden wealth, ultimately due to his uncle's mercantile success, raises the former captive to a position of mastery over both the Orient and his inamorata, enabling him to return from exile and to claim the right to marry her. But his power over her acquires a more concrete narrative form on his way home, when he hears of a beautiful Christian lady recently sold in the slave market (211). After buying this woman out of sympathy, Philidore discovers that she is Placentia, who had lost her fortune through the sudden return of her brother and had then left England in search of her former servant. Part of Haywood's gambit here involves the absolute reversal of master and slave within the romance plot, as the formerly powerful woman finds herself first destitute and then bought, under the absolute terms associated with Oriental slavery, by her former "Egyptian slave."

A return to a female-centered captivity plot, with its standard images of male sexual power and female subjugation, enables Haywood to give her heroine a comeuppance that replicates the progress of English courtship. At the beginning of the novel, Placentia is bold and presumptuous in her economic and sexual independence, and the interpolated tale that recounts her journey through the Orient plays with an Aubin-like vision of female self-assertion before ultimately highlighting female dependence on the Western male. Throughout Placentia's slavery she looks for ways to kill herself, and, when a fellow slave shows sexual aggression, she tries unsuccessfully to kill him with her master's scimitar. Even as she proves incapable of fully wielding this phallic symbol, the novel elsewhere accentuates the dependence that results from her journey to the Orient. For example, the text calls her a "charming slave" even after Philidore's purchase has freed her from slavery (220). Even more tellingly, when the formerly reticent Philidore discovers the identity of the woman so completely in his power, "joy now gave him boldness to seize what before he shunned out of too great a respect" (212). At first Placentia tries to maintain some independence from this newly aggressive suitor, but after their return to England, her brother comes to his aid. Not only does the Baron's return home nullify her economic independence, but he insists that she grant Philidore "full possession" of her hand (227). Thus Haywood's novel finally contains the oddly paired powers of woman and the Orient. After subjugating its male protagonist to servitude and his double to Oriental slavery, sexual abjection, and castration, the plot closes by restoring masculine prerogatives, first Philidore's economic power and then also patriarchal patterns of courtship and inheritance.

But the novel's neatly resolved conclusion does not entirely efface the sensational narrative drive or the ironic sting of Placentia's initial independence, Philidore's servitude, and the castration plot, with its violent disruption of captivity fiction's standard images of male activity and female passivity. In this novel as in Haywood's other captivity episodes, the Orient, as an imaginary landscape saturated with sexuality and despotism, provides an opportunity for resisting the increasingly rigid gender ideologies of the early eighteenth century. Rather than follow Aubin and Chetwood in opposing European self-possession to Oriental carnality and female chastity to male activity, Haywood proffers variable characterizations of male and female, European and Oriental, whose variable interaction suggests a transcultural interdependence of sexuality, power, violence, and subjugation. Haywood's Orientalism, like that of the Oriental tale, focuses on despotism and self-indulgence as traits that Eastern cultures distill in peculiarly rarefied and satirically pungent forms. In her fictions of captivity, Oriental social structures provide extremely illustrative analogues and ironic counterpoints for Western social structures, ultimately revealing limits and problems within the character patterns that serve the West's domestic ideology.

Taken together, the fictions of Aubin, Chetwood, and Haywood mark the 1720s as the apex of the Oriental captivity narrative in English fiction. In 1744 two fairly developed episodes within the anonymous *Lady's Drawing Room* (1744) adapted the plot of Oriental captivity to Orientalized settings in Malaysia and the Indian subcontinent. Following Aubin's vision of the Oriental sexual despot, the persecuted European maiden, and the ineffectual European male, these episodes earned steady reprintings through the end of the century.[37] Much briefer episodes of Oriental captivity also continued to dot the fictional landscape of the later eighteenth century, within novels such as John Shebbeare's *Lydia* (1755), Alexander Bicknell's *The Benvolent Man* (1775), and Ann Yearsley's *The Royal Captives* (1795). The theme also surfaced in such popular pamphlet fictions as the *Lives* of *Ambrose Gwinett* (1770) and *Captain Winterfield* (1798). The captivity episodes within these fictions generally served as single instances within extended narrative catalogues of affliction, so that Oriental slavery shared the spotlight with other forms of captivity, in a Mexican mine, a French prison, or the woods of North America.

When novelists once again turned to an extensive treatment of Oriental captivity towards the end of the century, they approached the subject from perspectives that diverged sharply from the fictions of the 1720s. A particularly intriguing combination appeared amidst the many moral tales interpolated in Robert Day's novel for children, *Sandford and Merton* (1783–1789). Day juxtaposed an episode focused on a European's slavery in Tunis against one focused on a Turk's slavery in Venice, with the clear agenda of creating sympathy for injured merit across ethnic boundaries. On the other hand, Robert Bage's *The Fair Syrian* (1786), shifting towards the satirically dismissive Orientalism of James Morier's *Hajji Baba of Ispahan* (1824), portrayed the Orient as decadent, effeminate, and weak, scarcely capable of rumpling the unflappable demeanor of its urbane male captive. In a final contrast, Royal Tyler's early American novel, *The Algerine Captive* (1797), framed itself as a realistic counterpoint to earlier romances of Oriental captivity, insisting on the absolute abjection of the captivity experience as part of a broader antislavery platform.[38] Despite this variety of perspectives, the steady reprints of Chetwood's *Robert Boyle*, flowing well into the nineteenth century, suggest that the popularity of this novel largely obviated the need for newcomers, so that it came to occupy a definitive position within the Anglo-American imagination of Oriental captivity.

The importance of the Oriental captivity narrative for the early evolution of the English novel lies not only in the popularity and ideological transparency of Chetwood's fictions but also in the broader experimentation of Aubin's versions and in the ironic sting of Haywood's parodies. In the very sharpness of their resistance, Haywood's reversals of the gender paradigms employed by her predecessors indicate the powerful ideological force of the Oriental captivity plot in the 1720s. Aubin's fictions, however, offer a fuller and clearer prototype for the subsequent development of English fiction. Compared with her works, subsequent English novels diminished the transgression and active self-preservation of female characters. But as her works provide a particularly clear demonstration, the Oriental captivity plot enabled a variety of characterizations that remained important for the later English novel: the improvisational subject who masters an alien environment, the insular subject who defends her or his virtue, the divided subject who mediates internal conflicts and tensions, and the transgressive subject who crosses boundaries of ethnicity, class, and gender. In the 1720s the fictional plot of Oriental captivity provided a prominent, even seminal mode of representing subjugation, alienation, and individualist triumph in fiction.

Although after the 1720s the plot of foreign captivity inspired only occasional episodes in British fiction, much more prominent narrative patterns such as the virtue-in-distress plot, the Gothic, and the bildungsroman adapted the plot of subjugation and alienation to increasingly domestic environments of social tyranny. *Pamela* is one of many eighteenth-century novels that focus in whole or in part on a domestic captivity plot. In many a novel of sensibility or virtue-in-distress, heroines suffer from the sinister designs of libertines, ranging from rape and kidnapping to forced marriage. And as literary scholarship has long recognized, the Gothic is another genre centrally concerned with motifs of imprisonment and escape, such as a mysterious doorway always seeming to permit egress from the most dingy and formidable of prisons.[39] Other subgenres of eighteenth-century fiction address the theme of captivity less obviously. The castaway novel, even if it does not also include actual episodes of foreign captivity, still concentrates on physical confinement as a figure for colonial practice, much in the manner of the captivity plot. Increasingly within later eighteenth-century fiction, however, the protagonist's alienation was no longer, as with the captivity narrative or the castaway plot, a matter of forced exposure to a foreign culture, but rather a matter of the individual's opposition to his or her own culture.

Like the early fictionalized captivity narratives of the 1720s, later eighteenth-century fictions produce subjective interiority through representations of dependence, doubt, frustration, hesitation, internal conflicts and resolutions. They thrive on tensions between subjugation and rebellion, conformity and transgression. In bildungsromans such as Fielding's *Tom Jones* and Burney's *Evelina,* although the main plots avoid the melodrama of physical confinement, the subplots still contain minor episodes of imprisonment, kidnapping, and forced marriage. But these canonical eighteenth-century fictions work more substantially to diffuse the concentrated constraint of physical captivity into a multiplicity of minor constraints, a host of circumstances that conspire to limit the self-assertion of the protagonist. An important aspect of this development is the shift away from captivities in alien environments and towards constraints within British society. Localizing constraint makes it more familiar, more recognizable, and more immediately threatening. Localization also permits a greater diffusion of constraint within a host of particular, because familiar details. Burney's later heroines are endlessly trapped by a host of picayune circumstances pointing to a sinister context of gender and class relations, while concrete institutions such as the workhouse, the debtors' prison, and the court of chancery fill the bleak, imprisoning landscape of Dickens's novels. Nineteenth-century realism concentrates on individuals struggling against strictures of marriage, gender, and class, while the historical romance retains a partial dependence on more overt episodes of kidnapping and escape. Such continued revisions and transformations of the subjugation plot testify to its influential place in the evolution of the novel, a genre continually obsessed with an isolated protagonist who is both alienated by an oppressive social environment and internally divided by efforts to form an accommodation with that environment. As the novels of Chetwood, Aubin, and Haywood make clear, the plot of foreign captivity provided a significant early means of imagining such a protagonist.

FIVE

Resisting Americans in British Novels of American Captivity

The scholarly tendency to assimilate British captivity narratives to American patterns becomes particularly problematic in the case of eighteenth-century British novels that include episodes of American captivity. The most obvious problem results from chronology, since London novels began to incorporate American episodes as early as 1720, long before such novelists of the early American republic as Ann Eliza Bleecker and Charles Brockden Brown turned to captivity for what critics have often celebrated as "uniquely American material" in the formation of a national literature.[1] Another problem results because British episodes imagined the American captivity experience according to a pattern that differed greatly both from later American fictions and from factual prototypes published on either side of the Atlantic. Until well into the nineteenth century, and with only occasional exceptions, factual accounts of American captivity tended to dwell heavily on the abject bondage of the captive, a figure isolated from friends and family, forced to witness the torture of other captives, often hungry and physically weak or wounded, unable, finally, to comprehend the inexplicable language and culture of the natives. Conversely, the dozen episodes of American captivity in eighteenth-century British fiction imagined such abject scenes only very briefly, raising an initial fear and excitement before concentrating more substantially on displacing those emotions. This displacement occurred through a consistent narrative pattern, one that represents a significant counterpoint to the later American myth of cross-cultural brotherhood and adaptation to the wilderness, as expressed in the fictions of James Fenimore Cooper, Conrad Richter, or *Dances with Wolves*.

In a metropolitan response to the terrors of the factual accounts, British novelists rewrote the American captivity experience by focusing first on the threat of native violence, then on the native custom of adopting captives, and finally on the failure of adoption to effect permanent changes in British character.[2] Thus eighteenth-century British novelists anticipated later American novelists by taking an interest in the Amerindian custom of treating military capture as the basis for an affiliation or alliance, with adopted captives often serving as replacements for lost family members. Beginning with the influential 1711 *Spectator* tale of Inkle and Yarico, a wide range of episodes in British fiction centered on the figure of a powerless male adventurer, who escapes the threat of violence through native desire for an affiliative bond, whether marital, fraternal, or filial. Imitations or transformations of the John Smith narrative or the Inkle and Yarico plot, with their focus on cross-cultural marriage, appear in William Rufus Chetwood's *The Voyages of Richard Falconer* (1720), in the anonymous *Female American* (1767), and in the anonymous *Adventures of Thomas Barry* (1800). On the other hand, a genteel British protagonist finds an adoptive father in Henry Mackenzie's *The Man of the World* (1773) and an adoptive mother in Charlotte Lennox's *Euphemia* (1790), while cultural exchange results from brothers-in-arms relationships in Edward Kimber's *The Life of Mr. Anderson* (1753) and in Charlotte Smith's *The Old Manor House* (1793). Curiously, this persistent narrative pattern developed without published factual prototypes, since extensive narratives concerning adopted captives did not enter the American press until the early nineteenth century.[3] Even without such models, adoption seized the imagination of eighteenth-century Britons more than any other aspect of the captivity experience.

Over the century's course, these fictional visions of captivity and adoption involved a persistent if somewhat paradoxical emphasis on cultural disparity, and this emphasis helped to mediate a shifting range of anxieties about the colonial project in America. The current chapter will analyze this continuity and change through a chronological survey of the novels. In pondering varied forms of adoption, British writers throughout the century explored the possibility that captives or other British colonists might "go native," abandoning their original culture and redefining themselves within the framework of Amerindian culture. The novels might seem to take some pride in native regard, or even find an initial excitement in the possibility of transculturation. However, they nearly always close by rejecting native culture, and ultimately they reduce it to the level of surface trimming, figured by the alien clothes which the captives don only temporarily. Although the natives formally adopt the captive Briton, these ceremonies fail to produce a substantial cultural transformation. The novels portray an unbridgeable gap between Amerindian and Briton, as the captive's interior essence seems to remain palpably British, genteel, and civilized while struggling against the imposition of a culture that appears irredeemably alien, barbaric, simple, and archaic. While this emphasis on cultural disparity remained constant throughout the century and implicit in the basic formula of the failed adoption plot, individual novels turned significant variations on the formula as they connected it to larger structures of novelistic plotting and social commentary. For readers and writers in Britain, these variations soothed a range of anxieties about the American colonial experience, from fears of Amerindian physical and cultural power to uneasiness about the moral and political implications of colonialism. While novels in the early part of the century tried unsuccessfully to subjoin the adoption plot to narratives of colonial heroism, later novelists harnessed its tensions for increasingly overt yet still highly anxious criticism of the colonial project in America.

The most obvious anxiety expressed by the failed adoption plot concerns the captive's subjugation among a putatively inferior and violent people. In nearly every British fiction of American captivity, the capture of a male protagonist leads to an initial evocation of the standard horrors of captivity before the captive's adoption circumvents their fulfillment. Each of these novels, sometimes long before its captivity episode actually begins, sets an initial interpretive framework for the capture through stereotypical images of native violence. Characters might briefly attest to the "savage" disposition of the natives, or the captors might temporarily threaten murder, torture, or even cannibalism. A few novels even portray their protagonists at the point of sacrifice, in the manner of the John Smith captivity. However, as with the intervention of Pocahontas, most of these novels quickly rescue their British captives from slavery, torture, and other forms of abjection. A famous exception is the very brief episode in Smollett's *Humphry Clinker* (1771), which, in reporting Lismahago's experiences of captivity and torture among the Miamis, delights in their monstrous mutilation of his body. But Smollett is nearly unique among British novelists in actually subjecting a British character to such violence. Most of these novels, after briefly raising fears of native violence and power, quickly move to soothe them through what seems an obsessively repeated insistence on the natives' desire for affiliation. Because the Amerindians so readily eschew violence for affiliation, adoption seems in many of these novels to furnish the British with political advantages over a people given to such naive customs. At another level, adoption also acts as a sign of a fundamental native regard for the British people, especially as the novels rarely clarify the cultural logic behind the custom and instead treat it as an inexplicable vagary of native character. Thus these episodes translate the Amerindian custom of adopting captives into a seemingly inevitable recognition of British merit, a reassurance that British captives stand fundamentally superior to the putatively inferior people who have only momentarily gained power over them.

The physical and political powers of the natives ultimately pose a much less important problem within these novels than do their cultural powers. After quickly displacing terror of native violence, the failed adoption plot turns to a more extended displacement of British anxieties about American transculturation, by representing the custom of adoption as quaint, naive, and fruitless. One function of this vision of cultural contact was to furnish ideological compensation for British failures in America. Depicting adoption as archaic and ineffectual compensated for metropolitan awareness of British losses in what James Axtell has described as a three-way "contest of cultures" among the natives, the British, and the French.[4] Although converting Amerindians to Christianity and civility formed an explicit component of Britain's colonial agenda from the days of the Roanoke colony, the British largely failed in their slight efforts to fulfill this goal, especially in contrast with the more spectacular Jesuit successes in Canada. While Protestant missionaries could report only the most modest of evangelical successes, Amerindian students at English schools earned a notorious reputation for running away, and travel narratives and colonial histories often commented on an "obstinate" adherence to ancient customs among the natives in general.[5] Over the course of the eighteenth century, as Roy Harvey Pearce has argued, the British gradually abandoned hopes for converting the Amerindians, and contemporary observers of the American scene increasingly acknowledged an invincible "integrity" within native culture, citing the force of ancient customs as proof of an essential disparity between the two cultures.[6]

Even more disturbingly for British cultural pride, London received accurate reports throughout the century that native Americans had proven far more successful in converting Britons to native lifestyles than had Britons in converting natives to British lifestyles. The French also managed to persuade some British captives to embrace Catholicism and to remain in the small settlements of Canada. But the most troubling and troubled reports on the contest of cultures, at least from the British perspective, concerned "white Indians," captives or other British travelers who had redefined themselves as natives and even refused opportunities to rejoin white civilization. British astonishment at the thoroughness of such transculturation often centered on the prisoner exchanges following various treaties among the British,

French, and Amerindians. The contrast between native and British conversion rates is formulated in particularly stark terms at the conclusion of Cadwallader Colden's popular *History of the Five Nations,* a 1727 portrait of the Iroquois that included a description of British difficulties in persuading Anglo-American captives to rejoin the fold at a 1699 prisoner exchange:

> No arguments, no Intreaties, nor Tears of their Friends and Relations, could persuade many of them to leave their new Indian Friends and Acquaintance; several of them that were by the Caressings of their Relations persuaded to come Home, in a little Time grew tired of our Manner of living, and run away again to the Indians, and ended their Days with them. On the other hand, Indian Children have been carefully educated among the English, cloathed and taught, yet, I think, there is not one Instance, that any of these, after they had Liberty to go among their own People, and were come to Age, would remain with the English, but returned to their own Nations, and became as fond of the Indian Manner of Life as those that knew nothing of a civilized Manner of living. What I now tell of Christian Prisoners among Indians, relates not only to what happened at the Conclusion of this War, but has been found true on many other Occasions.[7]

A similar account of an Ohio valley exchange reached London in 1766, as William Smith reported that many Anglo-American captives preferred their adopted culture and even tried to escape from what they regarded as a second captivity among the British. Smith struggled to explain away the preference of these adoptees for native culture: "For the honor of humanity, we would suppose those persons to have been of the lowest rank. . . . For, easy and unconstrained as the savage life is, certainly it could never be put in competition with the blessings of improved life and the light of religion."[8] Smith was forced to invoke the category of social class in order to restore a hierarchy of civility that the success of native adoption had forcibly disturbed.

But the most widely distributed and influential formulation of the contrast between British and native conversion rates appeared in Crèvecoeur's *Letters from an American Farmer,* whose first London edition of 1782 led a panoply of reprints through the end of the century. The farmer's famous comments on native adoption mark a tense moment of hesitation in the climactic letter, the "Distresses of a Frontier Man." Torn between conflicting allegiances to the British constitution and to the Anglo-American rebels, the farmer resolves them by choosing to relocate amidst a native tribe, although he fears the effects of this move on his children's development, as a result of "some great intoxication among the Indians." His most concrete expression of this fear occurs when he considers the parallel case of adopted captives, children "so perfectly Indianized" that they refused opportunities to rejoin their British parents. Equally as stunned and bewildered by such captives as Smith, he wonders, "By what power does it come to pass, that children who have been adopted when young among these people, can never be prevailed on to re-adopt European manners?" Compared to Smith, however, Crèvecoeur answers this question in a manner far more generous to the natives and far more disturbing to the assumed superiority of European civilization. He speculates that the adoptees find among the natives "the most perfect freedom, the ease of living, the absence of those cares and corroding solicitudes which so often prevail with us." He insists that "there must be in their social bond something so singularly captivating, and far superior to any thing to be boasted of among us; for thousands of Europeans are Indians, and we have no examples of even one of those Aborigines having from choice become Europeans! There must be something more congenial to our native dispositions, than the fictitious society in which we live."[9] Laced with paradox as with a Rousseauvian social vision, this passage imagines a "perfect freedom" and an ideal "social bond" produced through the experience of captivity. Despite the momentary hesitation produced by the thought of adoptees, the farmer ultimately looks forward to finding a life closer to "nature" amidst his chosen tribe. Thus the success of native adoption both excited and frightened the European mind, and the American adoptee provided an important figure for meditation on the roles of European civilization, the American landscape, and the American aborigines in the making of a new American identity.

British anxiety about American cultural contact reflected a deep-seated dualism pervading the most common European images of native Americans. From the earliest reports of Columbus's first encounter, double images of good and bad Indians marked European travel literature on the Americas, and this dualism continued when the British press started to carry the first-hand accounts of settlers in the seventeenth and eighteenth centuries. In much the same way that visitors to particular Islamic cultures offered observations on Islamic peoples in general, European travelers in the Americas generalized observations of local tribes into sweeping claims about the natives of America. This general commentary, however, frequently mixed admiration and condemnation. One traveler might describe cannibals while another might describe noble savages. Depending on which locality a traveler visited (and on which culture the traveler called home), he or she might describe all native Americans as either consistently devoted to liberty, attached to despotic government, or possessed of no government at all. Whereas

the French Jesuits favored images of the noble savage, the British emphasized indolence and violence, providing ideological justification for large-
scale settlement and encroachment on native lands. Beyond these widely
varying national responses, equally wide variations marked the responses of
British travelers as a group, and many individual texts, like those of Smith,
Colden, and Crèvecoeur, integrated both positive and negative images. Some
Britons praised the simplicity of Amerindian lifestyle while others damned
its destitution. Travel narrators sometimes highlighted native hospitality and
generosity, but they also insisted heavily on native superstition, especially as
manipulated by the "trickery" of shamans. The British might admire native
courage, stamina, and ability to withstand torture, or they might deplore an
implacable disposition towards incessant warfare, revenge, and torture. If
travel writers often celebrated the liberty of Amerindian government, they
also protested that the freedom and indolence of native hunters depended
on the drudgery of native women. The liberty of Amerindian culture might
seem to entail a sexual liberation for British men, especially when assisted by
a relative lack of clothing and sexual modesty among native women, but the
British also condemned the natives for polygamy, promiscuity, and divorce.[10]
Since native culture held both positive and negative qualities according to
the estimates of British writers, it seemed to offer appeals for British settlers
that metropolitan readers could comprehend, if not approve.

Like the broader anxieties expressed in such imagery, British anxiety
about cultural contact with the natives ultimately reflected the nature of the
colonial project in America, especially as it contrasted with British colonial
projects in other lands. In the Middle East or in India, British colonial strategy since the sixteenth century had involved the creation of small enclaves of
transient traders, soldiers, and bureaucrats, who tried to negotiate and eventually to commandeer existing political structures, while remaining firmly
British in cultural orientation. On the other hand, American colonialism since
the early seventeenth century had involved the transplantation of many permanent settlers, who survived in large part by exploiting the cultural strategies of a rapidly waning native population, as historians are increasingly coming
to recognize.[11] Although British success in America resulted partially from
the unplanned ravages of old world diseases, it also depended heavily on
British mastery of such Amerindian cultural resources as the production of
beaver pelts, maize, and tobacco, as well as on the alteration of European
cultural resources to suit the American environment, resulting in such hy-
brids as the skipjack and South Carolina rice. Moreover, the success of the
American colonial project also depended on achieving military mastery in
the American landscape, especially a mastery of what the British described

as native techniques of guerrilla warfare.[12] Because the British perceived themselves as fundamentally civilized, they often described their own violence as unnaturally forced upon them by the demands of colonialism, even by the alleged nature of the "savages" themselves. In a number of ways, then, the British could interpret the success of American colonialism as a transformation of British character to suit American circumstances, if not as a resignation of civility for an accommodation with native culture. Imaginative exploration of this transformation was often facilitated by the figure of the adopted captive, who aroused high anxiety in the writings of both metropolitan Britons and transplanted Euramericans such as Crèvecoeur, although the two groups resolved this anxiety in very different ways.

In response to the troubling reports of cultural conversion rates in colonial America, and to the even more troubling speculations about the cultural implications of these rates, British novelists persistently reimagined American cultural contact according to the pattern of the failed adoption plot. One effect of this focus on the native practice of adoption was to occlude the history of British efforts in cultural conversion. If the novels considered the negative results of British efforts at all, they blamed those results on the natives themselves, as a sign of cultural inferiority or intransigence. More pervasively and insistently, the failed adoption plot represented transculturation as a foolish and alien custom, a sign of Amerindian depravity rather than British civility. Within these works, it seems as if only savages would try something that fails so consistently as cultural conversion, while the civilized seem marked by an understanding that conversion must fail. What seems the inevitable failure of native efforts in cultural conversion helps to celebrate British civility as capable of withstanding the effects of American cultural contact. At the same time that these novels mediated fears of total immersion within an alien culture, they also soothed fears that any level of cultural contact or colonial experience might force Britons to adopt the imputed features of native culture or to alter themselves to suit the American environment. Within these works, adoption acted as a figure for British adaptation to America, a figure concerned especially with imagining the colonial world's potential effects on that central agent of British expansion, the adventurous male. As these novels repeatedly highlighted the adoptees' failure to adopt American customs and techniques, they suggested that truly civilized British captives ran counter to the colonial environment and its peoples, whether Amerindian or Euramerican. Thus fictional episodes of failed adoption helped to posit British civility as potentially compromised by the colonial experience but ultimately capable of resisting its threats, appeals, and demands. At the same time, however, the anxiety expressed through the figure of a passive and inept British adventurer often provided a vehicle for more overt opposition to American colonialism. When British novelists turned to the troubling material of American transculturation, their works opened a site of tension and even of opposition within colonial ideology, signaled particularly through troubled gender roles.

The failed adoption plot's concentration on an inept male adventurer marks a significant departure from the patterns of colonial heroism that distinguish the Oriental fictions of Chetwood and Aubin. In the 1720s their fictions adapted the Oriental captivity plot to develop characters who actively master the skills of colonial adaptation, trade, and violence within the most adverse of colonial settings, amidst a culture that British trade had penetrated only marginally and that had still posed a considerable threat to British shipping in the previous century. In a telling contrast, British fictions of American captivity focused on male captives who prove unsuccessful colonists within an environment that the British had exploited economically since the early sixteenth century and that had provided their most populated sites of colonial settlement since the early seventeenth century. While sometimes verging on the patterns of heroism that mark Chetwood's and Aubin's fictions, these novels turn more consistently to figures who disrupt these patterns, especially a passive British adventurer and an active Amerindian female. Instead of celebrating active colonial males, failed adoption episodes continually reduce the British adventurer to passivity if they do not also develop overt ethical critiques of masculine or colonial aggression.

   The figures of the passive male captive and the active native female produced sharp gender reversals within two of the most prominent Anglo-American legends of cultural contact, the tales of John Smith with Pocahontas and of Inkle with Yarico. Each of these tales represents an early and influential version of the failed adoption plot; in each case a powerless British adventurer finds rescue and affiliation through the energetic intervention of a native female, before he ultimately rejects her and returns home.[13] Whereas the Pocahontas story offered independent Americans a myth of national origins and destiny, the tale of Inkle and Yarico offered eighteenth-century Britons a problem requiring continual resolution. After Richard Steele's *Spectator* version adapted the tale from an incident in a contemporary travel narrative, the eighteenth century saw a host of poems, plays, and prose retellings, most of which tried to extend or transform his spare outlines. Steele frames the tale through Mr. Spectator's visit to Arietta, a woman of "Taste and Understanding," who invokes the episode in conversation, as a counterexample to a misogynist's attacks on female "Levity" and sexual inconstancy.[14] In Arietta's telling, after Inkle travels to the West Indies as a colonial trader, his party enters the wilderness and meets violence from local Amerindians. He escapes and hides in the woods, where he meets the young Yarico, they become amorous, and she protects and sustains him. After she helps him to find a British ship, he immediately sells her into slavery. Even in this sketchy form, developed in only two pages, the tale already contains the rudiments of the failed adoption plot. Although the text does not label Inkle a "captive," it applies the term "Confinement" to his situation in hiding, and the standard horrors of torture and captivity would always lurk as possibilities for eighteenth-century Britons imagining his situation. Furthermore, although Inkle is never formally adopted, Yarico initiates an affiliation with him, one which he ultimately rejects in the manner of the failed adoption plot.

Designed explicitly as an example of male perfidy, this seminal formulation of the tale poses its crisis of manhood in specifically colonial terms, as indicated by a fundamental disjunction in Inkle's character that subsequent retellings would attempt to resolve. On the one hand, this representative Englishman boasts a genteel form and manner, but this demeanor belies a mercantile disposition, produced because his parents took "particular Care to instill into his Mind an early Love of gain, . . . giving him a quick View of Loss and Advantage." This disjunction in his character affects the tone of narration, as Arietta gives him the ironic labels, "the Hero of my story" and "Our adventurer." Within the context of her argument in favor of women, these terms broaden the attack on Inkle into an attack on masculine heroism and adventure in general. And indeed Inkle proves far from heroic in negotiating the American world, as his party first meets Amerindian violence because they "unadvisedly marched a great distance from the Shore into the Country." Following this attack, the inept Inkle gains from Yarico not only food but also "a great many Spoils," as well as clues for eluding her violent people. After she enables him to negotiate the colonial environment, the disjunction in his colonial character finally forms the basis of narrative closure, as he sells his paramour after beginning "to weigh with himself how many Days Interest of his Mony he had lost during his Stay with Yarico." Thus mercenary calculation comes to mark the nature of colonial activity in America, and Inkle's failure to handle the wilderness serves to underscore the depths of his moral failure in selling his benefactress. In an accurate colonial critique, the tale suggests that Anlgo-Americans survived the colonial world only with the aid of those they dispossessed. After beginning as a tale of Inkle's potential subjugation, the episode ends as a tale of Yarico's subjugation, and thus it rather neatly reminds eighteenth-century readers that Europeans rather than natives were the principal subjugators in the colonial world.

For the remainder of the eighteenth century, European writers tried to resolve the colonial dilemma posed by Inkle and Yarico. In the many plays and verse epistles that gave voice to Yarico's complaints or to Inkle's regrets, European writers continually replayed the problem of his colonial failures, both moral and physical. Some revisions tried to enact formal resolutions for the plot's disjunctions, either by punishing the Englishman's perfidy with prison, death, or remorse, or by rewarding his repentance with a concrete consummation, such as the couple's happy reunion.[15] An altogether different kind of resolution for the Inkle and Yarico problem developed in the many novels that organized episodes of American captivity around the figures of a passive British male and an active Amerindian female. Whereas the direct revisions of Inkle and Yarico blame the English adventurer for spurning a native desire for affiliation, later episodes of failed adoption portray the native desire for affiliation as fundamentally naive. Whereas the Inkle and Yarico plot implies a connection between Inkle's moral and physical failures, later failed adoption episodes adduce the captive's physical incapacity as evidence for his opposition to an American environment that seems a proper sphere for native energy even as it leads, especially in novels from the end of the century, to British moral corruption.

Because eighteenth-century British episodes of American captivity return so persistently to the adoption of a male adventurer, they pose a caveat, or at least a counterpoint, for what has become a standard point of literary critical analysis of the American captivity genre: that women occupied a crucial position in its formation both as historical and as imagined captives.[16] The female captive is especially important in the American context because patterns of American settlement placed women in an unusual proximity to an alien culture, heightening fears of their vulnerability to alien men, and also because, as the spotty historical record suggests, female captives tended to assimilate to native culture more successfully than did male captives.[17] Both the possibility of female adoption and the possibility of rape and torture played prominent roles within the propagandistic captivity narratives that became increasingly important with the colonial and revolutionary wars of the late eighteenth century. Following factual and propagandistic prototypes published in the colonial press, several early American novels of the republican period developed images of passive, domestic, and innocent white women in the power of Amerindian men, ending sometimes in violence and sometimes in peaceful adoption. In Catherine Sedgwick's best-selling *Hope*

Leslie, the heroine's sister enters captivity as a child, finds a happy marriage with a native husband, and experiences such a thorough transculturation that she forgets English and refuses an opportunity to rejoin her natal family. Likewise, Cooper's Leatherstocking novels abound with female captivities while celebrating the figure of an energetic and happily acculturated frontiersman.[18] By contrast, the few British novels that include female captivities, such as Lennox's *Harriot Stuart* (1751) and Gilbert Imlay's *The Emigrants* (1793), take pains to avoid representing their captives amidst native culture. In both novels the heroines escape the potential rigors of captivity not through adoption but through more conventional contrivances of romance plotting.

The difference between eighteenth-century British and early republican visions of captivity and gender becomes clearer when we consider one of the first American novels, Ann Eliza Bleecker's *Maria Kittle* (1790–1791). In a manner typical of many later American novels, Bleecker's work places a female captive in a plot that closely follows the formulae of contemporary factual accounts.[19] After a brief new world idyll sets an initial scene of domestic happiness, Indian captivity intrudes and teaches the heroine a lesson about the instability of worldly expectations and the need to rely on God's providence. Not only does the heroine endure severe hunger and a long forced march, but she also witnesses several graphically detailed scenes of carnage, all much in the manner of the factual accounts. Throughout the novel, as many critics have observed, the terrifying motifs of Amerindian captivity furnish Bleecker with a means of defining her heroine's depths of emotive sensibility.[20] As this novel in particular demonstrates, American writers took an early and persistent interest in the experiences of the female captive, and they quickly and easily married the captivity narrative to the Gothic motifs of the virtue-in-distress novel.[21] That British novelists largely avoided this route indicates the force of metropolitan as opposed to early republican views of captivity. Whereas permanent settlers feared the native threat to the domestic, metropolitans feared the possibility of acculturation, and thus they focused on the primary agent of colonial expansion, the colonial male.

If metropolitan Britons resisted contemplating the experience of the white female captive, they found a peculiar interest in the relationship between the passive British male and the active native female. Images of these figures played a prominent role in expressing British anxiety about American acculturation, especially when focused on "Indian traders" who spent years in isolation amidst native cultures and often took native wives. As early as 1709, Londoners could read of such converts from civility in John Lawson's Carolina travel narrative: "we often find, that English Men, and other Europeans that have been accustom'd to the conversation of these savage Women, and their way of Living, have been so allur'd with that careless sort of Life, as to be constant to their Indian Wife, and her Relations, so long as they liv'd, without ever desiring to return again amongst the English, although they had very fair Opportunities of Advantages amongst their Countrymen."[22] This passage formulates the possibility of cultural assimilation in peculiarly sexual terms of passivity and action, placing the European converts in a feminized role of "constancy" with regard to the closely linked, active "allures" of native women and native culture. Both in eighteenth-century travel narratives and in novels employing the failed adoption plot, British anxiety concerning American transculturation often centered on the ideologically disruptive figures of the isolated, passive British adventurer and the active native female.

Even Chetwood, the creator of such an enormously aggressive colonial hero as Robert Boyle, portrays British adventurers as passive and inept when faced with American captivity, adoption, and transculturation. Building directly on the materials of the Inkle and John Smith plots, Chetwood develops two failed adoption episodes within the omnibus structure of his first novel, *The Voyages, Dangerous Adventures, and Imminent Escapes of Captain Richard Falconer* (1720).[23] The first full-length novel to include a failed adoption episode, this imitation of Defoe follows its protagonist through a series of adventures in colonial lands, mostly the Caribbean islands, mixing inset sections of pure travel description with accounts of colonial warfare, piracy, and shipwreck. These adventures help compose a persistent opposition between British and Spanish national characters, linking the latter with torture and tyranny, while the former earn the good will of the native Caribbeans. But if this novel imagines ample opportunity and justification for British colonialism, they both seem to vanish with the threat of capture and adoption by native Americans. Whereas *Robert Boyle* represents Oriental captivity as the hero's inauguration into a life of colonial mastery, *Richard Falconer* treats Amerindian captivity as a fundamental problem for British colonial expansion, one that the captive adventurers cannot solve. *Robert Boyle* portrays Oriental culture as a parody of European civilization, relatively familiar and thus easily assimilable and mastered, but the captivity episodes in *Richard Falconer* suggest an unbridgeable gap between native American and European. Within this novel, the gap between cultures seems so large as to preclude any possibility that the British might convert or rule the natives effectively.

The novel's first captivity episode is an interpolated tale narrated by

J. Cole Sculp.

The frontispiece and title page of Chetwood's first novel make
Amerindian captivity its primary sales pitch. What we now regard
as a standard image of American captivity and, indeed, of American
identity, here opens a 1720 London text concerned with defining
an English hero. (This item is reproduced by permission of *The
Huntington Library, San Marino, California*.)

Falconer's spiritual mentor, Thomas Randal. The episode begins by invoking the standard horrors of native captivity, when a shipwreck on Cape Charles, at the tip of the Delmarva Peninsula, leads to Randal's capture by a local tribe and their immediate threat to burn him, "drink [his] Blood, and feed upon [his] Flesh" (2:24). But the natives also explain that their violence stems from a desire "to be reveng'd of your Brothers at Jamestown, who kill us many Indians" (2:24). Although the novel portrays the natives as ferocious, it also traces their violence to an originary moment of British colonial expansion, the moment when British colonial methods most resembled the Spanish method of conquest over an extensive political power, in this case Powhatan's empire in tidewater Virginia. In a pattern that recurs in later failed adoption episodes, the novel suggests that British violence has both initiated the extreme violence of captivity and compromised the possibility of more peaceful cultural interaction.

In an early version of a heroic pattern more fully elaborated with Boyle, Chetwood portrays the captive Randal as a shrewd and resourceful colonial hero, a British man of science amidst ignorant and violent captors. The extreme threat of native violence quickly evaporates when his captors discover his medical instruments. When he explains that his lancets serve "to Bleed," an Amerindian demands "in a great Passion" if he uses them to kill native prisoners (2:25). While the natives immediately interpret these seemingly mysterious devices through the lens of "passion," as instruments of violence, the man of science calmly details their function within the early eighteenth-century curriculum of medical science, and later he demonstrates their practical efficacy by curing the tribe's chief of a fever. As a reward for this scientific mastery, the tribe invites him and his companions to join them, marry Amerindian wives, and fight against whites. In this early version of the failed adoption plot, the Amerindian desire for affiliation results from an intellectual gap between cultures. The efficacy of the lancets seems to render the natives eager for and dazzled by the benefits of science and civilization, and thus susceptible to the influence of Europeans. Furthermore, because cross-cultural affiliation here stems from the natives' misinterpretation of Randal's scientific prowess, their version of intercultural contact appears hopelessly naive in comparison with the modern systems of knowledge that guide the Briton. With stereotypical premodern naivete, a chief observes this new tribesman taking a pulse and imagines that he can use this technique to gain knowledge about the military goals of their common British enemies. The chief not only misinterprets the captive's scientific abilities, but also falsely imagines that the tribe's immediate cultural influence might outweigh his allegiance to the British nation. When the wily captive explains that pulse-taking requires physical contact with the British, the chief permits him to visit them, and he seizes this opportunity to quit his adopted tribe (2:29–30). Ultimately the novel portrays the Briton's faith-breaking as a commonsensical maneuver amidst the threats of colonial violence. However terrible cultural contact according to the native system may at first seem, the novel finally treats this system as so hopelessly naive that it represents only a minimal threat to the ingenuity of the British captive.

Chetwood further emphasizes the gap between cultures when Falconer himself later enters a captivity that partially replicates the experiences of his spiritual mentor. Even before this second episode of failed adoption begins, the novel lays its groundwork through images of native violence and cultural inferiority. Before recounting his captivity, Falconer offers a brief section of travelogue that describes the friendly natives of Dominico and highlights in particular their paltry housing, promiscuous sleeping arrangements, and inability to negotiate the most basic elements of European culture. Fond of liquor but easily made drunk, Falconer's Dominicans also show desire for European clothing but prove comically incapable of putting it to proper use. During his captivity, this native simplicity seems concomitant with an overwhelming ferocity. Like Randal, Falconer prefaces his adoption narrative with terrifying intimations concerning the potential results of capture. At several points before his capture, encounters with various Caribbean tribes provoke immediate thoughts of torture. In the first encounter, he and his companions adopt the heroic resolve typically celebrated in accounts of Barbary captivity, determining "to defend our selves to the last Drop of Blood, chusing rather to die by their Hands in Fight, than to be tortur'd after the Manner as they inflict upon all the Whites they get into their Hands" (2:110). But Falconer's actual capture, after he wanders aimlessly into a village inhabited by hostile natives, undermines this vision of heroic resolve. There he hides and sees the torture of a friendly Amerindian in a scene that replays both the violent imagery and the psychological profile of factual American captivities. Witnessing a decapitation and a disembowelment renders Falconer "so confus'd, that I might justly say I never thought at all . . . but yet when my Senses were compos'd, I put my Trust in God that he wou'd deliver me from this Danger"(3:135). The torture scene serves as a reminder of the standard British conception of Amerindian captivity, creating dramatic tension through an impression of the extremes of violence and abjection that await the passive protagonist.

Escape from the extremes of premodern violence occurs in a fashion typical of the failed adoption plot, not through the captive's own exertions but rather through a young native woman's Pocahontas-like intervention and his subsequent adoption through marriage. In an incident rather clearly modeled on the Smith story, the woman stops one of her tribesmen on the point of killing the hero. Chetwood heightens the sexual component of the Pocahontas fantasy when the natives insist that Falconer "shou'd take her to be [his] Mate, or Bedfellow, or suffer Death" (3:141). The forced-marriage motif quite clearly permits a carefully displaced European sexual fantasy about native women, blaming European sexual predations on native interest and even coercion. At the same time, however, this motif undermines the hero's self-mastery by linking him to a feminized position of sexual victimization. Falconer's release from his adopted tribe widens the gap between native and Briton, again emphasizing his incapacity and their connection with violence. Falconer tries but fails to escape by deceiving his new family. He tricks his wife by pretending exhaustion during a hunt, so that she lies down to rest and falls asleep. But when he runs away, he finds himself "immediately seiz'd" by his tribesmen and prepared for death by burning (3:149–51). After he weakly and vainly tries to break his bonds, he must finally depend on others for release, first through the chance invasion of an enemy tribe, and then through a second intervention on the part of his wife, who suddenly arrives to "put her head under [his] Feet" (3:152). When a hostile warrior aims a sword at him, his wife throws herself in front of the blow and receives a mortal wound. At one level her death gives closure to the sexual fantasy by freeing the protagonist from any permanent emotional attachment, but the marriage episode as a whole tends to separate him from the realm of the heroic and to portray him as passive and ineffectual in handling native culture on his own. After the invading tribe also decides to adopt him, he escapes through the accidental arrival of some British sailors and the assistance of a devoted Dominican, whom Falconer rewards by making him a servant. The Briton and the Indian, it seems, can never meet on terms of equality but only on terms of mastery and subjugation. Faced with what seems an inevitable native disposition towards capture, the Briton must manipulate the gap between cultures for his own benefit while seeking allies among his countrymen rather than among the natives.

Falconer's extended sojourn among two different tribes would seem to open ample space for acculturation, but the novel consistently highlights his failure to adopt or even much appreciate Amerindian customs. He experiences his wedding not as a ceremony of affiliation but rather as particularly glaring proof of cultural distance. In recording the occasion, he scorns native culture as a paradoxical, animalistic parody of European civilization. When he suddenly hears a "rude Noise," it turns out to be an "Epithalamium," and the wedding ceremony involves "mad, rude, monkey Gambols, that put me in mind of the mad Feasts of the Bachii in Virgil" (3:142–43). This palpable impression of cultural distance seems to explain, within the logic of this novel, the adoptee's rather implausible incapacity to "learn any of their Speech, but here and there a common Word" (3:146). So strong is Chetwood's insistence on cultural distance that he violates the standard European image of the native division of labor by portraying Falconer's wife as a "very dexterous" huntress while he himself remains "such a Bungler at it, that I cou'd never do any execution" (3:145). His hero utterly failing in comparison with the mastery of native culture celebrated in such heroes as Natty Bummpo, Chetwood portrays adoption as an utterly humiliating and even feminizing experience for the adventurous Briton.

Although Falconer's marriage fulfills a European sexual fantasy, the sharp ambivalence that the novel attaches to the marriage partially deprives the fantasy of its force. The cultural gap seems to preclude true affection for this couple, as Falconer rather vaguely comments that his wife can only show her "great Love" for him in "her Way" (3:145). Much of the apparent distance between husband and wife results from an apparently unbridgeable gulf in intellect, signaled by disparity in language and religion. Just as he cannot learn the native language, she cannot learn English, as "he cou'd never get her to repeat whole Sentences" but merely to echo minor physical sounds, "like a Parrot" (3:147). European religion seems equally baffling for the native wife. When he prays, she "look'd upwards too, with a kind of Concern . . . as if she had a mind to see something as she thought I look'd at" (3:145). Apparently limited to physical approximations of his language, spirituality, and personal affection, Falconer's wife seems less a simple innocent than a slave to the material, incapable of mastering what seem the higher forms of European culture. Among his second adopted tribe, Falconer puts more effort into evangelism but finds that he cannot convert this people because "their Understandings are so infirm, that without a Miracle there will be no curing 'em" (3:160). Again native worship seems bound to the physical, as Falconer declares that he could never "perceive these Indians worship'd any thing, except the Moon" and that their "Stargazing" leads to "Jumping and Capering like so many mad things" (3:161). This portrait of native worship serves partially as an explanation for British failures to convert the natives, while the novel's broader portrait of American encounters suggests that no true cultural exchange can ever occur between Britons and Amerindians.

Whereas Chetwood's *Robert Boyle* imagines the career of a colonial privateer as one of unlimited possibilities, *Richard Falconer*'s failed adoption episodes imagine a set of limits that accompany those possibilities, bringing the tensions of colonial ideology to the forefront. Throughout this novel the

American landscape seems to offer much danger and little colonial potential, as Falconer's American captivities conclude a colonial career that falls
considerably short of Boyle's spectacularly lucrative success. Falconer and
his mentor might create an impression of cultural superiority over their captors by occasionally concocting a successful trick, but such apparent superiority does not lead automatically to colonial success. Despite his extended
cultural contact, Falconer manages only one successful convert, gains no
spoils, and instead returns among his countrymen disheveled, filthy, and
broke. Large-scale conversion, peaceful settlement, and even trade all seem
impossible because of the extreme distance between British civilization and
native "savagery." Although the novel hints that native violence stems from
European aggression, the native inclination for violence and capture seems
so strong as to overwhelm the possibility that Britons might control the terms
of cultural contact. Within the natives' seemingly overpowering system of
cultural interaction, their efforts to emulate European culture prove comic,
while their willingness to make the captive a part of their culture only serves
as a further illustration of their naivete, especially as Falconer's continual
failure to acculturate suggests the foolishness of any attempt at transculturation. Thus although this novel touts the superiority of British civility, this
apparent superiority so completely separates the British from the natives
that key elements of the colonial project seem impracticable.

Thus the first failed adoption episodes in an English novel raised considerable tension within its author's otherwise unified strategies for imagining
colonial heroism. Following the early lead of Chetwood's plot structure, British
novelists often imagined American captivity as marking an end to colonial
activity. Whereas the Oriental captivity plot imagined the protagonist's slavery as a colonial apprenticeship, British novelists generally placed episodes
of American captivity near the ends of novels and often used these episodes
to mark a final moment of danger and liberation at the end of a sensitive
protagonist's checkered colonial career. The persistent recurrence of this
pattern, linking a release from Amerindian captivity with a climactic release
from the colonial environment, indicates that the failed adoption plot provided an important means for metropolitan Britons to conceive of the colonist as a captive. Separated from the seat of civility, the protagonists of these
novels often lament life in America as an isolation from friends, family, or
British society. Despite sharp criticism of British behavior in America and
despite occasional sympathy for its rebels, many of these novels ultimately
suggested that, ideally, civilized Britons were better off avoiding its problems entirely. In narratives celebrating the happy return of genteel protagonists to England, the closure of the failed adoption plot constituted a rejection

of the American colonies and the systems of subjugation that seemed to typify both native and European practice there. Thus the plot enabled a critique of the colonial project in America, but one that worked by trading on metropolitan fears of alien peoples and by renouncing America as a world where any level of acculturation might corrupt British civility. Linked to extreme violence, cultural debasement, and cultural distance, American captivity offered British novelists a more dismal and troubling prospect for imagining colonial heroism than did Oriental captivity. After Chetwood's early effort, North American captivity largely disappeared from English fiction through the middle of the century, except for the very brief episodes in Edward Kimber's *Life of Mr. Anderson* (1754) and Lennox's *Life of Harriet Stuart* (1751). In the latter third of the century, however, British novelists found significant ideological and argumentative potential in the tensions of the failed adoption plot.

Even more clearly than Chetwood's episodes of American captivity, the episodes in Kimber's fiction provide an index of the ideological struggles that mark British efforts to imagine the Anglo-American experience. Three decades after Chetwood, Kimber included American episodes first in *The History of Mr. Anderson* (1754) and second in *The Life of Neville Frowde* (1758). Both of these episodes pose the native American practice of taking captives as a threat to colonial trade. In the second, Frowde enjoys a lucrative career as a globe-trotting merchant, although he constantly faces the threat of capture from Barbary pirates or Spanish miners, before finally enduring an actual captivity among the natives of the Argentine coast. This episode focuses on the violence and abject drudgery of Frowde's captivity, which puts an end to his colonial career, as he afterwards retires in order to become a model country gentleman. Within this fairly straightforward vision of colonial success, South American captivity seems to provide both an unambiguous warning of the potential dangers awaiting the colonial trader and a justification that he will earn his fantastic wealth. Curiously, this novel represents a rare case in which a British novelist imagined a South American captivity, and also one of the few cases in which a British novelist admitted the standard horrors of factual captivity accounts.[24] Kimber could reproduce the standard patterns of his factual prototypes, even to the point of suppressing the possibility of transculturation, when portraying captivity in South America, a land where the British might trade but not settle, a land, as the novel suggests, already ruined for the British by a history of Iberian "barbarities" and violent native reactions.[25] Conversely, like most other British novelists concerned with American captivity, Kimber proved unwilling to dwell on its stereotypical horrors and intent on the problem of transculturation when, in *Mr. Anderson,* he turned to a North American setting, one where a large population of British settlers faced real questions of adaptation and cultural contact in an alien environment.

Poised on the high stakes of a North American setting, *Mr. Anderson's* brief captivity episode shares in the troubled colonial themes that mark the novel as a whole. The episode occurs after Tom, the young hero, has overcome a childhood of indentured "slavery," improved himself as an enlightened plantation overseer, and finally acquired a position of colonial prominence as a wealthy Indian trader and Indian fighter. The novel dwells very little on his colonial successes and quickly ends his career as a frontiersman by subjecting him to captivity among "a barbarous gang of savages!"[26] Tom's captors, however, just as quickly veer away from the savage and towards the ridiculous. When he plays a flute for them, they respond with "ridiculous gestures" of enthusiasm, and his gift of the flute leads to a ritual of exchange and friendship, "so sacred a compact amongst the Indians, that it is never broken" (141–42). Like Chetwood's novel, Kimber's failed adoption episode imagines the natives as childlike and gullible, easily placing trust in Europeans, even forming an absolute, lifelong alliance based on the captive's chance possession of a toy. Although the genteel Tom does not take advantage of their naivete, it nevertheless serves the dual purposes of keeping the hero from the rigors of captivity and of containing any threat posed by native culture.

The novel later negates its rather brief and insignificant alliance between native American and European, even as solemnized by its ritual of affiliation, by creating a similar and more significant bond between English and French gentlemen, involving a more permanently efficacious ritual of affiliation. Just before he falls into the hands of the Indians, Tom captures some Frenchmen in a border skirmish and treats his prisoners "with the utmost humanity" (131). He forms a particular alliance, moreover, with the Chevalier du Cayle, based partially on the their mutual suffering from parental courtship interference. This alliance with a nobly named Frenchman serves to heighten Tom's standing within the genteel structures of romance plotting, not only by creating a noble parallel for his own romantic suffering, but also by giving him the opportunity to release the Frenchman with a treaty based on the gentleman's word of honor: "Let my generosity make you a friend to any English subject, you may see a captive with your nation" (134). Tom's genteel treatment of the French redounds to his favor after his Amerindian captors transfer him to the Quebecois, who grant him a merely nominal captivity and then a happy trip to France. When several Parisians help Tom regain his liberty, his captivity ends with much less emphasis on savagery and subjugation than on gallantry, generosity, and the brotherhood of European gentlemen. In Kimber's novel as in later works that also follow this pattern, episodes of captivity among the French serve to displace terror of native transculturation, reassuring British readers that the power of civility outweighs the cultural impact of the colonial world.

But if this captivity episode foregrounds the gap between native American and European, the novel's multiple plots and subplots tend to confound this opposition. Even before Tom's captivity actually begins, an interpolated tale portrays a noble savage held captive by a depraved European. This Amerindian proves passionately devoted to liberty and to the English, and his wife's extended sexual persecution at the hands of a French officer ultimately entails her death and her husband's reduction to "a secret and perpetual prisoner" (122). Within this tale Kimber imagines an exceptional native capable of meeting the British on their own ideological terms of liberty, fortitude, and limited respect for women, while the French seem naturally allied with the novel's stereotypes about the native majority. At one level the episode's chart of alliances and enmities supports an ideology of increased British power in North America, but the variable captivities developed within the plot as a whole so completely reverse the terms of this chart that a profoundly confused ideological vision ultimately results. Not only does the novel depict Amerindian capture of a European, not only does it depict a debased European capturing a noble savage, but its main plot concerns a European gentleman enslaved by colonial planters, and its attack on planters grows so strong that it expresses considerable sympathy for the rebellion of African slaves. Within this novel, neither tyranny nor liberty nor subjugation seems attached to any particular culture, but rather all cultures seem capable of despotism in colonial America, while only the exceptional gentleman, of whatever cultural origin, can remain free of taint. The novel can resolve the ideological confusion produced by these multiform captivities only through a romance plot that withdraws its hero from colonial chaos to a genteel English home.

After American captivity episodes raised such ideological confusion in the works of Chetwood and Kimber, subsequent British novelists attempted a variety of methods for resolving it. The sudden flurry of American captivity episodes that marks British fiction after 1767 tried to resolve the colonial anxieties of the adoption plot by suppressing, rearranging, or recasting many of its key elements. One pattern involved continued experimentation with the gender roles associated with American captivity, as the novels increasingly mollified or fully suppressed the active native female while more ex-

tensively connecting male captivity to the oppression of sensitive British heroines. Several novels followed Kimber's lead in situating their episodes of
American captivity within serial patterns of colonial captivity, patterns that
align British debtors' prisons and military structures with native American
captivity as systems of subjugation typifying the colonial world. In a more
pointed attack on colonial endeavor, several novels followed Chetwood's lead
in attributing their captivity episodes as much to the aggressive violence of
European colonialism as to an inherently tyrannical disposition within the
natives. In 1767, for example, this variation on the failed adoption plot enabled the anonymous *Female American* to attack a masculine colonialism
driven by trade and violence and to recommend its replacement with a female-centered program of Christian evangelism. In 1773 Henry Mackenzie
similarly applied an episode of American captivity to a satiric attack on the
aggressive, violent disposition of *The Man of the World.* During this period,
just before and after the war for American independence, the failed adoption plot became increasingly frequent, experimental, and critical of colonial
policy, suggesting an intellectual effort to mediate the rising conflicts between homeland and colonies.

In a vividly formalized resolution of British colonial anxieties, the anonymous *Female American; or, the Adventures of Unca Eliza Winkfield* reframes
the failed adoption plot in order to deflect and redirect the ideology of colonial individualism, by imagining a hybrid, mixed-race female as an ideal agent
of cultural contact.[27] Narrated in the first person by its eponymous heroine,
the daughter of a European male and an Amerindian female, the novel opens
with an account of the father's captivity and consequent marriage. Whereas
most other episodes of failed adoption occur as climactic moments, near the
ends of novels, this novel places its captivity episode near its opening, where
it serves as an initial frame tale that provides both an explanation and a sharp
contrast for the unusual life of the hybrid "Female American." The captivity
episode to which this protagonist traces her origin occurs soon after the British settlement of Jamestown and largely replays while also transforming John
Smith's captivity among the Powhatans and his rescue by Pocahontas. Within
this novel, what seems the originary captivity episode of American experience does not represent a triumph for an Englishman's colonial prowess but
rather reveals a gap between cultures that women must take the lead in closing. To solve the problems of a violent colonial past, the novel suggests, women
must shift the colonial project from conquest to evangelism.

The opening captivity episode offers a sharp attack on the male-domi-
nated, secular, and exploitative colonialism of Jamestown. With considerable

historical accuracy, the novel suggests that the Virginia project initially focused on trade and violence and fell far short of its lofty ideological justification in terms of evangelism among the natives. Criticism of this most famous of colonial endeavors begins with the novel's early scenes in Britain, just prior to the ships' departure, when William Winkfield, the father of the "Female American," receives an ominous warning from his brother: "We have no right to invade the country of another, and I fear invaders will always meet a curse" (1:8). As in *Robinson Crusoe* and a number of factual captivity narratives, a warning against overseas travel initiates a providential interpretive framework that treats captivity as a just consequence of worldly ambition. The brother's warning proves prophetic when William falls into captivity as a result of a Powhatan massacre, but the novel somewhat mitigates this stereotypical violence through an effort to fathom its motives. As the natives explain to their captives, "the evil being who made you has sent you into our land to kill us; we know you not, and have never offended you; why then have you taken possession of our lands, ate our fruits, and made our countrymen prisoners?" (1:12). White violence and capture of natives, the novel intimates, cause native violence and capture of whites.

The novel further develops its critique of aggressive male colonialism through its failed adoption episode, which intensifies the gender reversal of the Pocahontas plot, portraying the colonial male as utterly hapless and dependent on the intervention of a native female. The captured father of the eponymous heroine must depend on the aid of her mother, also named Unca. Like Pocahontas, the elder Unca uses her position as the daughter of a powerful chief to rescue a powerless English captive from the violent extremes associated with native males. The novel repeatedly emphasizes William's docility, first as the captives "were drove, like sheep, many miles up the country," then as Unca "pulled him by his chain" to signal her marriage choice, and finally as the chief "gave him as a captive to his daughter, who, immediately breaking the chain from around his neck, threw it at his feet" (1:9, 15–16). At first the transaction between father and daughter seems a ritualistic exchange of property, so that the novel grants her considerable autonomy within the tribe, enough, at least, to restore the passive Englishman to a position of relative mastery. When she further distinguishes him with the gift of native slaves, he follows the captivity plot's standard movement from slavery to mastery, but here this crucial structural shift occurs entirely through the agency of a native female.

However, this cross-cultural marriage, far from suggesting the possibility of a happy transculturation, entails further threats to the passive European male, especially as the novel introduces a second sexually aggressive native woman in the person of Unca's sister. While her sexual forwardness once again fulfills a male fantasy about native women, this subplot also ultimately reduces the Englishman to passivity. When he refuses the sister's advances, she orders her slaves to "Seize that white infidel . . . and in an instant all power of defence or flight was equally taken from him" (1:25). She reduces the passive William to further weakness through poison, but the active and perspicacious Unca quickly rescues him: "her quick apprehension soon suggested what had happened; and as the Indians are remarkable for their knowledge of poisons, and no less so for their skill in antidotes, she instantly sought, and as quickly found" the right one (1:27). These scenes suggest the colonial male's utter incapacity to manage by himself the features of the American landscape, from female forwardness to locally grown antidotes. He can negotiate this landscape only as a result of his marriage, by depending on a wife who already knows and controls the landscape. The novel quickly ends this spectacle of masculine subjugation and dependence when the sister kills Unca, leading the stricken husband to abandon the colonial landscape, like so many male captives in the failed adoption plot, and to return home with his daughter.

The doubled Indian sisters represent, respectively, a poisonously dangerous and a moderately salutary version of female action. Modeling female aggression and self-reliance in the figure of the native woman provided a means of briefly fantasizing about the extreme possibilities of female action before ultimately containing them. The novel aggressively deplores the sister's sexual aggression and must even kill off the more moderate version of female action in the person of mother Unca. And because these two sisters dominate the novel's early scenes of native culture, their sexual aggression and exaggerated social power come to represent the Powhatans as a people whose social structures pose a considerable threat to European colonization. However, the novel solves both the problem of female action and the problem of cultural contact through the evolution of the main plot that follows the early captivity episode. Through the figure of the mixed-race daughter, the novel develops an idealized portrait of female action, by carefully circumscribing her physical activity to a coastal American island, and by carefully circumscribing her social activity to religious conversion of native Americans.

At first, however, the uncomfortable conflict of cultures that Unca experiences in England suggests that miscegenation entails problematic results. In England, as she explains, "My tawny complexion, and the oddity of my dress, attracted every one's attention, for my mother used to dress me in a kind of mixed habit, neither perfectly in the Indian, nor yet in the European taste" (1:43). The physical activity encouraged by her native upbringing creates further problems in assimilation, especially when her cousin begins to court her, and she erects a cultural and sexual roadblock for this quiescent male by telling him that she "would never marry any man who could not use a bow and arrow as well as I could" (1:50). In order to resolve the confusion in identity patterns that surrounds this displaced hybrid, the novel shifts her back to an Atlantic island, a point midway between American and British cultures. As in *Robinson Crusoe* and other fictions of colonial captivity, shipwreck and island confinement provoke a revolution in the protagonist's cultural identity. The novel portrays her as a moderately active and successful female Crusoe, who achieves a life of adequate physical comfort through her extraordinary application of the island's limited and alien resources, although she occasionally succumbs to the qualms and fears typically ascribed to sensitive heroines. Like Defoe's work, this novel frequently compares the circumscribed space of the island to a "captivity" or a "slavery," and it punctuates her life there with a series of physical traps and escapes. This novel also follows its predecessors in Defoe and in spiritual autobiography by framing the experience of physical captivity as an analogue for human life in the terms dictated by a Christian god. Through a long internal dialogue, Unca gains a renewed appreciation for a religious life of subjection to God's providence, learning that such subjection entails a paradoxical liberation of the spirit, that an island captivity "may be called a state of liberty" (1:113). As in *Robinson Crusoe,* the situation of island captivity grounds the formerly errant and unstable spirit of the captive in a firmly established Christian subjectivity, although here that shift involves some suppression of the captive's hybrid character.

Another form of captivity threatens when, again as in *Robinson Crusoe,* a group of Amerindians pay an annual ceremonial visit to the island, but the novel transforms the threat of captivity into an experience of European mastery over the native, albeit one that overtly displaces colonial exploitation in favor of a missionary ideal. When the Amerindians arrive, Unca takes advantage of a gigantic statue that greatly magnifies her voice in order to speak to them as a seemingly supernatural exponent of Christian doctrine. Like many a European missionary in America, she thus adapts elements of native religion to serve Christian indoctrination, but unlike the typical British missionary, she finds the natives "generally of a docile disposition" and soon gains an entourage of faithful converts, "a whole nation, all ready to serve me" (1:148–49, 2:56). The novel, however, carefully separates her position of mastery from that of exploitative colonialism. When an English ship arrives and spoils her evangelical idyll, she fears that her adopted people might suffer an aggressively exploitative colonialism: "their country might be discovered, and probably invaded, and numbers of the people be carried away into slavery" (2:66). But the boat luckily contains her cousin, now an ordained minister, who assists her missionary work, finally gains her consent to marriage, and helps her plunder the temple of its golden treasure, which they use to buy books and other goods for their adopted people. Once they stock themselves for a life of Christian leadership, the couple work to isolate their island from further European interference.

According to this novel, women must take the lead in diverting the colonial project from aggression to conversion. The initial captivity episode suggests that masculine colonialism inevitably backfires, as the intended captors become the captives, as aggression finishes in violence, passivity, and debasement. After posing its failed adoption episode as a problem related to the passive colonial male and the active native female, the remainder of the plot acts as a solution to this problem. The mixed-race daughter represents an idealized if bizarre mediator between cultures as well as a compromise between female aggression and female passivity. Not only does she control the terms of her courtship, but she also sets the initial terms of the conversion project, and finally blocks the possibility of further aggression from other European colonists. But if the novel makes a somewhat radical choice in its cross-gendered and mixed-race heroine, it also portrays the native contribution to this character as limited to a moderate physical activity, one that must be supervised, moreover, by Christian civility. To enforce the need for such a limit, the novel depicts her conversion in captivity as a necessary apprenticeship for her leadership. The novel's final vision of an idealized society allows for some cultural mixture but rests firmly on the British foundations of Christian conversion and the image of the colonist as captive.

Six years later Henry Mackenzie used the failed adoption plot for a different kind of anticolonial argument, with an even more virulent condemnation of masculine aggression, in *The Man of the World* (1773).[28] Published two years after his popular bible of sensibility, *The Man of Feeling*, Mackenzie's second novel develops a foil for Harley, the "Man of Feeling," in Thomas Sindal, a wealthy, powerful, and transparently named "Man of the World." Most of the novel concerns the various tricks, thefts, rapes, and imprisonments perpetrated by Sindal against a genteel, virtuous, and naive brother and sister, William and Harriet Annesley. After Sindal seduces William to a life of crime, the duped victim suffers a series of colonial misfortunes, beginning with transportation to America and culminating with adoption by an American tribe. Although William departs from other adoptees in his eager pursuit of adoption, Mackenzie uses this pursuit for satiric purposes, ultimately rejecting both native culture and the colonial system because they foster a mind-set that encourages worldly predation.

Developed as an interpolated tale near the end of the novel, William's autobiography expands the scope of Mackenzie's satire of the aggressive, masculine "World" of social predation, as the broader world of the colonies proves full of men like Thomas Sindal, and as William proves continually duped by them. At one level, the novel employs its adoption episode as a satiric counterpoint to British forms of social enslavement. William's incorporation into an astonishingly violent tribe climaxes a series of captivities at the hands of various British institutions, from the judiciary to the military. Mackenzie's satire, however, targets not only British systems of social organization but also William's naive adherence to men of the world and their false values, especially the manly ideal of "resolution." When William's various experiences of British enslavement lead to his hatred for British civilization, his consequent endorsement of native savagery provides the final target of Mackenzie's satire, which operates through sharp reversals of conventional captivity plotting. Rather than resist Amerindian capture and culture, William seeks native adoption and struggles to emulate native resolution by eagerly embracing the stereotypical horrors of captivity. But these horrors are so graphically portrayed as to undermine William's admiration for the natives, who emerge as the novel's most extreme instance of the violent, predatory disposition that marks "men of the world" across the globe.

In the first half of the novel, William follows the familiar novelistic pattern of learning the wisdom of resignation and self-control through the experience of physical confinement, which results directly from his failure to negotiate the masculine "World." His youthful warmth of spirits makes him an easy dupe for the conniving Sindal, who introduces him to metropolitan corruption, gaming, debts, criminality, and prison. Prison effects a revolution in William's psychological disposition along the lines carved out in both spiritual autobiography and novel. After his incarceration, he experiences a brief "delirium" but then finds opportunities for extensive introspection; through these he learns the kind of self-mastery that Defoe or Chetwood would have adduced as necessary for mastering masculine landscapes such as the colonies. After William receives a sentence of American transportation, he reveals at his departure a "determined sort of coolness not easily expected from one of his warmth of feelings, at a time of life when these are in their fullest vigour" (1:225). At this point in the novel, calm acceptance of the limitations imposed by colonial servitude seems to signal a mature rejection of a young man's aggressive appetites.

After disappearing for most of the second volume, William returns near the end of the novel to recount his colonial experiences, including his sojourn among the Amerindians. This interpolated tale has drawn little critical comment, although one scholar has described the natives as positive, even utopian figures.[29] But the episode serves ultimately to portray the colonies less as a pristine environment of innocent rebirth than as an extension of the masculine "World." Like many a mid century interpolated tale of colonial experience, Mackenzie's adoption episode represents the colonies as a land of trial but not of triumph, a world that continually tests a hero's resignation and fortitude but offers no concrete rewards except the possibility of a return home. Mackenzie pushes this narrative pattern to its satiric edge by portraying the suffering narrator's experiences not only in terms of physical abjection, but also in terms of psychological abjection, as he foolishly embraces the colonial landscape's nastiest forms of servitude.

Colonists as well as colonized form part of the larger world of masculine aggression to which the misguided William seems attuned. In America he shows such a strong disposition towards resigned submission that he joins the colonial military after his master's death releases him from indentured bondage. William's resilience under servitude seems to fit him for success within the colonial military as well as within the physical environment of colonial America. Although his extraordinary discipline earns advancement through the ranks, the novel undermines this success by portraying it as a result of William's subscription within a corrupt culture of violence, one whose false ideals of honor, resolution, and fortitude ultimately recoil on its votaries. He earns a court-martial for trying to uphold his "honor" by beating a fellow soldier who has insulted him. After receiving a sentence of "five hundred lashes" and suffering the first one hundred, he "resolved . . . to escape by an act of suicide" (2:170–71). William's experiences in the colonial military unmask the masculine code of honor, discipline, and resolution as a code of violence, one that promotes indifference to suffering and finally indifference to life itself. Even his suicide attempt backfires, leading to escape rather than death. In this novel the masculine resolution of the captive protagonist seems transmuted into the depths of psychological abasement to which the masculine world can push its victims.

When William's retrogression leads him to seek Amerindian adoption, the novel develops the sharpest reversals of standard captivity plotting in all of eighteenth-century fiction. After reaching and escaping the nadir of violence, debasement, and ineptitude marked by his suicide attempt, he immediately "formed the resolution" to join the natives (2:172). Still impetuous after all his captivities, William continues to form what Mackenzie represents as bizarre and reprehensible resolutions, snap decisions that always backfire, attempts to escape captivity that serve only to push him into further captivities. Rather than heroically resist native capture and the features of native culture that threaten to undo his own, William foists himself on the Amerindians, tries to redefine himself as one of them, and actively chooses to undergo the most feared trials of captivity. Within the context of his various subjugations in British cultural systems, this eager pursuit of American captivity and culture works partially to satirize British culture, by suggesting that it might force its victims to seek its putative opposite. However, within the novel's larger satirical economy, native culture does not offer a positive foil, but rather a negative parallel to British culture. Mackenzie does not represent native culture as a utopian system free of subjugations, but rather as a society predicated on extremes of violent subjugation, far more savage than noble. Only William's retrogression can explain his desire to embrace the native culture represented by this novel.

Mackenzie portrays violence as the key to William's transculturation and thus as the key to Amerindian culture. Soon after he meets the tribe, when a native patriarch questions his reasons for joining them, he reveals the wounds on his back and declares "my friendship to his countrymen and hatred to my own" (2:174). Stripes of bondage signal William's opposition to the British in a language of violence that seems immediately intelligible to the natives. Despite his proven enmity to the colonists, he must further demonstrate an ability to endure pain, an ability that will earn his right for adoption and prove his connection with the native. To test him, the Amerindians place some "oppressively heavy" baggage on his back, "whose flesh was yet raw from the lashes I had received; but as I knew that fortitude was an indispensable virtue with the Indians, I bore it without wincing" (2:175). As William uses ethnographic knowledge to withstand various bodily subjugations, Mackenzie reverses the motif of the captive's ethnographic mastery. Where Robert Knox or Robert Boyle would use ethnographic knowledge to resist and capitalize on native cultures, William's knowledge of native Americans helps him to make his way in the tribe and presumably motivates his desire to join them in the first place.

In its pointed insistence on violence as the key to native culture, Mackenzie's novel depicts the custom of adoption as predicated on rituals of torture and endurance, so that the natives' vision of personal and cultural identity seems to rest entirely in terms of extreme bodily subjugation and personal resolve. Although some American tribes did initiate captives through rituals such as the gauntlet, although they often tested new adoptees with rigorous treatment, and although initiation into adulthood sometimes involved ritual torture, Mackenzie's portrait of native culture, like much Anglo-American writing about the Indians, tends towards an exaggerated and exclusionary emphasis on torture and personal fortitude. William can join the tribe only when he masters the extremes of violence and bodily pain that seem to constitute the truth of native culture. During his initiation, the native patriarch becomes a father figure, schooling him in the violent customs of the tribe. First he must witness the torture of captured enemies, described in a vaguely exaggerated language typical of European writing on torture: "You can hardly conceive a species of inventive cruelty, which they did not inflict on the wretches whom fortune had thus put into their power; during the course of which, not a groan escaped from the sufferers" (2:177). Observing these tortures constitutes a crucial lesson in William's education, as the old Indian points expressively to one of the calm sufferers, "as if he had desired me to take particular notice of his resolution" (2:178)—that word again. When William himself undergoes torture on the next day, the novel lavishly describes the "experiments of wanton cruelty," endured through an extraordinary "patience, with which nothing but a life of hardship, and a certain obduracy of spirit, proceeding from a contempt of existence, could have endowed me" (2:180). In this passage, as the storyteller reflects on his own experience, he himself recognizes the falseness within the ideals of personal fortitude and resolution that he had so arduously mastered and that had merited his adoption by the old man.

Ultimately Mackenzie portrays William's enthusiasm for native culture not as a reflection of its inherent attractions but rather as a result of the old man's dangerous personal influence, which seems to hold the adoptee in thrall. As William explains, during the life of his adoptive father, "scarce any inducement could have tempted me to leave the nation to which he belonged" (2:182). However, when the old man's death ends William's subordination and makes him an "independent member of the community" (2:187), he suddenly decides to return to civilization, as if uncomfortable with his independence, or unwilling to endure native culture without the old man's restraining influence. Like William's earlier tutors, Thomas Sindal and the hierarchs of the colonial military, the old Amerindian is a man of the world who takes advantage of William's manly character flaws, his impetuousness and veneration for the false ideal of resolution. Each of these tutors gains a masterful influence over William, forces him into some kind of bodily subjugation, and indoctrinates him into a false system of values that teaches him to accept his subjugation. Under the guidance of these false tutors, William undergoes a series of degrading transculturations, first remaking himself as an Oxford playboy, then as a colonial soldier, and finally as a native American. Thus the novel's episode of native adoption represents the most extreme moment of the world's ascendancy over the mind of its feckless male victim.

After he leaves the Amerindians, William's subsequent colonial experiences further destabilize the standard oppositions between European civilization and Native American savagery, with the ultimate goal of revealing that savagery characterizes all men of the world. On his return to white civilization, he undergoes a series of cheats and captivities, beginning with the chicanery of a self-styled Indian expert. Then another colonist, hearing of this cheat, wonders "how a Christian could be guilty of such monstrous dishonesty . . . no better than one would have expected in a Savage" (2:195). Ultimately proving just as culpable as the man he criticizes, this next charlatan helps William with food and shelter but then expects him to become a servant in return, and, when he refuses a task of "menial servility," commits him to debtors' prison (2:197). After William's release and subsequent voyage homeward, his ship falls into the hands of the French. However, unlike other fictional episodes of French captivity, this one emphasizes the similarities rather than differences between a European confinement and the Indian captivity that precedes it. William's fellow British captives take consolation in thinking, "We are not . . . among savages, as you were," yet he finds himself "thrust into a dungeon, dark, damp, and loathsome; where, from the number confined in it, and the want of proper circulation, the air became putrid to the most horrible degree" (2:200). Both before and after his Amerindian captivity, William undergoes a series of European confinements, from a London gaol to a colonial debtor's prison, suffering from both British military discipline and French treatment of prisoners of war. Explicitly juxtaposed against the captivity episode in an ironic counterpoint, such incarcerations under European legal systems suggest that Europeans can match the horrors of Indian captivity and that masculine social aggression extends from London to the colonies and from the supposedly civilized to the supposedly savage, deeply penetrating every facet of the colonial world.

In a somewhat unsatisfying attempt at sentimental closure, the novel reunites William with his niece, Harriet's daughter, and marries her to an idealized country gentleman. Because the novel concludes with this family reunion and with the daughter's happy restoration to wealth and legitimacy, it locates its moral center within the domestic, the genteel, and the feminine, rather than with the Indians. The natives of America teach William no moral lesson and make no improvements in his personality, but rather reinforce previously established character flaws. All of his transformations under false guides remove him further from the female center of domesticity and gentility in the English countryside, and all of them involve some form of incarceration. His physical captivities parallel his psychological subordination to the false ideals propounded by men of the world, and native transculturation represents the most extreme moment of this subordination. Thus the natives stand as the ultimate men of the world, men physically located, from a British perspective, in the greater world of the colonies, far from the domestic seat of feeling and civility in the British countryside.

While Mackenzie's novel posits the natives as prototypically masculine, it completely suppresses the figure of the native female and replaces her with oppressed British women. In doing so the novel extends a pattern begun in Kimber's *Mr. Anderson* and further developed in eighteenth-century Britain's final spate of American captivity episodes, within three novels of the 1790s. American captivity and European oppression of women are closely linked in Lennox's *Euphemia* (1790), Smith's *The Old Manor House* (1793), and Imlay's *The Emigrants* (1793), three works informed by the period's feminist thought and engaged with the possibility of feminist, or feminine, transformation among men. Within each plot a climactic captivity episode marks a defining moment in the production of an idealized man who sympathizes with oppressed women and even takes the lead in their liberation. Within each plot the threats of captivity and transculturation precede a denouement focused on the reunion of a sensitive and genteel British couple. Thus by the 1790s, within the evolution of the failed adoption plot, a passive British heroine of sensibility had fully supplanted the active native female as the consort of the passive adventurer. Over the course of the century, moreover, episodes of American captivity gradually transformed him from a tense figure of colonial failure to a figure of idealized and even feminized sensitivity, while images of native female action gradually gave way to images of British female oppression.

Within the novels of Lennox, Smith, and Imlay, moreover, American captivity and female oppression are closely tied to the problematic aftermath of American independence. All three works reflect the politically charged atmosphere of the 1790s, when the French Revolution transformed the implications of American independence, producing heated debates on the nature of government, Enlightenment, and women. All three novels develop a troubled critique of British colonialism in tandem with their troubled critique of eighteenth-century gender roles, although Imlay's approach to these issues differs substantially from that of the women novelists. Like Mackenzie, Lennox and Smith connect the problem of female oppression in Britain to the problem of masculine transculturation in America. While Mackenzie uses the adoption plot in order to satirize the masculine virtues of fortitude and aggression, the women's episodes posit the male captive as an idealized figure of masculine sensibility. Not only does the captivity of their male protagonists enforce a lesson of male identification with the oppressed women of Britain, but their captivity further marks an opposition to the aggressive colonialism represented in other British males. While the women writers produce sensitive, passive, feminized gentlemen by subjecting them to native capture, Imlay turns an already-enlightened quasi-feminist into a romance hero, capable of moderate activity in rescuing a female captive. The three novels adopt equally divergent perspectives on the question of American independence, as Lennox baldly rejects America as a land of deprivation and tyranny, Smith offers a troubled meditation on British colonial iniquities, and Imlay celebrates America as the land of Enlightenment progress.

In *Euphemia,* her final novel, Lennox returns to the American setting and captivity theme of her first novel, *The Life of Harriot Stuart,* published forty years before in 1751. Her debut rescues its heroine from the ostensible horrors of Amerindian captivity by revealing that her supposed Amerindian captors are really a predatory European gentleman and his servant in disguise. As Susan Kubica Howard has suggested, this very brief captivity episode serves merely as a "red herring," which Lennox ultimately displaces through the novel's protracted focus on "less exotic, more domestic figures of violence and cruelty," and on "the savage nature of relationships between men and women" in Europe.[30] Like Haywood's *Idalia,* the bulk of this first novel follows its heroine through a series of abductions, attempted seductions, and near-rapes, and its captivity episode seems designed to transfer female readers' fear of alien peoples to the more palpable threats of European men.

Lennox adapted the failed adoption plot for a different kind of feminist argument in *Euphemia* (1790),[31] which treats the oppression of marriage rather than the pitfalls of courtship. This novel also includes the most extensive and intricately plotted episode of American captivity in eighteenth-century British fiction, as well as the most carefully informed, if only occasionally sympathetic, vision of native Americans and adoption. The failed adoption plot allows Lennox to develop a limited feminist agenda by imagining the production of a polite, modest, ideally feminized British gentleman through experiences first in Indian and then in French captivity. When Edward, the son of the eponymous heroine, himself undergoes a positive transformation in captivity, he represents the promise of a feminine transformation of British culture, one that complements his mother's own liberation from a life of marital bondage. But the happy outcome of his captivity results less from a successful adaptation to native culture than from the application of a moderate French veneer over a resilient British essence, a combination that forms a sharp contrast to the novel's array of male tyrants, both colonists and colonized. Ultimately the novel forms its ideal gentleman by carefully displacing the threat of native transculturation with the promise of a feminine transformation that requires a rejection of colonial America.

Edward's experiences in captivity serve to replicate, complement, and fulfill Euphemia's own life of subjugation through marriage to the tyrannical Neville, a dissipated wastrel whose uncle refuses to recognize his nephew's claim on his inheritance. Proud and overbearing, Neville exacerbates his oppressive treatment of his wife by insisting on a colonial military career. After they reach America, his love of rule leads him to drag the unwilling Euphemia to an isolated wilderness outpost at Schenectady. While the novel depicts the supposedly unpeopled American landscape as an attraction for such colonial tyrants as Neville, for Euphemia it represents an utter banishment from the pleasures of British society and female companionship. To maintain these pleasures, she exchanges the letters that compose the novel with a friend at home. This correspondence often laments their oceanic separation and portrays Euphemia's colonial banishment in a language of injured sensibility and virtue-in-distress, so that the colonial world seems closely allied with patriarchal dominion. Despite Neville's attraction to the unpeopled colonial landscape, he proves ineffective in handling it. His son's disappearance and captivity result both from his father's desire to live in the wilderness and from his failure to monitor the child's whereabouts during a wilderness ramble. Later, Neville's foolish obstinacy strands his family at a remote plantation with few supplies to carry them through a harsh winter. When the novel describes this experience as a "captivity," it draws an explicit correlation between the mother's subjugation and the son's (4:25). Within this larger portrait of female subjugation, the captivity episode constitutes a climactic moment of female suffering and endurance. Losing her son to the Indians appears as the worst possible outcome of Euphemia's colonial banishment and the keenest affliction in her life of marital captivity.

Moreover, when Edward returns from captivity towards the novel's conclusion, his release parallels his mother's liberation from marital captivity. The conclusion happily resolves the heroine's predicaments by returning her home, where her sensitive treatment of the dying uncle leads him to alter his will, granting her an economic independence from her husband. This happy liberation shortly follows Edward's own release, which provides a climactic moment of reunion just before Euphemia's return to cosmopolitan England, her reunion with her epistolary friend, and her assumption of economic independence. The son offers a parallel to the mother not only in that they experience simultaneous captivities and liberations, but also in that his captivity links him with the virtues of female sensibility and virtue-in-distress.

Even before the captivity episode itself, images of Amerindians form an important part of the novel's negative portrait of the aggressive masculinity that marks the colonial world, especially as the novel assigns them several ethnographic similarities that parallel the faults of Neville. As soon as the heroine reaches the wilds of Albany, her letters home adopt a loco-descriptive framework and echo common stereotypes about a native disposition for overindulgence in sleeping, eating, and drinking. She repeats the standard European characterization of the native distribution of labor, asserting that the men indulge themselves in hunting while the women "work in the fields" and "bring home heavy burdens, their husbands being too lazy and too insolent to partake their labours" (3:191).[32] Within the violent, masculine wilderness of America, peopled by European as well as native tyrants, the heroine often finds a refuge in the enclosed space of the fort at Albany, which provides another metonym for her confinement both within a bad marriage and within a violent masculine world. On one occasion, when Euphemia and some female friends try to perform the domestic ritual of a tea party outside the walls of the fort, the violent interruption of some drunken Amerindians drives them back inside. An even more threatening image of the colonial world arises when Euphemia mentions "an alarming account of an intended insurrection of the negroes at New-York." Although she seems to sympathize with the rebels when she abhors the resulting "prosecutions, tortures, and death," ultimately she transfers this abhorrence to the colonial landscape as a whole, declaring, "There is no safety, I think, any where but in the Fort" (3:195). Once again the confined space of the fort represents a domestic refuge from an American violence that subsumes European and non-European alike.

Adoption first enters the novel as an aspect of this landscape of fear. Long before Edward's captivity episode begins, some local Mohawk chiefs perform a ceremony of adoption for Euphemia and another European woman, but Lennox's treatment of the episode creates an impression of cultural scorn, distance, and finally fear. As Euphemia describes the incident, an "Indian chief thought proper to confer the honour of adoption upon Miss Clara, as his brother did upon me. This is considered as a high mark of respect among them, which conferred upon us all the rights and claims of a Mohawk by birth" (3:193). At first the epistolary heroine maintains a cultural distance from the natives through this mildly ironic application of the urbane language of British social forms, but her irony soon turns to fear and concrete images of cultural distance when she recounts the details of the ritual itself: "The ceremony concluded with one of their terrific dances," full of heavy drinking, which "made them very quarrelsome, as usual; but we, safe behind our walls, suffered no inconvenience from them" (3:194). Here adoption seems not only quaintly naive but violently chaotic, a custom that the colonists can suffer only to limited extent.

The terror surrounding this initial adoption multiplies when the novel turns to Edward's more extensive experience of transculturation. After his sudden and inexplicable disappearance, Euphemia imagines her son "torn in pieces by wild beasts, or mangled by those savage hunters of men, who, when hunger presses, devour their species" (3:215). An air of mystery and Gothic supernaturalism surrounds his disappearance, his return, and the broader motif of adoption. Young Edward bears the significant birthmark of a bow and arrow on his chest, as if born under a sign of native identity or of native violence. Moreover, Euphemia experiences portentous palpitations before his disappearance and afterwards foresees his return in a dream about his ghost. Such Gothic trappings serve to heighten the failed adoption plot's initial moment of raw terror.

On Edward's return the novel follows the typical movement of the failed adoption plot from creating fear of horrible death to raising fear and excitement about the possibilities of transculturation. Much of this fear results because the novel frames the captivity experience through the lens of feminine sensibility. Rather than narrate captivity from Edward's personal perspective, the novel records his experience through several layers of emotional mediation, as Euphemia's confidante, Mrs. Benson, takes over the heroine's epistolary task, since her son's return leaves her too overwhelmed to write. Mrs. Benson herself suffers from terror and misrecognition at the first appearance of the returned captive, because both Edward and his faithful servant William have temporarily assumed native clothing in order to escape, so that the latter "appeared a perfect Indian, his hair being already cut in their frightful fashion" (4:238). Fear mixes with attraction when she recognizes the disguised Edward: "In the countenance of this Indian boy I perceived a strong resemblance to my Euphemia" (4:197). This mysterious correspondence is explained when he "bared his bosom, and shewed me the mark of the bow and arrow with which he was born" (4:198). The birthmark now seems to have signaled the young boy's exotic identity, his inborn connection with the native, a connection now confirmed by his sudden appearance in a native costume that neatly encapsulates a narrative of capture and transculturation. The inevitability of this connection receives further confirmation when Euphemia first sees her son in Indian dress and exclaims, "the very form I saw in my dreams" (4:203). A mysterious fate thus seems to have given Euphemia a son born for Amerindian adoption, connecting her through her son to a pair of conflicting subaltern positions, the captive and the native.

After powerfully evoking British fears of going native, the novel then undermines them by revealing that young Edward has managed to maintain a seemingly incorruptible British essence. When the novel finally turns to narrating the captivity experience itself, a happy adoption dissipates the potential horrors of violence and subjugation. Ethnographic details suggest the possibility of peaceful bonds between European and Indian, especially through the mediating influence of a female sensibility that seems capable of crossing cultures. The novel's invocation of sensibility begins with the boy's adoption by a Huron woman, "on whom the beauty of little Edward had seemed to make some impression" and continues as the frightened child feels "encouraged by those signs of compassion that were strongly marked in her countenance" (4:211–12). The novel represents such sensibility not as an isolated case but as an ethnographic characteristic: "The Indian women are extremely fond of their children, and take the utmost care of them while they are young" (4:213). However, the novel quickly brings the adoptive mother to her deathbed, where the final call of female sensibility forces her to insist on Edward's return to his natural mother. In this reformulation of the adoption plot, Lennox transforms the native female paramour, marked by aggressive courtship, into a native mother, marked by energetic sensibility. What *The Female American* represented as the mediating influence of a specific hybrid female character here becomes abstracted into a motherly sensibility that crosses the cultural gap and resolves the difficulties of cultural interaction as represented by the problem of captivity.

The novel further deflects British fears of going native through the common technique of shifting from confinement among the alien and "savage" Americans to confinement among the French, who represent a more familiar and manageable threat to British self-possession as well as a potential improvement to British civility. After the death and legacy of Edward's adoptive mother reduce the possibility of native transculturation, he enters a French captivity when the priest responsible for his return to British territory decides to take him in, educate him, and convert him. Although the novel celebrates Edward's successful resistance to Catholic proselytism during his double captivity, temporary transculturation still seems to provide limited benefits for this young Briton's character formation. As a result of his French captivity, Mrs. Benson declares, "our handsome Indian" has become "a good classical scholar," acquiring "a polite as well as a learned education" (4:209). Furthermore, she praises the "handsome Huron" in a language that sharply underscores the value of mixing European cultures: "His French education has given him an air and manner, so unembarrassed, so polite, and even gallant, which, joined with a true English solidity of understanding, makes him pass for a prodigy" (4:248). French cultural traits seem, like Edward's Huron clothing, to reside at the level of a polished surface and thus provide a positive overlay for the rational British base that enabled him to resist the blandishments of Catholic proselytism. The novel's constant use of the expression, "handsome Huron," suggests that native adoption also contributed to his idealized character formation even if the novel never details his native personality traits and even as it carefully delimits the potential effects of native culture. After the family's return to London, a foolish old gentleman comments that "our handsome Huron . . . had not an *outlandish* look; and piously hoped he never worshipped the devil when he was among the cannibals" (4:253). Notwithstanding the novel's scorn for the stereotypes of this cultural chauvinist, they help to show that the transculturated Edward can satisfy the most rigorous of British standards. Thus the novel undermines fears of transculturation most forcefully by suggesting that Edward's captivity allowed him not only to gain a properly genteel education but also to achieve an ideal balance between cultures.

Edward's cross-cultural education in captivity produces an ideally feminized gentleman, modestly adhering to what the novel posits as female authority and female standards of decorum, presumably through the influence of his feminine mentors, the sensitive native stepmother and the French priest. Even on Edward's first appearance in Indian costume, he "yielded submissively" to the guidance of the women and "modestly drew back" when his sister shows fear at their reunion (4:200, 205). His feminized gentility takes further shape against the foil of his imperious and prodigal father, especially during a journey to London, where Neville tries to guide his son through a brief education in the metropolitan enclaves of clubbish masculinity. In contrast to his debauched father, Edward resists such temptations with the help of his captive education, what the novel calls his "early habits of study and retirement" (4:257). Further contrasts between Edward's passive gentility and the aggressive masculinity of the colonial world develop as the novel narrates his escape from captivity. As so often in the failed adoption plot, the protagonist escapes not through his own exertions but through those of another, in this case the servant William. When the escapees attempt to return to British civilization, they meet the villainous Lieutenant Blood and must negotiate "the fierce and haughty air of this petty commander" (4:228). By this point the novel has established Blood in the role of petty military tyrant, through his jealousy of Neville's paltry power and through his abuse of the soldiers in his command. When Blood finds his rival's son in his power, he decides to imprison the escaped captives, falsely declaring them Canadian "criminals" and planning to return them, "under guard," to Montreal (4:236). Far from rescuing captives, this colonial officer as petty dictator attempts to return escaped captives to a second captivity. This episode leads to another significant reversal of the standard captivity plot when some local Amerindians come to the aid of the escaped captives. The garrison's doctor helps them escape Blood's clutches with the aid of two Mohawks, "both sensible and honest fellows . . . highly provoked at the cruelty and injustice of the Lieutenant" (4:237). For helping the escapees, the doctor himself faces imprisonment but trusts that one of the natives will travel to the colonial governor with an "account of Mr. Blood's tyranny and injustice" (4:239). Portrayed as reliable, rational, and devoted to justice and liberation, these Native Americans find ways of releasing captives rather than taking them.

Despite these positive native exemplars, the novel subsumes its occasional suggestions of positive cultural interaction within a narrative pattern geared towards a closure of withdrawal from the American landscape. With very little to show for their experiences of native adoption, Euphemia and her son ultimately settle into the British countryside for a life of gentility and reunion with her friends. This pattern of withdrawal simultaneously serves a feminist and an anticolonial critique. Within the structure of the failed adoption plot, Lennox's placement of the heroine's son in the role of the passive captive not only undoes the problem of male passivity, by explaining it as a result of his youth, but also turns it to positive account. Edward's feminized captivity, passivity, and happy withdrawal from the colonial world confirm a gentility that stands in sharp contrast with his father's aggressive penetration of the wilderness and the petty tyrannies of the colonial military. Furthermore, Edward's captivity not only distances him from his father's colonial aggression, but also marks his connection with his mother's marital oppression. The experience of native adoption, especially as transmuted through exposure to French urbanity, thus seems to produce a male feminist in late eighteenth-century terms, a man who refuses to follow in his father's hypermasculine footsteps and who thus seems destined to show greater respect for women.

A similarly feminist plot and character structure animates Charlotte Smith's *The Old Manor House*,[33] published only three years later. Like Lennox, Smith places a feminized gentleman into American captivity near the close of her novel, and his captivity likewise proves analogous to the more protracted captivity of a female protagonist. However, whereas Lennox finally rejects

America as a land of subjugations, Smith shows more sympathy for its prospects, even if her novel lacks Lennox's detailed knowledge of its landscapes and peoples. Of all the writers surveyed in this chapter, Smith reaches furthest towards the possibility of transculturation, but finally she too rejects it as her conclusion simultaneously brings her captive home and resolves the female dilemmas at the heart of her plot. When her novel ends with a happily feminized vision of ideal British gentry, it suggests that Britons can remain civilized only if they leave America to its rebellious colonists. Within this variation on the failed adoption plot's anticolonial agenda, the novel mixes an attack on British policy during the Revolution with a deeply ambiguous portrait of the Amerindian place in America.

Female confinement and economic dependence provide the focus for the main plot, which centers on the physical confinement of Monimia, the impoverished niece of Mrs. Lennard, who is herself housekeeper to the wealthy, proud, and elderly Mrs. Rayland. As a seeming vagary of her character, Mrs. Lennard locks Monimia every night in a turret isolated from the rest of the house. This physical confinement results from and also symbolizes her economic and social dependence on her aunt and her degrading position as household servant to Mrs. Rayland. Monimia's status as a dependent, furthermore, eventually renders her liable to the sexual persecutions of a neighboring gentleman, Sir John Belgrave. Despite her restricted situation, however, she also awakens the interest, sympathy, and love of a sensitive young gentleman, Orlando Somerive, the son of a distant and less wealthy relative of Mrs. Rayland. Orlando's feelings for this impoverished captive link him to the feminine and the confined, as his love grows partly out of sympathy for her dependence, and his attentions in turn lead her aunt to watch and confine her more closely. Further feminized through his own economic dependence, Orlando tries to accommodate his family's hopes that Mrs. Rayland will make him her heir, and he agrees to her proposal to uphold the family's honor as a military officer in the struggle with the American rebels. When he falls into Amerindian captivity as a result of his aunt's military obsessions, this physical captivity acts as a concrete realization of the twin "captivities" of economic dependence that afflict him and Monimia. Even more thoroughly than *Euphemia*, this novel identifies native capture of a sensitive young gentleman with female oppression in British social structures.

In the American episode itself, native violence and mastery of the wilderness seem to leave both the British in general and Orlando in particular entirely passive and ineffectual. The episode allows Smith to portray the British cause in America as mismanaged, treacherous, and debasing. She links Orlando's capture to the fate of General Burgoyne's expedition and capitalizes on contemporary knowledge of its disasters, portraying the British army as poorly managed and incompetent in negotiating the wilderness, so that they must rely heavily on native guides. Like a number of revolutionary and postrevolutionary captivity narratives printed in the fledgling republic, Smith's novel portrays British use of native troops as a betrayal of civilization and a tacit endorsement of "savage" depredations among "innocent" planter families (360). In Smith's account the British betrayal backfires when their diplomatic failures with the Indians turn these former allies into enemies who prey on Briton and Anglo-American alike. After Orlando's capture, he learns that the natives attacked because "the English had not dealt fairly with them" (378). Smith's account of the capture emphasizes the passivity of both Orlando and his fellow Britons, who can offer only a "random" and ineffectual resistance before a head wound robs him of consciousness (377). The wound renders him "Giddy and disturbed," so weak that a friendly native must support him on the long march through Indian territory (379), and thus it acts as a metonym for British colonial mismanagement as much as for his own subjugation.

Orlando's Indian captivity appears as one of several confinements that interrupt his military career, eventually remove him from action, and continually undercut the standards of aggressive masculinity that his culture would expect from a military officer. Even on the original transport voyage to America, the young officer feels confined within "a little crowded vessel," and Smith compares the plight of his soldiers to "that which the miserable negroes endure in their passage to slavery" (345). After his capture and release from the Iroquois, he learns that American troops had captured his regiment during his absence, giving him an ambiguous military standing: since he is perhaps "included in their captivity," he is effectively disbarred from further action (388). Then, on his return from Quebec to New York, his vessel falls into the hands of the French, and he finds himself "once more a prisoner" (388) and transported to France. There his generous captors allow him to return to England with some smugglers, who take advantage of wartime chaos by robbing him. Although he "yielded . . . to this robbery with as good a grace as he could," his sword falls overboard as a result (391). Through the series of subjugations that constitute Orlando's military career, and especially through the absolute disappearance of the phallic metonym that signifies his military prowess, the novel consistently feminizes its hero by forcing him into situations that parallel the plight of its central female captive.

Given the novel's overt critique of British colonial warfare, we might expect that Orlando's captivity would lead to some level of positive cultural contact, but the novel's view of transculturation remains fundamentally ambivalent. Even before his capture, Orlando's attitude towards the natives mixes attraction and repulsion: "Their savage appearance, and the more savage thirst of blood which they avowed—that base avidity for plunder, with an heroic contempt of danger, pain, and death, made them altogether objects of abhorrence, mingled with something like veneration" (360). The novel encodes this ambivalence more concretely through the figure of Wolf-hunter, the native who supports Orlando in his weakness. From their first meeting, Orlando distinguishes this Amerindian from the rest of his people, "remarking his more open countenance—his more gentle manners. . . . The secret sympathy between generous minds seems to exist throughout the whole human kind; for this young warrior became soon as much attached to Orlando as his nature allowed him to be to any body" (361). This carefully delimited gentility, simultaneously distributed through all human nature and opposed to Indian nature, serves primarily to rescue the British hero from the horrors of captivity. In the typical pattern of failed adoption, Orlando, on finding himself a "prisoner," initially "concluded he was reserved for those horrid tortures of which he had heard so many terrific descriptions," but soon discovers that Wolf-hunter "had saved him, and was his sworn friend" (377–78). But this impression of cross-cultural brotherhood ultimately capitulates to an emphasis on Orlando's subjugation. When the captive asks if he can leave, Wolf-hunter refuses with "some resentment" (381). The inexplicable behavior of this native "brother" holds him in the realm of the arbitrary and the alien.

This ambivalent vision of the natives also affects Orlando's transculturation, as his experience among the Iroquois verges on the later American myth of the "white Indian" who attains an idealized "brothers-in-arms" relationship with a native. Through contact with Wolf-hunter, Orlando learns the local language and even manages "to acquire a good deal of the customs of the Indians of North America" (362). But many aspects of his transculturation carry notes of ambivalence, and he remains largely passive during its most substantial moments: "His friend the Wolf-hunter had equipped him like an Indian warrior. His fine hair was cut off, all but a long lock on the crown of his head—and he was distinguished from the Iroquois by nothing but his English complexion" (380). Moreover, his adaptation to Amerindian behavior often results from crafty calculation, based on safety rather than sympathy. He devotes particular effort to transculturation during his attempts to obtain release, when he "endeavored to conform himself to the modes of his savage hosts, and was indeed become almost as expert an hunter, in their own methods, as the most active among them" (383). As in the later fiction of Cooper or Richter, the white Indian masters native culture so well that he becomes one of its most proficient exemplars, and his success creates an

impression of the simplicity of native customs, especially since he emulates
them only in order to escape.

Although Orlando outwardly conforms to native culture, the novel portrays this change as external to his inward depths of sensibility, especially as
these depths permit the action of genteel sympathy across the boundary between Briton and Frenchman. Despite the novel's intimations of cross-cultural friendship, at one point it emphasizes Orlando's heavy suffering at the
thought that he must spend an entire Winter "among these barbarians, deprived of all human intercourse, and in a kind of living death" (381). Here
even Wolf-hunter seems excluded from the realm of human interiority.
Orlando's release further enforces the distance between him and his native
captors, as he follows the advice of some French Canadians as to the "means
of conciliating this his Indian master," and negotiates his release by offering
the Iroquois trade in spirits and other goods (383). Any possibility of ennobling transculturation and cross-cultural friendship seems to dissolve with
the suddenly restored emphasis on Orlando's subjugated status, the degrading effects of colonial trade, and received European wisdom for handling
Amerindians. Further connections between Orlando and the French occur
when, as in Kimber's *Mr. Anderson* and Lennox's *Euphemia*, a French captivity follows the hero's Amerindian one. Among the French Orlando finds
that "his captivity was . . . much less terrible than that he had formerly sustained," as the commander proves a "generous captor" (388–89). Once again
capture by the French seems to offer a consolatory contrast to captivity among
Native Americans, suggesting that sympathetic bonds can form across the
barriers between European gentlemen even if the barriers between native
American and European remain impassable.

Orlando's captivities ultimately teach him to sympathize less with the
plight of Native Americans than with the plight of Anglo-Americans, especially as the novel suggests an identification of his subjugated position with
that of the rebel colonists in their struggle against Britain, and further, an
identification of the plights of his loved ones and their own. Before he enters
Indian captivity, he meets an Anglo-American prisoner concerned about the
fate of his family, suffering from an "anguish with which Orlando well knew
how to sympathise" (360). The prisoner's experience parallels his own in
America. Even before he falls into native hands, the novel constantly treats
his American journey as a captivity separating him from loved ones who need
him, and his capture exacerbates this problem. As he recovers from his physical wound, he "felt infinitely more miserable in supposing that he should live
in such insupportable anguish as his fears for Monimia and his family would
inflict upon him—condemned probably as long as his life lasted, to drag on a

wretched existence among the savage tribes of the American wilderness, and cut off from all communication with his country" (379). As a soldier captured by "savages," Orlando learns in a particularly telling manner how colonial warfare can separate men from their families, leaving them dependent, unprotected, subject to capture. As he travels with the Iroquois, they "attacked the defenceless villages of the English Americans, whose men were out with the army; and destroyed the women and children, or led them away to captivity infinitely worse than death" (380). Orlando's identification with the rebels grows more concrete after he returns to England, where he reads newspaper accounts of the war, and "his heart felt for the sufferings of the oppressed . . . fighting in defence of their liberties" (450). In this novel, then, native capture serves partially to illustrate the threat that British colonial policy posed to its former colonists, and partially to ally its genteel protagonist with their sufferings.

Throughout his American experience, Orlando's strongest sympathetic bond focuses on Monimia, and the novel constantly highlights the contrast between his physical distance from her and her imminent presence in his thoughts. After he reads a letter describing Sir John Belgrave's persecutions, Orlando "started up to demand instant satisfaction . . . when he found himself, by the distance of many thousand miles, deprived of all power of protecting his Monimia" (376). Dependent, persecuted, and confined, Monimia provides a female center for the captivity episode as well as for the novel as a whole. In this novel's treatment of the failed adoption plot, no native female appears as a figure of potential cultural mediation, and instead the possibility of transculturation attaches to a native brother. After rejecting the violence of this brother and the violence of the American world, the novel concludes by returning Orlando to the heart of the feminine in the English countryside. Not only does he inherit the fortune of Mrs. Rayland, but the novel's final image of his married life focuses particularly on the philanthropy of this formerly subjugated couple. In this novel, then, while the active native female has completely disappeared, the passive domestic female attains a power of sympathy over the British male that finally culminates with their transformation into idealized gentry.

Like Lennox, Smith resolves both the problems of the passive adventurer and the possibility of transculturation by disclaiming America as a world of masculine violence that threatens to reduce the Briton to the putative level of the native. While her novel celebrates the formation of sympathetic bonds across national, economic, and sexual barriers, the barrier between Native American and sensitive Briton appears finally insuperable. The novel's final impressions of the natives highlight predation and link them to other predators, such as Sir John Belgrave, the French smugglers, or the British army in America. All of these figures, moreover, act as foils for the protagonists' pacific sensitivity, a quality most concretely produced, and ideologically enforced, by the experience of subjugation at the hands of such predators. Such manifold captivities as the protagonists suffer, however, serve as an apprenticeship for their final transformation into ideal gentry. In this novel, the generosity of the ideal gentleman, even as much as his ability to identify with the "feminine" experience of subjugation, seems to correlate with his experience in Native American captivity. As this experience confirms his sympathy for dependent women, debtors, and other Anglo-Americans who suffer oppression, his sympathetic nature emerges partially by contrast with native capture, violence, and indifference to suffering.

Another way of assessing the anti-American tendency of these novels is by comparing them with Imlay's *The Emigrants,* a novel that paints America as the land of freedom and the land of the future. Like *Euphemia,* this epistolary work opens with an emphasis on its correspondents' painful Atlantic separation, as economic distresses force some of them to migrate to the "back settlements" of the American frontier. But whereas the failed adoption plot normally concludes with the captive's happy return to the seat of civility, Imlay closes by bringing all his correspondents together in an America that stands as a refuge from European tyranny. Couched in the language of 1790s radicalism, Imlay's attack on the tyranny of European institutions focuses particularly on female oppression under British marriage laws, as the impossibility of divorce forces several female characters into a "savage" marital captivity that the novel correlates with its somewhat anticlimactic episode of Native American captivity. This episode works partially to sustain the somewhat contradictory agendas of feminism and romance, but ultimately it treats captivity from the postrevolutionary perspective of the American frontier, a perspective that tends to erase the natives from the landscape and to eschew any possibility of transculturation.[34]

Whereas novels with failed adoption episodes generally reject what they represent as the "savagery" of colonial America, Imlay works to correct this image after initially indulging it. Like these novels, *The Emigrants* initially portrays emigration as a kind of captivity, focused in this case especially on Caroline, the youngest representative of the impoverished family of genteel emigrants. Although the novel initially describes her as "entombed" in America, she soon finds romantic pleasure in the frontier landscape and a host of cultured Anglo-Americans in Pittsburgh and Louisville, including a romantic suitor, Captain Arl—ton; a wealthy sponsor, Mr. Il—ray; and a long-lost uncle, Mr. P—.[35] These three emigrants act as the novel's political authorities, attacking such European shortcomings as monarchy, debtors' prisons, and commercialism, so that America emerges as a land of enlightened freedom rather than savage captivity. The novel's most sustained development of this vision of American freedom relates to marriage. All of the correspondents, male and female alike, deplore the effects of "tyrannical" and "despotic" marriage laws. Uncle P— furnishes one of several subplots offering concrete dramatization of European marital captivity. He narrates his love for a woman married to a tyrannical peer who forces him into debtors' prison after discovering the affair before the couple eventually escape to America. Several female characters find a refuge in America, freed from tyrannical British husbands and married a second time to more equitable American settlers.

But if America represents political and feminist progress, the novel does not allow the natives to share in its vision of the future but rather cites them as its most concrete instance of a despotism that seems to have corrupted all the world's men except Anglo-American emigrants. As Il—ray praises "the advantages of liberty" that England has enjoyed, he avers that "all the rest of the world, for I will leave America out of the question, has been fettered and groaning under the most diabolical tyranny" (299). This amorphous global barbarism is illustrated most concretely through native capture of Anglo-American women, a threat that pervades the novel from beginning to end. P—'s tale of escape from British marital tyranny concludes with the native capture of his wife and children, so that American captivity seems both to complement and to fulfill the novel's attack on the marital despotism of Europe. On Caroline's first journey through the Appalachians, she meets some settlers and speculates that they "perhaps have lost a wife, a mother, or a child; for I am told that savages have no regard for age or sex?" (28). Caroline does enjoy some peaceful encounters with Amerindians, but these moments are buried under more vivid and terrifying images of native capture. After she records a second encounter in a letter home, her domestic correspondent responds with a rhapsody of terror: "I thought I saw you insulted, and liable to be carried off by those Indians, whose image was so forcibly impressed upon my mind . . . that I have never been able to obliterate that impression" (201). After all these hints, Caroline is finally captured at the novel's climax, and one correspondent labels her predicament a "barbarian slavery" (305). Thus Native American capture of white women provides the novel's clearest instance of the female oppression that Euramerican settlers have supposedly left behind.

That the novel adopts such a frontiersman's perspective on the natives appears most clearly in its handling of Caroline's captivity itself. In a sharp divergence from its fictional predecessors, the novel represents captivity mostly through the correspondents' vague speculations as to the possible experiences of the captive rather than through a precise narration of personal experience. Writing very much in the language of early republican captivity narratives, Il—ray wonders, "How will her sensible heart palpitate in the agonizing dereliction? How will her tender limbs support the fatigue of being hurried through briary thickets? How will her lovely frame be able to rest, without other covering than the cloud deformed canopy of the heavens? . . . after the effervescence of our passions, our cooler judgment searches for more stable ground to act upon; and it is from the loss we all have sustained, we are bound to demand that Caroline shall be given up; otherwise the whole race of savages, must expiate with their lives the robbery they have committed" (246). Like much early republican writing on captivity, this novel reveals not only a repetitious obsession with the wilderness's physical marks on the body of a female captive, but also an overt contemplation, as a supposed result of rational "judgment," of genocide.[36]

From its frontiersman's perspective, the novel finally subjoins the captivity plot to the purposes of romance, bringing star-crossed lovers together in a manner that underscores frontier heroism. The captivity episode serves primarily to resolve their troubled courtship, which, according to the conventional patterns of late-century novels of sensibility, stalls through a series of misunderstandings, especially when a jealous sister forges a letter in Caroline's name. All problems evaporate, however, when Arl—ton meets and rescues Caroline while exploring the wilderness in an effort to forget her. The novel's connection between captivity and romance becomes almost laughably overt after her release, when one correspondent likens escape from the natives to escape from the epistolary machinations of the jealous sister: "how did I tremble when Mr. Il—ray related to me the particular and horrid circumstances of your captivity with the savages, and the more wicked one of the note?" (305).

Concerned with romance and frontier heroism rather than with the possibility of transculturation, the novel's account of Caroline's captivity offers only the vaguest images of the natives and instead focuses on her rapturous rescue at the hands of her frustrated paramour. It is Il—ray rather than the female captive who assures British readers of what emerges as the most crucial details of her experience among the Amerindians: "she never felt in the least harassed, or alarmed for her safety, as she had, from the moment she was captured, a presentiment that Arl—ton would retake her; and . . . the Indians treated her the whole time with the most distant respect, and scrupulous delicacy" (258). From the moment of her capture, the novel suggests, the impossibility of cultural interaction seems confirmed by the certainty of masculine prowess within the romance plot. In the few pages where Caroline herself recounts her captivity, she describes it as an experience of "exploring" the wilderness rather than an experience of cultural contact (256). Moreover, she relies on the vague, ecstatic, and erotically suggestive language of romantic landscape description, painting the environment in terms that largely evacuate its native inhabitants. Writing to her sister in England, she traces a climactic moment of her passion: "It was in the wild regions of the country of the Illinois, where the sweetened breezes attune the soul to love . . . and it was at that instant . . . when I felt an obligation for a deliverance from captivity, that made my high-beating heart at the recognition of Arl—ton, almost burst from its confines—Yes, Eliza, he rescued me from the savages" (274). The natives participate in this landscape only to the extent that they enable the romance plot, which completely overwhelms any suggestions of cultural contact.

As it subjoins the captivity plot to romance, the novel returns to romance's linguistic games with captivity and sexuality, suggesting that Arl—ton has replaced the natives as Caroline's captor. In describing the rescue, he dwells at first on the overwhelming emotional prospect of "the most divine woman upon earth, torn into shatters by the bushes and briars, with scarcely covering to hide the transcendency of her beauty, which to be seen by common eyes is a profanation"; these lurid anxieties, however, quickly evaporate with the announcement of his personal triumph: "Caroline has fallen into my hands!" (251). *The Emigrants* raises sexual excitement by placing a white woman in the hands of the natives and then transferring that excitement to her unregulated contact with a white male in the wilderness. As Arl—ton elsewhere exults, "What a change has happened in the fortune of your friend?—Every thing conspires to make me the happiest man living—I have been almost three days alone, as it were, with Caroline" (254). Another correspondent similarly plays with the language of captivity, referring to Caroline as Arl—ton's "fair captive" (264). Within this novel, the vague but extreme threat of Amerindian captivity serves partially to authorize a more moderate sexual aggression for the Anglo-American male.

Imlay's novel adopts a perspective typical of many frontier captivities of the early nineteenth century, celebrating the future possibilities of a land whose native inhabitants enter the picture primarily as a threat to white womanhood. In developing this perspective, he follows the failed adoption plot's first pattern of displacement, raising but also quelling the terrors of subjugation. But he never even approaches the second pattern of displacement. Instead of raising and displacing fears of going native, he completely suppresses any suggestions of transculturation and even any of the captive's personal thoughts on her contact with the natives. His focus on masculine concern and effort for the female captive suggests a shift towards confidence in the power of male republicans to handle the American world. This novel imagines the Anglo-American male as a moderate yet still forceful agent of Enlightenment progress, through his success in wilderness exploration and native warfare, through his enlightened plans for equitable government, and through his enlightened yet also directive sympathy for the plight of women. In this view of the American future, the problems raised by the British plot of failed adoption, including the passive British male, the active native female, native culture, and the possibility of transculturation, all disappear.

The failed adoption episodes of eighteenth-century fiction anticipated many of the narrative patterns that typified fictional accounts of captivity published in nineteenth-century America. Many of the colonialist topoi that characterized Chetwood's and Aubin's fictions of Oriental captivity did not develop in novels with American settings until the nineteenth century. Throughout that century, popular American fictions began to exploit the Amerindian captivity plot in order to develop such character types as the guileful male captive who tricks his way out of native culture and returns home laden with booty, and the assertive heroine who maintains self-possession through a carefully circumscribed violence. Some nineteenth-century American narratives also continued to explore problems in the gender ideology of active male and passive female, though without the persistent obsession with a single narrative pattern that marks eighteenth-century British fictions.[37]

But such parallels to nineteenth-century American patterns distinguished eighteenth-century fictions of American captivity much less than a metropolitan approach to the problem of transculturation, one that largely disappeared with the rise of three dominant American myths of cultural interaction. Adopting a frontier perspective on cultural interaction, all three of these myths explore the problem of developing a new national identity within a colonial environment, through a vision of a transplanted people, severed from its homeland and transformed in relation to the indigenous people it has come to dominate. The first of these myths dwells on images of native violence threatening domestic femininity. Such images have long provided inspiration for male violence, as the perspective adopted in Imlay's British novel has found a much wider distribution in American venues, from the visceral propaganda of the late eighteenth-century Manheim anthology to "classic" Westerns such as *The Searchers*. The second of these myths retells the story of John Smith and Pocahontas as a prophecy of manifest destiny, suppressing all traces of native adoption while transforming the active native female into a figure of romantic love, cultural generosity, and divination of her people's seemingly inevitable demise.[38] The third of these myths, initiated by the Leatherstocking narratives and their images of a vanished cross-cultural brotherhood, transforms the material of native adoption into a positive vision of an Anglo-American cultural transformation built partially through the brotherly contributions of the seemingly doomed native population. These myths gained such cultural dominance in the nineteenth century, influencing European as well as American visions of cultural contact, that they largely overwhelmed eighteenth-century Britain's metropolitan vision of cultural contact in America.

From a metropolitan perspective, British novelists of the eighteenth century so strongly asserted the power and the value of British civility that they denied the possibility of transculturation. Their accounts of the captivity experience were an attempt to negotiate the disturbing images of cultural interaction that emanated from the contact zone throughout the century, undermining the assumed opposition between British civility and native savagery. Reports of happily adopted Britons excited but also disturbed British writers at home, inspiring them to recast experiences of captivity and adoption in a surprisingly persistent manner. The failed adoption plot centered on the figure of the passive male captive and the active native female partially because the intermarriage of British colonists with native wives provided a locus for metropolitan anxiety about American transculturation. These novels insisted on an unbridgeable gap between native and Briton in order to explain away the embarrassing reports of British failure in converting natives and the disturbing reports of native successes in converting Britons. In suggesting that native efforts in transculturation would inevitably fail because of their protagonists' civilized superiority, whether of intellect or sensibility, the novels offered fantastic counterexamples to the generally acknowledged pattern of American cultural conversions. At the same time, the failed adoption plot also suggested that British failures in conversion resulted from an insuperable recalcitrance in native character. Within these captivity episodes, the natives' foolish determination to impose their own culture on Britons seemed concomitant with a refusal, or perhaps an inability, to emulate or even approach British civility. Even if later writers abandoned Chetwood's insistence on native intellectual inferiority, physical violence continued to dominate their portraits of native character, and the later novels increasingly used images of violence and the native ideal of indifference to pain as counterpoints to their protagonists' sensibility. These portraits of native character thus created an impression of a vast cultural difference, which no efforts in cultural conversion, whether initiated by natives or Britons, could possibly overcome.

This obsessively reproduced cultural gap raised ideological tensions in the earliest versions of the failed adoption plot, by Steele, Chetwood, and Kimber, before it contributed to an increasingly explicit but still highly ambivalent critique of the colonial project within the later British fictions of American captivity. Whereas colonial fictions such as *Robinson Crusoe, Robert Boyle,* and the Leatherstocking saga suggested that Anglo-American mastery of the colonial world depended on adaptation to it, the failed adoption plot suggested that adaptation to the American world would bring adventurous Britons too close to its indigenous inhabitants, turning Britons into Americans. Within these novels, the natives acted as a metonym for America and for the British colonial project there. Captivity, native adoption, and intermarriage all provided figures for British attachment and adaptation to America. These novels subverted the colonial project by depicting the colonial experience as itself a kind of captivity, both as a separation from the seat of civility and as an experience that led inevitably to capture and unwanted exposure to native culture. By portraying cultural contact as a debasing and empty experience for the captured Briton, and by insisting on the impossibility of transculturation for genteel Britons, the failed adoption plot suggested that they could not adapt to and succeed within the American world because it would remain fundamentally alien to civility.

Six

Utopian Captivities and other "African" Paradoxes

Nothing could more fully illustrate the close connection between classical liberalism and the captivity genre than liberal utopias that draw heavily from the plot structures of captivity. Three prominent English utopian novels of the eighteenth century develop plots in which an experience of captivity under an African people provides an important moment of crisis and resolution in a protagonist's progress towards utopia. Captivity plotting provides a frame tale for utopia in the first of these novels, Simon Berington's *Adventures of Sigr Gaudentio di Lucca*, as its protagonist describes how enslavement in Turkish Egypt led to his adoption into an isolated African utopia. First published in 1737, this minor best-seller inspired twenty-five printings by 1821, reaching four languages and both sides of the Atlantic.[1] Another important mixture of captivity and utopia appeared in 1750, when Robert Paltock published *The Life and Adventures of Peter Wilkins, a Cornish Man*, a work that exerted an especial influence on nineteenth-century luminaries such as Coleridge and Dickens. In Paltock's novel a brief episode of captivity in Angola acts as a prelude for the main theme, the protagonist's creation of a technological and political wonderland in a fantastic setting near the South Pole.[2] At the very end of the century, George Cumberland partially followed Berington's model in *The Captive of the Castle of Sennaar*, a novel that describes not one but two African utopias through the voice of a European prisoner, incarcerated by a petty despot on the upper Nile.[3]

Significantly, the utopian novels of Paltock and Cumberland were the only two eighteenth-century English fictions to include episodes of European captivity in equatorial or southern Africa, in contrast with the many novels that portrayed European captives on the Barbary coast. Sub-Saharan captivity carried particular appeals for authors of liberal utopias, not least because a forced journey into the deep south could offer some explanation for the protagonist's otherwise implausible discovery of a fantastic land previously unknown to Europeans. For each of these novelists, however, the eighteenth-century understanding of Africa and African captivity contributed more to the political than to the geographical rationale of the utopian setting. Simultaneously stressing chaos, confinement, and cultural depravity, Europe's early modern images of Africa furnished a setting that enabled these utopists to explore the relationship between the self and the state in extreme terms, especially through an ambivalent image of the subject as a captive to the state. In each case the African material supported the development of utopian ideals not simply by offering a foil for them but further by initiating a constantly iterated dialectic, first an oscillation between the poles of self and society, liberty and confinement, power and abjection, and then a synthesis built around the paradox of liberty in confinement, the liberal subject's ideal accommodation with social order.

In their mixture of captivity, utopia, and a European protagonist's penetration of sub-Saharan Africa, these novels represent a significant departure from the more mainstream fictional pattern of setting captive heroes on the Barbary coast. As we have seen in chapters 2 and 4, both factual and fictional captivity narratives set on the coast often asserted the superiority and inevitability of British liberties by demonstrating the captive's maintenance of an internal freedom of thought and will against an alien environment represented as inherently corrupt and despotic. Although a similar vision of captive heroism occasionally informs the novels of Paltock, Berington, and Cumberland, all three novelists greatly complicate this basic cultural opposition. Like Chetwood's *Voyages and Adventures of Captain Robert Boyle,* Paltock's novel portrays captivity as an apprenticeship for colonial heroism, but he extrapolates this narrative pattern onto a utopian scale, as his captive protagonist defeats fantastic colonial obstacles, gains fantastic colonial rewards, and finally perfects a morally cleansed version of British colonialism that substitutes capitalist freedom for native slavery. And in an even sharper departure from Oriental captivity fictions, the colonial progress of Paltock's protagonist seems to depend on an internal discipline originally inculcated by an African mentor. On the other hand, Berington and Cumberland portray protagonists who fail to muster the aggressive impulses of captive heroism and even come to embrace what seems its opposite. Under the tutelage of their adoptive African utopias, each protagonist learns that the ideal state rests within a paradox, as it guarantees freedom for its subjects by teaching them, and the European protagonist, the internal discipline of self-regulation. Each of these three novels celebrates a hero whose individual progress in self-regulation is wedded to the progress of an idealized non-European state, and in each case progress advances as the protagonist internalizes concrete lessons taught by figures of African wisdom. To varying degrees, these novels contemplate the possibility of an African cultural influence on a European protagonist, and their willingness to do so forms a sharp contrast with contemporary fictions of American captivity, which, as we have seen in the previous chapter, struggled to deny the possibility of cross-cultural transformation. In contrast, the novels of Berington, Paltock, and Cumberland pose African transculturation as a sign for a needed disordering of European character. Each novel ties its protagonist's psychological career to a set of personal paradoxes that build on the central paradox of the utopian genre, the placement of an ideal state within Europe's antitypical landscape.

In order to envision an ideal society, the Western tradition of utopian writing has long turned to unfamiliar and confined settings. Thomas More's eponymous utopians initiate their ideal polity by creating their own South Seas island, cutting it off from a depraved mainland, while the female sanctuary of Charlotte Perkins Gilman's *Herland* is hidden in a remote South American valley, surrounded by nearly impassable mountains.[4] The isolated geography of utopian settings serves a number of purposes. First, an island, a desert oasis, or an isolated valley increases the plausibility of utopian narratives by explaining not only the discovery of a previously unknown land but also the perfection of a society whose isolation preserves it from the vices attributed to other polities. Second, setting an ideal society far from Europe helps to shock readers out of complacent acceptance of European social institutions. Producing tones of confusion and playful discovery, the geographical disjunction of utopia creates a sense of political disjunction, as the utopist strives to dislocate an audience's imagined seat of cultural and political superiority, and to remind them of the gap between European social ideals and European social reality. This gap is also reinforced by the trope of geographical confinement, which at one level suggests the limitation of the ideal in relation to the real. Imagined through a geography of isolation, the ideal seems difficult to access, difficult to remember, and difficult to imitate, although these very difficulties create moods of preciousness, urgency, and moral obligation. But a final reason for utopian confinement, and one most germane to the novels discussed in this chapter, is that it serves to highlight the paradox of freedom that sits at the heart of many utopias.

Although a tension between subjective liberty and social order characterizes the utopian tradition in general, this tension became increasingly marked with the rise of classical liberal thought at the end of the seventeenth century. As Krishan Kumar has suggested, utopia was "born with modernity" and thus shares "the central dilemmas of complex modern societies . . . the often conflicting pulls of the need for order and the desire for freedom."[5] Ideals of social regulation generally distinguished English utopias of the seventeenth century, as they responded to the period's political and social upheavals. By contrast, those of the following century turned increased attention to individual fulfillment, especially as they mixed the static narrative structure of utopia with the dynamic structures of the developing novel.[6] This increased emphasis on freedom and fulfillment reflected the rise of liberal individualism in late seventeenth-century political theory. Individual freedom from governmental oppression and the rights of individual property owners were equally important for the two most important strands of late seventeenth-century political theory: classical republicanism as represented by James Harrington's *The Commonwealth of Oceana* (1656) and classical liberalism as represented by John Locke's *Two Treatises of Government* (1690). Significantly, both of these enormously influential texts relied on utopian strategies of conceptualization. Explicitly formulated as a description of an ideal but fictional polity, Harrington's seminal republican vision imagined freedom from tyrannical violence and social chaos through a mixed government or a separation of powers, a carefully regulated distribution of political activity among various powerful segments within society.[7] Less explicitly utopian but even more influential for modern political thought, Locke's work argued that the individual's rights to liberty and property provide the logical foundation for his contractual submission to government. To demonstrate the priority of those rights, Locke produced a rather utopian account of their origins in a state of nature, one clearly modeled on contemporary accounts of Native Americans. For each theorist, utopia helped to resolve the paradox inherent in the concept of freedom as an aspect of social order or government. In each case utopia served to explain how a government or social order can guarantee individual freedom.

A paradoxical play with the languages of liberty and order dominated English utopian writing in the eighteenth century. This emphasis partially reflected the increasing dissemination and sophistication of liberal political thought, but it also reflected the deep social ironies of an era signaled by absolutism, revolution, the expansion of centralized government, and the growth of the slave trade. In general, eighteenth-century visions of the ideal state still tended to favor classical republicanism over classical liberalism, emphasizing the liberties of the subject less than the responsibilities of the citizen, ideals of personal virtue, and the threat of societal corruption. But as authors linked this corruption to such figures as James II or Robert Walpole, utopian celebration of independence from tyranny often coalesced into visions of broader franchise and constitutional liberties, especially with the increasing importance of democratic ideas amidst the late-century revolutions. While constantly proclaiming ardent devotion to subjective liberties, however, eighteenth-century utopias also placed much value on social deference. If they sometimes celebrated technological liberation from the severity of the material world, they also attacked the social consequences of economic individualism and advocated technological simplicity, careful regulation of desire, and even communal ownership of goods. Throughout the century, the genre took much interest in the social position of women, and a single text might advocate female liberation through the companionate marriage while also vesting most social authority in a patriarchal hierarchy. Although utopias such as Berington's experimented with deistic thought, others based their ideals of virtue in Christian simplicity, which could encompass both equality in the eyes of God and puritanical rigors of moral discipline.[8] Many of these particular tensions within eighteenth-century utopias may ultimately reflect more fundamental contradictions within the utopian genre as a whole. The unified harmony of its social architecture is insistently normative even for texts that celebrate deviation from the received norms of their audiences; nevertheless this very deviation produces moods of playful experimentation and liberation even in utopias that idealize the most conservative and ordered of polities.[9] With such a wide-ranging potential for paradox, the utopian genre provided a field for exploring the intellectual tensions involved in the eighteenth-century's faltering movement towards individualism and democracy.

As eighteenth-century utopists explored the tensions between individual liberty and social order, their omnibus narratives often juxtaposed utopian materials against thematic and narrative elements borrowed from the captivity genre. Such mixtures entailed two important paradoxes: first, as the European traveler finds a model for European social improvement in a non-European landscape marked by the savage possibility of captivity, and second, as he finds utopian freedom through the experience of captivity. Mixtures of utopian and captivity plotting turn up in narratives with many different settings, even in narratives with Australian settings. This is surprising because the period saw no factual models narrating Australian captivity, although the ancient western myth of a southern continent lying at Europe's "antipodes" had long furnished a vehicle for imagining Europe's cultural and political antitype.[10] At the century's beginning, Hendrik Smeeks's 1708 Dutch narrative, *The Mighty Kingdom of Krinke Kesmes,* included an interpolated tale concerning the El-Ho ("free man"), a European traveler captured first by the savage natives of a South Seas island and then recaptured by its utopian colonists. A better-known example is Lemuel Gulliver, who experiences variable mixtures of captivity and distopia all over the Pacific. Beyond the South Seas, America, Africa, and the Orient also occupied important positions within the Western geographical imagination, and they could also play the role of Europe's antitype or provide appropriate settings for mingling captivity narrative and utopia. One such mixture appeared within Ambrose Evans's 1719 novella, *The Adventures, and Surprizing Deliverances of James Dubordieu.* After the title character is captured by pirates and then marooned on a voyage to the West Indies, he discovers a utopia happily isolated among seemingly impassible mountains and characterized by a fantastic level of personal liberty, as the people "had no form of government among them, but liv'd . . . without magistrates, or any rule, which might contradict the inclinations of every particular or individual."[11] Another mixture of captivity and utopia appeared in the anonymous 1757 novel, *The Voyages, Travels, and Wonderful Discoveries of Capt. John Holmesby.* After the hero's kidnapping and sale into North American indenture, a shipwreck strands him in South America, where he becomes a "Servant to a Savage," but finds in his master the venerable remnant of a lost utopian state.[12] Whatever its setting, the captivity genre's simultaneous invocation of the themes of subjugation and liberty made it a particularly strong vehicle for simultaneously engaging the paradox of freedom and the paradox of utopia, the ideal but confined state.

Although eighteenth-century utopists routinely turned to settings beyond the reach of contemporary geography, Berington, Cumberland, and Paltock could explore the paradox of freedom with particularly destabilizing results by turning to African settings. Compared to Australia, South America, or Siberia, Africa offered unique opportunities because Europeans associated it not only with the geographically unexplored but with the geographically, ethnically, and politically extreme. Africa, for eighteenth-century Europeans, carried an especially strong reputation as a land of vast deserts, raging rivers, impassable mountains, tyranny, carnage, and cannibalism. In turning to African settings, the utopists could count on their readers' familiarity with a well-established tradition of European writing about the "dark continent," which tended to generalize a wide range of African cultures and political entities under broad headings of despotism, superstition, and cultural depravity. For many European writers, African cultures seemed an extreme fulfillment of the stereotypes associated with the Orient, especially as the tyrannical corsair kingdoms of the northern coast seemed to find equally tyrannical counterparts in the slaving kingdoms of the Western coasts. Although the European image of Africa retained the same broad outlines throughout the early modern period, its particular uses and associations changed with the increasing importance of the slave trade and with an increased European interest in developing interior colonies within the continent. During the Renaissance, European commentators regarded native African polities as ineffective and anarchic, much in the manner of the most common accounts of Native American government. Over the seventeenth and eighteenth centuries, with the expansion of the slave trade, British commentators placed increased emphasis on African tyranny, although they linked this tyranny to unstable revolutions rather than to solid absolutism. Both sides of the late eighteenth-century debate over the slave trade assigned its origins, if not full responsibility for its continuation, to the violent despotism of native slaving kingdoms. The West Indian planter Samuel Martin declared, in a popular proslavery tract, that "all the kingdoms of Africa are slaves, from the highest to the lowest, to the arbitrary power of lawless tyrants, who have the lives and properties of their subjects absolutely at their disposal."[13] Abolitionists often produced equally damning and generalized portraits of African cultures, especially at the end of century, as they increasingly argued for a liberal, Christian, and capitalist transformation of these cultures from what seemed an inherent disposition towards despotism and slavery.[14]

The potential for both African civilization and African depravity seemed augmented when European writers imagined the little-known interior. Some writers imagined that the interior would reveal greater virtue, civilization, and opportunity than the coast, and even hoped to find modern counterparts to the medieval fable of Prester John's lost Christian kingdom.[15] Other writers, however, especially slave traders, imagined that the peoples of the interior must possess the same damning characteristics as their coastal neighbors, but to an even greater degree. One of the most notorious legends of interior despotism concerned the conquest of the coastal slave kingdom, Whidah, by the interior kingdom of Dahomey, especially as described in the oft-reprinted and clearly biased account of William Snelgrave, a slave trader. In Snelgrave's version, the conquest occurred partially because the once formidable Whidah had degenerated to the stature of a petty Oriental kingdom, ruined by luxury, polygamy, the king's "Effiminacy," and the tyranny of his upstart subordinates. Turning to the invasion itself, Snelgrave portrays widespread cannibalism, huge piles of moldering heads, and ritual sacrifice for the sake of a "Fetish or Guardian Angel." Even after victory, the king of Dahomey, according to Snelgrave, proved continually cruel to his own people because he constantly feared rebellions, and the result of such government was a "desolation" of all trade in the surrounding areas.[16] Dahomey retained this reputation through the end of the century, in such texts as Robert Norris's 1789 *Memoirs of the Reign of Bossa Ahadee* and Archibald Dalzel's 1793 *History of Dahomy, an inland Kingdom*. Because interior kingdoms such as Dahomey could suggest to English readers both mysterious peoples and horrible despotism, they offered particularly surprising and thus particularly effective settings for utopia.

Setting utopias in sub-Saharan Africa gained additional shock value from the widespread yet muted role played by captivity within European writings on the region. Scenes of European detention and subjugation at the hands of native rulers saturate these writings, even to the extent that there is no recognizable genre of African captivity narrative comparable to that of the Oriental or American genres. Though the precise boundaries of these latter categories are somewhat vague, we can still trace the persistent efforts of writers and editors to center a genre on the concept of captivity as a violation of what they implied should be a norm of free British access to Mediterranean waters and North American soil. British writers could assume a norm of free trade and travel in the Mediterranean basin because of British naval power, while American captivity violated assumed rights of travel and settlement in the "unpeopled" American wilderness, as supported by a network of garrisons and militias. But the few early modern Britons who ventured south of the Mediterranean coast of Africa could not rely on the support of significant military or administrative intervention, and their texts did not assume a norm of free travel. In early modern travel literature on sub-Saharan Africa, captivity does not seem a violation of the norm meriting a genre of its own but rather a constant and normal aspect of travel. With the single exception of Robert Drury's *Madagascar*, English narratives of captivity south of the Sahara appeared in the course of longer, more generally focused travel narratives and geographies. At the close of William Smith's conventional *Voyage to Guinea* (1744), for example, appears a letter from the Dahomeyan captive Bullfinch Lambe, which merely requests aid from a British governor and does not construct the experience of captivity as a curiosity or an outrage for English readers.[17] On the other hand, the general run of early European travel writing on sub-Saharan Africa is laced with scenes of detainment, trial, and coercion. From Jerome Lobo's early seventeenth-century *Voyage to Abyssinia* (translated by Samuel Johnson in 1735) to James Bruce's 1790 *Travels to Discover the Source of the Nile*, and even in the reports of slave traders such as Snelgrave, progress from one land to another often occurs as a series of accommodations with rulers who assumed an absolute prerogative over anyone in their domains, so that the threat of imprisonment looms constantly rather than intermittently.[18] Even when not actually imprisoned, the British protagonists of these texts seem to travel in a condition bordering on captivity in its dependence on the sufferance of native rulers.

As European travelers in Africa, the protagonists imagined by Berington, Paltock, and Cumberland face constant threats of subjugation. In each case, the journey that brings the protagonist to utopia begins by passing through parts of Africa known for wild geography and violent despotism, before reaching points further south, in unknown lands of paradox and further extremity, the improbable but still possible realm of the ideal. Paltock's protagonist passes through Angola, a land known to Europeans for Portuguese slavery and colonial wars, and there he meets captivity, a crocodile, and the African mentor who embarks him on a career of utopian liberation amidst an imaginary winged people living near the South Pole. Berington and Cumberland, on the other hand, set their utopias in unexplored portions of Africa that their narrators reach by journeying down the Nile past Egypt. Penetrating an area that would provoke the curiosity of Europeans for years to come, the narrators pass by immense deserts, along a river known for fertility and flooding, through a region envisioned by Europeans as formerly civilized but now ruled by Ottoman despots. Berington sets Mezzorania and Cumberland sets Jovinia, the second utopia of his narrative, within the fabled Mountains of the Moon, a legendary geographical feature supposedly situated between the Sahara and the West African jungle. Cumberland situates his first utopia on an island in what he calls Lake Zambre, probably referring to one of the great lakes of Eastern Africa. The extreme contrasts of African geography, in all three of these novels, seem to match the extreme contrasts of African politics, which place utopia against despotism in a mutually illuminating juxtaposition. That the protagonists find utopias of freedom, self-regulation, and Christian virtue within lands associated with despotism, chaos, and Islam represents the most basic paradox of these narratives, one that foregrounds the notion of freedom through subjugation as their central concern.

Paltock's novel imagines an ideal society produced through European civilization of a decidedly un-European world. Far more spectacular than even the colonial career of Robert Boyle, Peter Wilkins's utopian project at the south pole is nothing less than a fantastically complete transformation of a fantastically alien world into a model society based on enlightened ideals of liberty, economy, and progress. This extreme fulfillment of a European fantasy of social perfection and personal power concludes a dialectic of freedom and subjugation that begins, as in Chetwood's novel, with the protagonist's captivity in an African state associated with despotism and depravity. Wilkins's Angolan captivity leads to a set of African experiences that are explicitly formulated as his initial lesson in colonial agency, a lesson that comes to occupy an enabling position within his psychological makeup during the novel's later sections of utopian creation.[19]

In portraying this transformation from African captivity to utopian colonialism, Paltock imagines the colonial project as the fullest resolution of what he portrays as an inevitable predicament for the world outside of Europe, an inevitable dialectic of confinement and mastery. Wilkins's utopian colonialism replicates the narrative structure of his captivity both on the small scale of personal psychology and the grand scale of technology and government. Within this early version of what we now call science fiction, the hero's political captivity anticipates a series of physical confinements imposed by the fantastic possibilities of the natural world, so that political liberation becomes closely correlated with scientific rationality and the liberation from material abasement that it enables. At another level of the dialectic, the hero attains liberation from material abasement through what begins as a mutually beneficial colonial relationship, as both he and his colonized friends contribute to the progress of liberty and enlightenment. Somewhat surprisingly, the impetus for this progress often seems to originate with the colonized themselves, especially with the Angolan mentor who befriends Wilkins in his initial captivity. After the protagonist internalizes the lessons provided by this mentor, they enable him to obtain a role of decisive leadership in his colonial utopia. This dialectic of confinement and mastery identifies the colonist with the colonized even as the plot grants them separately scaled roles within its colonial synthesis.

Paltock's novel begins by following colonial fiction's standard dialectic of confinement and liberation but soon pushes that dialectic into sharper relief, contradiction, and paradox. In the novel's opening picaresque frame, as so often in narratives of colonial adventure, the voyage of colonial trade appears closely and ambiguously bound to a psychology and a political rhetoric of personal freedom. Just like Robinson Crusoe or Robert Boyle, Peter Wilkins suffers from a youthful desire "of seeing the World" (16).[20] In the standard pattern of the voyage novel, his first pursuit of colonial freedom results in a disaster formulated as a reversal of the poles of liberty and slavery. Designed for the African coast and thus implicitly for African slaves, Wilkins's first voyage ends abruptly when he enters a horrible captivity among some French pirates. As he describes the fate of his crew, the pirates "chained us two and two, and turned us into the Hold," where they "lie for six Weeks; till the Fetters on our Legs had almost eaten to the Bone, and the Stench of the

Place had well nigh suffocated us" (38). Here the would-be slavers meet the hardships of the middle passage themselves.

After a rescue by the French navy, the protagonist enters a second captivity in Angola, a land well-known to Europeans because its long-standing Portuguese colony had penetrated the interior and fought a series of internecine wars with various native rulers, producing much vivid material for eighteenth-century geographical surveys.[21] Beyond the many captives obliquely described in general histories of these wars, Samuel Purchas's huge collection of voyages included a long personal narrative from Andrew Battell, who experienced Angola as a series of captivities and accommodations among a variety of tyrannical authorities, both native and Portuguese.[22] Battell's narrative seems to have furnished a model for Wilkins's captivity in a number of its details.[23] After his capture by the Portuguese, he finds himself "imprisoned, and almost starved" in Angola, and finally "set to Work in removing the Rubbish and Stones of a Castle" (43). Thus the novel initially represents Wilkins's colonial career through a descending scale of minute particulars, moving from youthful desire for familial liberation through an increasingly abject series of captivities, with the nadir set in Angola. The protagonist's Angolan captivity climaxes a series of reversals that seem to punish this paradigmatic colonial agent with the effects usually experienced by the colonized.

Again in the typical pattern of colonial fiction, this seemingly inevitable failure of the protagonist's initial colonial efforts soon provides the occasion for his development of the colonial skills of self-fortification and improvisation, although this novel first models these skills within an unusual mentor. Just as the feckless Wilkins seems resigned to slave labor, he meets Glanlepze, a fellow slave of African descent who rekindles the Cornishman's smothered impulse for liberty, and who eventually comes to occupy an important position within his conscience, acting as a continually useful memento of liberty, activity, and enlightenment.[24] During their captivity, Glanlepze becomes a spokesman for liberal doctrine, voicing the standard formula for expressing the core dilemma and the heroic resolve of captivity fiction: "for my part, immediate Death, in the Attempt of Liberty, is to me, preferable to a lingering Life of Slavery" (44). As a voice of liberation and a leader of their escape effort, the African exhibits the typical virtues of the captive hero.

After their escape Glanlepze continues to support and educate the Cornishman, especially when the latter proves incapable of handling the daunting physical environment of Angola. As Wilkins admits to his friend, "I was in an unknown World, and would follow wherever he should lead me" (46). When they meet a crocodile, Wilkins remains passive ("My Blood ran chill within me") while Glanlepze faces the beast "without the least Dismay" and displays considerable wit and agility in subduing it (49). The episode offers a crucial moment in Wilkins's education, as his mentor codifies his heroic action within a system of rational planning worthy of Crusoe himself: "Why Peter, says he, there is nothing but a Man may compass by Resolution, if he takes both Ends of a Thing in his View at once, and fairly deliberates on both Sides. . . . What you have seen me perform, is only from a thorough Notion I have of this Beast, and of myself, how far each of us hath Power to act and counter-act upon the other" (50). The African here becomes a spokesman for the skills of observation, assessment, and improvisation so often celebrated in the colonial or captive hero. When, much later in the novel, Glanlepze's resolution returns to Wilkins's memory in a time of great personal anxiety, he declares that the memory "ought to be engraven on Brass, as I wish it was on my Heart" (212). Glanlepze's guidance during Wilkins's Angolan sojourn, moreover, extends from psychological resolution to ethical standards, as mentor and protégé refuse to join what seems the most prominent local business: "as to Excursions for Slaves, which is a Practice in many of those Countries, and what the Natives get Money by, since our own Slavery, Glanlepze and I could not endure it" (56). In this novel, it is an African male who initially occupies the role of the native female within *The Female American,* providing the narrative occasion for redirecting the ideological impetus for colonialism from plunder to enlightenment.

After Wilkins leaves his mentor, his education in what seem the twinned colonial impulses of liberty and rationality initially results in failures that more or less explicitly correlate political confinement and the material challenge of the natural world. When the Cornishman hears of some European sailors confined in a nearby Portuguese prison, his renewed zeal for liberty inspires him to lead their escape and to confiscate a Portuguese ship, but his plan to avoid all shores backfires when a storm leaves him alone on the ship. After escaping from political tyranny, he faces a more terrible subjugation in the fantastic power of the natural world to thwart human will, instanced most concretely in a giant rock that acts as a lodestone and drags the ship hundreds of miles into the Antarctic. Wilkins tries to escape the rock in the ship's boat but soon finds himself sucked into a cataract that flows into a cavern. Bizarre natural forces seem to thwart the will of the budding colonist far more effectively than did the machinations of petty tyrants. The novel renders explicit the equation between social confinement and human prostration before the material when Wilkins describes spending five weeks in the cavern, "like a poor condemned Criminal, who knows his Execution is fixed for such a Day, nay such an Hour, and dies over and over in Imagination" (74). The natural world finally seems to produce a perfect prison after

Wilkins emerges from the cavern into a valley shaped "like an Amphitheatre": "above all, appeared the naked Rock, to an immense Height," and "as perpendicular as a regular Building" (76–77).

The bizarre natural landscape of Paltock's imagination is a fantastic amplification of the problems of confinement and resolution that his protagonist initially encountered in African captivity. Trapped within his amphitheater for a number of years, Wilkins emulates Crusoe in his ready production of a comfortable, English-seeming home, even making bread, cheese, and lamp oil out of the bizarre raw materials that fill this most exotic and most confining of physical landscapes.[25] After basing a limited material utopia on the ingenuity of an isolated Western protagonist, Paltock's novel then turns more substantially than Defoe's to developing a material and social utopia based on colonial interaction and the problem of subjugation. For Wilkins, complete freedom from physical confinement in an alien landscape occurs with the introduction of a people native to that landscape, Paltock's famous winged aliens, who look like ordinary Anglo-Saxons with wings. As with Crusoe's man Friday, the novel first introduces its native population through a single representative, creating a simplified portrait of cultural interaction. When Wilkins discovers the beautiful Youwarkee, she is badly wounded, grounded, and separated from her people, and he nurses her back to health before they fall in love and marry. Despite the extreme fairness of her skin, this marital connection carries overtones suggestive of a mutually beneficial colonial relationship. Once his nursing restores her capacity to fly, she helps him retrieve crucial European supplies that remain stranded on his ship. After his initial doubts concerning her capacity both to select useful supplies and to manage their transportation, her subsequent success removes his doubts and forces him to "admire" the "Sagacity" of native women (151). As an antidote to colonial exploitation, the novel imagines an ideal relationship between Briton and non-European along the lines of the companionate marriage, as the husband carries a mild and seemingly benevolent authority over the wife, and they share a mutual tenderness, respect, and obligation.[26]

This colonial model develops through an ambiguous connection between the winged female and other objects of British colonial interest. Wilkins's reassessment of his wife's capacities leads to another important invocation of the African mentor within his conscience: "Alas! Thinks I, what narrow hearted Creatures are Mankind? Did not I heretofore look upon the poor Blacks in Africa as little better than Beasts, 'till my friend Glandlipze convinced me . . . that my own Excellencies might have perished in a Desert, without his Genius" (151). The implicit connection between Glanlepze and Youwarkee marks an important shift in the novel's plotting of colonial relationships. After an

African male initially plays the role of native mediator, the novel develops that role more thoroughly in the figure of a native woman. Glanlepze may perturb the opposition between a British self and an African other because he resembles a captive hero in his fortitude and devotion to liberty, but Youwarkee pushes this disorder to a more extreme level. Like the "Female American," she is a hybrid figure. While her pale skin makes her seem European, her wings mark an extreme form of racial difference. Furthermore, while she behaves like a specific African, Glanlepze, the novel hints at no racial connection. Combined with surprising and multiple signs of familiarity, her fantastic otherness produces a puzzle of identity that destabilizes British notions of colonial selves and others.

Through the novel's fantastic formulation of the relationship between colonizer and colonized, it renders explicit what usually remains an implicit connection within early modern colonial discourse, that between the colonial trader's confinement within an alien world and his mutual dependence with the native. Restoring Youwarkee to health earns concrete material benefits for the confined Wilkins, as they come to resemble colonial and native participants in a trading factory, often through explicit reliance on the language of colonial shipping. While the native wife undertakes repeated journeys to retrieve supplies from the distant ship, the husband remains confined within the limited space of the "Arkoe," or natural amphitheater, like an Anglo-African trader in a factory or fortress. Although she generally tries to follow his guidelines in selecting particular supplies, she also makes some choices of her own, before loading them into casks and tossing them into the flow of seawater that runs through the cavern into the Arkoe. During these operations, Wilkins calls his wife his "Factor," and, with the arrival of a particularly large set of casks, he declares that "any one who had seen the Arrival of her Fleet would have taken it for a good Ship's Cargoe" (137, 237). The material improvements produced by this "shipping" carry further colonial overtones as Wilkins describes their work as a civilizing process, the fulfillment of his earlier labors in Crusoe-like isolation: "Youwarkee and I having fixed ourselves by degrees into a settled Rota of Action, began to live like Christians; having so great a Quantity of most sorts of Necessaries about us" (154). The civilizing process thus seems fulfilled through a mutual interaction and dependence between colonizer and colonized, as the colonist depends on the people he civilizes even as he wins their affection with the sympathetic, tender, and mildly paternal aid characteristic of a companionate husband.

The mutual dependence celebrated in this relationship results especially from heightened emphasis on the always implicit problem of the colonist's physical limitation, signified in this case through the contrast between

Wilkins's wingless confinement and the astonishing physical powers of the natives. At one level the power of flight suggests limitless possibilities of human action. The native word for their wings is "Graundee," suggesting an aggrandizement of human potential. Such extraordinary powers as Youwarkee possesses highlight not only her husband's physical weakness but also the vicarious power conferred by her service. When he expresses anxiety about his incapacity, she tells him, "Fear not . . . for you have a Wife will hazard all for you, tho' you are restrained: And as my Inclinations and Affections are so much yours, that I need but know your Desires, to execute them, as far as my Power extends; surely you, who can act by another, may be content to forego the Trouble of your own Performance" (136). The colonist is thus empowered by his very confinement, raised to a position of executive authority by a skillful and empathetic handling of the gap between his physical incapacity and the superior might of an alien people.

This vision of a mutually beneficial colonial pairing despite racial difference is later broadened to encompass Youwarkee's people as a whole, especially as Wilkins's winglessness leaves him anxious about his own insignificance among them. His anxiety develops especially when his wife leaves him to visit her family in their homeland, Swangeanti,[27] hoping to establish a broader level of contact between her European husband and her people. Fearing that she will abandon him, he becomes obsessed with his winglessness and its effect on their children, some of whom cannot fly and must therefore remain "imprisoned" in the Arkoe (175). When his wife returns, he regrets his inability to venture towards her homeland: "if I was as others here are, I might make a better Figure than they, by my superior Knowledge of things, and have the World my own" (211). Lack of flight now seems correlated with the confined space of the Arkoe, both serving as signs of the physical limitations of the colonist and his consequent dependence on the aid of natives.

Compensation for flightlessness and physical dependence, the novel suggests, must come from the kind of wary intellectual acumen taught by Glanlepze. When some of Youwarkee's relatives first visit Wilkins in his Arkoe, he allows them to believe that he can control the underwater movements of fish, describing himself as "well enough pleased they should think me excellent for something, as I really thought they were on account of the Graundee" (195). Even an ostensible intellectual mastery offers compensation for physical inferiority. When Wilkins's frustration with his physical limitation grows desperate, he once again recalls the resolute example of his African mentor: "O Glaulepze, Glaulepze! says I, I shall never forget thy Speech after engaging the Crocodile; that every thing was to be attained by Resolution, by him that takes both Ends of a thing in his View at once, and fairly deliberates what may be given, and taken" (212). Here an African spokesman for improvisation and resolution helps a confined European colonist to find the confidence to begin subduing a physically daunting people. Wilkins overcomes the problem of confinement through an intellectual device that both enables his escape from the Arkoe and raises him to a position of social mastery: he concocts a platform on which several native slaves will carry him to the capital. Thus European intellectual and social mastery seems an almost inevitable correlative of European physical dependence within a fantastically alien landscape, even a solution sponsored by the colonized themselves.

Once Wilkins reaches Swangeanti, the novel formulates his rapid rise to political leadership as an increase of liberation and enlightenment eagerly sought by the majority of the natives. He becomes an agent of freedom particularly in helping a local monarch to subdue a set of rebels who seem intent on emulating the stereotypical features of African despotism. As one of the king's loyal supporters explains to Wilkins, the rebels threaten to "render us all Slaves to an usurped Power. . . . We have no hopes but in your Destruction of the Tyrant-Usurper" (240–41). Wilkins's enemies emerge as a fractious minority who favor political repression and idol worship, whereas his role involves goading a docile majority to follow what seem their natural impulses towards liberty and rationality. Although the novel celebrates the natives' progress in rationality, liberty, and Christianity, Wilkins promotes these values through the captive-hero's traditional skills of subterfuge and manipulation. His role as liberator and enlightener seems to entail stratagem and self-aggrandizement even in its most concrete and far-reaching component, the abolition of slavery. This project begins with his initial journey to Swangeanti, when he suddenly seizes the authority to insist on the manumission of the slaves who will sustain his flight from the Arkoe. At this point he declares "what an Enemy I was to Slavery; and . . . as I am about to undertake what no Man upon Earth ever did before; to quit my Country, my Family, my every other Conveniency of Life, for I know not what . . . I must insist upon every Man present alighting with me in Safety, being made free the Moment we touch the Ground" (252). The personal sacrifice of the colonial traveler here seems to justify his seizure of authority. A more transparently self-seeking motive for this act surfaces when Wilkins explains to the reader that he believed it "would make the Men more zealous in my Service" (253). His efficacy as an agent of freedom always seems intertwined with his personal power as a demagogue.

This mixture of persuasion, manipulation, and outright confiscation of authority continues when Wilkins introduces freedom to Swangeanti as a whole. After he liberates the city, his plans to visit other territories within the kingdom produce unrest among the citizens: "the whole City was in an Uproar, especially those who had been freed by me. What? says I, have they so soon forgot their Subjection, to misapply their Liberty already? . . . they all said wherever I went, they were determined to go and settle with me; for if I left them, they should be reduced to Slavery again" (313). When these citizens promise to "obey [him] in any thing" (313), it becomes clear that Wilkins's role as liberator leads to nearly autocratic authority, gained both through the populace's enthusiasm for him and through his ready judgment of the ways they apply their liberty. With such a forceful political leader, Swangeanti no longer needs the guidance of its king, who accepts his transformation to the status of figurehead, calling Wilkins his "Father," and declaring to him, "I have been frequently, since I knew you first, in doubt of my own Existence; my Life seems a Dream to me; for if Existence is to be judged of by one's Faculties only, I have been in such a Delusion of them ever since, that as I find myself unable to judge with Certainty of any other thing, so I am subject to doubt, whether I really exist" (366). Although at one level the king's words celebrate the supercession of monarchy by liberty, they also suggest a crisis of identity produced by the complete transformation of a native society under an alien system of colonization.

Further elements of Wilkins's power develop as he replaces native systems of slavery with a European economic system built on mercantile colonialism, a system that he imposes without the full understanding or even the full awareness of the natives. In explaining his motives for abolishing slavery, he outlines his plan for a capitalist system: "I would only have every serving Man at Liberty to chuse his own Master, and every Master his own Man" (301). The conceptual gap between native slavery and European capitalism becomes particularly apparent when Wilkins tries to explain his plans in greater depth to his father-in-law. When the Cornishman discusses the division of labor, he finds that the venerable native "could not well understand all I said; and I found by him, that all the Riches they possessed were only Food and Slaves; and, as I found afterwards when amongst them, they know the want of nothing else: But, I am afraid, I have put them upon another way of thinking, tho' I aimed at what we call civilizing of them" (215).[28] This momentary regret, however, does not vitiate the otherwise triumphant tone that suffuses Wilkins's economic transformations. Later he explains to his father-in-law that "my Meaning in giving Liberty is . . . for the Introduction of Arts" (324), and eventually the people are fully "supplied not only with the Conveniences, but Superfluities of Life" (372). The paradisiacal features of Paltock's utopia take shape first through the language of liberty and then

The frontispiece to Chetwood's *Robert Boyle* develops a standard
early modern vision of colonial warfare, pitting superior technology against vast numbers of primitives, all for the reward of a
beautiful, exotic, and undeveloped land. (By permission of the
British Library.)

through the language of trade and commodities. By representing the natives as appreciative of such novelties despite an initial failure to understand them, the novel offers justification for an aggressive policy of colonial penetration.

Under Wilkins's guidance, liberty not only promotes civilization for his adopted people at home but also launches their colonial power abroad.[29] This process begins when he overhears a local myth about nearby Mount Alkoe, allegedly a den of torture and slavery. When Wilkins discovers that it is in reality a land of mines and smelting, he forms an immediate resolution to "turn the Profit of the Country my own way; and make it pass thro' our Hands" (331). This mixture of personal and national improvement continues with his successful appropriation of this alien resource. At Alkoe he finds an established slave system ruled by a tyrannical governor, who represents another colonial power, the "Zaps" of the "Born Isles." This system closely resembles the Spanish colonial program as described by British propaganda: the mines cause a high death rate among the slaves, and the governor asserts his power by torturing them to the point of death.[30] Once Wilkins overthrows this governor, the latter reveals a "Roughness in his Nature, which drove him to Extremities with the poor Slaves," and he defends his system by asserting that, "where Slavery abounds, it is necessary to act, or at least be thought to do so, in a merciless Manner" (341). Despite this hardened and rationalized despotism, the enlightened Wilkins rapidly converts the tyrant to able and lenient government by installing a wage system. Wilkins's first order is to "maintain Freedom; but, says I, let no Man eat, who will not work, as the Country and the Produce is the King's" (342). As for the Zaps, Wilkins initiates trade with them, buying their ships with the produce of the mines. Both at the national and individual level, then, he replaces a system of baldly physical compulsion with a system of economic compulsion under his distant but effective management. His alterations lead to an abundance of trade and an increase of settlement, with "scarce a Family but was of some Occupation or other" (369). The novel portrays two other colonial ventures as well, and in both cases Wilkins recruits colonists from among the formerly enslaved, improving both their material prosperity and the defensive posture of Swangeanti. Thus the novel rationalizes colonial intervention by imagining a utopia showing that European-style capitalism produces greater economic abundance than native systems of slavery.

Drawing from the closely intertwined discourses of manumission, capitalism, and colonialism, Paltock imagines a utopian version of British colonialism in a sanitized Africa of the imagination, an Africa made as perfectly appealing to the British colonist as he himself is to its people. Despite their fair skin and the markedly alien feature of their wings, the natives of Paltock's utopia resemble contemporary images of Africans in a number of ways: physical prowess, idol worship, tyrannical government, cultural simplicity. The imagined culture of Swangeanti resembles that of Europe's imagined Africa just as the bizarre natural landscape of Swangeanti resembles the startling Africa of European travel literature. Paltock sets a colonial utopia within this fantastic landscape, moreover, as an extension and fulfillment of his protagonist's initial colonial experience in African captivity. Wilkins's personal progress through subjugation, transformation, and resolution in Angola remains an always implicit background as well as a sometimes explicit parallel for the subjugations and transformations that he experiences in the course of building his utopia. The twinned spheres of his colonial triumph, furthermore, encompassing both the material innovations of capitalism and its displacement of slavery, occupy the same ground as his African debasement, since he falls into captivity during the course of a slaving expedition. In portraying this transformation from African debasement to colonial utopia, Paltock's novel turns a significant variation on the captivity narrative's causal displacement of the colonial project. Whereas a novel such as *Robert Boyle* simply blames European aggression on the prior aggression of a non-European people, *Peter Wilkins* splits the causes for European expansion among the colonist's initially aggressive disposition, the harsh political and physical realities that seem inevitable outside of Europe, and a voice of psychological and moral rigor embodied in the exploited. As the novel juxtaposes these factors in a dialectical process of personal and utopian development, they combine to displace the actual evils of British practice in Africa to the fantastical realm of the colonial ideal.

Although the utopian systems of Berington and Cumberland similarly emerge through a dialectic of mastery and confinement, their novels offer a decidedly different formulation of the relationships among Africa, Europe, liberty, and enlightenment. Part of this difference results from the settings of their narratives and the nationalities of their protagonists. By setting an enlightened Cornish protagonist first in a remote portion of the African interior and then in a fantastically sanitized analogue for Africa, Paltock represents cultural interaction largely as the projection of British know-how into the heart of the unknown. Building a sharp dichotomy between high civilization and low, he only occasionally intimates that the high has anything to gain from the low, and such gains occur primarily in terms of moral and psychological inspiration. Berington and Cumberland, by contrast, more thoroughly subvert the national dichotomies of civilization and savagery. Both authors focus on Italian protagonists, representatives of a land that English readers would associate with high civilization but also with moral degeneracy and political tyranny, with Michelangelo but also with the cicisbeo and the Inquisition.[31] In each novel, moreover, the Italian protagonist meets tyranny on both sides of the Mediterranean, although he also reaches a nadir of despotism with a captivity in the Nile region, similarly regarded as an ancient site of both civilization and tyranny.

The North African setting permits the novelists to mix stereotypes of tyranny and depravity drawn from contemporary descriptions of African and Middle Eastern lands. Images of overlapping political authorities, social chaos, and the threat of captivity often saturated texts centered on Egypt, the upper Nile, and Ethiopia. Johnson's 1735 translation of Jerome Lobo's narrative hit the press two years before Berington's utopia, and a similar portrait of the region characterized John Campbell's lightly fictionalized *Travels and Adventures of Edward Brown,* published two years after Berington.[32] In exploiting the region's reputation for chaos and confinement, Berington and Cumberland borrowed several patterns from the Barbary captivity narrative, and in both of their texts, as in captivity narratives more generally, the threat of a tyrannical Orient provides the ultimate rationale for and validation of the possibility of enlightened freedom. Both authors, however, exploit the region's reputation for political chaos in order to develop a vision of tyranny and depravity that threatens to engulf Europe as well as North Africa. In Africa, moreover, the protagonists discover not only a nadir of despotism but also a utopia of liberty, so that the continent offers starkly illustrative examples of both political extremes. Whereas Paltock only briefly reverses his prevalent opposition between British enlightenment and alien simplicity, the utopias of Berington and Cumberland involve a constant conflation of this opposition, most fully and consistently because they set their utopian models of liberty and enlightenment within what English readers would have imagined as the heart of tyranny.

Placing an ideal state in the presumed heart of tyranny is one of many paradoxes that the authors exploit in constructing their visions of ideal and practical politics. Each novel exploits the paradoxical potential of the captivity framework in order to develop a utopian model of liberty which is paradoxically predicated upon subjection and restraint. At the concrete level of novelistic plotting, each protagonist finds utopian liberty as a direct result of falling into an abject captivity among a stereotypically debased African people. The individual experience of the captive protagonist parallels the collective experience of his adoptive utopian people, who appear as a captive nation surrounded by a world full of despotic peoples, European, Oriental, and

African. Each narrative ensures the freedom of both its utopian people and its European immigrant by secluding them from the outside world in an isolated geographic location, a paradoxically liberating form of national captivity. The paradox of liberation through confinement, furthermore, is central to each utopia's model of civil polity, as the pinnacle of human liberty results from subjection within an ideal system of social organization, one predicated on self-control and social deference rather than law and coercion. After the protagonist's initial captivity isolates him as an absolute subject suspended among stark dichotomies of liberty and subjugation, the utopia offers a vision of his accommodation within a system stressing moderation for both the individual and the state. Such utopian ideals of moderation, moreover, take further shape against a panoply of counterexamples furnished by the variable motifs of captivity plotting: abject confinements, insatiable predators, headstrong libertines, and semi-enlightened patriarchs. Each narrator, finally, recounts his experiences of utopian accommodation while in prison, a setting that enables him to demonstrate the continuing integrity of a liberated mind through forthrightness, composure, and resignation under the rigors of physical confinement. Thus in both cases the framework of the captivity narrative serves to enhance utopian explorations of the limits, conflicts, and paradoxes of liberal thought.

This effort to destabilize Western political ideas works partially by disrupting the dichotomy between an internally free European captive and non-European despotism. Within Berington's utopia and within each of Cumberland's utopias, the European traveler eagerly embraces the "alien" culture of the utopian people and comes to occupy a position of respect within it. The convert leaves his adoptive people only under compulsion, and in each case he seems to internalize their cultural disposition, which provides a source of inner strength if not an active political agenda after he returns to Europe. The possibility of an "African" cultural colony in the Italian countryside emerges with surprising clarity at the end of Cumberland's novel, although this colony forms merely one strand within a broader utopian project of Christian colonialism directed towards Africa as well as towards Europe. For both Berington and Cumberland, moreover, the protagonist's conversion seems less an acceptance of African culture than a return to a cultural perfection that originated outside of Africa, since the utopian peoples first came from lands such as the Indus River valley or Italy itself. Thus, although both authors broach the possibility of Europeans' learning from idealized African polities, they do so in a manner that carefully limits the effects of this cultural movement to a calculated disruption of

European political complacency. Instead of advocating cultural pluralism or even relativism, this project serves to measure the gap between the ideals and reality of European society.

Berington's dislocation of received European social wisdom emerges especially from his paradoxical mixture of an African utopia with an Oriental captivity narrative. Not only does an experience of Egyptian captivity enable his protagonist to find a utopia, but other subplots further capitalize on the standard plotting of Oriental captivity in order to reinforce the text's paradoxical themes. But if the novel draws many devices from the Oriental captivity narrative, the protagonist (Gaudentio di Lucca, whose name suggests his enlightenment) eventually comes to embrace a very different set of ideals from those commonly celebrated in the captivity plot. Whereas Oriental captivity provides a colonial apprenticeship for protagonists such as the historical Francis Knight and the fictional Robert Boyle, Berington's 1737 novel, like other utopian fictions of the eighteenth century, offers mild criticism of colonial aggression.[33] While he places an aggressive desire for colonial mastery in a minor villain, his protagonist openly rejects offers of imperial power and instead easily accommodates to situations of limitation and even confinement. The closing vision of the protagonist is one of successful internalization of his adoptive people's ideals despite his physical separation from them, as he puts the doctrine of liberation through limitation into practice north of the Mediterranean. Basing the hero's novelistic progress on his conversion to alien cultural ideals forms a central component within Berington's larger effort to complicate British political ideas by complicating the Oriental captivity narrative's standard vision of heroism and cultural interaction.

Much of this complication results as Berington sets his utopia within the frame of not one but two captivity narratives, the first an inquisition narrative and the second a Barbary narrative.[34] The title concentrates primarily on the protagonist's inquisitorial captivity: *The Memoirs of Sigr Gaudentio di Lucca: Taken from his Confession and Examination before the Fathers of the Inquisition at Bologna in Italy. Making a Discovery of an unknown Country in the midst of the vast Deserts of Africa . . . Copied from the original Manuscript kept in St. Mark's Library at Venice: With Critical Notes of the Learned Signor Rhedi, late Library-Keeper of the said Library. To which is prefix'd, a Letter of the Secretary of the Inquisition, to the same Signor Rhedi, giving an Account of the Manners and Causes of his being seized.* As the title indicates, the initial inquisition narrative serves both as an authenticating device and as a frame surrounding the utopia with an atmosphere of systematic, world-ranging confinement. The text itself opens with further authenticating devices, first a preface from the English "Publisher," and then a more extensive introduction written by the Secretary of the Inquisition himself, so that the captive's utopian narrative carries the weight of a juridical authority enhanced by its very tyranny. In the course of this introduction, we learn that the inquisitors asked di Lucca for a full autobiographical narrative, insisting on novelistic standards of verisimilitude, and threatened dire punishments if they detected any falsehoods, so that di Lucca seems to provide a fully documented utopian narrative because his life depends on it. As a result of this narrative frame, the authenticity, practical effectiveness, and cultural appeal of the African utopia seem offered as counters for the injustice and subjugation of European institutions.

As the Inquisition's request for a full autobiography simultaneously invokes verisimilitude and provides a pretext for the utopian narrative, the meaning of the protagonist's life coalesces with the ideals of the Mezzorain utopia, and both stand together against an inquisitorial atmosphere of tyrannical authority and panoptic observation. From the preface we learn that, even before his confinement, the Inquisition spent time observing di Lucca, reading his letters, and investigating his correspondents. The logic of this panoptic frame continues to develop as he delivers his autobiography, struggling to convince a hostile inquisitorial audience of his forthrightness by constructing a past life of integrity. Not only does the Secretary allude to their efforts to "catch him tripping in his Story" (39), but the text itself further documents these efforts as the inquisitors constantly interrupt his narrative with questions and comments. Through these interruptions of the utopian narrative, the text constantly reminds its readers that di Lucca's act of narration occurs before an inquisitorial audience, in an effort to obtain freedom from a tyrannical confinement. While subject to inquisitorial power, di Lucca exudes moderation and composure as seemingly essential aspects of his personality. The publisher's preface, moreover, confirms that "the Man stands to the Truth of it with a Stedfastness that is surprizing" (ix–x). As the plotting of the subsequent narrative indicates, di Lucca's composure shows that his conversion to Mezzorain cultural ideals holds against the most hostile investigations of the most suspicious and chauvinistic of European cultural authorities, even compelling their admiration.

Berington mitigates the radical critique implied in this cultural conversion by introducing a second frame tale, based on Oriental captivity, within the frame of the inquisition narrative. Following the generic pattern of the Barbary captivity plot, di Lucca's inquisitorial confession begins with a youthful voyage of colonial trade, but his first voyage, like that of Wilkins, ends with capture, in this case by Algerian pirates. The standard pattern of Barbary plotting continues as the protagonist and his companions adopt the standard resolution of the captive-hero, "that we had better die honourably than be made Slaves," although they cannot escape transportation to the slave market at Cairo (32). The Barbary captivity section characterizes the young protagonist as a headstrong agent passionately devoted to personal liberty, against the background of a Mediterranean world that seems permeated with social systems predicated on subjugation. However, the conventional captivity pattern collapses as di Lucca learns that his sale into slavery will ultimately lead to liberation. Whereas captivity teaches Robert Boyle the skills of colonial mastery, di Lucca's captivity introduces him to a world where masters and slaves do not exist. His buyer turns out to be a Pophar, patriarchal leader of the utopian Mezzorains, who promises his new "slave" a life of absolute liberty if he will journey to their homeland: "I know no just Laws in the Universe, that can make a Free-born Man become a Slave to one of his own Species. If you will voluntarily go along with us, you shall enjoy as much Freedom as I do my self: You shall be exempt from all the barbarous Laws of these inhuman Countries" (54). As in Oriental captivity narratives more generally, ideals of liberty take shape in opposition to the alleged practices of Oriental peoples, but Berington's novel subverts the narrative logic of the captivity plot. In keeping with their utopian ideals, di Lucca's new "captors" do not keep watch over his movements, so that he could easily escape. Although he feels a compulsion for liberty, he decides to remain with the Mezzorains. This voluntary subjugation on the part of the formerly defiant captive provides a concrete, individual fulfillment of the utopia's abstract social vision of freedom through captivity. Later di Lucca describes himself as made "fortunate by my Captivity" (233), after his voluntary confinement within the ideal state has produced a life of material prosperity and personal freedom. Such manifold departures from the conventions of captivity plotting indicate a shift from an absolute, individualistic dichotomy of liberation and captivity to a more complex vision of multiple tensions between liberty and subjugation, the individual and society.

When di Lucca learns the history of his adoptive people after reaching Mezzorania itself, their experience comes to stand as a collective parallel for his individual experience of freedom through Oriental captivity. Their history involves an experience of national captivity, national escape, and national liberation. Originally peaceful residents of ancient Egypt, the Mezzorains left their ancestral homeland because of attacks from the violent, rapacious Hicksoes, the apparent originators of Oriental despotism, invaders who practiced a "Tyrannical way of Living" and "made Slaves of their Brothers" (136–37). Adopting the captive-hero's resolve on a national scale, the future utopians "resolv'd to fly to the farthest Parts of the Earth, rather than fall into the Hands of those Inhuman Monsters" (123). As they plunge deep into the Sahara in search of a safe haven, an oasis offers them "the happiest Banishment they could wish" (135). Thus the origin of this utopia of absolute freedom is directly and paradoxically related to the imagined origin of Oriental tyranny, as the tyrannical ancestors of contemporary Oriental despots threaten to imprison the Mezzorains on a national scale, and their attempt to escape such tyranny leads to a happier national confinement within their isolated utopia.

This vision of national captivity continues as the novel defines the relationship between the Mezzorains and the surrounding lands of North Africa according to the standard dichotomies of early modern Orientalism. On their occasional journeys to Egypt, the Mezzorains maintain a distinct insularity from local corruptions, much in the manner of a captive hero: "They seemed not only to have a Horror of the barbarous Manners and Vices of the *Turks,* but even a Contempt of all the Pleasures and Diversions of the Country" (60). In Cairo, particularly, they must defend themselves against the temptations of "the most voluptuous and lewd Town in the whole *Eastern* Empire," where "the young Women seem'd ready to devour us" (61). On their return, much like escaping captives, they are careful to avoid any chance that Turkish authorities might follow them and discover their hidden land. Like captivity protagonists, the Mezzorains travel through the Orient with an eye towards its dangers, in order to resist them.

As an isolated outpost of enlightenment surrounded by what seems the pervasive tyranny of the Orient, Berington's utopia occupies a political situation that parallels its geographic situation as a desert oasis, and both of these situations serve as concrete embodiments for the cornerstone of his social and political theory: the paradox of liberty through subjugation. In Berington's complex narrative structure, this paradox appears as a necessary mediation for the complexities of social organization. Whereas his novel portrays the surrounding Orient as stricken by absolute hierarchies of mastery and slavery, his utopia represents a more practical, because more moderate, accommodation with the tensions of liberation and subjugation that seem to accompany every facet of human existence, affecting even his utopia's material prosperity. The land itself is so productive that every Mezzorain can pursue whatever occupation, or rather pastime, that he or she likes. While surveying the country's material prosperity, di Lucca experiences "with infinite delight the effects of Industry and Liberty" in permitting a profusion of technological achievements (257). Despite this liberation from material concerns, the Mezzorain religion seems predicated on a vision of life as a subjugation to the material. As di Lucca explains, a fundamental Mezzorain belief envisions life as "a state of banishment and mourning; wandering in sunburnt Deserts, and tost with the storms of innumerable lawless desires, still sighing after a better Country" (164). Here the external physical pressure of the desert surrounding the oasis seems correlated with the internal physical pressure of passion, both suggesting material limitations on the potential for absolute freedom.

This humanist vision of subtle yet pervasive psychological conflicts between liberty and confinement lays the foundation for Berington's utopian government, which mediates these conflicts through ideals of communal affiliation and internal discipline. When the Pophar is proclaimed ruler of the people at his return from Egypt, the people "prostrated themselves before him" (152), following a pattern of stereotypically Oriental subordination. However, di Lucca observes that this behavior represents a moment of purely voluntary and filial submission within an enlightened and liberated patriarchy. As he attests, "I never saw such an Air of a Freeborn People in my Life, as if they knew no other Subjection but what was merely Filial" (104). The text formulates this notion of freedom through filial subjection in a number of paradoxes, some explicitly labeled as such. Di Lucca observes at one point that the brotherly Mezzorains "are all Masters, and all Servants," and at another point that "the Paradox of this Government consists in this, that they are joint Lords, acknowledging no inequality" (214, 216). This principle of classless equality guarantees everyone a seemingly absolute independence, limited only by "natural" principles of affiliation: "What is most peculiar in this Government, is, that they are all absolute in some manner, and independent, as looking on themselves as all equal in Birth; yet in an entire dependency of Natural Subordination or Eldership" (211). This paradox is explained partially through an attribute found in many eighteenth-century utopias, although not in the utopian tradition as a whole: the goal of keeping the laws "as few, and as simple as possible" (235). Within this unregulated system, authority naturally gravitates towards those best able to rule, such as the aged Pophar, whose very skill in leadership entails that he will never rule his subjects any more heavily than they naturally need or desire. Another paradox results as individual freedom from positive laws, even as much as freedom from tyrannical leaders, requires and thus promotes a strict discipline of self-control. Di Lucca ultimately decides that this paradox renders the Mezzorain government fundamentally alien, if not incomprehensible, to Europeans: "every Thing they do is a sort of paradox to us, for they are the freest and yet strictest People in the World" (232). Believing in the fundamental goodness of human nature when unfettered by regulation, Berington suggests that a natural limitation of selfish desire results from a natural desire for social well-being.

The novel's most extensive illustration of the paradox of freedom through self-regulation concerns di Lucca's courtship and marriage.[35] Although the Mezzorains grant children, especially females, an absolute prerogative in marriage choice, parents still interfere in courtship once they suspect their children's inclinations, by creating "vast Difficulties, contrived on purpose, both to try, and enhance their Constancy" (228). When the Pophar sees the growing mutual affection between his daughter and di Lucca, he tests the young couple by insisting that the newcomer "must either solemnly renounce all Pretensions to her, or be shut up for ever without any Commerce with his People, till Death" (277). Di Lucca passes this test of self-regulation by surrendering himself to captivity and torture: "take me, shut me up, kill me, cut me in a Thousand pieces" (277). Based on a notion of internal "constancy" established through the separations and confinements of the lovers, the well-judged interference of the Mezzorains paradoxically leads to a more perfect fulfillment of the children's choices.

The novel further refines its ideal of rationally constrained freedom by developing a subplot that illustrates the dangerous results of unrestrained liberties. On an exploratory journey south of the utopian land, di Lucca and his adoptive people discover an English hermit, a former captive who has escaped from "some strange Barbarians," and sought refuge deep in an uninhabited stretch of mountains (293). After the Mezzorains save the Englishman from physical confinement and the threat of recapture, he proves a "*European* Savage," representative of "Libertines" and "Free-thinkers" more generally (293), especially in his efforts to corrupt and conquer Mezzorain society. The novel links his efforts in social corruption particularly to the appeal of unrestrained liberty: "his great aim, was to pervert our Youth, enticing them into all manner of Liberties" (294). He tries to seduce di Lucca with the appeal of unrestrained colonial power, insisting that the two of them could easily "make our selves Lords and Masters of all" (294). But the Italian has internalized the Mezzorain doctrine of self-restraint too thoroughly to find any appeal in colonial despotism, and he immediately betrays the plans of the Englishman. After the Mezzorains take the libertine to Cairo in order to free him, another captivity plot develops as he reports them as a threat to the local government. But the Turks soon recognize his machinations and reward him with what seems a fitting punishment: "sent to the Gallies for Life" (304). As the libertine serves to demonstrate, excess of will, embodied in colonial ambition as well as in an attempt to form an accommodation with Oriental political systems, ultimately entails the most absolute of subjugations, as marked by the Turkish galleys.

With the return to the Mediterranean, the novel closes its utopian vision and returns to the setting and plot structures of the captivity narrative, which reaffirm the contrast between Mezzorain political ideals and Mediterranean despotism. As di Lucca sails back towards Italy, he is again seized by the Turks but luckily discovers that a former admirer has become the Sultaness of the empire. She offers him "the first Post of the *Ottoman* Empire" as her husband, and his refusal reveals a full adherence to the Mezzorain ideal of liberation through self-regulation, as well as a full opposition to the aggressive heroism commonly celebrated in the captivity plot (322). After the novel rejects absolute power by projecting it onto the figure of a spurned Turkishwoman, yet another subplot reframes the hero's resistance to seduction and absolute power within a European setting. After di Lucca finishes his utopian narrative, the inquisitors enjoin a brief narration of his subsequent life in Italy, which, if verified, "might purchase him his Liberty" (326). He complies by recounting a final episode illustrating the principles of freedom through self-regulation, as he avoids the "ensnaring Airs" of a courtesan who had "enslav'd several Persons of the first Rank" (330). This lowly European counterpart to the imperial seductress serves to draw a parallel between Oriental and European failings. When di Lucca's story of resisting the courtesan seems to assist his release from the Inquisition, the Mezzorain doctrine of freedom through self-regulation seems again to grant its adherent enormous powers of self-fortification, forthrightness, and autonomy. In these parallel instances of di Lucca's adherence to Mezzorain ideals, the return from utopia through first an Oriental and then an Italian frame serves to integrate Europe and the Orient within a mutual opposition to the ostensibly non-Western ideals of Mezzorania.

In the long-standing utopian tradition of dislocating European complacency about the value of European civilization, Berington's novel simultaneously undermines and reaffirms the standard opposition between European civilization and Oriental depravity. On the one hand, the novel weakens the opposition between Oriental slavery and European liberty by introducing an interpolated tale concerning di Lucca's mother, whose abduction and sale to a Corsican merchant remind us that Mediterranean slavery was a feature of Christian as well as Islamic shores. That the most depraved figure of the novel is an Englishman further weakens the opposition between European civilization and Oriental depravity, especially as the libertine seems peculiarly identified with the Orient both in personal disposition and in narrative dispensation. On the other hand, the Oriental captivity plot that fills much of the novel relies on a standard set of stereotypical motifs, such as circumcision, rampant female sexuality, and the seductions of absolute power. Moreover, as the novel consistently defines Mezzorain principles of freedom in opposition to Oriental despotism, these principles sometimes seem allied with Europe. As the Pophar explains to di Lucca, "I have been informed . . . that your Laws are not like these barbarous *Turks,* whose Government is made up of Tyranny and Brutality, governing all by Fear and Force, and making Slaves of all who fall under their Power. Whereas, the *European Christians,* as I am told, are govern'd by a Divine Law, that teaches them to do good to all" (57). In its hopeful naivete, the passage carries an ironic potential for upbraiding Europe's failure to match its ideals, but this potential ultimately reflects Mezzorania's standing as an analogue for the mythical kingdom of Prester John, a fantastic reproduction of European ideals within the heart of the non-European world. At one point di Lucca observes that among the Mezzorains he "enjoy'd the same Liberty that I cou'd have had, if I had been in *Italy*" (61). That Italy stands sometimes as a sign of liberty and sometimes as a sign of confinement reveals the novel's primary concern with measuring the gap between European ideals and European practice.

Berington's critique of European institutions emerges through a constant play with parallels and oppositions between Europe and Africa. Far from celebrating a nationalist or pan-European triumph over Africa's imputed failings, his varied captivity plotting discloses parallels between the protagonist's Oriental captivity, his European experiences, the national experiences of his adoptive utopia, and, finally, the prospect for any individual's liberty within society. Ultimately these parallels suggest that no people, whether Oriental, European, or utopian, can escape the vexing and interrelated problems of liberty and subjugation. The novel's captivity plotting exposes the flaws of resolving these problems in absolute terms of despotism, slavery, libertinism, and self-will, while its utopian portion imagines more complex and nuanced resolutions for their tensions. As a prelude to utopian idealism, the opening captivity sections display absolute dichotomies of liberty and slavery that both demand the resolution of utopian moderation and define it as a mediation of these opposing extremes. In the denouement that follows the utopian narrative, captivity plotting helps to reveal the successful deployment of utopian ideals within the moderate frame of the protagonist's psychological growth. Within the somewhat muted novelistic pattern of di Lucca's life, captivity teaches him to reject youthful self-will and to embrace utopian ideals of self-regulation as a necessary accommodation with the subjugation imposed by any and all polities. The application of utopian idealism to the individualistic reform of a novelistic life becomes an even more prominent and explicit concern of Cumberland's work.

Like Berington's novel, Cumberland's two-part utopia emerges through a complex narrative structure, organized as a dialectic of captivity and liberation. After publishing the first part of *The Captive of the Castle of Sennaar* in 1798, he wrote a second part around 1800, but it reached print only in 1991.[36] In the first part, an unnamed narrator speaks from the prison of the title, recounting a series of personal misfortunes that culminate with his African incarceration. This first-person narration provides a frame for his encounter with a fellow prisoner, Lycas, whose name, like that of Berington's di Lucca, suggests enlightenment. The bulk of Cumberland's first part focuses on the life story of this mentor-narrator, especially his many years among the utopian Sophians (people of wisdom). When the original narrator resumes his personal history in the second part, he first identifies himself as Memmo (a rememberer), and then records the death of Lycas, his own escape from Sennaar, and a subsequent series of captivities that lead ultimately to a sojourn among the utopian Jovinians (people of rule?). Like the enlightened Lycas and di Lucca before him, Memmo must leave the utopian people he so admires, and the second part closes with his efforts to create his own utopia on an isolated Italian estate, based on both the Sophian and Jovinian models. The utopia narratives of Lycas and Memmo complement each other, with the Sophians offering a vision of an ideal polity based on natural reason alone, and the Jovinians offering a distinct yet reciprocal vision of the ideal state, this time based on biblical revelation.

This double utopian structure both imitates and extends Berington's method for simultaneously developing a critique of European social institutions, a concrete model for European reform, and a novelistic vision of personal progress. In Berington's manner, Cumberland mingles utopian and captivity plotting in both of his narratives. Likewise, he organizes the social structure of both his utopias around a paradoxical mixture of social liberation and personal discipline. And much more clearly than Berington, Cumberland poses his visions of utopian captivity as explicit models for personal mastery over affliction, where captivity and tyranny are identified with the passions, and their restraint enables physical and political liberation. For both authors, enlightened liberation is something lost to Europeans but obtainable within the heart of a prison, within the heart of tyranny, within the heart of Africa, as long as one follows principles of moderation and self-regulation. Thus at one level Cumberland's imagined Africa, like Berington's, is a landscape devoted to exploration of tensions and possibilities in the European mind. But Cumberland also gives more generous attention to concrete problems of cultural interaction in Africa, such as religious diversity and the slave trade, and he develops a more overt critique of European colonialism through contrast with a utopian colonialism based on moderation and Christianity. As a fulfillment of this utopian colonialism, Cumberland's second part closes with a vision of its African utopia developing a colony of enlightened Christianity in Italy, and this colony itself represents Memmo's fullest internalization of utopian ideals and the climax of his novelistic progress. Whereas the utopian structure of Berington's narrative implies that the ideals of an imagined Africa can improve European society, Cumberland's novel renders this implication concrete by imagining a process of utopian colonization that reverses the eighteenth-century expansion of European power.

Like Berington, Cumberland highlights the paradoxes of his ideal society by setting its narrative within a frame tale centered on captivity within an African land that British readers would have associated with the despotic, the exotic, and the depraved. What little knowledge contemporary readers might have possessed of the minor principality of Sennaar would have come primarily from one of the eighteenth-century's most notorious travel narratives, James Bruce's *Travels to Discover the Source of the Nile.* From its 1790 publication, this enormous journal gained its author a reputation for self-promotion, exaggeration, and even outright fabrication, leading one scholar to describe him as "perhaps the most widely read but also the most severely maligned traveler to come out of the British isles."[37] In recounting his journey among the region's minor states, this traveling doctor describes constant rebellions and conspiracies, autocratic rulers, summary executions, terrified subjects, and his own efforts to propitiate a constantly shifting spectrum of petty potentates. When Bruce reaches Sennaar, near the headwaters of the Nile, the "peevish" monarch asks him to examine some fifty wives in the royal harem, and he feels "obliged to attend them." Monstrous imagery saturates his description of the women, "corpulent beyond all proportion," with stereotypically dangling breasts and bizarre, physically abusive jewelry. Although known in Britain for his imposing stature and physical aggression, the narrator nevertheless reaches a crisis of personal agency when his "patients" take the lead in stripping naked: "it was not without great astonishment that I heard the queen desire to see me in the like dishabille. . . . Refusal, or resistance, were in vain. I was surrounded with fifty or sixty women, all equal in stature and strength to myself." Thinking that this situation may entail the violent revenge of the king, Bruce feels "disgusted" at his own powerlessness.[38] What is particularly striking about this incident is how the traveler frames the material of triumphant colonial action—penetrating the harem, gaining exotic and extensive sexual opportunities, displaying intellectual mastery through medical practice—within a narrative pattern of detention, coercion, and accommodation. This contemporary image of Sennaar as a land of exotic subjugation provided Cumberland with a particularly abrasive framework for a utopia of liberation, just as Paltock and Berington produced similar disjunctions by juxtaposing their utopias against other African lands where captivity seemed always a possibility.

Like Berington's novel, Cumberland's first utopian narrative opens within the framework of captivity. With the initially published title, *The Captive of the Castle of Sennaar*, Cumberland clearly placed his work in the category of captivity narrative, with echoes of Barbary captivity, African despotism, and Gothic castles. The novel confirms this generic imprimatur with Memmo's opening words: "Immured within the walls of a chamber constructed of Egyptian granite . . . how can a man, habituated to confinement, better pass away some of his vacant hours, than by recording the singular relations of a departed friend . . . who partook, while life remained, of the same restraint; and kindly taught the companion of his fate to mitigate its extreme severity?" (5). While Cumberland thus frames the "singular relations" of Lycas's utopian experiences as a means of teaching reconciliation to confinement, the prison stands as a background against which the narration of liberty takes shape. At one point Memmo describes how the light from outside, "arrested by the bars of a rude grating, chequers the paper" he uses to write (5), and his narration is often interrupted by reminders of its prison setting, such as rattling keys, drawing bolts, and a falling drawbridge, which function in a manner similar to the inquisitorial interrogation of di Lucca. Thus the prison setting retains an implicit presence during the course of the utopian narrative, suggesting that utopian idealism always emerges in relation to captivity, not only that utopian ideals remain always available to any kind of prisoner, but also that the inevitable subjugation within any social order requires such an idealistic response in the first place.

The novel further frames its utopian principles as consolation for any kind of affliction or subjugation with its account of Memmo's entry into the prison and his initial encounter with Lycas. On entering his cell, Memmo swoons under its burdens and the intensity of his passions, but he wakes to find the elderly Lycas, who thus represents wisdom for the mind enthralled by passion. The headstrong young captive asks, "Have confinement and chains any thing to offer me in exchange for freedom, probably for ever lost?" (6), but the elderly captive replies with reference to his own experience in captivity: "Yet am I now tranquil, easy, nay almost content, after a long and solitary confinement" (9). A series of such questions and answers set a personal level of interpretation for the utopian narrative, indicating that its ideals of regulation within confinement apply at the level of personal psychology if not of social practice.

Memmo's personal subjugation to passion results from a youthful experience of political tyranny, as he reveals to his mentor through a brief autobiography. This account takes the form of a progress through increasingly barbaric tyrannies, establishing a vision of global tyranny that seems to engulf both European and non-European and thus to provide a frame of confinement for the isolated outpost of the ideal state. Memmo's journey begins as a result of familial tyranny in his native Italy. His parents try to arrange a marriage for him, but he resists out of devotion to another woman. His parents then force his paramour into a convent and even lock their son in "an accursed state-dungeon" (11). Released four years later, and "Disgusted with every species of arbitrary power," he leaves Italy to see "the miseries under which France groaned, the despicable state of the Spaniards, and the horrors of African tyranny; the brutal stupidity of the Turks, and the stupid brutality of the Egyptians" (12). Within the experience of this narrator, then, European tyranny seems to provide an initial impetus for the passion that drives him into lands of more extreme tyranny. At the climax of this narrative progress through a world full of despotic states stands the minor principality of Sennaar, ruled by a "Cruel, accursed tyrant" (8) and dominated by the monumental prison of the title, which seems not only the fullest manifestation of this tyrant's power but also the defining feature of Sennaar as a locality. Memmo despairs of escape from a land that so greatly outdistances European modes of tyranny: "From the Bastiles of Europe, an escape might have been meditated with some prospect of success; but here, where the whole country is a prison, and its sovereign the jailor, what hope is left me[?]" (13). Defined by imprisonment, Sennaar stands as a global nadir of despotism and subjugation, as well as a personal nadir of unenlightened passion.

Memmo's autobiographical progress through a global landscape of tyranny precedes Lycas's own life narrative, which encloses his utopian experience within yet another frame stressing personal subjugation and political tyranny. As a Greek subject of the Turkish empire, Lycas represents a people anciently free and wise but now captive to despotic overlords, according to the standard enlightenment assessment of Mediterranean history. Within the harem at Constantinople, he achieves a fairly powerful position that eventually leads to disgrace and a desire to journey far away from his native land. Once he reaches Sophis, he describes the Ottoman state to his utopian listeners in terms that frame it as the polar opposite of their ideals. He undertakes to describe the Turkish military, as he explains to the Sophians, in order "to confirm you in your mild customs," linking it with "the most arbitrary power" and a reduction of "the most valuable privilege of our nature, free-will" (76–77). Once he leaves the utopia, his narrative closes with his confinement within the prototypical African state of Sennaar, which thus seems to coalesce with the prototypical Oriental polity of Turkey as instances of a global tyranny that surrounds the Sophian utopia both geographically and within the narrative structure of Lycas's autobiography.

As in Berington's novel, the movement of the utopian narrator from subjugation to liberty parallels the historical experience of the utopian people, who inhabit a captive land, a limited territory surrounded by a barbaric world and deliberately isolated from it. Physically the utopia rests on an island within lake Zambre, an isolated locale known to British readers only as the stuff of legend.[39] When the utopians detail their national history, Lycas learns that the "customs" of "foreign nations" provided the original "reason of the *Sophians* separating themselves from the world" (67). As the utopia's founder meditated on the means of achieving an ideal state, "he had long perceived that it could only flourish, free from interruption, in a perfect solitude" (75). In his search for solitude, the founder led his people from their ancient home in the Indus valley across "large spaces of sand" until he reached the lake "(which so happily encircles our islands), and found himself free from the persecutions of mankind" (74). Desert and oasis, lake and island all suggest multiple levels of geographical enclosure, as well as the potential that such enclosure offers for perfecting material and social well-being. Lycas confirms this vision of safe enclosure when he informs the Sophians that he has found, "except in this island," an evil state of society "every where," with "tyrants framing arbitrary laws, and by hereditary force, over-awing the multitude" (78). In the national experience of the Sophians as well as in Lycas's personal experience, recognition of the tyranny that seems to dominate global politics fulfills a necessary precondition for appreciation, if not creation, of the ideal state.

Again in the manner of the Mezzorain utopia, the Sophian state achieves liberation both through geographical confinement and through personal confinement, through a careful balance between individual freedom within society and the moral restraint of self-control. Like the Mezzorains, the Sophians cultivate both freedom and dependence through a reduction of restrictive laws. Individual freedom extends only to what the utopians regard as the natural limitations of reason and desire. Because they believe that human reason is "circumscribed," they embrace the goal of "restraining themselves to the proper enjoyment of the mundane natures," so that restraint becomes a central component of their educational system: "prudence . . . or the restraining art, must be inculcated early" (63, 73, 83). Inculcation of personal restraint and the absence of restrictive laws mutually reinforce each other, so that each individual is free to follow what seem the natural dictates of social restraint. In practical social terms, these ideals entail a form of communism that prohibits class distinctions and private property. Lycas observes that some Sophians temporarily occupy positions of leadership, but when he asks an agricultural leader if a piece of land is his "exclusive property," the Sophian wonders if Lycas regards him as a slave-driving tyrant (47). As another leader explains, true liberty means that all social distinctions arise from differences in personal merit: "Equal citizens of our free country, we can conceive no distinctions, but those of superior beauty, virtue, talents, or experience" (70). Freed from regulations and rigid structures, the ideal state becomes a communal meritocracy.

Like Berington, Cumberland develops an extensively detailed model for his utopian vision of social freedom through a focus on courtship and the position of women. Sophian devotion to freedom encourages courtship even among the very young, and parents avoid interference because they ascribe an essential goodness to natural impulses of affection and sexuality: they "*respect the innocent will in all things*" and are "fully sensible of the dangers arising from the suppression of the natural fires" (44). When the Sophians ask Lycas about the outside world, they sicken at his description of Turkish marriage customs, especially at the thought of "tyrants" who choose partners for their children (67). As so often in the mild feminism of eighteenth-century Britain, the bald subjugation of the harem provides a negative foil for a less restrictive valorization of female character.[40] Quickly converted to the Sophian method of courtship, Lycas looks forward to an informal marriage with his Sophian paramour, "if constant attention, tender regard, and everlasting love, could bind her" (67, 71). Thus the novel formulates a utopian ideal of companionate marriage as a liberating confinement, a less coercive bond than a legalistic marriage.

When Lycas concludes his utopian narration, the text turns to the possibility of spreading Sophian enlightenment throughout the surrounding world of tyranny and depravity. After leaving Sophis from despair over his lover's death, Lycas plans "to go out a missionary to mankind, to spread, if possible, the noble customs of this select nation among my fellow creatures" (90). Initially this project of cultural colonialism targets black Africans, who seem, in this novel, most in need of its offerings. Lycas achieves some moderate success until he reaches Sennaar, where "in proportion as I succeeded with the people, I excited the jealousy of their cruel rulers. Liberty, justice, and humanity were here almost unknown. . . . No sooner were my principles understood, than my liberty was in danger" (91). The selfish tyranny of Sennaar's rulers marks not only the diametrical opposite of the self-regulating freedom of Sophis, but also the limits of Sophian colonialism.

But if political colonialism fails in the novel's first part, it suggests that personal transformations are more successful and significant than social ones, and this contrast in itself illustrates the Sophian doctrine of liberation through limitation. Two personal transformations form the basis of the complex narrative structure of the first part, as Lycas's account of the Sophian utopia and his own transformation forms the key component of a wider effort to accustom his pupil to the practice of Sophian wisdom. With the prison providing an ideal setting for teaching the paradox of liberation through confinement, Memmo must learn to accept his bounded situation, to achieve as much as he can within its limitations, and even to resist the urge to escape. Cumberland provides some rather implausible details of the productive and comfortable life attained by the prisoners in their "spacious" and "elegantly furnished" apartment (7), their time filled with drawing, music, physical fitness, philosophy, and philanthropy. Despite his confinement, Lycas remains "at the station of humanity" by spending much of his time at a window overlooking a dangerous rock in the current of a well-traveled river. As he explains to Memmo, he had suffered heavy despair following his first imprisonment, but after witnessing the fatal wreck of a riverboat on the hidden rock, he had devoted himself to warning subsequent travelers to avoid it, finding in this service "some compensation for perpetual confinement" (10). This highly implausible example is meant to suggest not only that there are worse fates than confinement, but also that philanthropic as well as personal discipline can overcome personal oppression.

The novel documents Memmo's psychological education in such discipline during the progress of Lycas's utopian narrative. At first the pupil struggles to emulate his mentor's resignation to confinement, admitting his fear that "it will be long before I shall possess sufficient resignation to keep me from admitting, into my mind, flattering dreams of escape" (33). But the plot soon rectifies his doubts by giving him proof of the dangers entailed by the desire for liberty. From their prison window they see "a poor fellow-prisoner," who had attempted to climb down a rope from his window, but cut his rope too short, and thus hung suspended, "nearly exhausted, and ready to drop into a deep and watery hole" (59). After rescuing the prisoner, they interpret his dangling situation as an allegorical tableau teaching the lesson that "imprudence may augment even the miseries of captivity for life" (60). A further lesson in the same doctrine occurs when Memmo reveals an inclination to accept his gaoler's offer of escape. In response, Lycas asks indignantly, "have I, in imagination, conveyed you to *Sophis* only to see you return to this ignoble selfishness?—Freedom is, doubtless, inestimably, *immeasurably sweet*, but, in base society, there is no true liberty" (60). Against a selfish desire for personal liberty, Lycas opposes the Sophian doctrine of resignation, here posited as an imaginative journey to the isolated utopian land itself. He quickly clarifies the nature of his objection by pointing out that their pursuit of physical liberty will entail the imprisonment of another, their gaoler (60). Such wisdom in itself can immediately suppress Memmo's desire for physical freedom, as he explains: "the magnanimous sentiment exalted my soul, and seemed thereby to have softened my captivity" (60). True liberation results from the moral discipline of resignation to adversity, illustrated here through a refusal to harm others in escaping adversity.

With such incidents framing the utopian narrative, the first part of Cumberland's novel documents both a successful personal conversion to Sophian enlightenment and the failure of broader attempts at cultural conversion in the face of Sennaar, a defining instance of political tyranny. Part two offers a second vision of personal enlightenment, this time through Memmo's journey to the Christian utopia of Jovinia. After the death of Lycas and a rebellion in Sennaar, Memmo escapes and decides to search for the Sophians. But his path takes him to Jovinia, whose Christian version of the doctrine of liberation through confinement seems to offer a more powerful, if still limited, model of social transformation. Cumberland's second utopian vision flirts with the possibility of an enlightened, Christian colonialism expanding from the heart of African tyranny, but ultimately the novel retreats to a more moderate transformation, one operating within the limits imposed by a seemingly inevitable tyranny afflicting both Europe and Africa.

After Memmo's escape from Sennaar, his subsequent experiences return to the personal dialectic of liberty and subjugation, power and dependence, that marks his autobiography in the original frame narrative. With the support of a loyal native slave, he indulges himself in a leisurely idyll, sauntering about an Africa that seems temporarily free of governmental intrusions and blessed with enormously satisfying material comforts. But confinement quickly ends this idyll as the traveler undergoes a series of captivities, first through his ineptitude at handling Africa, when he traps himself in a cave, and then through the stereotypical problems of African government, when he is captured by a native tribe. After destroying Memmo's idyll of personal liberation, his abject captivity among a stereotypically depraved African people provides the narrative prelude for his social accommodation with a liberated utopian people. As captive to a petty king, Memmo finds himself "stripped, and dressed in the costume of his servants," and forced to "fatiguing and laborious employment" (121). The novel exacerbates this vision of captive abjection through a stereotypical description of the captive-taking people: "fierce, warlike, cruel, and superstitious, dirty in their habits, rude in their manners, overreaching and treacherous" (126). Nevertheless, Memmo reconciles himself to his abject condition with the thought that even if he escaped from this people back to Sennaar, "a second captivity less salubrious than this . . . might have lasted to the end of my days" (121). The overarching threat of more terrible captivities constantly haunts this section of the novel, especially when Memmo's new owner mentions an even more terrifyingly cruel and despotic people whose rapacity threatens even the first utopia's nadir of despotism, Sennaar itself. Safe in a moderate captivity from the threat of more terrible captivities, Memmo abandons his African wanderings. At this point in the novel, just as the threat of absolutely despotic Africans establishes the limits of personal freedom, Memmo learns of the utopian Jovinians in a manner that serves to crystallize the dichotomy between the two peoples. He learns of the two peoples at nearly the same time and from the same person, his captor. The increasing enlightenment and kindness of this captor, moreover, means an increase in social integration for the isolated, exiled captive, especially when he is permitted to join the Jovinians. Captivity under a moderate African patriarch not only provides a refuge from dangerous extremes of despotism and personal autonomy, but also initiates the final stage in the protagonist's transformation into a utopian subjectivity of moderation.

As in Berington's novel, the protagonist's personal experience of liberation through captivity parallels the utopians' historical experience and geographical position as a captive people. In this case, however, the experience of collective captivity and escape initially emerges through European rather than Oriental tyranny, as Memmo soon learns after reaching Jovinia. This ideal polity originated as an "oppressed" Christian sect, who followed the teachings of a heretical Italian monk, Jovinian, and whose flight to Africa permitted their enrollment as God's "servants," in "an independent church" (164). After the monk leads his followers south, they find a refuge "Shut up on one of the highest plains of these mountains," surrounded by a "wild and rocky . . . barren region" (124, 136). According to the paradoxical logic of utopian geography, this "sterile barrier" becomes a "happy circumstance which has determined our settlements, and has afforded us that protection from the dark nations" (136, 139). Once again the fantastic possibilities of an imagined Africa permit a geography of confinement, sanctuary, and voluntary withdrawal from what seems the region's defining political and cultural regimen. If temperate Europe provides the initial site of Jovinian persecution, the extremes of Africa permit starker definitions of political depravity, political sanctuary, and political potential.

The Jovinians imagine their geopolitical confinement in specifically Christian terms of subjugation, depravity, and cultural perfection. As they explain, "we are crucified to the world and the world to us" (152), subjugated in their isolation from the larger world but thereby saved from its depravity. Geographical isolation in the midst of pagans not only recalls the myth of Prester John but further supports an ideal of Christian discipline as a withdrawal from the sins of the world. In the midst of "idolatrous and cruel nations," surrounded by "corruptions," the Jovinians yet manage to preserve "the wholesome discipline of our religion and language in equal purity" (174, 237). Christian discipline also suffuses this utopia's variation on the ideal social balance between freedom and subjugation. In this case political freedom results from "a genuine republic founded on Christian principles, freedom of conscience, and equal rights, the imprescriptible privilege of man" (176). Despite this emphasis on freedom, subjugation to the divine will enforces a system of self-regulation that keeps citizens in their places: "All are capable of perceiving their general duties and believing in a ruling power, and obeying his laws; but it is only given to a few to combine these feelings with the talents necessary to direct and govern for the general good" (232). At first somewhat skeptical, Memmo soon learns to accept the paradox that serves as a motto for this utopia: "here the service of God and man might with truth be said to be perfect freedom" (236). As in Berington's novel, Cumberland's formulations of utopian freedom rely heavily on a language of regulation, limitation, and confinement.

Memmo resolves this ostensible conflict by recognizing that the Jovinian social system relies on individually internalized precepts of self-regulation. Even more than the Mezzorain and Sophian utopias, this one constitutes "a system of self-denial," celebrating "Temperance" and "sobriety of manners" as resignation to the divine will (149, 152). Jovinian freedom results from a regulation of the passions because they impose a tyranny on the will. Once again a concrete example emerges with courtship, as the utopians believe that greater freedom results from rapidly arranged marriages than from extended courtship, because "we know the force of the passions, and endeavour to restrain their power by shortening the duration of their tyranny" (216). The self-regulation that enables such freedom encompasses not only sexual desire but also social decorum and material production: "Excess in all things was positively prohibited," and "temperance" was "universally adopted" as the "main spring" of social happiness (155, 236). As expressed in the Jovinian utopia and in Memmo's personal progress, civilization involves an internal-

ized system of spiritual and social regulation, a personal accommodation with
material limitation.

The Jovinian utopia provides an alternative model for British society not
only in its inward structure but also in its outward intercourse with other
societies. Whereas utopian narratives generally stress the enclosure and withdrawal of the ideal society from surrounding corruptions, the second part of
Cumberland's narrative, written on the cusp of British imperialism, combines this stress with an emphasis on specific methods for exporting the utopian ideal. Not only do the Jovinians serve as a model for a Christian variety
of colonialism, but colonialism seems fundamental to the origins and organization of the ideal state. Looking back at the utopia's infancy, one Jovinian
leader labels it a "colony" (167). Another connects the outlines of their social
structure and the effects of their material prosperity to a seemingly natural
process of colonial growth: "colonists are sent from all overpeopled districts,
and a new community is soon formed, resembling the works of certain in-
sects, from parents, to families, to colonies. Such is the general outline of our
civil polity" (210). Besides this internal expansion within the utopian enclosure, the Jovinians feel a call for an external expansion directed at the surrounding African peoples and built on the twinned goals of "civilization, and
conversion" (154). Within the text's framework of captivities, this Jovinian
project finds its justification and its concrete formulation as a divinely ordained reversal of their national captivity. As the utopians explain, "we hold
an opinion that we are reserved and placed in this sanctuary, with a commis-
sion to spread the genuine doctrines of our religion among the benighted
men that surround us" (143). The generic isolation of utopian geography
comes to stand, within Cumberland's rendering, as a sign of the necessarily
captive and necessarily colonial nature of the ideal state.

Much of the Jovinian plan reflects British plans for Africa at the end of
the century, building on widespread arguments concerning abolition, savagery, Africa, and the responsibilities of enlightened, Christian Europe. Imagining their project as quiescent improvement rather than aggressive
exploitation, the Jovinians plan to build a "Propaganda-College" in order to
train "armies, not of soldiers, but of martyrs" (165). In their plans for improvement, as in those of Peter Wilkins, capitalism appears as an enlightened substitute for native systems of despotism. Through a "liberal diffusion
of our superfluous products," the Jovinians hope to convince their neighbors
"to cultivate the earth" instead of pursuing "gold-dust and slaves" (153). Like
many abolitionist plans for the aftermath of the slave trade, Jovinian colonialism appears as a solution for what were described as inevitable native
tendencies towards tyranny and disorder. The utopians quickly succeed in

their first colonial project, which concerns the small tribe of Memmo's old master, the semi-enlightened Foozoo. Although Christian agency occupies the leading place within the novel's vision of colonial progress, it also suggests that enlightenment can draw from many cultures in a mutually beneficial synthesis. Thus Foozoo emerges as the novel's most vociferous critic of European slavery: "I abhor the trade, which is connected with every atrocity; my family slaves constitute my support, and I provide for theirs. . . . But report says you Europeans tear them from their relations to work them like cattle, give them no instruction as to moral conduct or religion, abuse their females and make drudges of their mixed breed" (251). Jovinian guidance augments his progress in enlightened despotism, helping him to repress the local aristocracy, and convincing him to take the role of benevolent "president" rather than rapacious autocrat (246). While this reformed African autocrat strives to conciliate the Christian colonists, they retain their cultural insularity within a special enclosure, "guarded from all intrusions from the ignorant natives" (245). Much in the manner of British missionaries, the Jovinian colonists guide the natives but remain separate, retaining the insularity that marks their geography and their history, representing a utopian fulfillment of British colonialism.

When Memmo decides to transplant the Jovinian model of confined colonialism to his European home, this decision provides a climax for the progress in personal enlightenment that began with his liberating experience of African captivities. His conversion to the Jovinian principle of liberty through self-denial is so complete that it forces him, in yet another paradox, to leave this land of liberty and to return to a life of seeming captivity as a European reformer. He anticipates his role as reformer in terms that parallel the national position of the captive yet colonial utopia, as he plans to "make the cloister my home—from whence to send abroad my systems of reform" (238–39). Whereas a captivity narrative normally projects the return to Europe as a return to freedom, Memmo's return is a journey from utopian liberation to a world saturated with tyranny. After leaving Jovinia, he must first pass through Darfur, a land dominated by "selfish merchants, slave dealers, and an arbitrary government," and then through Egypt, ruled by "a despotism the most coercive" (249, 260). Even when crossing the Mediterranean from Africa to Europe, he must fend off the machinations of an Italian corsair.

The presence of an Italian rather than an African corsair marks the first instance within a broader pattern of reversal that transforms Renaissance Italy into the text's final scene of despotism and reform, one that serves to shift the aim of Cumberland's social criticism closer to home. Whereas Africa revealed occasional instances of isolated enlightenment amidst widespread despotism, Italy seems at first a land of unrestrained tyranny, especially when the encounter with the corsair leads Memmo to a broad indictment of "European government! And in what is it better on the seas, than in an Indian forest among savages? And Venice? Venice my birth place, the pride of Italy, the Mistress of the Adriatic, the polished corner of the temple of politeness—in what is she better? A depraved moral government . . . the paradise of priests and tyrants, where the multitude are sacrificed to the few—a republic in name, but a despotism in reality . . . a community of slaves and tyrants, mutually detesting and detested" (263). Just as the Italian corsair supplants African figures of predation within the novel's character structure, European savagery comes to supplant non-European savagery as the novel's final political target.

In order to accomplish reform within the overarching tyranny of Italy, Memmo must imitate the captive, colonial, and Christian methods of the Jovinians. After achieving personal liberation through his successive captivities in Africa, he experiences his European homeland as a captivity entailed by the difficulties of reform. The threat of "a solitary cell in the Inquisition" constantly hounds him during his plans for reform and ultimately forces him to abandon Venice for a family estate in a remote rural district (267). Perched high among some remote mountains near the Swiss border, the estate becomes a miniature version of the Jovinians' captive utopia, a confined but liberated sanctuary from the threat of imprisonment under a political despotism that seems to pervade the larger social realm. His worldly Venetian friends imagine the estate a confinement, but Memmo, on his first night there, "tasted freedom and repose, and dreamed of the innocent and affectionate *Jovinians*" (276). As Memmo's dream intimates, he follows a parallel course with the Jovinians, voluntarily a captive through his refusal to form an accommodation with the tyranny of European society.

In his recreation of the Jovinian ideal, Memmo introduces new levels of social liberty to his familial dependents while retaining authority as an Old Testament patriarch, enlightened autocrat, and colonial planner. In order to render his fulfillment of the patriarchal ideal more concrete, the text suddenly reveals that his reforms follow the precedent of his grandfather; as Memmo speculates, "I suppose I was born to carry on his plans of emancipating the minds of all around him" (279). This simultaneous fulfillment of his birthright and of Jovinian ideals entails some loosening of the estate's social hierarchy, but the novel generally formulates Memmo's utopian production of liberty as an autocratic imposition of reform through patriarchal channels. He asks his dependents to treat him as a father, and he installs a Jovinian system of discipline, what he calls a "grand scheme, of subjecting all my tenants to a system of pure morality" (290). This mini-utopia resembles the Jovinian even in the colonial ambitions consequent on its captive situation. As Memmo assesses the situation, "all we have to fear is the envy of our neighbouring states—to repress whose jealousy we seek every occasion of serving them, thereby hoping to enlarge our boundaries, and soften the line of partition, by converting them to our institutions" (296). The Jovinian model for colonizing Africa now clearly serves as a model for colonizing Europe with political reform.

In imagining an African cultural colonization of Europe, Cumberland introduces yet another political paradox to be resolved at the level of personal psychology and face-to-face relationships, just like the paradox of an African utopia or the paradox of a utopian captivity narrative. The personal resolution needed for these paradoxes becomes clearest with the novel's closing assessment of Memmo's life, his African experience, and his work as a reformer. After settling in Italy, the narrator decides that his life story, punctuated especially by his experiences in Africa, provides, "however slightly, a foundation on which to build by degrees a reform" (247). Confining social change to the moderate levels of psychological transformation and personal contact, Memmo comes to regard his life as a powerful instance of liberation through confinement, with his various political captivities leading to a necessary personal reform, a positive suppression of youthful passion that enables adulthood liberation and assumption of responsibilities. Under the influence of the Jovinians, the adult narrator assesses his captivities as fitting punishment for the youthful passion that had led him to disobey his parents: "What intemperance, what follies had I not committed, through giving way to excitement, and self will?" (260). After his return to Italy, a like-minded reformer soothes the protagonist's anxieties by inviting him to compare his current situation with the role he would have played if he had followed the dictates of his father: "you would now probably have been a Senator sworn to promote the objects of a remorseless and intriguing government, chained to a misalliance," but instead "your passions repressed flung you violently out of a vortex of crime by their own eccentricity, and the Castle of *Sennaar* by its coercion restored their equilibrium" (294). Even the central captivity of the title, within a land posited as the heart of despotism, now stands as an instance of the psychological reform that lays the groundwork for political reform.

In their structural movement from personal confinement to utopian liberation and then back to moderate accommodation, the two parts of Cumberland's narrative repeat the pattern of Berington's while accelerating the radical drive of its juxtapositions and paradoxes. *The Captive of Sennaar* likewise begins with a focus on problems of personal captivity and liberation before reframing those problems in terms of what ultimately emerge as more significant questions of social freedom, organization, and interaction. Much more fully than in Berington, however, the social resolution of these questions within a utopian setting depends on an analysis of personal psychology and personal reform, especially as Cumberland formulates the recurring problem of captivity as one of learning to subordinate personal desires to questions of social cohesion. The novel's explicit concern with social cohesion, moreover, extends from the ideally confined and integrated polity of utopia to the problems of interaction between polities, problems that are imagined here in specifically colonial terms. Within this novel, envisioning an African colonization of Europe enacts both a general critique of European polities and a specific critique of European abuses in Africa. By imagining such a colony, Cumberland flouts not only the standard opposition between European enlightenment and African savagery, but further the opposition between European cultural agency and African receptivity. This conclusion amplifies the radical critique implicit in his predecessors' vision of cultural contact, broadening their paradoxical vision of African transculturation from the level of an individual protagonist to the level of European society.

In the utopian novels of Paltock, Berington, and Cumberland, cultural interaction in the contact zone begins according to a common narrative structure but then diverges according to varying political agendas. Each novel's first vision of cultural contact involves a captivity. From the personal perspective of the protagonist, the opening framework of captivity creates a mood of abjection as a contrasting prelude for the joy of utopian discovery. At the same time, the captivity framework serves to define the protagonist as an absolute subject, punished for excessive self-will, cut off from society, and opposed to an absolutist government. In each novel the stark opening captivity provides the starting point for an extended dialectic of subjugation and liberation, mastery and dependence. A synthesis for each dialectic results through the utopian society's paradoxical mediations of the absolute poles of liberty and subjugation, especially through internalized precepts of self-regulation, societal accommodation, and patriarchal deference. Even the spectacularly masterful Wilkins constantly remembers his paradoxical dependence on an African mentor, met in captivity, while the utopian educations of di Lucca and Memmo rest firmly on the paradox of social liberation through self-regulation.

The three novels diverge in their visions of the process of utopian creation. In a fantastic fulfillment of colonial ideology, Paltock celebrates an

Englishman's personal creation of an ideal state in an alien land, and this fantastic creativity seems to depend on the master's consciousness of what it means to be subordinate, on his adherence to the kind of principles, such as opposition to slavery, that seem best taught by an experience of captivity. For Paltock an ideal master seems to guarantee an ideal state, and the ideal state is fundamentally colonial in nature. On the other hand, Berington takes a more traveled route within the utopian tradition, envisioning the utopian state as a distant, unreachable ideal, fundamentally alien to European institutions and practicable only at the personal level. Thus his novel closes with the protagonist unhappily separated from his adoptive people, still practicing their principles on his own, but seemingly incapable of recreating them at the societal level. For this protagonist, moreover, utopian ideals forbid participation in empire. Although for Cumberland utopia seems a similarly distant prospect, his vision of an Italian patriarch enlightened through experiences in African captivity suggests, on a much smaller scale than Paltock's, that a master conscious of the experience of dependence can recreate his own utopia of self-regulating freedom. While Berington largely ignores colonial issues, Paltock and Cumberland develop the two most complex experiments with the colonist-as-captive figure in eighteenth-century fiction. Both authors transform the captive into a utopian colonist. Whereas a series of captivities marks the progress of Paltock's colonist in the twinned ideals of economic prowess and resistance to slavery, Cumberland identifies the limitations of captivity with the very practice of utopian reform. As these two novels reveal in a particularly telling manner, the figure of the captive offered eighteenth-century Britons opportunities for imaginative exploration of the cultural consequences, moral implications, and final destiny of the colonial project.

Conclusion

In 1759 Samuel Johnson's *Rasselas* revisited the same fantastic geography explored by Berington twenty years earlier and revisited once again by Cumberland at century's end. But Johnson's plot, characters, and agenda ran almost directly counter to those of his utopian predecessor and successor. The most obvious contrasts were, first, Johnson's creation of an African dystopia rather than an African utopia, and, second, his choice of Abyssinian rather than European protagonists. Although his evocation of setting partially reflected his research into the European literature describing Abyssinia and Egypt, his handling of the material involved so many echoes and reversals of Berington's narrative as to suggest that the older work had provoked a direct response.[1] Berington's utopia, with its intricate mixture of captivity and freedom, would have offered both attractions and problems for a civic humanist such as Johnson. He might have admired Berington's treatment of confinement as a metonym for the "human" requirements of personal discipline and personal acceptance of limitations. But Johnson would have found unpalatable the suggestion of human perfectibility implied by utopia. And he would also have found unpalatable Berington's use of an Oriental captivity plot, with its attendant visions of individualistic liberation, absolute government, and stark cultural oppositions. In fashioning similar narrative materials, Johnson developed a plot that not only undermined Berington's vision of captive utopia but also throttled the drive for individual liberation so important to earlier captivity fictions, especially the enormously popular *Robert Boyle*. In *Rasselas* we find a conservative, humanist response to the liberal individualism and cultural antagonism of the captivity plot, and thus a brief discussion of Johnson's work offers a suitable route for beginning a reassessment of the British captivity tradition as a whole.

Johnson's dystopia resembles Berington's utopia in several ways. First, in Johnson's Happy Valley, the ostensibly paradisiacal abode of Rasselas and other royal children, we find a more extreme version of Berington's isolated geography. Johnson's valley is "surrounded on every side by mountains, of which the summits overhang the middle part"; the only entrance is a constantly guarded cavern "closed with gates of iron."[2] More direct echoes turn up when he describes those outside the enclosure as "slaves of misery," living in "regions of calamity, where discord was always raging, and where man preyed upon man" (11–12). In describing the blissful life inside the enclosure, Johnson retains Berington's emphasis on paradox, but the trope now works to support a dystopian rather than a utopian vision. On the positive side, the inhabitants enjoy a "blissful captivity" in their "prison of pleasure"; outsiders wishing to join them are called "competitors for imprisonment" (10, 164). On the negative side, two chapter titles refer to "The discontent of Rasselas in the Happy Valley" and "The wants of him that wants nothing" (11, 14). And as Imlac declares of the valley's immigrants, "They envy the liberty which their folly has forfeited, and would gladly see all mankind imprisoned like themselves" (55). Thus the most enduring paradoxes concerning the Happy Valley treat it a symbol of one of Johnson's favorite themes, the dissatisfaction that inevitably follows satisfied wishes. As Rasselas comes to recognize, the valley is ultimately a "fatal obstacle that hinders at once the enjoyment of pleasure, and the exercise of virtue" (18). Once he discovers that free choice and the possibility of misfortune are necessary for human happiness, he comes to view the valley as a prison and begins searching for an escape route. The notion that an enclosed utopia would restrict the conversational benefits and moral complexities of social life is a clear rejection of the utopian tradition as a whole, but Johnson's paradoxical Abyssinian setting points to the more specific target of Berington's African utopia.

By placing his utopian prison at the opening of his tale, Johnson partially recapitulates Berington's narrative structure and partially reverses its import. Each plot opens with its protagonist trapped by confining institutions, and each juxtaposes this initial captivity against his later discovery of a personal ethic based on tempering liberty with limitation. But the similarities in plot structure end there. Whereas di Lucca's Oriental captivity precedes and even enables his utopian discovery, Johnson reverses that sequence by beginning with utopia, then turning to escape, and finally introducing an Oriental captivity plot near his close. Furthermore, whereas Berington's novel moves from Europe to Egypt and then down the Nile to a land whose geography seems Abyssinian, Johnson begins in Abyssinia before moving to a fuller exploration of the Orient. The interpolated autobiography told by Rasselas's mentor, Imlac, allows for a brief itinerary of Middle Eastern lands before Rasselas and his friends settle down for an extended exploration of the varied social possibilities of the Nile valley. But the final and most important contrast between Berington's and Johnson's plot structures relates to their protagonists' political progressions. Whereas di Lucca moves from absolute captivity to utopian liberty-in-confinement, Rasselas moves from a false liberty-in-confinement to a sort of confinement-in-liberty, an apparently unlimited geographical exploration undercut by the limits of human psychology. Di Lucca moves from captivity to liberty through the vehicle of an idealized polity, based on a social enforcement of limitation on radically individuated subjects. Conversely, Rasselas moves from captivity to liberty by escaping a falsely idealized polity, and throughout the text Imlac enforces the Johnsonian dictum that no political institution can achieve perfection, while the best bet for human happiness involves individual recognition of human limitations. Although both authors stress the need to limit self-assertion, Berington does so by creating a perfected social model for personal transformation, while Johnson's skepticism about the possibilities of complete social and personal transformation lead him to reapply Berington's ethic through a reversed plot structure, one that stresses constant striving for individual improvement.

Johnson's echoes and reversals of the Oriental captivity tradition are not limited to its earliest utopian exemplar. *Rasselas* also echoes the rationalist and individualist escape routines that are central to the Oriental captivity tradition as a whole. As Johnson devotes two entire chapters to Rasselas's attempt to escape the Happy Valley, the protagonist becomes something of an Abyssinian Robert Boyle, spending "week after week" searching for an aperture, receiving Imlac's guidance in cultivating "perserverance," and finally fixing a plan based on observation of animal behavior (21, 58). By assigning the heroic rationalism of escape to Abyssinian characters, Johnson undermines the standard British association of such behaviors, in such latitudes, with European characters. Rasselas's rationalist escape thus initiates a narrative pattern that will continue after the journey to Egypt, as the text includes some local echoes of Orientalism's stereotypes while working more broadly to undermine its totalizing generalities. In Egypt Rasselas meets some merchants who suffer fear of local tyrants, and his respect for the Bassa ends with some typically Orientalist revolutions in government: surrounded by "plots and detections, strategems and escapes, faction and treachery," the

Bassa ends up in chains, before his successor is likewise deposed when the Turkish Janissaries murder their Sultan (91). But Johnson employs such examples to illustrate the instabilities of human rather than Oriental life; he loosens the Orientalist bent of these examples by developing prominent counterexamples and a globe-ranging social analysis that ultimately work to undercut standard European oppositions between Orient and Occident. As Imlac declares, "Oppression is, in the Abyssinian dominions, neither frequent nor tolerated; but no form of government has been yet discovered by which cruelty can be wholly prevented" (32). For Johnson, the faults of Abyssinian government are human faults, not Oriental ones. Even more tellingly, Imlac's youthful journey through the lands of the East reveals varied dispositions among different peoples, and his famous analysis of European technological success works to undermine European triumphalism: "The Europeans . . . are less unhappy than we, but they are not happy. Human life is everywhere a state in which much is to be endured, and little to be enjoyed" (50). Johnson's humanism may have retained Orientalist stereotypes when it found them locally useful, but his global definition of humanity required some resistance to narrative patterns celebrating British nationalism.

This partial retention of Orientalist motifs in order to undermine them is also typical of what stands as the tale's only true captivity episode, that of Pekuah's kidnapping by an Arab raider. In its digression from the tale's main themes, the episode has always somewhat mystified literary critics, although it rather clearly participates in the tale's development of a mild form of antiromance. This role becomes especially clear when we consider how the episode resists the narrative patterns of earlier captivity fictions. On first hearing of Pekuah's kidnapping, the sanguine Rasselas, like a romance hero or one of Chetwood's protagonists, wants to ride off to her rescue, but Imlac soon determines an alternative course of action, based not on aggressive plans for rescue, but rather on prudent negotiations for ransom. The episode further reverses the customary patterns of captivity romance after Pekuah recollects her experiences in confinement. Immediately after capture, she recalls, she feared the effects of "perpetual confinement" and any passing "caprice of cruelty," but she quickly found her captor "far from illiterate," knowledgeable of the "rules of civil life," and willing to make her the "sovereign" of his camp (132–37). Although he keeps a harem, this most Orientalist of motifs provides little occasion for titillation but rather enables Johnson's protagonists to pity both the ignorance of the women confined there and the ennui of the master exposed only to such women. Hints of his sexual interest in the educated Pekuah occur in highly chivalric terms before finally vanishing with some anticlimactic negotiations for her release: "The Arab, according to the custom of his nation, observed the laws of hospitality with great exactness" and "restored her with great respect to liberty" (131). Pekuah recalls her captivity as moderately civil, even enlightening, but finally overlong and even dull, certainly a far cry from the captivities of Aubin's heroines. Ultimately Johnson's treatment of this episode rejects the standard plotting of Oriental captivity, with its customary expression of radical self-assertion, and replaces it with a narrative of negotiation and compromise.

Another important departure from the common run of captivity plotting comes in Johnson's choice of an Arab captor, since there was no European tradition of factual texts or fictional episodes exploring extensive captivities among the desert Bedouins. The choice of a Bedouin captor was central to Johnson's purpose in the Pekuah episode, bringing the theme of liberty to the fore. Eighteenth-century travel literature tended to associate the Bedouins with the freedom of a wandering life and to oppose them to the allegedly degraded empire of the Ottoman Turks. Johnson plays on these associations by making the Arab an exponent of liberty. Although Pekuah attributes his depredations to greed, she also quotes his own explanation for his actions. He identifies his goals with libertarian politics, describing his people as "the natural and hereditary lords of this part of the continent, which is usurped by late [Turkish] invaders, and low-born tyrants, from whom we are compelled to take by the sword what is denied to justice" (134). As liberty and civility overstrike false expectations of cruelty and lust, the Arab acts as a repudiation of the stereotypical Orientals of earlier captivity fictions.

Pekuah's captivity episode is immediately followed by one that scholars usually have a much easier time explaining: the episode of the astronomer, whose excessive observation of the skies leads him to the notion that he controls the weather, illustrating the danger of indulging the imagination. The effect of closely juxtaposing the two episodes is to replace what Johnson regarded as a less significant kind of captivity with what he regarded as a more significant kind, at least with respect to the moral education of his eighteenth-century readers. For a civic humanist such as Johnson, a plot based on captivity by another culture was an inflated myth, the stuff of romance and escape fiction; for a civic humanist intent on educating a domestic audience, the greatest threat of captivity came from the weakness of the human mind. Johnson fills his tale with expressions such as "tyranny of reflection" (66), exploring humanist psychology in terms of liberation and subjugation, and these expressions become most pronounced and most dense in the episode of the astronomer. Under the force of the astronomer's example, Imlac insists that "airy notions" can "tyrannize" anyone's mind and that the "reign of fancy" can easily grow "imperious, and in time despotic" (150–52). Compelled by this example, Pekuah and Rasselas confess and reject visionary schemes for self-aggrandizement. Thus the astronomer provides the text's climactic, most telling example of humanist psychology and moral education, and the immediate precedent of the anticlimactic episode of Oriental captivity acts both as a false lead and an ironic counterpoint to the true climax. In sum, an ironic retelling of a plot that normally entails radical self-assertion acts as a prelude for a plot illustrating the dangers of radical self-assertion.

Like the utopian narratives of Berington and Cumberland, Johnson's captivity episodes are intellectual revisions of a popular narrative form, attempts to probe philosophical questions and to educate a leisured audience by complicating a plot structure that must have seemed quite familiar to British readers by the middle of the eighteenth century. As a form that reached many middle- and upper-class readers in its own day and fired the imaginations of intellectuals, the captivity narrative now sits at the edges of our own canon of eighteenth-century British literature. Fairly extensive episodes of American captivity turn up in minor novels by minor authors such as Charlotte Lennox, Henry Mackenzie, and Charlotte Smith, but the most famous such episode is the very brief and very unusual one in Smollet's most famous novel. The captivity narrative also occupies a small place in the Defoe canon. The genre inspired minor incidents in *Robinson Crusoe* and *Captain Singleton,* provoked a controversy over the authorship of a major text, *Madagascar,* and finally provided a source, in Knox's *Ceylon,* that Defoe retold once and may have imitated more extensively throughout his fictions. But if the captivity narrative is somewhat marginal to our own literary canon of the British eighteenth century, the genre inspired several eighteenth-century best-sellers that have disappeared from our reading lists: Chetwood's *Robert Boyle,* most notably, but also Berington's utopia and the bulk of Aubin's fiction. Although the captivity narrative occupies a securer place in the American literary canon, especially as determined by the Rowlandson text, that canon has ignored a number of later best-sellers, most notably cross-Atlantic sensations such as the accounts of Jonathan Dickinson and Peter Williamson, as well as nineteenth-century transculturation narratives such as Mary Jemison's. The captivity narrative thus occupies an important though not fully appreciated place in the Anglo-American tradition of publishing for popular audiences.

Stories of protagonists held captive by powerful others are, of course, important in many cultures, and they remain a potent force in late twentieth-century film. As the cinema clearly demonstrates, the plot of an unjustly subjugated rebel who single-handedly overcomes a tyrannical system remains one of Western culture's most cherished myths. Narratives of heroic endurance and escape quite simply saturate the films that Hollywood dispenses to much of the planet. Heroes from Rambo to Tank Girl resist elaborate forms of imprisonment, graphically detailed tortures, and tyrannical systems of oppression in the most thinly veiled allegories of freedom. Moreover, films such as *Gunga Din* and its nostalgic reenactment *Indiana Jones and the Temple of Doom* show that the Western narrative of resisting captivity can still serve both as an allegory of freedom and as a displacement of colonial agency, one that portrays Western adventurers as liberators rescuing native peoples from their own systems of oppression. The latter film, particularly, in its nostalgic zeal for recapturing the essence of colonial material, reaches gothic extremes in its elaboration of a plot focused on motifs of exotic captivity. Not only does it follow its predecessor in celebrating active Western heroes who rescue an innocent yet passive Indian population from an ancient cult devoted to murder, but in this case the cult's favorite mode of execution involves a cage that immobilizes the body in the shape of crucifixion before lowering it into a fiery pit. In this captivity narrative as in Chetwood's *Robert Boyle,* the allegory of freedom is an allegory of Western freedom, posed as a modern innovation that triumphs over the allegedly slavish and oppressive dispositions of primitive, non-Western peoples. The colonial history of the captivity plot is still very much with us.

The modern captivity narrative's significance for literary history lies especially in its transformation of what was, at bottom, a very ancient and widespread pattern of storytelling. Stories of capture, subjugation, and escape are fundamental to much of the world's traditions of myth and folklore. A series of captivities marks the journey of Odysseus, for example: not only is he captured by monsters and witches, but Penelope endures an extended captivity in her own home. In cultures from the Mediterranean to Africa and America and Oceania, the hero's archetypal journey and his status as culture bringer often depend on captivity, whether he is confined in an underworld, an otherworld, or a land of the dead. Sometimes a hero must rescue his wife from captivity, as do Odysseus and Tiny Flower, the hero of a Tewa (Native American) folktale; sometimes a heroine rescues herself, as does Yombo in some versions of a Mende (African) tale.[3] But although the folkloric motif of captivity shares some superficial similarities in plotting with the early modern genre of the captivity narrative, the intellectual and social significance attached to the captivity experience differs greatly in the two contexts.

Both the mythic and the modern versions of captivity associate it with an increase in knowledge. But whereas mythic narrative links captivity to sacred knowledge, the modern captivity narrative transforms the captive into a bringer of mundane knowledge, rendered through the scientific schema of travel description. In a pattern typical of mythic captivity, Tiny Flower's wife is held by a thunder god, and her name, White Corn, indicates that her captivity and escape represent the seasonal return of thunder, rain, and the planting cycle. Yombo, on the other hand, like many another culture bringer, steals technological powers from the otherworldly spirit who confines her. According to the ethnographic rhetoric of the early modern captivity narrative, however, a captive can return with few cultural gifts from an alien, inferior, captive-taking culture. The captive's primary acquisition is knowledge, but of a kind very much unlike the cultural know-how obtained by Yombo. Whereas a culture bringer obtains the technological knowledge that enables the community to work, an early modern captive obtains a knowledge that promotes the individual reader's interest in the Western state. Perhaps the former captive's knowledge can demonstrate the horrors of life under a foreign government, lacking liberty, perhaps it can buttress comparisons favoring the material benefits of Western civilization, or perhaps it can contribute to colonial exploitation of an alien people's strengths and weaknesses. Whatever the specific rhetorical application of the captive's knowledge, the widespread reliance on scientific schema such as lists, standard headings, and the plain style ultimately makes the captive's knowledge-gathering seem an ordinary kind of skill, practicable by any Westerner who falls into the extraordinary situation of captivity in an alien land.

The difference between these two versions of captive knowledge, in the folktale and in modern narrative, is related to a difference in their visions of the alien. The women of the folktales are held by bizarre, enormously powerful supernatural beings; the thunder god who holds White Corn challenges her husband to a series of grotesque and seemingly impossible contests. Similarly, the protagonists of dream vision narratives often journey to mysterious caverns where they sojourn with the ancient spirits of nature. Humans in myth and folklore, then, are held captive by the powerful sacred forces animating the natural world. Even Odysseus is held captive by Poseidon's son. As mythic motifs contributed to the development of European romance, captivity continued to play an important role as a motivator of plot, a shaper of identity, and a sign of the sacred. In *Sir Gawain and the Green Knight*, the hero suffers several debasing subjugations at the hands of a supernatural whose bizarre powers mock the complacent chivalry of Arthur's court. More generally, one of our most basic notions of Western romance concerns a princess's rescue, by her knight in shining armor, from the castle of a terrible knight. All of these narrative conventions portray humans held captive by the supernatural, by the sacred, or at least by the mysterious. None of these narrative conventions devotes much attention to detailing the experience of captivity, by describing prison, labor, or other particulars of abjection, but rather they paint captivity in a few quick brush strokes designed to launch the heroism of the protagonists.

Like the folktale, the early modern captivity narrative portrays subjugation and escape in a location associated with alien power, but it portrays a very different kind of alien. Myths and folktales represent captivity in a singular otherworld, the realm of the sacred; no matter who the captivating spirit, no matter what the route by which the protagonist journeys to meet the alien, the features of the otherworld itself remain constant in their opposition to the everyday world of community life. The modern captivity narrative and the novel, on the other hand, represent a variety of specifically distinguished other worlds; one goal of such genres is to define the specific features of the captivating environment, distinguishing it from other environments in its class. The otherworld of myth is bizarre, almost inexplicable, comprehensible only as metaphor and allegory. The other worlds of captivity narratives and novels are foreign but easily explicable, easily documented through such intellectual schema as travel description. The otherworld of myth is experienced only through arduous efforts, such as the spirit quest or dream vision. The other worlds of the captivity narrative are experienced through accident, such as when Robert Boyle falls overboard, or through the alleged degradation of an alien culture, its supposedly rare disposition for taking captives. Although the captivity narrative's antagonist is still an alien, the genre devotes much effort to rendering his strangeness familiar, as the discursive strategies of travel description portray alien customs as debased counterparts to European ones. Rather than portray the captor as a mysterious entrant from a sacred plane of existence that informs and determines the real world, the early modern genre of the captivity narrative portrays the captor as a debased competitor for the protagonist, from another part of the real world. Rather than portray captive-taking as an inevitable yet inexplicable aspect of the sacred, the modern captivity narrative portrays captive-taking as a debased custom resorted to by cultures that are made to seem not merely ordinary, but inferior. The protagonist of a modern captivity narrative is held by degraded representatives of an allegedly inferior culture, just as, within the larger generic field of the novel, the protagonist is usually held by degraded representatives of an allegedly inferior class, belief, or proclivity, such as Richardson's aristocratic libertines or Austen's insufferable boors.

Subjugation to the alien is closely related to cultural identity both in folkloric captivity and in the modern captivity genre, but the captive's relationship to his or her culture is utterly transformed in early modern narratives and the novels and films that later imitated them. In folklore the protagonist's escape implies a full reintegration with the tribal community, even to the point of defining collective identity around the experience of captivity. In the stories of Tiny Flower and Yombo, cultural identity is defined through the technological devices or the natural cycles that seem to originate with the captive's escape and reintegration into the communiꞇy; captivity thus helps to define the hero as one who suffers for the community's benefit. In early modern narrative, on the other hand, subjugation among powerful aliens serves to define individualistic liberty rather than community integration. The difference is especially clear when we consider how the two narrative types portray captive heroism. Although Tiny Flower, somewhat like Robert Boyle, effects his wife's escape by defeating her captor in a series of contests, the secret knowledge that enables his victories comes from a helpful deity, Spider Woman, who rewards his respect for her and for the natural world that she symbolizes.

Conversely, the rhetoric of the modern captive hero celebrates absolute self-reliance. Even as John Rawlins's 1622 escape narrative venerates the contribution of laboring men to the English state, it formulates his captivity experience as an opportunity for personal cleverness and personal renown. Likewise, although Robert Boyle and Aubin's heroines follow Yombo and Tiny Flower in taking important things from powerful aliens, the novels treat such thefts as mere additions to personal riches. Culture heroes gain items of community benefit, such as a ritual device or knowledge concerning the proper means of handling the planting cycle, whereas Chetwood's and Aubin's protagonists take gold, jewels, or slaves. Within the colonial careers of adventurers such as Robert Boyle, an early experience of foreign captivity authorizes an unlimited personal license for individualistic economic and colonial activity. He starts on the road to captivity after serving a lackluster apprenticeship and inspiring his uncle to sell him into indentured service; in captivity he bests an Irish renegado, and in freedom he bests a number of Spanish colonists in America. Thus his return home in wealth and triumph stands as a victory over his European neighbors as well as a victory over the peoples of the non-Western world. The depredations of this modern captivity protagonist seem to mark him as a successful challenger within an international framework of competition that pits the English against other, seemingly inferior opponents. Within myth and folklore, the plot of captivity, escape, and theft represents the community's cycle of antagonism and harmony with nature, but within the early modern captivity narrative, the plot of captivity, escape, and theft represents a Western individual's successful mastery of what seems his natural antagonism to the multiethnic operators of a modern, competitive, colonial world.

It may seem surprising that the British captivity tradition tends towards the scientific and the individual rather than the sacred and the corporate, given the prominent role of religious rhetoric within the early American tradition. But even the earliest English travail narratives, dating from the turn of the seventeenth century, contain surprisingly little in the way of explicit religious commentary. Captivity among Islamic or Catholic cultures may entail brief descriptions of spiritual struggles or the comfort of Christian belief, but these themes occupy relatively small portions of text. Both in their titles and in the texts themselves, these narratives place primary emphasis on the curios of their protagonists' observations and the details of their experiences in captivity. Although the motifs of captivity and travail invited application to Christian beliefs concerning sin and salvation, the texts only rarely make these applications explicit. As the captivity genre grows beyond the confines of the chapbook over the course of the seventeenth century, nationalist and ethnographic perspectives become increasingly dominant, expansive, and refined. Only one British captivity narrative, William Okeley's 1675 *Ebenezer*, is as explicitly framed within and as extensively committed to the generic conventions of spiritual autobiography as are the American texts of Mary Rowlandson, Jonathan Dickinson, and John Williams. If Robert Knox sometimes borrows motifs from spiritual autobiography, these motifs make scarcely any impression within a text organized palpably as a description of an alien land. Compared to our own textual world, early British captivity narratives may show a greater tendency towards the spiritual. But compared to the generality of English texts from the late sixteenth through the eighteenth century, the British captivity narrative is a distinctly secular genre. Understanding the secularism of the British captivity tradition helps us to place in a properly limited context the distinctly spiritual variation developed in Puritan New England. Spiritual impulses were easily grafted onto the captivity tradition, but its roots grew out of the modernist, secular impulses of science, liberalism, nationalism, and individualism.

Another intriguing point of divergence between the American and the British captivity traditions involves the gender of the typical captive. Although the female captive has long played a central role in the scholarship on the American captivity tradition, she has played only a minor role in my own study. My treatment of gender has tended to concentrate on images of masculinity more than on images of femininity, and this concentration has largely resulted from an effort at broad coverage of the British material. That factual captivity narratives focus on female captives much more often in a North American context than in other geographical contexts should by now be quite obvious. There are some intriguing exceptions. In 1769 appeared a London text attributed to a Mrs. Crisp, titled *The Female Captive: A Narrative of Facts which Happened in Barbary in the Year 1756*. And in 1806 appeared a Boston text titled a *History of the Captivity and Sufferings of Mrs. Maria Martin Who Was Six Years a Slave in Algiers, Two of Which She Was Confined in a Dark And Dismal Dungeon, Loaded With Irons*. These are the only published works in English focused exclusively on female captivity in Barbary, with the Martin text occupying a much larger place among the few American texts set there than does the Crisp text among the many British texts set there. The female captive continued to play a greater role in the American press than in the British over the course of the nineteenth century, especially with the rise of self-consciously American fiction. With the prominent exception of Aubin, British novelists of the eighteenth century tended to portray female captives much less often than did their American successors of the following century. An obvious explanation for this divergence lies in the geographical differences in British and American colonial practice. Female captivity would most likely occur, and would raise the most interest, in a setting such as America, where large-scale familial settlement had determined the shape of colonial practice and eventually of national identity.

The divergence between the American and British captivity traditions is also important for assessing the captivity narrative's relationship with American slavery and the slave narrative. The British captivity tradition, since it deploys the rhetoric of liberty much earlier, much more often, and much more thoroughly than its American counterpart, reveals much closer parallels to the slave narrative and implicates American slavery much more directly. With its plot of oppression, abjection, and climactic liberation, combined with its explicit themes of cultural alienation, culture-crossing, and national belonging, the British captivity tradition offers at least an important precedent for the American slave narrative, even if no captivity account initially published in Britain ever furnished a direct model for the author or editor of a slave narrative. Both genres, moreover, show significant parallels to a third Anglophone tradition of writing about oppressed individuals: the discourse of indenture. Former indentured servants produced accounts of personal abjection and American life as early as the mid seventeenth century, and these texts show many more parallels, such as the use of travel description, with the British captivity tradition than with the American one. Since Anglophone indenture narrators sometimes claimed that they were kidnapped, often described themselves as slaves, and directly compared the situations of black and white servants in North America, this tradition offers an important point for investigating the connection between the slave narrative and other forms of Anglophone writing about subjugation. Whereas any narrative of foreign captivity addressed an audience already somewhat predisposed to accept the captive's vituperation of an alien culture, an indenture or slave narrative lodged its attack on institutions practiced or condoned by its audience.

Despite this difference in rhetorical address, the British captivity tradition still offers closer parallels to the context of American slavery than does the American captivity tradition. Although the most common pattern of enslavement for British captives outside America involved familial servitude, they still sometimes endured conditions, such as gang labor or extreme forms of corporal punishment, that offer modest parallels to the horrors of plantation slavery. Explicit discussion of American plantation slavery, however, was almost entirely absent from the British tradition of captivity narratives. Such a discussion would be less likely in the earlier British captivity narratives, which hit the press before the rise of the English plantation system on the North American coast and its subsequent turn to African slave labor. But even in captivity narratives published after this transformation, meditations on British liberties and the tyrannies of foreign peoples developed almost entirely without reference to Anglo-American practices of slavery and indenture. One prominent exception, Robert Drury's narrative of Malagasy captivity, only provides a further illustration of the rule. This text acknowledges no contradictions even as it repeatedly celebrates the protagonist's deliverance from oppressive enslavement, sometimes proclaims the moral worth of the Malagasy, and finally records his cheerful participation in their enslavement. Even with narratives set in America, Anglo-American institutions of servitude and the captive-taking practices of non-European peoples seem to inhabit different conceptual plains.

The tendency to avoid a critical comparison of institutions continues in eighteenth-century fictions of foreign captivity. Chetwood's fiction, in its treatment of settings from Barbary to the New World, would seem to encourage a comparison of slaving institutions, but his presentation reduces both European enslavement of non-Europeans and non-European capture of Europeans to a personal contest of subjugation and advancement: A journey outside of Britain, Chetwood's novels suggest, amounts to joining an inevitable game of capture or be captured. If Englishmen succeed in this game better than other cultures, their success results from individual prowess rather than institutional practice. A more common pattern of portraying European practices of slavery in captivity novels involves using black slaves for ironic counterpoint and narrative disjunction rather than institutional critique. For example, Aubin's omnibus, globe-trotting plots sometimes include characters in the manner of Aphra Behn's Oroonoko, black slaves who seem to merit sympathy because of their noble births, and not because of any inherent injustice within the institution of American slavery. The later British fictions of American captivity tend to adopt settings in the northern colonies and so address the question of black slavery in only the most oblique ways. Lennox's *Euphemia,* for example, portrays a black slave revolt as a minor incident of terror for its heroine, offering no possibility of comparison to her son's captivity. Much of Edward Kimber's *Mr. Anderson* develops an ambivalent critique of American indentured service and even of American slavery, but the protagonist's brief experience in Amerindian captivity seems entirely divorced from that critique. The eighteenth-century fictions of foreign captivity that invite the most direct correlation between African slaves and European captives are two that portray Europeans in African captivity: the utopian novels of Paltock and Cumberland. Paltock's novel treats captivity as an implicit punishment for its protagonist's participation in a slaving expedition; this strategy becomes much more explicitly and extensively developed in Royall Tyler's *The Algerine Captive.* No British captivity narrative of the seventeenth or eighteenth century, whether factual or fictional, would draw such an explicit parallel between the captivity of Westerners in foreign lands and the enslavement of Africans in America.

The Anglophone tradition of foreign captivity narratives thus furnishes a vivid illustration of David Brion Davis's analysis of the fundamental contradictions in Western notions of slavery.[4] Within both factual and fictional accounts of enslavement outside America, the rhetoric of national outrage often grows so strong as to imply the injustice of any practice of enslavement, and sometimes the rhetoric of native British liberties spills over into a discourse of human rights. That this rhetoric implicates Anglophone slavery in America is a question that British captivity narratives do not face. Perhaps some explanation for the post-1739 decline of British captivity narratives, both factual and fictional, lies in the rise of British antislavery literature. Increasing awareness of American slavery may have made the rhetoric of liberty seem contradictory or hypocritical when applied to British captives in other lands, or accounts of American slavery may have supplanted accounts of British captivity in providing readers with a vehicle for identifying with abject experience, feeling the value of liberty, and rousing moral indignation.

In assessing the British captivity tradition's relationship with its American counterpart, we need finally to return to the question of the captivity genre's relationship with the novel. In its modern, secular, British context, the captivity narrative underwent an initial development and subsequent expansion that paralleled those of the early novel. The captivity narrative began, at the turn of the sixteenth century, as a chapbook genre, inhabiting a medium that also provided an early home for popular fiction. Protagonists in the early chapbook captivities gave little impression of psychological interiority and instead served as neutral mouthpieces for curious observations; the observational rhetoric might apply the same bland tone to nautical minutiae, to myths inserted by an editor, or to the tortures undergone by the narrator. After these inauspicious beginnings, the genre gradually expanded in length over the seventeenth century, much in the manner of prose fiction, until some captivity narratives commanded multiple volumes and novelistic page counts in the eighteenth century. From the late sixteenth through the eighteenth century, the captivity narrative, again like prose fiction, involved increasingly sophisticated experiments with documentary strategies. Job Hortop's tally of imprisonments gave way to the more fully developed schema of formal travel description, which reached a capstone with Robert Knox's 1681 account of Ceylon. On the other hand, Robert Drury's captivity narrative eschewed formal description in developing a verisimilitude that firmly subordinated ethnographic observations to the psychological process of the protagonist's experience. The Drury narrative thus climaxes a long process of expansion and experimentation with narrative treatment of captive psychology. After the empty mouthpieces of the sixteenth century, seventeenth-century narratives gradually increased the emphasis on the psychological struggles entailed by subjugation in an alien environment, with Okeley's 1675 narrative standing as the fullest British adaptation of a captivity experience to the framework of spiritual autobiography. Compared to such a culturally insulated captive as Okeley, however, transculturated captives such as Drury, Pellow, and John Dunn Hunter often displayed even greater psychological conflict, and their experiences provided the basis for the longest, richest, and most popular captivity narratives in eighteenth-century Britain and nineteenth-century America.

But the captivity genre was more than just a parallel for the early novel's experiments in narrative form. As a direct influence on the suppositional plotting of eighteenth-century British fiction, the captivity genre played a prominent role in the novel's early evolution. In the 1720s, Oriental captivity or the threat of captivity could provide a novel's primary plot line, animating several extensively detailed episodes, as is the case in Chetwood's *Robert Boyle* and Aubin's *Count de Vinevil*. Oriental captivity could also provide the most common thread within a multithreaded, omnibus novel, such as Aubin's *The Noble Slaves* and *Count Albertus*. Although *Robert Boyle* and *The Noble*

Slaves were among the most popular of all the novels that I have discussed, they did not initiate a vogue for basing whole novels on the theme of captivity in alien lands. Instead novels after the 1720s generally followed the pattern established by the earliest fictional episode of foreign captivity, in Richard Head's *The English Rogue.* This pattern involved a brief captivity episode marking an important moment of transition or counterpoint within a protagonist's domestic career. For many a captive male protagonist, the Middle East often seemed to provide a gateway from feckless youth to colonial heroism. In utopian novels with brief episodes of African captivity, subjugation marks the protagonist's transition either into or out of libertarian utopia. Brief transitional episodes of captivity became more common in the latter half of the century, within novels that treated American captivity as a sign that genteel Britons should abandon America because its endemic violence would threaten British character. After the eighteenth century, however, even such brief episodes of non-Western captivity would become much less prominent in British fiction, as extensive portraits of captive protagonists relied increasingly on domestic, institutional, and Gothic settings.

The eighteenth-century shift from extensive treatment to brief episodes of captivity in British novels is related to a contemporaneous shift from an aggressively nationalist agenda to discomfort with the colonial project. Early in the century, the most popular treatment of foreign captivity in British fiction, Chetwood's *Robert Boyle,* also embraced the most aggressively vengeful and predatory colonial plotting and developed the most extensive section of travel description in any captivity novel. Likewise, the constant iteration of captivity episodes in Aubin's *The Noble Slaves* was introduced by a preface that cited the most sweeping and damning of Orientalist generalizations as a key for interpreting the episodes. In these early works, lengthy portraits of the indignities endured by European protagonists were matched by portraits of their heroic patience, perseverance, and rationality, themes requiring slow and careful plotting. But the shorter episodes that followed these early ones rarely devoted energy to ethnographic method or to detailing careful plans for escape. A few bold strokes sufficed for painting the protagonists' passivity and abjection, and on the rare occasions that they engineered their own escapes, the narratives did not concern themselves with detailed contrivances. If the early Orientalist novels emphasized the captives' potential for rational mastery of alien lands, the later American episodes concentrated on brief evocations of sensibility.

To understand the cultural reasons for this shift in the imaginative revisions of the captivity experience, we need to consider the broader role that the captive, whether factual or fictional, might have played in British views of colonialism. The colonial cycle of British intervention and non-Western dependence proceeded at very different rates in different settings, and the variable results of this process produced variable narrative shapes within the British captivity tradition. The British initiated the process in the sixteenth century, sending adventurers to America, Russia, the Ottoman Empire, Persia, and India. Although the process produced rapid and early political transformations in the case of North America, several centuries of trading factories were needed before Bengali rulers acquiesced in British seizure of political power during the 1760s, and British trade in the Middle East, active since the sixteenth century, did not lead to imperial administration until the nineteenth. In response to these regional variations, British novelists imagined regional variations on the captivity experience. Novels that transformed the captive into an aggressive figure of colonial heroism tended to adopt Oriental settings, reflecting Britain's eighteenth-century relationship with Middle Eastern lands as the sites of colonial footholds, trading factories that might have formed the basis of territorial expansion. Novels that attempted an experimental mixture of captivity narrative and utopia adopted sub-Saharan settings, choosing uncharted territory as a suitable vehicle for imagining not only a perfected state, but also a perfected colonialism, in which the movement of ideas outstripped the movement of peoples and material goods. Novels that expressed anxieties about colonial iniquities or the effects of cultural interaction on British colonists tended to take American settings, reflecting metropolitan attitudes towards colonies with a long history, an advanced institutional apparatus, and a large settler population. Where the colonial project was already quite advanced, metropolitan writers were more likely to contemplate its faults.

Even before the production of these self-consciously fictional revisions of the captivity experience, the stories told by returned captives deeply disturbed and excited metropolitan authors. Even before they responded to the captivity experience with imaginative fiction, they felt a need to intervene in the production of "factual" accounts of captivity experience. As a result, the factual captivity genre incorporated not only the perspective of actual captives, but also the perspective of Britons who never left home. Metropolitan editors displayed a variety of responses to the experiences of former captives in the course of polishing, retelling, and sometimes even fabricating the material of captivity for publication. If the editors of the earliest British captivity narratives occasionally embellished the plain tales of the captives with references to already well-established features of the exotic, a countervailing effort to transform captivity into a basis for scientific knowledge became increasingly important over the course of the seventeenth century, reaching an apotheosis with the Royal Society's sponsorship and direction of Robert Knox's account of his Ceylonese captivity. Whereas Knox's editors helped him to mold his experiences into a scientific framework, other captivity editors often surpassed their narrators in developing the significance of the individual captive experience for an understanding of national politics. An especially clear case of an editor's deriving political inspiration from captive experience occurs with Robert Drury's narrative. The political implications of Malagasy culture fired Defoe's imagination, leading him to speculate on the origins of parliaments if not to place liberal sentiments in the mouths of Drury's captors. In an even more telling sign of editorial intervention, this text so greatly resembles a Defoean bildungsroman as to provide some justification for scholarly identifications of the work as one of Defoe's novels. The picaresque sections of Thomas Pellow's narrative likewise suggest that editors sometimes could not contain their impulses to add fabricated incidents and to draw from established fictional patterns in reshaping captive experience. Each of these varied forms of editorial intervention involved an effort to render the strange familiar, by reshaping and adding material that would fit recognizable generic conventions, but the resulting inconsistencies in style, voice, and frame often ended up rendering the strangeness of captivity even more fundamentally strange.

The captivity genre's situation at the borders between fact and fiction, travel narrative and novel, reflects the fundamental extremity of the captivity experience and the consequent rhetorical exigency to render that extremity plausible. The captivity narrative imposed a rhetoric of scientific rigor on an experience whose very nature involved a violent deviation from Western norms of peaceful travel, domestic comfort, and authorial autonomy. Some texts turned the exoticism of foreign captivity to positive account, aggressively exploiting the notion that captives, as servants and converts who witnessed alien cultures from the inside, gained more intimate experiences of them than did other travelers. On the other hand, the deep cultural insights retailed in captivity narratives often served to illustrate extreme differences between British culture and the cultures of captive-taking peoples. Compared to other travel narratives, captivity narratives more thoroughly documented the outlandish, the shocking, and the brutal, often stressing the enormity, even the implausibility, of customs such as torture. And since the captives sometimes underwent torture themselves, often suffered other forms of abjection, and always complained of their subjugation, their accounts documented crises of extraordinary personal experience as much as the quotidian truths of alien cultures. These crises of personal experience often centered on the problem of transculturation. Accounts of personal transculturation created a vivid impression of psychological tension because the former captives struggled to organize their experiences within rhetorical frameworks stressing British nationalism and ethnographic distance. The retrospective imposition of such frameworks on the extraordinary experiences of foreign captivity created an impression of a subject under siege, struggling to resist the forcible imposition of alien cultural forms, but also tempted by their appeal and even capable, sometimes, of forming an accommodation with them. If the captivity narrative, like the novel, relied heavily on documentary strategies stressing the plausible and the customary, the driving force behind these strategies was often rhetorical justification for textual inclusion of the implausible, the exotic, and the forbidden.

As a result of this fundamental tension, the captivity narrative was not a genre that merely enshrined an aggressive colonialism, but rather one that also registered, and posed in its turn, fundamental problems in national identity and character. For metropolitan Britons, the notion of a captive's forced subjugation and submersion within an alien culture demanded an aggressive assertion of national character precisely because it raised such troubling visions of divided, corruptible, transgressive identity. Celebrations of liberal subjectivity, cultural allegiance, and contributions to national well-being could grow from portraits of captive gentlemen and tradespeople, merchants and seamen, Quaker women and emigrants from other European lands. Within all of these representatives of British nationality, the experience of captivity and escape could serve as an illustration of inborn liberty, whereas the repetition of despotic motifs across a global range of cultures suggested that all the world beyond Britain possessed an inherent disposition for tyranny. But the very vehemence of the captivity genre's nationalist rhetoric often stands as an attempt to smooth over a fundamental sense of crisis at the heart of national identity . The effort to publish and sell captivity in the print marketplace was an attempt to exploit a set of questions and problems raised inevitably by the experience of forced participation in an alien culture. Could a captive retain a British identity when forced into a subordinate position among an allegedly barbaric people? How would a British captive react when his captor turned out to be an Irish renegado, proof of the benefits obtained through cultural conversion? What if the captivity lasted twenty-three years? What if the captive took a native spouse or occupied a position of power and respect in a culture that Britons associated with savage oppressions? Other implicit questions developed through recurring narrative structures. Was there something peculiar in British identity that made it capable of withstanding alien oppressions or abject experiences, even of turning them to positive account? Could British gentility survive the experience of American colonialism, with its overwhelming pressure to savagery? Did the experience of captivity imply a colonial destiny for the British people?

My goal in this book was to illustrate this variety of questions as raised within the British captivity tradition. I have focused this book on "British captivity narratives" and confined myself to texts in English partly out of limitations on my scholarly resources, and partly out of the polemical goal of undoing the notion of a uniquely American captivity genre. But this label should not be understood as an attempt to restrict the genre to a nationally or linguistically defined group. As briefly indicated in chapter 1, the earliest European captivity narratives came from the pens of continental writers who entered Islamic slavery. Whether covering the sufferings of captives in general or limited to the experiences of a single captive, texts focused on Islamic captivity appeared in Latin, German, Dutch, Spanish, French, and Italian. Like their counterparts writing in English, continental authors also sometimes adapted the materials of the factual captivity narrative to fiction. Some early examples occur in Alonso de Castillo Solorzano's *La Garduna de Sevilla* (Spanish, 16??), Hendrik Smeeks's *The Mighty Kingdom of Krinke Kesmes* (Dutch, 1708) and Simon Tyssot de Patot's *Voyages et Avantures de Jacques Massé* (French, 1710). Much better known today are the Oriental captivity episodes in *Don Quixote* (1605), as well as Prévost's explorations of Islamic captivity in his *Histoire d'une Grecque Moderne* (1740) and of American captivity in *Le Philosophe Anglois; ou, Histoire de Monsieur Cleveland* (1731). *Krinke Kesmes* and *Monsieur Cleveland* develop mixtures of captivity and utopian plotting in a manner similar to that employed by Berington and Paltock. Rather clearly, more research and a comparative study are in order, and it may be that the captivity narrative is a far more international genre than my own study has suggested.

For the captivity narrative is, finally, no more a British genre, nor even an Anglophone genre, than a Western one. The captivity narrative is concerned with Western identity as much if not more than with American or British identity. From the central European narratives of the late medieval period to Hollywood's retelling of the colonial oppression plot, the captivity genre has defined an isolated Western hero against the Oriental, the barbaric, or the savage, primitive foils for the West's modernity. The captivity narrative is a modern genre in the sense that it is a self-conscious celebration of the modern, of new information organized in a new way, handled with the sophisticated care of science, and framed as evidence for the superiority of the modern West over the primitive non-West. But the modernity of the captivity narrative is always an uncomfortable, tenuous modernity, because the evidence for the West's modern superiority is offered by someone who temporarily lost, or even discarded, his or her modernity. Although captives could and often did plead compulsion, many narratives do not stop short of expressing pleasure and pride in personal assimilation to the supposedly primitive. The captivity narrative, then, is a genre that speaks as much to the permeability as to the rigidity of Western identity. It is a genre determined by no nation's origins, progress, or triumph. Instead it is a genre that speaks to the history of the modern West's exploration, exploitation, and interaction with other cultures. This history largely concerns the West's exportation of many modern beliefs and practices, such as the libertarian, individualistic, and scientific impulses of the captivity plot. But this history also concerns the West's importation of what it liked to describe as alien beliefs, practices, and experiences. And it also concerns the West's own troubled assumption of a modern identity. The captivity narrative provides particularly rich and concrete evidence that the conceptual systems of modernity were not simply a Western imposition on the rest of the world, but emerged in tandem with the West's colonial expansion in a process that transformed Westerners and their others alike.

Notes

Introduction

1. This quotation comes from the introduction to the anthology by Vaughan and Clark, *Puritans among the Indians*, 2. Although Baepler has recently acknowledged that British narratives of enslavement in the Barbary states provided a precedent for the American captivity tradition, his work still concentrates on the place of the Barbary narratives in American literature. See Baepler, "The Barbary Captivity Narrative in Early America" and *White Slavery in Africa*.

2. Even as recently as 1997, in a generally excellent study, Sayre has identified the Indian captivity narrative as an "Anglo-American genre" and Rowlandson's text as "the foundational captivity narrative"; see Sayre, *Les Sauvages Américains*, 258.

3. Earlier studies of captivity narratives set in the Barbary states have sometimes recognized their potential impact on the American captivity tradition but not their full extent and distribution. See Starr, "Escape from Barbary," 35–52; Lewis, "Savages of the Seas," 75–84; and Baepler, "The Barbary Captivity Narrative in Early America."

4. Said, *Orientalism*. While Said concentrates on the fully developed Orientalism of nineteenth- and twentieth-century literature, the concept of an aggressive rhetoric common both to academic and to popular literature is also quite useful in understanding the West's writing on the "Orient" in earlier centuries, as long as one recognizes that Orientalism was still a rhetoric in formation during that period. Developing gradually through the centuries when the West acquired an increasing dominance of Middle Eastern lands, Orientalism came gradually to dominate other Western modes for describing those lands.

5. Annesley, *Memoirs of an Unfortunate Young Nobleman* (1743); Kimber, *The*

History of the Life and Adventures of Mr. Anderson (1754); and *The Adventures of a Kidnapped Orphan* (1747). For a fuller discussion of indenture narratives, see Van Der Zee, *Bound Over,* and Snader, "Caught between Worlds," 301–65.

1. Travel, Travail, and the British Captivity Tradition

1. Hortop, *The Travailes of an English Man* (1591), 23. Further citations appear in the text.

2. Vail initiated this misapprehension, speculating that the Hortop text was "apparently the first story of the Indian captivity of an Englishman," based on a description of the text as given in Jones, *Adventures in Americana,* 1:51. For Vail, see *The Voice of the Old Frontier,* 8, 94. Americanist scholars have often accepted Vail's assessment without investigation.

3. This theme runs throughout Bhabha's essays, collected in *The Location of Culture.*

4. Derounian-Stodola and Levernier, *The Indian Captivity Narrative,* 11.

5. For a modern English edition, see Schiltberger, *The Bondage and Travels of Johann Schiltberger* (1427), ed. Neumann, trans. Telfer.

6. Georgijevic, *The Ofspring of the House of Ottomanno* (1569).

7. For further discussion of these and other accounts, see Beck, *From the Rising of the Sun,* 26; and Wolf, *The Barbary Coast,* 341–42.

8. On both the history and the myth of the Inquisition, see Peters, *Inquisition.*

9. Saunders, *A True Discription and Breefe Discourse* (1587), B2v.

10. See Hakluyt, *The Principal Navigations* (1589), for the captivity of Thomas Saunders (3:139–55) and the travels of Job Hortop (6:336–54). Purchas includes many more captivities in *Hakluytus Posthumus, or Purchas his Pilgrimes* (1613). See, for example, the narratives of John Rawlins (6:151–71), Lewis Barthema (9:78–83), and Nicholas Roberts (9:311–21).

11. See, for example, the effort by Derounian-Stodola and Levernier, *The Indian Captivity Narrative* (216–24), to establish a standard set of title abbreviations, based primarily on the last names of captivity authors.

12. The first American edition to follow the British naming convention was Rowlandson, *A Narative of the Captivity* (1770). See Vail, *The Voice of the Old Frontier,* 290.

13. I have counted both preface and text, using the fullest eighteenth-century editions.

14. See, for example, the anthology edited by Levernier and Cohen, *The Indians and Their Captives.*

15. Armstrong and Tennenhouse, "The American Origins of the English Novel," 386–410; rpt. in *The Imaginary Puritan,* 196–216. The authors claim incorrectly that Rowlandson appeared in thirty editions by the end of the eighteenth century (a seventeenth imprint appeared in 1800), and that the "fifth" American edition of 1720 also appeared in Britain (for correct details, see Vail, *The Voice of the Old Frontier*).

16. Derounian, "The Publication, Promotion, and Distribution of Mary Rowlandson's Indian Captivity Narrative in the Seventeenth Century," 248. Derounian cites some evidence of the text's promotion in England but acknowledges that any evidence for English readership is largely "conjectural" (256).

17. Vail, *The Voice of the Old Frontier*, 328. Besides Williamson's account, the other two most popular narratives were those of John Marrant (1785) and Mary Jemison (1824), rather than Rowlandson's. Like Williamson's narrative, Marrant's succeeded first in the British press.

18. Vail, *The Voice of the Old Frontier*, 263.

19. For a particularly Americanized version of Williamson's narrative, see Van Der Zee, *Bound Over*, 209–27.

20. Carleton, "The Indian Captivity," 169–80; Pearce, "The Significances of the Captivity Narrative," 1–20.

21. Derounian-Stodola and Levernier, *The Indian Captivity Narrative*, 40.

22. Rowlandson, *The Sovereignty and Goodness of God* (1682), in *Puritans among the Indians*, ed. Vaughan and Clark, 33.

23. VanDerBeets, introduction to *Held Captive by Indians*, xx–xxiv. This introduction encapsulates the stance taken throughout VanDerBeets's writings on American captivity narratives; his essays are collected in *The Indian Captivity Narrative*.

24. Ebersole, *Captured by Texts*.

25. Dickinson, *God's Protecting Providence* (1699), ed. Andrews and Andrews, 52.

26. Williams, *The Redeemed Captive Returning to Zion* (1707), ed. Vaughan and Clark, 167–226.

27. See, for example, Castiglia, *Bound and Determined;* Kolodny, *The Land before Her*, 6–67; Gherman, "From Parlour to Tepee"; Person, "The American Eve," 668–85; Namias, *White Captives*. Rowlandson's text plays a crucial role in these works and has inspired two extended treatments of her retrospective efforts to impose a Puritan discursive order on memories of extreme personal suffering, alienation, and strangeness. See Howe, *The Birth-Mark*, 89–101, 123–28; and Breitweiser, *American Puritanism and the Defense of Mourning*.

28. McKeon, *The Origins of the English Novel*, especially 39–52.

29. Davies, *A Trve Relation* (1614), C1v.

30. Davies, *A Trve Relation*, C1r.

31. At least two reprints appeared, in 1592 and 1600. I have used the 1592 printing.

32. Webbe, *The Rare and Most VVonderfull Things*, D3r, D1v.

33. Lithgow, *The Totall Discourse* (1632), 56.

34. Okeley, *Eben-ezer* (1675), 15–16.

35. Okeley, *Eben-ezer*, 17.

36. VanDerBeets, introduction, xii.

37. Wolf, *The Barbary Coast*, 341. For a useful overview of early modern historiography concerning the Barbary Coast, see 341–42.

38. For a fuller discussion, see chapter 2 below.

39. Goonetileke, introduction to Knox, *An Historical Relation of the Island Ceylon* (1681), xv. See also Goonetileke, "Robert Knox in the Kandyan Kingdom, 1660–1679," 81–151.

40. Nasir, *The Arabs and the English,* 31.

41. See Oliver, introduction to Drury, *Madagascar* (1729), ed. Oliver, 10. Further citations appear in the text. For specific examples of Drury's influence, see Secord, *Robert Drury's Journal,* 4, 62–63.

42. *Philosophical Transactions,* 1 (1665–1666): 140–43.

43. Churchill and Churchill, eds., *A Collection of Voyages and Travels* (1704), 1:lxxiii–lxxvi. The directions for travelers were also expanded for Boyle, *General Heads for the Natural History of a Country* (1692).

44. *Philosophical Transactions,* 1 (1665–1666): 186.

45. *Philosophical Transactions,* 1 (1665–1666): 188.

46. Churchill and Churchill, eds., *A Collection of Voyages and Travels,* lxxv.

47. Frantz, *The English Traveller and the Movement of Ideas.*

48. Pitts, *A True and Faithful Account* (1738), xv, vi. Further citations appear in the text.

49. Sayre, *Les Sauvages Américains,* 24–25, 79–143.

50. Knox, *A Historical Relation of Ceylon . . . ,* ed. James Ryan, xxx. For more details on the work's publication, see Goonetileke, introduction to *An Historical Relation of the Island of Ceylon* (1681), ix.

51. Sayre, *Les Sauvages Américains,* 259.

52. Thomas Sprat, *The History of the Royal Society* (1667), 62.

53. The voluminous scholarship on the plain style is conveniently summarized and carefully reformulated in Robert Adolph, *The Rise of Modern Prose.* For the plain style's importance in travel writing, see Frantz, *The English Traveller and the Movement of Ideas,* 57–68; and McKeon, *The Origins of the English Novel,* 100–13.

54. *Philosophical Transactions* 9 (1676–1677): 552.

55. Phelps, *A True Account* (1685), 26.

56. Starr, "Escape from Barbary," 36–37.

57. Coustos, *The Sufferings of John Coustos* (1746), 62–63.

58. Coustos, *The Sufferings of John Coustos,* 68.

59. For a particularly strong discussion of these issues, see Fitzpatrick, "The Figure of Captivity," 1–26.

60. For particularly strident examples of either extreme, see Castiglia, *Bound and Determined,* 45–52; and Ebersole, *Captured by Texts,* 15–60.

61. Hawthorne's retelling appeared under the title "The Duston Family," in *The American Magazine of Useful and Entertaining Knowledge* (1836), and Thoreau included a brief retelling in *A Week on the Concord and the Merrimack Rivers* (1849). They are reprinted and analyzed in Levernier and Cohen, *The Indians and Their Captives,* 156–59, 224–30. Dustan's violence provides the crucial instance of what

Fiedler has seen as a central archetype within American mythology; see Fiedler, *The Return of the Vanishing American,* 91–108.

62. For sources related to Defoe's possible role in the Drury narrative, see Moore, *DeFoe in the Pillory;* and Secord, *Robert Drury's Journal,* 1–71.

63. Pellow, *The History of the Long Captivity* (1739), 28–29.

64. Davies, *A True Relation* (1614), A4r.

65. Evans and Chevers, *This is a Short Relation of some of the Cruel Sufferings* (1662).

66. Vaughan, *The Adventures of Five Englishmen from Pulo Condoro* (1714), 71.

67. See Saunders, *A True Discription and Breefe Discourse* (1587), especially C2v.

68. Evans and Chevers, *This is a Short Relation of some of the Cruel Sufferings* (1662), 17.

69. During the eighteenth century, Dickinson inspired a dozen printings and retellings, split equally between Britain and America. Williamson inspired a dozen in Britain alone. For details, see Vail, *The Voice of the Old Frontier.*

70. Dickinson, *God's Protecting Providence* (1699), ed. Andrews and Andrews, 52.

71. Brooks, *Barbarian Cruelty* (1693), 31–34, 84.

72. Williamson, *French and Indian Cruelty* (1757), 45. Further citations appear in the text.

73. This use of the captivity narrative to fortify the Puritan community is especially evident in Mather, *Humiliations Follow'd by Deliverances* (1697), *Decennium Luctuosum* (1699), and *A Memorial of the Present Deplorable State of New-England* (1707). Scholars have long recognized this use of the captivity genre, but see especially Fitzpatrick, "The Figure of Captivity," 1–26; and Ebersole, *Captured by Texts,* 61–76.

2. The Captive as Hero

1. This understanding of the captivity genre is especially important for Armstrong and Tennenhouse's argument for a connection between captivity narrative and novel. See "The American Origins of the English Novel," 386–410; rpt. in *The Imaginary Puritan,* 196–216.

2. This recognition is implicit in such broad surveys as Derounian-Stodola and Levernier's *The Indian Captivity Narrative* and Namias's *White Captives.* It becomes an explicit point of argument in Mitchell Breitwieser's *American Puritanism and the Defense of Mourning;* in Castiglia's *Bound and Determined;* and in Burnham's *Captivity and Sentiment.*

3. As David R. Sewell has argued in relation to the American texts, captivity narratives "are, at root, ethnographies. By describing and interpreting the experience of captivity, the captive reverses after the fact the 'natural' power relations between 'savage' and 'civilized' that imprisonment has temporarily reversed. The Indian,

whatever his actual power during the event, can be captured and tamed once and for all in the written narrative." See Sewell, "So Unstable and Like Mad Men They Were," in *A Mixed Race,* ed. Shuffleton, 42.

4. For a study that recognizes the tension between passivity and activity within American accounts, see Burnham, *Captivity and Sentiment,* especially 51–60.

5. Davies, *A True Relation* (1614).

6. Webbe, *The Rare and Most VVonderfull Things* (1590).

7. Hasleton, *Strange and Wonderfull Things* (1595), B3v.

8. Lithgow, *The Totall Discourse* (1632), 468.

9. Williamson, *French and Indian Cruelty* (1757), 3. Further citations appear in the text.

10. *A Narrative of the Capture and Treatment of John Dodge,* 13; according to Derounian-Stodola and Levernier (*The Indian Captivity Narrative,* 28–30), portions of this text were reprinted in *The Remembrancer* in 1779.

11. Pearce, "The Significances of the Captivity Narrative," 6–13; VanDerBeets, *The Indian Captivity Narrative,* 13–24; Denn, "Captivity Narratives of the American Revolution," 575–82; Sieminski, "The Puritan Captivity Narrative and the Politics of the American Revolution," 35–56; Derounian-Stodola and Levernier, *The Indian Captivity Narrative,* 23–36, 63–73.

12. Webbe, *The Rare and Most VVonderfull Things* (1590), A3r–A3v.

13. Phelps, dedication page, *A True Account* (1685).

14. *The Famous and Wonderfull Recoverie* (1622), A2r–A3r.

15. T. S[mith], *The Adventures of (Mr. T. S.)* (1670), 5, 13. Further citations appear in the text.

16. Okeley, *Eben-ezer* (1675), A7r.

17. Phelps, preface, *A True Account* (1685).

18. Locke, *Two Treatises of Government,* ed. Laslett, 268. Further citations appear in the text. For a similar discussion in Hobbes, see *Leviathan,* ed. Tuck, 141.

19. For other equations between slavery and captivity, see Locke, 284, 322–23.

20. For detailed analyses of this language, see Dickinson, *Liberty and Property;* and Clark, *The Language of Liberty.*

21. Pellow, *The History of the Long Captivity* (1739), 2.

22. For an analysis of the American context at the turn of the nineteenth century, see Lewis, "Savages of the Seas," 75–84. For a discussion of early American dramas that employ the Barbary plot, see Montgomery, "White Captives, African Slaves," 615–30.

23. Martin, *The Tryal and Sufferings* (1724), A2r, A3r.

24. Coustos, *The Sufferings of John Coustos* (1746), viii.

25. Coustos, *The Sufferings of John Coustos* (1746), xxvi.

26. Knox, *An Historical Relation* (1681), 123. Further citations appear in the text.

27. Gyles, *Memoirs of Odd Adventures* (1736), in *Puritans Among the Indians,* ed. Vaughan and Clark, 105. Further citations from this anthology appear in the text as Vaughan and Clark.

28. For studies that adopt earlier perspectives than Said's influential *Orientalism,* see Doob, *Nebuchadnezzar's Children;* Metlitzki, *The Matter of Araby in Medieval England;* and Chew, *The Crescent and the Rose.*

29. Phelps, *A True Account* (1685), 8–9.

30. Vaughan, *The Adventures of Five Englishmen* (1714), 77.

31. Bumstead, "Carried to Canada!" 79–96.

32. Martin, *The Tryal and Sufferings* (1724), especially 23–34, 81–91.

33. Langbein, *Torture and the Law of Proof;* Peters, *Torture,* 74–102.

34. In Knox, *An Historical Relation* (1681), the plates face pages 22, 38, and 104.

35. Brooks's work first appeared in London in 1693, followed by an American printing in Boston, published by S. Phillips in 1700.

36. Saunders, *A True Discription and Breefe Discourse* (1587), C2v.

37. Hasleton, *Strange and Wonderfull Things* (1595), B2v.

38. Webbe, *The Rare and Most VVonderfull Things* (1590), C4v, A3v.

39. Knight, *A Relation of Seaven Yeares Slaverie* (1640), 26.

40. Vaughan, *The Adventures of Five Englishmen* (1714), 141, 73.

41. Vaughan, *The Adventures of Five Englishmen,* 84–85.

42. Burnham, *Captivity and Sentiment,* 52–91.

43. Drury, *Madagascar* (1729), 56.

44. Wadsworth, *The English Spanish Pilgrime* (1629), 40.

45. For examples and analysis of the gauntlet, see Axtell, *The Invasion Within,* 312–14.

46. Elliot, *A Modest Vindication of Titus Oates* (1682), 6.

47. Rowlandson's function as a "captive-commodity" forms an important element in Burnham's analysis of her cultural hybridity (see *Captivity and Sentiment,* 18–21).

48. Okeley, *Eben-ezer* (1675), 21, 42.

49. Elliot, *A Modest Vindication of Titus Oates* (1682), 3–10.

50. For Rowlandson's economic activity, see Vaughan and Clark, 52, 55. For feminist interpretations of this activity, see Ulrich, *Good Wives,* 227–28; and Burnham, *Captivity and Sentiment,* 28–30.

51. Vaughan, *The Adventures of Five Englishmen* (1714), 85, 106.

52. See the groundbreaking essay by Axtell, "At the Water's Edge."

53. Kupperman, *Settling with the Indians,* 171–81.

54. For India, see Spear, *The Nabobs,* and Marshall, "Taming the Exotic," 49; for the Middle East, see Wood, *A History of the Levant Company,* 229–45; for Africa, see Davies, *The Royal Africa Company,* 240–64.

55. Knight, *A Relation of Seaven Yeares Slaverie* (1640), 53, 55.

56. See, for example, the third edition of *French and Indian Cruelty* (1758).

57. Drury, *Madagascar* (1729), 63.

58. The providential framework is especially important for Ebersole's *Captured by Texts.* This study reads even nineteenth-century texts largely in terms of residual traces of providential discourse.

59. VanDerBeets, *The Indian Captivity Narrative*, 1–11; Vaughan and Clark, 1–28; Ebersole, *Captured by Texts*, 61–97.

60. Vaughan, *The Adventures of Five Englishmen* (1714), 142, 118–19.

61. For varying critical perspectives on these issues, see Watt, *The Rise of the Novel*, especially 60–92; Novak, *Defoe and the Nature of Man;* Hunter, *The Reluctant Pilgrim;* Starr, *Defoe and Casuistry;* Richetti, *Defoe's Narratives;* and McKeon, *The Origins of the English Novel*, 315–37.

62. An instructive parallel to Knox's dedication is in the famous preface to Mary Rowlandson's account, published a year after Knox's narrative and signed "Per Amicum," most likely Increase Mather. See Rowlandson, *The Soveraignty & Goodness of God* (1682), A2r–A3v. See also the analysis in Ebersole, *Captured by Texts*, 43–49.

63. Phelps, *A True Account* (1685), 24.

64. Knight, *A Relation of Seaven Yeares Slaverie* (1640), 27, 15.

3. The Perils and the Powers of Cultural Conversion

1. Armstrong and Tennenhouse recognize the problem of the captive's malleable cultural identity as a backdrop for what they see as Rowlandson's intense assertion of Englishness; see "The American Origins of the English Novel," 386–410; rpt. in *The Imaginary Puritan*, 196–216. For an interpretation of Rowlandson that stresses her participation in native culture, see Burnham, *Captivity and Sentiment*, 10–49.

2. Burnham, *Captivity and Sentiment*, 3.

3. Pellow, *The History of the Long Captivity* (1739), 2–3. Further citations appear in the text.

4. See the fourth edition of Pitts, *A True and Faithful Account* (1738). Further citations appear in the text. Rowlandson's text reveals similar shifts but in a much less pronounced manner; see Burnham, *Captivity and Sentiment*, 22–23.

5. For studies of the popularity, significance, and influence of these narratives, see Fiedler, *The Return of the Vanishing American*, 104–19; Drinnon, *White Savage;* and Namias, *White Captives*, 145–203.

6. Chew, *The Crescent and the Rose*, 375.

7. See the ironically titled *Modest Vindication of Titus Oates* (1682), sig. B1r and p. 22.

8. Knight, *A Relation of Seaven Yeares Slaverie* (1640), A3v.

9. Okeley, *Eben-ezer* (1675), 21.

10. For commentary on captive conversion in travel narratives, see the examples in Chew, *The Crescent and the Rose*, 373–77.

11. T. S[mith], *The Adventures of (Mr. T. S.)* (1670), 20.

12. Okeley, *Eben-ezer* (1675), 47–48.

13. Drury, *Madagascar* (1729), 162. Further citations appear in the text.

14. Vaughan, *The Adventures of Five Englishmen* (1714), 106, 108.

15. Henry, *Travels and Adventures* (1809); Seaver, *A Narrative of the Life of Mrs. Mary Jemison* (1824); James, *A Narrative of the Captivity and Adventures of John Tanner* (1830).

16. Knox, *An Historical Relation* (1681), 123.

17. Gyles, *Memoirs of Odd Adventures* (1736), in *Puritans Among the Indians*, ed. Vaughan and Clark, 105.

18. Knox, *An Historical Relation* (1681), 123.

19. Other scholars have analyzed Rowlandson's emphasis on food; see Ulrich, *Good Wives*, 229; and Derounian-Stodola and Levernier, *The Indian Captivity Narrative*, 92–93.

20. Williamson, *French and Indian Cruelty* (1757), 35.

21. Knox, *An Historical Relation* (1681), 169–70.

22. Moore, *Defoe in the Pillory.*

23. Secord, *Robert Drury's Journal*, 1–71.

24. One of the foremost Western scholars on Madagascar has shown particular skepticism of the work's political analysis, attributing them to editorial intervention; see Grandidier, *Histoire Physique, Naturelle et Politique de Madagascar*, vol. 4, tome 1, pp. 498–505.

25. On Defoe, see especially Schonhorn, *Defoe's Politics.*

4. Mastering Captivity

Portions of chapter 4 originally appeared as "The Oriental Captivity Narrative and Early English Fiction." *Eighteenth-Century Fiction* 9.3 (April 1997): 267-98.

1. Armstrong and Tennenhouse, "The American Origins of the English Novel," 386–410; rpt. in *The Imaginary Puritan*, 196–216.

2. Burnham, *Captivity and Sentiment*, 41–62.

3. Starr, "Escape from Barbary," 35.

4. Since Secord, Defoe scholars have recognized the importance of Knox's account of captivity in Ceylon as an important "source" or "influence" for Defoe's fictions of capitalist and colonial expansion, especially *Robinson Crusoe* and *Captain Singleton*. The arguments as applied to Knox could equally apply to Oriental captives such as Rawlins, *The Famous and Wonderfull Recoverie* (1622), and Okeley, *Eben-ezer* (1675). For Secord, see *Studies in the Narrative Method of Defoe*. For continued emphasis on the connection between Knox and Defoe, see Backscheider, *Daniel Defoe*, 429–30; and Faller, *Crime and Defoe*, 116.

5. See, for example, Richetti, *Popular Fiction before Richardson*, 216–29. For influence on Richardson, see McBurney, "Penelope Aubin and the Early English Novel," 245–67; Zach, "Mrs. Aubin and Richardson's Earliest Literary Manifesto (1739)," 271–85; and Beasley, *Novels of the 1740s*, 163–66.

6. Chetwood, *The Voyages, Dangerous Adventures, and Imminent Escapes of Captain Richard Falconer* (1720), *The Voyages, Travels and Adventures of William Owen Gwin Vaughan* (1736), *The Twins: or, the Female Traveller* (1742–1743); Barker, *The Lining of the Patch Work Screen* (1726), in *The Galesia Trilogy*, 195–98. Rowe included two episodes in the first edition of *Friendship in Death* (1728) and another in part 2 of *Letters Moral and Entertaining*, added to the third edition of *Friendship in Death* (1733). For the episodes themselves, see the Garland facsimile of the third edition, 26–29, 61–62, 123–25.

7. Said, *Orientalism.*

8. Khairallah, "Arabic Studies in England in the Late Seventeenth and Early Eighteenth Centuries"; Holt, *Studies in the History of the Near East;* Netton, "The Mysteries of Islam," in *Exoticism in the Enlightenment,* ed. Rousseau and Porter, 23–45.

9. Said, *Orientalism,* 62.

10. For a historical account of Barbary in this period, see Wolf, *The Barbary Coast.* For further scholarship on British images of the Orient, see Oueijan, *The Progress of an Image;* Beck, *From the Rising of the Sun;* Nasir, *The Arabs and the English;* and Chew, *The Crescent and the Rose.* Kabbani's *Europe's Myths of Orient* concentrates on British literary images of the nineteenth century.

11. For historical scholarship on Christian slaves, see Lewis, *Race and Slavery in the Middle East;* Wolf, *The Barbary Coast,* 151–74; Blunt, *Black Sunrise,* 71–85. For the sixteenth century, Braudel discusses both Christian and Moslem piracy and slavery in *The Mediterranean and the Mediterranean World,* trans. Reynolds, 2:743–55, 865–91.

12. The most developed analysis of these motifs appears in the work of Green, beginning with *Dreams of Adventure, Deeds of Empire.*

13. [John Rawlins], *The Famous and Wonderfull Recoverie* (1622), B4v. Further citations appear in the text.

14. Starr, "Escape from Barbary," 38.

15. Knight, *A Relation of Seaven Yeares Slaverie* (1640), 14.

16. Knight, *A Relation of Seaven Yeares Slaverie* (1640), 15.

17. Knight, *A Relation of Seaven Yeares Slaverie* (1640), 26.

18. Okeley, *Eben-ezer* (1675), 27. Further citations appear in the text.

19. Head, *The English Rogue* (1665), 239–41.

20. Defoe, *The Life and Strange Suprizing Adventures of Robinson Crusoe* (1719), ed. Crowley, 19–20. Further citations appear in the text.

21. See Defoe, *Robinson Crusoe,* 96, 137. At another point he laments, "I was a Prisoner lock'd up with the eternal Bars and Bolts of the Ocean" (113).

22. Chetwood, *The Voyages and Adventures of Captain Robert Boyle* (1726). Further citations appear in the text as *Robert Boyle.* Richetti (*Popular Fiction,* 212) has described Boyle as a Crusoe-like example of "the resourceful European artisan-technician."

23. See particularly Spacks, *Desire and Truth.*

24. Chetwood, *The Voyages, Travels and Adventures of William Owen Gwin Vaughan* (1736), 2:129.

25. Aubin, *The Noble Slaves* (1722), ix. Further citations appear in the text.

26. For a brief overview of Western images of sexually predacious Orientals, see Kabbani, *Europe's Myths of Orient,* 14–36; see also Grosrichard, *Structure du Sérail.*

27. Aubin, *The Life of Charlotta Du Pont* (1723), 100. Further citations appear in the text.

28. Nussbaum has argued more generally that images of the "other" woman played an important role in creating the domestic heroine, even in constituting eighteenth-century feminism; see Nussbaum, *Torrid Zones.*

29. Aubin, *The Strange Adventures of the Count de Vinevil* (1721), 87–92.

30. For varying views on female disguise in eighteenth-century fiction, see Castle, *Masquerade and Civilization;* Schofield, *Masking and Unmasking the Female Mind;* and Craft-Fairchild, *Masquerade and Gender.* Brown has argued that female clothing plays an important role in the mystification of colonial ideology; see *Ends of Empire.*

31. Aubin, *A Collection of Entertaining Histories and Novels* (1739), 228–29. Further citations appear in the text.

32. Haywood, *Idalia* (1724).

33. Haywood, *The Fruitless Enquiry. Being a Collection of Several Entertaining Histories and Occurrences, which Fell under the Observation of a Lady in her Search after Happiness* (1727), 57–59. The first edition appeared in 1727, and later printings appeared in 1739, 1767, and 1769. Further citations appear in the text.

34. Haywood, *Philidore and Placentia* (1727), 198–200. McBurney reprints the only eighteenth-century edition. Further citations appear in the text.

35. Haywood's fiction of the 1720s involves a broader effort to expose this fantasy and to reveal the material reality of female subjugation that it helped to obscure; see Schofield, *Eliza Haywood,* 43–81.

36. Schofield offers an insightful discussion of the novel's gender reversals but ultimately forces them into an overstated reading of the work as a "woman-oriented novel"; see Schofield, *Quiet Rebellion,* 38–41.

37. Subsequent printings of the full novel appeared in 1746 and 1748. The captivity episodes were excised and printed separately six times up to 1800.

38. Tyler's text seems at least partially directed as a response to the recent American reprintings of Aubin and Chetwood. Discussions of Tyler sometimes treat his antislavery platform in relation to the general context of Barbary captivity, but they miss the more specific context of earlier captivity novels; see Tanselle, *Royall Tyler,* 163–73; Davidson, *Revolution and the Word,* 192–211.

39. For older and more recent treatments of Gothic imprisonment, respectively, see Railo, *The Haunted Castle,* 7–45; Richter, *The Progress of Romance,* 80–81, 97–100. Also relevant to the novelistic treatment of imprisonment is Bender, *Imagining the Penitentiary.*

5. Resisting Americans in British Novels of American Captivity

1. See, for example, Haberly, "Women and Indians," 431–41; and Derounian-Stodola and Levernier, *The Indian Captivity Narrative,*185–91.

2. "Adoption" is a term used by anthropologists and historians to describe the native custom, along with "transculturation" and "assimilation"; see Hallowell, "American Indians, White and Black," 519–31; Heard, *White into Red;* Axtell, *The Invasion Within.* Eighteenth-century writers also applied the term "adoption" to the native custom, as exemplified in quotations from Crèvecoeur and Lennox below.

3. See particularly Smith, *An Account of the Remarkable Occurences* (1799); Seaver, *Narrative of the Life of Mrs. Mary Jemison* (1824); James, *A Narrative of the Captivity and Adventures of John Tanner* (1830). These and other such texts are discussed in Derounian-Stodola and Levernier, *The Indian Captivity Narrative,* 73–85.

4. This argument is most thoroughly developed in Axtell, *The Invasion Within.*

5. See Axtell, *The Invasion Within,* especially 131–217.

6. Pearce, *The Savages of America.*

7. Colden, *The History of the Five Indian Nations* (1727), 181.

8. Smith, *An Historical Account of the Expedition* (1765).

9. Crèvecoeur, *Letters from an American Farmer* (1782), 218–19.

10. For general discussions of the European vision of native Americans, see Berkhofer, *The White Man's Indian;* Kupperman, *Settling with the Indians,* 1–106; Williams, "Savages Noble and Ignoble," in Marshall and Williams, *The Great Map of Mankind,* 187–226; and Kiernan, "Noble and Ignoble Savages," in *Exoticism in the Enlightenment,* ed. Rousseau and Porter, 86–116.

11. See especially Axtell, "The Indian Impact on English Colonial Culture," in *The European and the Indian,* 272–315; and Jennings, *The Founders of America,* 167–207.

12. For an illuminating discussion of Anglo-American meditations on native warfare, see Sayre, *Les Sauvages Américains,* 249–83.

13. Scholars have sometimes interpreted Smith's account of his experiences as a failure to recognize a native adoption ceremony, leading to a national misapprehension of an adoptive sister, Pocahontas, as a romantic lead; for a recent overview and affirmation of this interpretation, see Lemay, *Did Pocahontas Save Captain John Smith?* 63–65.

14. Joseph Addison, et al., *The Spectator* (1711), 1:48. All further quotations come from 1:50–51.

15. British examples include Moore, *Yarico to Inkle* (1736); Jerningham, *Yarico to Inkle* (1766); a Young Gentleman of Trinity College, Dublin, *Yarico to Inkle* (1771); Weddell, *Incle and Yarico* (1742); and, most popularly, Colman, *Inkle and Yarico* (1787). Several of these are included in Price, *Inkle and Yarico Album.* Price also provides a bibliographic discussion and considers several continental examples. According to Merchant, the Inkle/Yarico story inspired another kind of revision in Robert Paltock's *Peter Wilkins* (1750), which portrays a happy transracial marriage and a

successful colonial hero; see Merchant, "Robert Paltock and the Refashioning of 'Inkle and Yarico,'" 37–50.

16. For studies that develop a strong equation between women, captivity, and American fiction, see Haberly, "Women and Indians"; Kolodny, *The Land before Her,* 6–67; Castiglia, *Bound and Determined;* and Burnham, *Captivity and Sentiment.*

17. Axtell, *The Invasion Within,* 304.

18. For other examples of early American novels that show an extensive interest in female adoption and transculturation, see Child, *Hobomok* (1824); Hentz, *Tadeuskund* (1825); and Sealsfield, *Tokeah* (1829). The female captive is central to Barnett's analysis of the nineteenth-century frontier romance; see Barnett, *The Ignoble Savage,* 48–70. See also Pearce, *The Savages of America,* 196–236.

19. Written in 1781, the novel first appeared as a serial in the *New York Magazine; or, Literary Repository* (1790–1791). It entered book form first in the *Posthumous Works* (1793), and then in a separately published volume, *The History of Maria Kittle* (1797). I have used the Garland facsimile of the 1797 edition.

20. Critical discussions emphasizing sensibility in the American narratives include Pearce, "The Significances of the Captivity Narrative," 13–14; Derounian-Stodola and Levernier, *The Indian Captivity Narrative,* 186–87; Ebersole, *Captured by Texts,* 98–143; and Burnham, *Captivity and Sentiment,* especially 92–5.

21. Examples include Holman, *The Prisoners of Niagara* (1810); and French, *Elkswatawa* (1836). Suppositonal propaganda often drew from the techniques of virtue-in-distress fiction; see especially *A Surprizing Account of the Captivity of Mrs. Hannah Willis* (1799); *An Affecting Narrative of the Captivity and Sufferings of Mrs. Mary Smith* (1815); and the analysis of these texts in Derounian-Stodola and Levernier, *The Indian Captivity Narrative,* 140–41.

22. Lawson, *A New Voyage to Carolina* (1709).

23. Further citations appear in the text.

24. An extremely fanciful episode of South American captivity, imagined along the lines of failed adoption, appears in *The Voyages, Travels, and Wonderful Discoveries of Capt. John Holmesby* (1757).

25. *The Life, Extraordinary Adventures, Voyages, and Surprizing Escapes of Capt. Neville Frowde* (1758), 172–73.

26. Kimber, *The History of the Life and Adventures of Mr. Anderson* (1754), 141. Further citations appear in the text.

27. *The Female American* (1767). Citations appear in the text.

28. Citations appear in the text.

29. Barker, *Henry Mackenzie,* 66–68.

30. Howard, introduction to Lennox, *The Life of Harriot Stuart* (1751), ed. Howard, 44, 46.

31. Citations appear in the text.

32. For a discussion and an effective rebuttal of this stereotype, see Axtell, *The Invasion Within,* 151–55.

33. Citations appear in the text.

34. On this postrevolutionary perspective, see Pearce, *The Savages of America*. On its place in nineteenth-century American fiction, see Barnett, *The Ignoble Savage*.

35. Imlay, *The Emigrants* (1793), 2–3. Further citations appear in the text.

36. The locus classicus here is the Manheim anthology, first published in 1793 and often reprinted and plagiarized thereafter. For discussions of this narrative and other propagandistic accounts, see VanDerBeets, *The Indian Captivity Narrative*, 13–24; and Derounian-Stodola and Levernier, *The Indian Captivity Narrative*, 26–36, 63–73.

37. For discussions of the American texts, see Castiglia, *Bound and Determined*, 137–79; and Ebersole, *Captured by Texts*, 231–36.

38. Tilton documents the explosion of this myth in *Pocahontas*. See also Fiedler, *The Return of the Vanishing American*, 69–90.

6. Utopian Captivities and Other "African" Paradoxes

1. For details, see Harvey and Racault, "Simon Berington's *Adventures of Sigr Gaudentio di Lucca*," 1–14. On the basis of its twenty-four printings before 1821, the authors call Berington's work "one of the best-selling novels of the eighteenth century" (2).

2. After inspiring nine eighteenth-century printings in four European languages, the work entered its heyday in the nineteenth century. For a list of printings, see Gove, *The Imaginary Voyage in Prose Fiction*, 321–24. On the novel's eighteenth-century influence, see Prica, *Daniel Defoe's Robinson Crusoe und Robert Paltock's Peter Wilkins*. On its nineteenth-century influence, see Roger Lund, "Robert Paltock," 348–55.

3. Considering Cumberland's debt to Berington, Bentley discusses many direct parallels of plot and setting in the introduction to his fine edition of *The Captive of the Castle of Sennaar* (1798), xxvii–xxxvi.

4. More, *Utopia*, 35–36; Gilman, *Herland*. For an illuminating discussion of the geography of More's utopia, see Marin, *Utopics*, especially 99–142.

5. Kumar, *Utopianism*, 51.

6. On the regulatory vision of seventeenth-century utopias, see Davis, *Utopia and the Ideal Society*. Much of Fausett's work argues for a connection between the rise of realist fiction and utopias with austral settings, especially those produced in the tradition of the French *voyage imaginaire;* see Fausett, *Writing the New World*, 158–79, and *Strange Surprizing Sources of Robinson Crusoe*. On the integration of utopia and novel in the eighteenth century, see Rees, *Utopian Imagination*.

7. On the political goals and influences of Harrington's work, see Pocock, *The Ancient Constitution and the Feudal Law* and *The Machiavellian Moment*.

8. See, for example, the selection in Gregory Claeys, ed., *Utopias of the British Enlightenment* (New York: Cambridge, 1994). Claeys provides a useful introduction and bibliography, vii–xxxii. See also Rees, *Utopian Imagination*, which covers a very

canonical and not entirely representative selection, but which offers a particularly strong discussion of gender issues.

9. Scholarship on utopia is generally split between an emphasis on its regulatory social architecture and an emphasis on its liberating experiments, and this split often reflects differences in historic and geographic focus. In *Utopia and the Ideal Society,* for example, Davis's focus on seventeenth-century British utopias leads him to define utopia in terms of regulation (see especially 36–39). On the other hand, Fausett's focus on austral utopias, especially those of the *voyage imaginaire* tradition, leads to an emphasis on playful, disruptive, and satiric imagery; see Fausett, *Writing the New World.* Marin's *Utopics* is especially strong on the inherent playfulness of utopian discourse, while Kumar's *Utopianism* emphasizes its subversiveness.

10. On the Australian setting, see Fausett, *Writing the New World,* and *Images of the Antipodes in the Eighteenth Century.*

11. Evans, *The Adventures, and Surprizing Deliverances* (1719), 79.

12. *The Voyages, Travels, and Wonderful Discoveries of Capt. John Holmesby* (1757), 31–41.

13. Martin, *An Essay upon Plantership* (1773), 3.

14. For studies of British images of Africa and Africans, see especially Barker, *The African Link;* and Curtin, *The Image of Africa,* v–57. For analysis of abolitionist discourse, see Sypher, *Guinea's Captive Kings,* and Ferguson, *Subject to Others.*

15. Curtin's *The Image of Africa* emphasizes British interest in the colonial promise of the interior. For discussion of the Prester John myth within European culture, see Slessarev, *Prester John;* and Gumilev, *Searches for an Imaginary Kingdom,* trans. Smith.

16. Snelgrave, *A New Account of Some Parts of Guinea and the Slave-Trade* (1734). Reprinted separately in 1754, the text also furnished material for continual excisions, abridgements, and criticisms in travel collections such as the extremely successful one edited by Thomas Astley, *A New General Collection of Voyages and Travels* (1745–1747), 2:485–519. Curtin (*The Image of Africa,* 12) calls the Astley collection "the inevitable mine of information for anyone concerned with African affairs during the second half of the century."

17. Lambe, "Letter on Captivity in Dahomy," in Smith, *A New Voyage to Guinea* (1744), 171–89. Lambe's narrative was reprinted in the widely distributed Astley collection; see 2:482–85.

18. See Johnson, trans., *A Voyage to Abyssinia* (1735), by Jerome Lobo, ed. Gold. Gold's introduction includes a useful discussion of the original text, its translations, and background (see xxiii–xlii).

19. Critical interpretations of Paltock generally downplay the African material; see, for example, Bentley's introduction to his edition of *Peter Wilkins* (1750), ix–xviii; and Fausett, *Images of the Antipodes,* 72–79. Rees (*Utopian Imagination,* 109) briefly notes the importance of the African episodes to Wilkins's psychological development, and Lund ("Robert Paltock," 353) discusses the place of slavery in his moral development.

20. Further references appear in the text, citing Christopher Bentley's edition of *Peter Wilkins*. Wilkins's Cornish identity might hint at the crucial role played by such provincials as the merchants of Devon and Cornwall in British expansion overseas.

21. See, for example, the fifteen folio pages in Astley, ed., *A New General Collection of Voyages and Travels* (1745-1747), 3:268–82.

22. "The Strange Adventures of Andrew Battell, of Leigh, in Angola and the Adjoining Regions" first appeared in Purchas's *Purchas his Pilgrimes* (1613), 6:367–406. Battell's narrative also appeared in the widely distributed Astley collection, *A New General Collection of Voyages and Travels*, 3:136–43.

23. For details on Paltock's debt to Battell and to other material from the Astley collection, see Bentley's introduction and notes, *Peter Wilkins* (1750), xii, 384–85.

24. As the spelling of this name changes within Paltock's text, I will allow these variants to stand within quotations, while adhering to "Glanlepze" within my own text.

25. Comparisons to *Robinson Crusoe* go back to a critic in the *Monthly Review* 4 (Dec. 1750): 157. More recent comparisons include Bentley, ed., *Peter Wilkins* (1750), x–xi; Lund, "Robert Paltock," 350–51; Rees, *Utopian Imagination*, 109–10; and Fausett, *Images of the Antipodes*, 73–74.

26. Rees (*Utopian Imagination*, 111) describes the couple's relationship as a companionate marriage but interprets it as a positive prescription rather than an ambiguous vision of colonialism. For readings that recognize the colonial ambiguities of the marriage, see Fausett, *Images of the Antipodes*, 197; and Merchant, "Robert Paltock and the Refashioning of 'Inkle and Yarico,'" 48–50.

27. I use this term as the most convenient. Wilkins renames the country from its original name, "Normbdsgrsutt," because he cannot pronounce it. The new name, "Sass Doorpt Swangeanti," means the "great Flight-Land" (*Peter Wilkins*, 304).

28. Critics often give this isolated passage too much weight in arguing that the novel criticizes colonialism; see, for example, Bentley, ed., *Peter Wilkins*, xviii; and Lund, "Robert Paltock," 359. Rees (*Utopian Imagination*, 112–13) and Merchant ("Robert Paltock and the Refashioning of 'Inkle and Yarico,'" 48–50) more successfully support this position, but the evidence for it seems slight when compared to the general drive of the novel's plot structures.

29. As noted by Rees, *Utopian Imagination*, 115.

30. Given the text's broader interest in utopian name-games, we might speculate that "Zaps" and "Born" are oblique anagrams for "Spanish" and "Iberia." On British propaganda against the Spanish empire, see Gibson, *The Black Legend*, and Maltby, *The Black Legend in England*.

31. For eighteenth-century views of Italy, see Kirby, *The Grand Tour in Italy*, 75–83; Mullenbrock, "The Politcal Implications of the Grand Tour," 7–21; Black, *The British and the Grand Tour*, 112–15, 170–92; and Redford, *Venice and The Grand Tour*, 5–80.

32. Campbell, *The Travels and Adventures of Edward Brown* (1739).

33. In both *Writing the New World* and *Images of the Antipodes,* Fausett shows that colonialism acts as a source of tension within early modern utopian fiction set in Australia.

34. Further citations appear in the text. For a more detailed discussion of the novel's complex narrative scheme, see Harvey and Racault, "Simon Berington's *Adventures of Sigr Gaudentio di Lucca* (1737)," 5–6.

35. As the works of Rees and Fausett reveal in particular, gender is a crucial question in seventeenth and eighteenth century utopias. Rees concentrates on the place of women in utopian visions of the ideal society, while Fausett considers gender-crossing as a sign for culture-crossing.

36. For a more detailed discussion of the novel's genesis and publication, see Bentley's introduction to *The Captive of the Castle of Sennaar* (1798), ix–x, xliii–lii. Although Cumberland may not have originally begun the work with two complementary parts in mind, the second part draws the rather unclosed materials of the first into a fairly developed bildungsroman. Further citations from this edition appear in the text.

37. Adams, *Travelers and Travel Liars,* 210. Adams (210–22) also documents the controversy that Bruce's reports aroused long before the publication of his book, beginning as early as 1774.

38. Bruce, *Travels to Discover the Source of the Nile* (1790), 4:447–50.

39. Bentley (*The Captive of the Castle of Sennaar* [1798], 310) offers some useful discussion of the contemporary British notion of the area.

40. See the examples cited in Nussbaum, *Torrid Zones,* 11–17, 192–93.

Conclusion

1. On Johnson's geographic researches, see Lockhart, "The Fourth Son of the Mighty Emperor," 516–28; and Weitzman, "More Light on *Rasselas,*" 42–58. For another argument suggesting a direct response from Johnson to Berington, see Bentley, "*Rasselas* and *Gaudentio di Lucca* in the Mountains of the Moon," 1–11.

2. Johnson, *Rasselas and Other Tales* (1759), ed. Kolb, Yale Edition, 16:7. Further citations appear in the text.

3. "The Stolen Wife," *American Indian Myths and Legends,* 285–90; "A Competition of Lies," *African Folktales,* 92–99.

4. The several books within Davis's project are well represented by the first, *The Problem of Slavery in Western Culture.*

Primary Bibliography

This chronological bibliography consists primarily of captivity narratives, both factual and fictional, both British and American. For settings outside America, I have included every captivity text that I am aware of. For America I have included captivity narratives referred to in my own study. In addition, I have included some peripheral materials such as travel narratives, general histories, and other texts that discuss captivity. I have included occasional explanatory notes, especially for works that I do not cover substantially in my own text. I have ordered the works by year of initial publication, and then by author's name within the year. Some entries carry two different dates. In these cases, the initial date (used to place the work in chronological order) is that of the original publication, and any subsequent publication date marks the date of a later edition that I have used in my own text.

1427? Johannes Schiltberger. *The Bondage and Travels of Johann Schiltberger, a Native of Bavaria, in Europe, Asia, and Africa, 1396–1427.* Ed. Karl Friedrich Neumann. Trans. J. Buchan Telfer. Works issued by the Hakluyt Society, 1st ser., no. 58. London: Hakluyt Society, 1879. Rpt., New York: B. Franklin, 1970.

1548. G.A. Menavino. *Trattato de Costume et Vita di Turchi.* Fiorenza: Lorenzo Torrentino, 1548.

1569. Bartolomej Georgijevic. *The Ofspring of the House of Ottomanno . . . Whereunto is added Bartholomeus Georgieuiz Epitome, of the Customes, Rytes, Ceremonies, and Religion of the Turkes: with the Miserbale Affliction of those Christians, whiche Liue vnder their Captiuitie and Bondage . . . Englished by Hugh Goughe.* London: Thomas Marshe, [1569?].

1587. Thomas Saunders. *A True Discription and Breefe Discourse, of a Most Lamen-*

table Voiage, Made Latelie to Tripolie in Barbarie, in a Ship Named the Iesus: VVherin Is Not Onely Shevved the Great Miserie, That Then Happened the Aucthor Hereof and His Whole Companie, Aswell the Marchants as the Marriners in That Voiage, According to the Curssed Custome of Those Barbarous and Cruell Tyrants, in Their Terrible Vsage of Christian Captiues. . . . London: Richard Iones, 1587.

1589. Richard Hakluyt. *The Principal Navigations, Voyages, Traffiques & Discoveries of the English Nation. . . .* 10 vols. London: J.M. Dent, 1927.

1590. Edward Webbe. *The Rare and Most VVonderfull Things vvhich Edvv. VVebbe an Englishman Borne, Hath Seene and Passed in His Troublesome Trauailes . . . VVherein Is Set Forth His Extreame Slauery Sustained Many Yeeres Together in the Gallies and Warres of the Great Turke. . . .* London: A[bel] I[effes], [1592?].

1591. Job Hortop. *The Trauailes of an English Man, Containing his Svndrie Calamities Indured by the Space of Twentie and Odd Yeres in his Absence from his Natiue Countrie. . . .* London: W. Wright, 1591. Facs. rpt., New York: Da Capo, 1972.

1595. Richard Hasleton. *Strange and Wonderfull Things. Happened to Richard Hasleton, Borne at Braintree in Essex, in His Ten Yeares Trauailes in Many Forraine Countries.* London: A[bel] I[effes], 1595.

1608. [John Reynard]. *The Admirable Deliverance of 266. Chistians by Iohn Reynard Englishman from the Captiuitie of the Turkes. . . .* London: Thomas Dawson, 1608.

1613. Andrew Battell. *The Strange Adventures of Andrew Battell, of Leigh, in Angola and the Adjoining Regions. Reprinted from "Purchas his Pilgrimes."* Ed. E.G. Ravenstein. Works issued by the Hakluyt Society, 2d ser., no. 6. Nendeln, Liechtenstein: Kraus Reprint, 1967.

1613. Samuel Purchas. *Hakluytus Posthumus, or Purchas his Pilgrimes: Contayning a History of the World in Sea Voyages and Lande Travells by Englishmen and Others.* London: William Stansby, 1625. Rpt., in 20 vols., Glasgow: J. MacLehose and Sons, 1905–1907.

1614. William Davies. *A Trve Relation of the Travailes and Most Miserable Captiuitie . . . of William Dauies, Barber-Surgion of London, Vnder the Duke of Florence. . . .* London: Nicholas Bourne, 1614.

1621. I.B. *Algiers voyage in a iournall or briefe reportary of all occurrents hapning in the fleet of ships sent out by the King his most excellent Maiestie, as well against the pirates of Algiers, as others. . . .* London: B. Alsop, 1621. A factual account of successful resistance to Barbary pirates.

1622. [John Rawlins]. *The Famous and Wonderfull Recoverie of a Ship of Bristoll, called the Exchange, from the Turkish Pirates of Argier. . . .* London: Nathaniel Butter, 1622.

1629. James Wadsworth. *The English Spanish Pilgrime. Or, a nevv Discouerie of Spanish Popery, and Iesuiticall Stratagems. VVith the Estate of the English*

Pentioners and Fugitiues vnder the King of Spaines Dominions, and else where at this Present Time. . . . London: Michael Sparke, 1629. Facs. rpt., New York: Da Capo Press, 1970. This factual text includes an Oriental captivity episode.

1630. John Smith. *True Travels, Adventvres, and Observations of Captaine Iohn Smith.* London: Thomas Slater, 1630. Facs. rpt., New York: Da Capo, 1968. This factual text includes an episode of captivity in central Asia.

1632. William Lithgow. *The Totall Discourse, of the Rare Adventures, and Painefull Peregrinations of long Nineteene Yeares Travayles from Scotland, to the most Famous Kingdomes in Europe, Asia, and Affrica . . . Together with the Grievous Tortures he Suffered, by the Inquisition of Malaga in Spaine, his Miraculous Discovery and Delivery thence. . . .* London: Nicholas Okes, 1632.

1640. Francis Knight. *A Relation of Seaven Yeares Slaverie under the Turkes of Argeire. . . .* London: T. Cotes, 1640.

1647. Alfonso de Dominici. *Trattato della Miserie, che Patiscono I Fideli Chistiani Shiavi de' Barbari. . . .* Rome, 1647.

1657. Richard Ligon. *A True and Exact History of the Island of Barbados.* London: Humphrey Moseley, 1657. This travel narrative includes the anecdote that inspired the Inkle and Yarico legend.

1662. Katharine Evans and Sarah Chevers. *This is a Short Relation of some of the Cruel Sufferings (for the Truths Sake) of Katharine Evans & Sarah Chevers, in the Inquisition in the Isle of Malta. . . .* London: Robert Wilson, 1662.

1665. Richard Head. *The English Rogue.* Boston: New Frontiers, 1961.

1665. Royal Society of London. *Philosophical Transactions giving Some Accompt of the Present Undertakings, Studies, and Labours of the Ingenious in many Considerable Parts of the World.* London: John Martyn, 1665. Facs. rpt., Amsterdam: Graaf and Israel, 1963–1964.

1667. Thomas Sprat. *The History of the Royal Society. . . .* 1667. Facs. rpt., Jackson I. Cope and Harold Whitmore, St. Louis: Washington Univ. Press, 1959.

1670. T. S[mith]. *The Adventures of an English Merchant Taken Prisoner by the Turks of Argiers. . . .* London: Moses Pitt, 1670.

1675. William Okeley. *Eben-ezer: or, a small Monument of Great Mercy. . . .* London: Nat. Ponder, 1675.

1676. Thomas Overbury. *A True and Perfect Account of the Examination, Confession, Tryal, Condemnation and Execution of Joan Perry . . . Likewise Mr. Harrison's Own Acount How He Was Conveyed into Turkey and There Made a Slave Above Two Years. . . .* London: Rowland Reynolds, 1676.

1681. Robert Knox. *An Historical Relation of the Island Ceylon in the East Indies. . . .* London: Richard Chiswell, 1681. Rpt., ed. James Ryan, Glasgow: James MacLehose and Sons, 1911. Facs. rpt., with an introduction by H.A.I. Goonetileke, New Delhi: Navrang, 1983.

1682. Adam Elliot. *A Modest Vindication of Titus Oates. . . .* London: Joseph Hindmarsh, 1682.

1682. Mary Rowlandson. *The Soveraignty & Goodness of God, Together, with the*

Faithfulness of His Promises Displayed; Being a Narrative of the Captivity and Restauration of Mrs. Mary Rowlandson. 2d ed. Cambridge, Mass.: Samuel Green, 1682. Facs. rpt., Garland Library of Narratives of North American Captivities, vol. 1, New York: Garland, 1977. Rpt. in *Puritans among the Indians: Accounts of Captivity and Redemption, 1676–1724,* ed. Alden T. Vaughan and Edward W. Clark, Cambridge: Harvard Univ. Press, 1981.

1685. Thomas Phelps. *A True Account of the Captivity of Thomas Phelps at Machaness in Barbary, and of his Strange Escape. . . .* London: H. Hills, 1685.

1689–1690. John Locke. *Two Treatises of Government.* Ed. Peter Laslett. New York: Cambridge Univ. Press, 1960.

1690. *L'Esclave Religieux et Ses Avantures.* Paris: Daniel Hartmels, 1690.

1692. Robert Boyle. *General Heads for the Natural History of a Country. . . .* London: John Taylor and S. Holford, 1692.

1693. Francis Brooks. *Barbarian Cruelty Being a True History of the Distressed Condition of the Christian Captives Under the Tyranny of Mully Ishmael, Emperor of Morocco. . . .* London: I. Salusbury and H. Newman, 1693. Rpt., Boston: S. Phillips, 1700.

1697. Cotton Mather. *Humiliations Follow'd by Deliverances. . . .* Boston: B. Green and J. Allen, 1697. Facs. rpt., Garland Library of Narratives of North American Captivities, vol. 1, New York: Garland, 1977.

1699. Jonathan Dickinson. *God's Protecting Providence, Man's Surest Help and Defence.* Philadelphia: Reiner Jansen, 1699. Ed. Evangeline Walker Andrews and Charles McLean Andrews. New Haven: Yale Univ. Press, 1961.

1699. William Hacke. *A Collection of Original Voyages: Containing . . . IV. Mr. Roberts's Adventures Among the Corsairs of the Levant. . . .* London: J. Knapton, 1699.

1699. Cotton Mather. *Decennium Luctuosum. . . .* Boston: B. Green and J. Allen, 1699. Facs. rpt., Garland Library of Narratives of North American Captivities, vol. 3, New York: Garland, 1978.

1704. Awnsham Churchill and John Churchill, eds. *A Collection of Voyages and Travels. . . .* London: Awnsham Churchill and John Churchill, 1704.

1704. Joseph Pitts. *A True and Faithful Account of the Religion and Manners of the Mohammetans, in Which is a Particular Relation of Their Pilgrimage to Mecca, the Place of Mohammet's Birth; and a Description of Medina and of His Tomb There. As Likewise of Algier and the Country Adjacent, and of Alexandria, Grand-Cairo, &C. With an Account of the Author's Being Taken Captive, the Turks Cruelty to Him and of His Escape. . . .* Exon: S. Farley for P. Bishop and E. Score, 1704.

1707. Cotton Mather. *A Memorial of the Present Deplorable State of New-England.* Boston: S. Phillips, 1707. Facs. rpt., Garland Library of Narratives of North American Captivities, vol. 4, New York: Garland, 1978.

1707. John Williams. *The Redeemed Captive Returning to Zion. . . .* Boston: B. Green, 1707. 3d ed. Boston: S. Green, 1758. Rpt. in *Puritans among the Indians: Ac-*

counts of Captivity and Redemption, 1676–1724, ed. Alden T. Vaughan and Edward W. Clark, Cambridge: Harvard Univ. Press, 1981.

1708. Hendrik Smeeks. *The Mighty Kingdom of Krinke Kesmes.* 1708. Ed. David Fausett. Trans. Robert-H. Leek. Atlanta: Rodopi, 1995. This Dutch novel contains episodes of captivity and utopia.

1708. John Stevens. *New Collection of Voyages. . . .* London: J. Knapton, 1708. This popular voyage collection includes some "Travels in the Kingdoms of Fez and Morocco during Eleven Years' Captivity."

1709. John Lawson. *A New Voyage to Carolina. . . .* London: n. p., 1709. Facs. rpt., March of America Facsimile Series, no. 35. Ann Arbor, Mich.: University Microfilms, 1966.

1711. Joseph Addison, et al. *The Spectator.* Ed. Donald F. Bond. 5 vols. New York: Oxford Univ. Press, 1965. Vol. 1, pp. 48–51, contains the most popular version of the Inkle and Yarico legend.

1713. Simon Ockley, ed. *An Account of South-West Barbary Containing What Is Most Remarkable in the Territories of the King of Fez and Morocco. Written by a Person Who had been a Slave.* London: J. Bowyer and H. Clements, 1713. Promises but does not deliver an actual narrative of captivity.

1714. Walter Vaughan. *The Adventures of Five Englishmen from Pulo Condoro. . . .* London: C. Bates and A. Bettesworth, 1714. Facs. rpt., New York: Garland, 1972.

1719. Daniel Defoe. *The Life and Strange Surprizing Adventures of Robinson Crusoe. . . .* 1719. Ed. J. Donald Crowley. New York: Oxford Univ. Press, 1972.

1719. Ambrose Evans. *The Adventures, and Surprizing Deliverances of James Dubordieu, and his Wife. . . .* London: J. Bettenham, 1719. Facs. rpt., New York: Garland, 1972.

1720. William Rufus Chetwood. *The Voyages, Dangerous Adventures, and Imminent Escapes of Captain Richard Falconer. . . .* London: Chetwood, 1720. Facs. rpt., New York: Garland, 1973.

1720. Daniel Defoe. *The Life, Adventures, and Pyracies of the Famous Captain Singleton. . . .* 1720. Ed. Shiv K. Kumar. London: Oxford Univ. Press, 1969.

1721. *An Account of the Extream Misery of the Christian Captives in Barbary.* London: J. Downing, 1721.

1721. Penelope Aubin. *The Strange Adventures of the Count de Vinevil. . . .* London: E. Bell et al., 1721. Facs. rpt., New York: Garland, 1973.

1721. *A Description of the Nature of Slavery among the Moors . . . To which is added, an Account of Capt. Stuart's Negociations for the Redemption of English Captives . . . written by one of the said Redeem'd Captives.* London: J. Peele, 1721.

1722. Penelope Aubin. *The Life and Amorous Adventures of Lucinda. . . . Taken by a Rover of Barbary, and Sold a Slave at Constantinople. . . .* London: E. Bell et al., 1722.

1722. Penelope Aubin. *The Noble Slaves: or, the Lives and Adventures of two Lords and two Ladies. . . .* London: E. Bell et al., 1722.

1723. Penelope Aubin. *The Life of Charlotta Du Pont, an English Lady; Taken From Her Own Memoirs. Giving an Account How She Was Trepan'd by Her Stepmother to Virginia. . . .* London: A. Bettesworth, 1723.

1724. Eliza Haywood. *Idalia. Or, the Unfortunate Mistress.* 3d ed. London: Dan Browne and S. Chapman, 1724. Facs. rpt. in *Masquerade Novels of Eliza Haywood*, with an introduction by Mary Anne Schofield. Delmar, N.Y.: Scholars' Facsimiles & Reprints, 1986.

1724. Isaac Martin. *The Tryal and Sufferings of Mr. Isaac Martin, who was Put into the Inquisition in Spain, for the Sake of the Protestant Religion. . . .* London: J. Osborn et al., 1724.

1726. Jane Barker. *The Lining of the Patch Work Screen. . . .* London: A. Bettisworth, 1726. Rpt. in *The Galesia Trilogy and Selected Manuscript Poems*, ed. Carol Shiner Wilson, New York: Oxford Univ. Press, 1997.

1726. William Rufus Chetwood. *The Voyages and Adventures of Captain Robert Boyle. . . .* London: John Watts, 1726. Facs. rpt., New York: Garland, 1972.

1727. Alonso de Castillo Solorzano. *Spanish Amusements: or, the Adventures of that Celebrated Courtezan Seniora Rufina Call'd, the Pole-cat of Seville. . . .* 2d ed. London: H. Curll, 1727. This fictional collection includes Oriental captivity episodes.

1727. Cadwallader Colden. *The History of the Five Indian Nations Depending on the Province of New-York in America.* Ithaca, N.Y.: Cornell Univ. Press, 1964.

1727. Eliza Haywood. *The Fruitless Enquiry. Being a Collection of Several Entertaining Histories and Occurrences, which Fell Under the Observation of a Lady in her Search after Happiness.* 2d ed. London: T. Lowndes, 1767.

1727. Eliza Haywood. *Philidore and Placentia; or L'Amour trop Delicat.* London: Tho. Green, 1727. Rpt. in *Four before Richardson: Selected English Novels, 1720–1727*, ed. William H. McBurney, Lincoln: Univ. of Nebraska Press, 1978.

1727. *A Voyage to Cacklogallinia.* London: J. Watson, 1727. Facs. rpt., New York: Garland, 1972.

1728. Penelope Aubin. *The Life and Adventures of the Young Count Albertus, the Son of Count Lewis Augustus, by the Lady Lucy: Who Being Become a Widower, Turn'd Monk, and Went a Missionary For China. . . .* London: J. Darby et al., 1728.

1728. Elizabeth Singer Rowe. *Friendship in Death. . . .* London: T. Worrall, 1728. 3d ed., with *Letters Moral and Entertaining.* 2 pts. London: T. Worrall, 1733. Facs. rpt., New York: Garland, 1972.

1729. Robert Drury. *Madagascar; or, Robert Drury's Journal, during Fifteen Years' Captivity on that Island.* London: W. Meadows et al., 1729. Ed. Pasfield Oliver, 1890. Rpt., New York: Negro Universities Press, 1969.

1733. Simon Tyssot de Patot. *The Travels and Adventures of James Massey. Translated from the French.* London: John Watts, 1733. The hero of this novel enters both the Goa Inquisition and Algerine slavery.

1734. William Snelgrave. *A New Account of Some Parts of Guinea and the Slave-Trade.* London: James, John, and Paul Knapton, 1734. Facs. rpt., Cass Library of African Studies, Slavery Series, no. 11, London: F. Cass, 1971.

1735. Samuel Johnson, trans. *A Voyage to Abyssinia. By Father Jerome Lobo, a Portuguese Jesuit. . . . With a Continuation of the History of Abyssinia . . . By Mr. Legrand. From The French.* London: A. Bettesworth and C. Hitch, 1735. Ed. Joel J. Gold. The Yale Edition of *The Works of Samuel Johnson,* vol. 15. New Haven: Yale Univ. Press, 1985.

1736. William Rufus Chetwood. *The Voyages, Travels and Adventures of William Owen Gwin Vaughan. . . .* London: J. Watts, 1736. Facs. rpt., New York: Garland, 1972.

1736. John Gyles. *Memoirs of Odd Adventures. . . .* Boston: William Dodge, 1736. Rpt. in *Puritans among the Indians: Accounts of Captivity and Redemption, 1676–1724,* ed. Alden T. Vaughan and Edward W. Clark, Cambridge: Harvard Univ Press, 1981.

1736. Edward Moore. *Yarico to Inkle. An Epistle.* London: Lawton Gilliver, 1736.

1737. Simon Berington. *The Memoirs of Sigr Gaudentio di Lucca. . . .* London: T. Cooper, 1737. Facs. rpt., New York: Garland, 1973.

1738. Joseph Pitts. *A True and Faithful Account. . . .* 4th ed. London: T. Longman and R. Hett, 1738. Facs. rpt., Farnborough: Gregg International, 1971. Greatly expanded from the first edition.

1739. Penelope Aubin. *A Collection of Entertaining Histories and Novels. . . .* London: D. Midwinter et al., 1739.

1739. John Campbell. *The Travels and Adventures of Edward Brown. . . .* London: J. Applebee, 1739. Facs. rpt., New York: Garland, 1973. A novel of travels in and below Egypt.

1739. Thomas Pellow. *The History of the Long Captivity and Adventures of Thomas Pellow, in South-Barbary. . . .* London: R. Goadey, 1739. Facs. rpt., New York: Garland, 1973.

1742. Weddell. *Incle and Yarico: A Tragedy.* London: T. Cooper, 1742.

1742–1743. William Rufus Chetwood. *The Twins: or, the Female Traveller. . . .* London: n.p., 1742–1743.

1743. James Annesley. *Memoirs of an Unfortunate Young Nobleman, Return'd from a Thirteen Years Slavery in America. . . .* London: J. Freeman, 1743. Facs. rpt., New York: Garland, 1975. This roman à clef begins with an extended indenture narrative.

1743. William Moraley. *The Infortunate: Or, The Voyage and Adventures. . . .* Newcastle: J. White, 1743. Rpt., ed. Susan E. Klepp and Billy G. Smith, University Park: Pennsylvania State Univ. Press, 1992. This indenture narrative includes an interpolated episode concerning Moroccan slavery.

1744. Bullfinch Lambe. "Letter on Captivity in Dahomy." In William Smith. *A New Voyage to Guinea: Describing the Customs, Manners. . . .* London: John Nourse,

1744. Facs. rpt., Cass Library of African Studies, Travels and Narratives, no. 22, London: Cass, 1967.

1744. *The Lady's Drawing Room. Being a Faithfull Picture of the Great World....* London: M. Cooper and A. Dodd, 1744. Facs. rpt., New York: Garland, 1974.

1744. *The True History of Henrietta de Bellgrave....* London: M. Cooper and A. Dodd, 1744. This captivity tale also appears in *The Lady's Drawing Room* of the same year.

1745–1747. Thomas Astley, ed. *A New General Collection of Voyages and Travels....* 4 vols. London: Thomas Astley, 1745–1747. Facs. rpt., Cass Library of African Studies, Travels and Narratives, no. 47, London: Cass, 1968.

1746. John Coustos. *The Sufferings of John Coustos, for Free-masonry, and for his Refusing to turn Roman Catholic, in the Inquisition at Lisbon....* London: W. Strahan, 1746.

1747. *The Adventures of a Kidnapped Orphan.* London: M. Thrush, 1747. Facs. rpt., New York: Garland, 1974.

1748. John Norton. *The Redeemed Captive.* Boston: S. Kneeland, 1748. American.

1750. Isaac Morris. *A Narrative of the Dangers and Distresses Which Befel Isaac Morris, and Even More of the Crew, Belonging to the Wager... on an Uninhabited Part of Patagonia, in South America; Where They Remained... 'Till They Were Seized by a Party of Indians, and Carried above a Thousand Miles into the Inland Country....* London: S. Birt, 1750. Rpt., New York: R.M. McBride, 1927.

1750. Robert Paltock. *The Life and Adventures of Peter Wilkins.* Ed Christopher Bentley. New York: Oxford Univ. Press, 1973.

1751. Charlotte Lennox. *The Life of Harriot Stuart, Written by Herself.* Ed. Susan Kubica Howard. Madison, N.J.: Fairleigh Dickinson Univ. Press, 1995.

1754. Edward Kimber. *The History of the Life and Adventures of Mr. Anderson....* London: W. Owen, 1754. Facs. rpt., Garland Library of Narratives of North American Captivities, vol. 7, New York: Garland, 1975. This novel contains a short Amerindian captivity and a much more extended treatment of indenture.

1755. John Shebeare. *Lydia; or Filial Piety.* 4 vols. London: J. Scott, 1755. Facs. rpt., in 2 vols., New York: Garland, 1974. This novel contains a brief Oriental captivity.

1757. *The Voyages, Travels, and Wonderful Discoveries of Capt. John Holmesby. Containing a Series of the Most Surprising and Uncommon Events, Which Befel the Author in His Voyage to the Southern Ocean, in the Year 1739.* London: F. Noble and J. Noble, 1757. This travel novel contains moments of utopia and captivity.

1757. Peter Williamson. *French and Indian Cruelty....* York: N. Nickson, 1757. Facs. rpt., Garland Library of Narratives of North American Indian Captivities, vol. 9, New York: Garland, 1978.

1758. Edward Kimber. *The Life, Extraordinary Adventures, Voyages, and Surprizing Escapes of Capt. Neville Frowde....* London: J. Wren, 1708 [1758].

1758. Peter Williamson. *French and Indian Cruelty.* . . . 3d ed. Glasgow: J. Bryce and D. Paterson, 1758. Facs. rpt., Garland Library of Narratives of North American Indian Captivities, vol. 9, New York: Garland, 1978. Expanded from the first edition.

1759. Samuel Johnson. *Rasselas and Other Tales.* Ed. Gwin J. Kolb. Yale Edition of *The Works of Samuel Johnson,* vol. 16. New Haven: Yale Univ. Press, 1990.

1764. Henry Grace. *History of the Life and Sufferings.* . . . Reading: printed for the author, 1764. Facs. rpt., Garland Library of Narratives of North American Captivities, vol. 10, New York: Garland, 1977.

1765. William Smith. *An Historical Account of the Expedition against the Ohio Indians, in the Year 1764, under the Command of Henry Bouquet.* . . . Philadelphia: William Bradford, 1765. Rpt., London: T. Jefferies, 1766. Facs. rpt., March of America Facsimile Series, no. 45, Ann Arbor, Mich.: University Microfilms, 1966. Describes American captives.

1766. Edward Jerningham. *Yarico to Inkle an Epistle.* London: J. Dodsley, 1766.

1767. *The Female American; or, the Adventures of Unca Eliza Winkfield. Compiled by Herself.* London: Francis Noble and John Noble, 1767. Facs. rpt., New York: Garland, 1974.

1767. Henry Mackenzie. *The Man of Feeling.* New York: Norton, 1958.

1769. Mrs. Crisp. *The Female Captive: A Narrative of Facts which Happened in Barbary in the Year 1756.* London: C. Bathurst, 1769.

1770. Isaac Bickerstaff. *The Life, Strange Voyages, and Uncommon Adventures of Ambrose Gwinett.* . . . 4th ed. London: J. Lever, [1771?].

1770. Mary Rowlandson. *A Narative of the Captivity.* . . . Boston: Nathaniel Coverly, 1770. The first American edition with the word "captivity" in the title.

1771. A Young Gentleman of Trinity College. *Yarico to Inkle.* Dublin: Stewart & Co., 1771.

1773. Henry Mackenzie. *The Man of the World.* London: W. Strahan and T. Cadell, 1773. Facs. rpt., New York: Garland, 1974.

1773. Samuel Martin. *An Essay upon Plantership.* . . . 5th ed. London: T. Cadell, 1773.

1775. Alexander Bicknel. *The Benevolent Man. Or, the History of Mr. Belville: In Which Is Introduced, the Remarkable Adventures of Captain Maclean, the Hermit.* London: J. Lewis, 1775. Facs. rpt., New York: Garland, 1974. Novel with brief Oriental captivity.

1779. John Dodge. *A Narrative of the Capture and Treatment of John Dodge.* Philadelphia: T. Bradford, 1779. American suppositional narrative.

1780. John Kingdon. *Redeemed Slaves: Being a Short Narrative of Two Neopolitans Redeemed from Slavery on the Coast of Barbary.* Bristol: W. Pine, 1780.

1782. J. Hector St. John de Crèvecoeur. *Letters from an American Farmer.* Gloucester, Mass.: Peter Smith, 1968. Includes famous comments on American captives.

1783–1789. Thomas Day. *The History of Sandford and Merton.* London: J. Stockdale,

1783–1789. Facs. rpt., New York: Garland, 1977. Children's novel with Oriental captivity episodes.

1784. John Filson. *The Discovery, Settlement and Present State of Kentucke.* . . . Wilmington, Del.: James Adams, 1784. Facs. rpt., March of America Facsimile Series, no. 50, Ann Arbor, Mich.: University Microfilms, 1966. Includes the original Daniel Boone captivity.

1785. John Marrant. *A Narrative of the Lord's Wonderful Dealings.* . . . London: Gilbert and Plummer, 1785. Facs. rpt., Garland Library of Narratives of North American Captivities, vol. 17, New York: Garland, 1978.

1787. Robert Bage. *The Fair Syrian.* . . . London: J. Walter et al., 1787. Facs. rpt., New York: Garland, 1979. Novel with Oriental captivity episodes.

1787. George Colman. *Inkle and Yarico: An Opera.* London: G.G. and J. Robinson, 1787.

1789. Robert Norris. *Memoirs of the Reign of Bossa Ahadee, King of Dahomey.* . . . London: W. Lowndes, 1789.

1790. James Bruce. *Travels to Discover the Source of the Nile, in the Years 1768, 1769, 1770, 1771, 1772, and 1773.* 5 vols. Edinburgh: J. Ruthven, 1790.

1790. Charlotte Lennox. *Euphemia.* 4 vols. London: T. Cadell and J. Evans, 1790. Facs. rpt., London: Thoemmes, 1992.

1792. James Bristow. *A Narrative of the Sufferings of James Bristow, Belonging to the Bengal Artillery, during Ten Years Captivity with Hyder Ally and Tippoo Saheb.* Calcutta: the Honorable Company's Press, 1792.

1793. Ann Eliza Bleecker. *Posthumous Works.* . . . New York: T. and J. Swords, 1793.

1793. Archibald Dalzel. *The History of Dahomy, an Inland Kingdom.* . . . London: T. Spilsbury and Son, 1793. Facs. rpt., London: Cass, 1967.

1793. Gilbert Imlay. *The Emigrants (1793) Traditionally Ascribed to Imlay, but, More Probably, by Mary Wollstonecraft.* . . . Facs. rpt., with an introduction by Robert A. Hare, Gainesville, Fla.: Scholars' Facsimiles & Reprints, 1964.

1793. Charlotte Smith. *The Old Manor House.* Ed. Anne Henry Ehrenpreis. New York: Oxford Univ. Press, 1969.

1795. Susanna Rowson. *Slaves in Algiers.* Philadelphia: Carey, 1795. Oriental captivity in dramatic form.

1795. Ann Yearsley. *The Royal Captives: A Fragment of Secret History Copied from an Old Manuscript.* 4 vols. London: G.G. and J. Robinson, 1795. Facs. rpt., New York: Garland, 1974. This man-in-the-iron-mask novel includes a very brief episode of Algerian captivity.

1797. Ann Eliza Bleecker. *The History of Maria Kittle.* . . . Hartford, Conn.: Elisha Babcock, 1797. Facs. rpt., Garland Library of Narratives of North American Captivities, vol. 20, New York: Garland, 1977.

1797. Royall Tyler. *The Algerine Captive.* Walpole, N.H.: David Carlisle, 1797. One of the first American novels.

1798. John Coustos. *Horrid Tortures: or, the Unparalleled Sufferings.* . . . Putney, Vt.:

Sturtevant, 1798. Rpt., Brookfield, Mass.: E. Merriam, 1800. American reprint of *The Sufferings,* 1746.

1798. George Cumberland. *The Captive of the Castle of Sennaar. An African Tale. . . .* London: Egerton, 1798. Ed. G.E. Bentley. Montreal: McGill-Queen's Univ. Press, 1991.

1798. *The Voyages, Distresses, and Adventures of Captain Winterfield. . . .* London: Ann Lemoine, 1798. This pamphlet fiction includes captivities and other global distresses.

1799. *Horrid Indian Cruelties! Affecting History of the Dreadful Distresses of Frederic Manheim's Family. . . .* Boston: James White, 1799.

1799. James Smith. *An Account of the Remarkable Occurences in the Life and Travels of Col. James Smith.* Lexington, Ky.: John Bradford, 1799. American transculturation narrative.

1799. *A Surprizing Account of the Captivity of Mrs. Hannah Willis.* Stonington-Port, Conn.: S. Trumbull,1799. American narrative.

1799. *The True History of Zoa. . . .* London: S. Fisher and T. Hurst, 1799. A captivity tale from *The Lady's Drawing Room,* 1744.

1800. *Narrative of the Singular Adventures and Captivity of Mr. Thomas Barry. . . .* Sommers Town [London]: A. Neil, 1800. Facs. rpt., Garland Library of Narratives of North American Captivities, vol. 24, New York: Garland, 1979. Fictional.

1801. *The Life and Travels of James Tudor Owen.* London: S. Fisher, 1801. Facs. rpt., Garland Library of Narratives of North American Captivities, vol. 25, New York: Garland, 1977. Fictional.

1806. Maria Martin. *History of the Captivity and Sufferings of Mrs. Maria Martin Who Was Six Years a Slave in Algiers, Two of Which She Was Confined in a Dark And Dismal Dungeon, Loaded With Irons.* Boston: W. Crary, 1806.

1809. Alexander Henry. *Travels and Adventures in Canada and the Indian Territories.* New York: I. Riley, 1809. Facs. rpt., March of America Facsimile Series, no. 43, Ann Arbor, Mich.: University Microfilms, 1966. American transculturation narrative.

1810. Jesse Lynch Holman. *The Prisoners of Niagara.* Frankfort, Ky.: William Gerard, 1810. Facs. rpt., Berea, Ky.: Kentucky Imprints, 1975. American fiction.

1815. *An Affecting Narrative of the Captivity and Sufferings of Mrs. Mary Smith.* Providence, R.I.: L. Scott, 1815. American.

1823. John Dunn Hunter. *Manners and Customs of Several Indian Tribes Located West of the Mississippi Including Some Account of the Soil, Climate and Vegetable Productions and the Indian Materia Medica, to Which Is Prefixed the History of the Author's Life During a Residence of Several Years Among Them.* Philadelphia: J. Maxwell, 1823. American transculturation narrative.

1824. Lydia Maria Child. *Hobomok, a Tale of Early Times.* Boston: Cummings Hilliard, 1824. Rpt. in *Hobomok and Other Writings on Indians,* ed. Carolyn L. Karcher, New Brunswick, N.J.: Rutgers Univ. Press, 1986.

1824. James Everett Seaver. *A Narrative of the Life of Mrs. Mary Jemison.* Canandaigua, N.Y.: J.D. Bemis, 1824. Rpt., with an introduction by June Namias, Norman, Okla.: Univ. of Oklahoma Press, 1992. American transculturation narrative.

1825. Nicholas Marcellus Hentz. *Tadeuskund, the Last King of the Lenape: an Historical Tale.* Boston: Cummings, Hilliard, 1825. American fiction.

1829. Charles Sealsfield. *Tokeah, or the White Rose.* Philadelphia: Carey, Lea & Carey, 1829. American fiction.

1830. Edwin James. *A Narrative of the Captivity and Adventures of John Tanner. . . .* New York: G. & C.H. Carvell, 1830. Rpt., with an introduction by Louise Erdrich, New York: Penguin, 1994. American transculturation narrative.

1836. James Strange French. *Elkswatawa; or the Prophet of the West.* New York: Harper & Brothers, 1836. American fiction.

Secondary Bibliography

Adams, Percy. *Travel Literature and the Evolution of the Novel.* Lexington: Univ. Press of Kentucky, 1983.

———. *Travelers and Travel Liars, 1660–1800.* Berkeley: Univ. of California Press, 1962.

Adolph, Robert. *The Rise of Modern Prose.* Cambridge, Mass.: MIT Press, 1968.

Armstrong, Nancy, and Leonard Tennenhouse. "The American Origins of the English Novel." *American Literary History* 4 (Fall 1992): 386–410.

———. *The Imaginary Puritan.* Berkeley: Univ. of California Press, 1992.

Axtell, James. "At the Water's Edge: Trading in the Sixteenth Century." In *After Columbus: Essays in the Ethnohistory of Colonial North America*, 144–81. New York: Oxford Univ. Press, 1988.

———. *The European and the Indian: Essays in the Ethnohistory of Colonial North America.* New York: Oxford Univ. Press, 1981.

———. *The Invasion Within: The Contest of Cultures in Colonial North America.* New York: Oxford Univ. Press, 1985.

Azim, Firdous. *The Colonial Rise of the Novel.* New York: Routledge, 1993.

Backscheider, Paula. *Daniel Defoe: His Life.* Baltimore: Johns Hopkins Univ. Press, 1989.

Baepler, Paul. "The Barbary Captivity Narrative in Early America." *Early American Literature* 30 (1995): 95–120.

———. "White Slavery in Africa: The Barbary Captivity Narrative in American Literature." Ph.D. diss., Univ. of Minnesota, 1996.

Barker, Anthony J. *The African Link: British Attitudes to the Negro in the Era of the Atlantic Slave Trade, 1550–1807.* Totowa, N.J.: Frank Cass, 1978.

Barker, Gerard K. *Henry Mackenzie.* New York: Twayne, 1975.

Barnett, Louise K. *The Ignoble Savage: American Literary Racism, 1790–1890.* Westport, Conn.: Greenwood Press, 1975.

Batten, Charles. *Pleasurable Instruction.* Berkeley: Univ. of California Press, 1978.

Baum, Rosalie Murphy. "John Williams's Captivity Narrative: A Consideration of Normative Ethnicity." In *A Mixed Race: Ethnicity in Early America,* ed. Shuffleton, 56–76. New York: Oxford Univ. Press, 1993.

Beasley, Jerry C. *Novels of the 1740s.* Athens: Univ. of Georgia Press, 1982.

Beck, Brandon H. *From the Rising of the Sun: English Images of the Ottoman Empire to 1715.* New York: P. Lang, 1987.

Bender, John. *Imagining the Penitentiary: Fiction and the Architecture of Mind in Eighteenth-Century England.* Chicago: Univ. of Chicago Press, 1987.

Bentley, G.E. *"Rasselas* and *Gaudentio di Lucca* in the Mountains of the Moon." *Revista Canaria de Estudios Ingleses* 9 (1984): 1–11.

Berkhofer, Robert F., Jr. *The White Man's Indian: Images of the American Indian from Columbus to the Present.* New York: Knopf, 1978.

Bhabha, Homi K. *The Location of Culture.* New York: Routledge, 1994.

Bissell, Benjamin Hezekiah. *The American Indian in English Literature of the Eighteenth Century.* New Haven: Yale Univ. Press, 1925.

Black, Jeremy. *The British and the Grand Tour.* London: Croom Helm, 1985.

Blunt, Wilfrid. *Black Sunrise: The Life and Times of Mulai Ismail, Emperor of Morocco, 1646–1727.* London: Methuen, 1951.

Braudel, Fernand. *The Mediterranean and the Mediterranean World in the Age of Philip II.* Trans. Sian Reynolds. 2 vols. New York: Harper & Row, 1973.

Breitwieser, Mitchell Robert. *American Puritanism and the Defense of Mourning: Religion, Grief, and Ethnology in Mary White Rowlandson's Captivity Narrative.* Madison: Univ. of Wisconsin Press, 1990.

Brown, Laura. *Ends of Empire: Women and Ideology in Early Eighteenth-Century English Literature.* Ithaca, N.Y.: Cornell Univ. Press, 1993.

Bumstead, J.M. "'Carried to Canada!': Perceptions of the French in British Colonial Captivity Narratives, 1690–1760." *American Review of Canadian Studies* 13 (1983): 79–96.

Burnham, Michelle. *Captivity and Sentiment: Cultural Exchange in American Literature, 1682–1861.* Hanover, N.H.: Univ. Press of New England, 1997.

Carleton, Phillips D. "The Indian Captivity." *American Literature* 15 (1943): 169–80.

Castiglia, Christopher. *Bound and Determined: Captivity, Culture-Crossing, and White Womanhood from Mary Rowlandson to Patty Hearst.* Chicago: Univ. of Chicago Press, 1996.

Castle, Terry. *Masquerade and Civilization: The Carnivalesque in Eighteenth-Century English Culture and Fiction.* Stanford: Stanford Univ. Press, 1986.

Chew, Samuel Claggett. *The Crescent and the Rose: Islam and England during the Renaissance.* New York: Oxford Univ. Press, 1937.

Claeys, Gregory, ed. *Utopias of the British Enlightenment.* New York: Cambridge, 1994.

Clark, J.C.D. *The Language of Liberty, 1660–1832: Political Discourse and Social Dynamics in the Anglo-American World.* New York: Cambridge Univ. Press, 1994.

"A Competition of Lies." In *African Folktales,* ed. Roger D. Abrahams, 92–99. New York: Pantheon, 1983.

Craft-Fairchild, Catherine. *Masquerade and Gender: Disguise and Female Identity in Eighteenth-Century Fictions by Women.* Philadelphia: Univ. of Pennsylvania Press, 1993.

Curtin, Philip D. *The Image of Africa: British Ideas and Action, 1780–1850.* Madison: Univ. of Wisconsin Press, 1964.

Davidson, Cathy N. *Revolution and the Word: The Rise of the Novel in America.* New York: Oxford Univ. Press, 1986.

Davies, K.G. *The Royal Africa Company.* New York: Longmans, 1957.

Davis, David Brion. *The Problem of Slavery in Western Culture.* New York: Oxford Univ. Press, 1988.

Davis, J.C. *Utopia and the Ideal Society: A Study of English Utopian Writing, 1516–1700.* New York: Cambridge Univ. Press, 1981.

Davis, Lennard. "The Fact of Events and the Event of Facts: New World Explorers and the Early Novel." *The Eighteenth Century: Theory and Interpretation* 32 (1991): 240–55.

———. *Factual Fictions: The Origins of the English Novel.* New York: Columbia Univ. Press, 1983.

———. *Resisting Novels: Ideology and Fiction.* New York: Methuen, 1987.

Denn, Robert J. "Captivity Narratives of the American Revolution." *Journal of American Culture* 2 (1980): 575–82.

Derounian, Kathryn Zabelle. "The Publication, Promotion, and Distribution of Mary Rowlandson's Indian Captivity Narrative in the Seventeenth Century." *Early American Literature* 23 (1988): 239–61.

Derounian-Stodola, Kathryn Zabelle, and James Levernier. *The Indian Captivity Narrative, 1550–1900.* New York: Twayne, 1993.

Dickinson, H.T. *Liberty and Property: Political Ideology in Eighteenth-Century Britain.* New York: Holmes and Meier, 1977.

Doob, Penelope Reed. *Nebuchadnezzar's Children: Conventions of Madness in Middle English Literature.* New Haven: Yale Univ. Press, 1974.

Drinnon, Richard. *White Savage: The Case of John Dunn Hunter.* New York: Schocken, 1972.

Ebersole, Gary L. *Captured by Texts: Puritan to Postmodern Images of Indian Captivity.* Charlottesville: Univ. Press of Virginia, 1995.

Edwards, Philip. *The Story of the Voyage: Sea-Narratives in Eighteenth-Century England.* New York: Cambridge Univ. Press, 1994.

Faller, Lincoln B. *Crime and Defoe: A New Kind of Writing.* New York: Cambridge Univ. Press, 1993.

Fausett, David. *Images of the Antipodes in the Eighteenth Century: A Study in Stereotyping.* Cross/Cultures, no. 18. Atlanta, Ga.: Rodopi; 1994.

———. *Strange Surprizing Sources of Robinson Crusoe.* Atlanta, Ga.: Rodopi, 1994.

———. *Writing the New World: Imaginary Voyages and Utopias of the Great Southern Land.* Syracuse, N.Y.: Syracuse Univ. Press, 1993.

Ferguson, Moira. *Subject to Others: British Women Writers and Colonial Slavery, 1670–1834.* New York: Routledge, 1992.

Fiedler, Leslie. *The Return of the Vanishing American.* Rev. ed. New York: Stein and Day, 1968.

Fitzpatrick, Tara. "The Figure of Captivity: The Cultural Work of the Puritan Captivity Narrative." *American Literary History* 3 (Spring 1991): 1–26.

Frantz, R.W. *The English Traveller and the Movement of Ideas, 1660–1732.* Lincoln: Univ. of Nebraska Press, 1967.

Gherman, Dawn Lander. "From Parlour to Tepee: The White Squaw on the American Frontier." Ph.D. diss., Univ. of Massachusetts, Amherst, 1975.

Gibson, Charles. *The Black Legend: Anti-Spanish Attitudes in the Old World and the New.* New York: Knopf, 1971.

Gilman, Charlotte Perkins. *Herland.* Introduction by Ann J. Lane. New York: Pantheon, 1979.

Goonetileke, H.A.I. "Robert Knox in the Kandyan Kingdom, 1660–1679." *Sri Lanka Journal of the Humanities* 1 (Dec. 1975): 81–151.

Gove, Philip Babcock. *The Imaginary Voyage in Prose Fiction. . . .* London: Holland Press, 1961.

Grandidier, Alfred. *Histoire Physique, Naturelle et Politique de Madagascar.* 39 vols. Paris: Imprimerie Nationale, 1885–[1954].

Green, Martin. *Dreams of Adventure, Deeds of Empire.* New York: Basic, 1979.

Grosrichard, Alain. *Structure du Sérail: La Fiction du Despotisme Asiatique dans l'Occident Classique.* Paris: Seuil, 1994.

Gumilev, L.N. *Searches for an Imaginary Kingdom: The Legend of the Kingdom of Prester John.* Trans. R.E.F. Smith. New York: Cambridge Univ. Press, 1987.

Haberly, David T. "Women and Indians: *The Last of the Mohicans* and the Captivity Tradition." *American Quarterly* 28 (1976): 431–41.

Hallowell, A. Irving. "American Indians, White and Black: The Phenomenon of Transculturization." *Current Anthropology* 4 (1963): 519–31.

Harvey, A.D., and Jean-Michel Racault. "Simon Berington's *Adventures of Sigr Gaudentio di Lucca.*" *Eighteenth-Century Fiction* 4 (Oct. 1991): 1–14.

Heard, J. Norman. *White into Red: A Study of the Assimilation of White Persons Captured by Indians.* Metuchen, N.J.: Scarecrow Press, 1973.

Hilger, Michael. *From Savage to Nobleman: Images of Native Americans in Film.* Lanham, Md.: Scarecrow, 1995.

Holt, P.M. *Studies in the History of the Near East.* London: Cass, 1973.

Howe, Susan. *The Birth-Mark: Unsettling the Wilderness in American Literary History.* Hanover, Conn.: Wesleyan Univ. Press, 1993.

Hulme, Peter. *Colonial Encounters: Europe and the Native Carribean, 1492–1797.* New York: Methuen, 1986.

Hunter, J. Paul. *Before Novels: The Cultural Contexts of Eighteenth-Century English Fiction.* New York: Norton, 1990.

———. *The Reluctant Pilgrim.* Baltimore: Johns Hopkins Univ. Press, 1966.

Jennings, Francis. *The Founders of America: How Indians Discovered the Land, Pioneered in It, and Created Great Classical Civilizations, How They Were Plunged into a Dark Age by Invasion and Conquest, and How They Are Reviving.* New York: Norton, 1993.

———. *The Invasion of America: Indians, Colonialism, and the Cant of Conquest.* Chapel Hill: Univ. of North Carolina Press, 1975.

Jenuja, Renu. "The Native and the Nabob: Representations of the Indian Experience in Eighteenth-Century English Literature." *Journal of Commonwealth Literature* 27 (1992): 183–98.

Jones, Herschel V. *Adventures in Americana, 1492–1897. . . .* 2 vols. 1928. Facs. rpt., New York: Cooper Square Publishers, 1964.

Kabbani, Rana. *Europe's Myths of Orient.* Bloomington: Indiana Univ. Press, 1986.

Khairallah, Shereen Nagib. "Arabic Studies in England in the Late Seventeenth and Early Eighteenth Centuries." Ph.D. diss., Univ. of London, 1972.

Kiernan, V.G. "Noble and Ignoble Savages." In *Exoticism in the Enlightenment,* ed. Rousseau and Porter, 86–116. New York: Manchester Univ. Press, 1990.

Kirby, Paul Franklin. *The Grand Tour in Italy (1700–1800).* New York: S.F. Vanni, 1952.

Kolodny, Annette. *The Land before Her: Fantasy and Experience of the American Frontiers, 1630–1860.* Chapel Hill: Univ. of North Carolina Press, 1984.

Kumar, Krishan. *Utopianism.* Minneapolis: Univ. of Minnesota Press, 1991.

Kupperman, Karen Ordahl. *Settling with the Indians: The Meeting of English and Indian Cultures in America, 1580–1640.* Totowa, N.J.: Rowman and Littlefield, 1980.

Langbein, John H. *Torture and the Law of Proof.* Chicago: Univ. of Chicago Press, 1977.

Lemay, J.A. Leo. *Did Pocahontas Save Captain John Smith?* Athens: Univ. of Georgia Press, 1992.

Levernier, James, and Henning Cohen, eds. *The Indians and Their Captives.* Westport, Conn.: Greenwood, 1977.

Lewis, Bernard. *Race and Slavery in the Middle East: An Historical Enquiry.* New York: Oxford Univ. Press, 1990.

Lewis, James R. "Savages of the Seas: Barbary Captivity Tales and Images of Muslims in the Early Republic." *Journal of American Culture* 13 (Summer 1990): 75–84.

Lockhart, Donald M. "'The Fourth Son of the Mighty Emperor': The Ethiopian Background of Johnson's *Rasselas.*" *PMLA* 78 (1963): 516–28.

Lund, Roger. "Robert Paltock." In *Dictionary of Literary Biography: British Novelists, 1660–1800,* ed. Martin Battestin, vol. 29, pt. 2, pp. 348–55. Detroit: Gale, 1985.

Maltby, William. *The Black Legend in England: The Development of Anti-Spanish Sentiment, 1558–1660.* Durham, N.C.: Duke Univ. Press, 1971.

Marin, Louis. *Utopics: Spatial Play.* Trans. Robert A. Vollrath. Atlantic Highlands, N.J.: Humanities Press, 1984.

Marshall, P.J. "Taming the Exotic: The British and India in the Seventeenth and Eighteenth Centuries." In *Exoticism in the Enlightenment,* ed. Rousseau and Porter, 46–65. New York: Manchester Univ. Press, 1990.

Marshall, P.J., and Glyndwyr Williams. *The Great Map of Mankind: Perceptions of New Worlds in the Age of Enlightenment.* Cambridge: Harvard Univ. Press, 1982.

McBurney, William H. "Penelope Aubin and the Early English Novel." *Huntington Library Quarterly* 20 (1957): 245–67.

McKeon, Michael. *The Origins of the English Novel, 1600–1740.* Baltimore: Johns Hopkins Univ. Press, 1987.

Merchant, Peter. "Robert Paltock and the Refashioning of 'Inkle and Yarico.'" *Eighteenth-Century Fiction* 9 (October 1996): 37–50.

Metlitzki, Dorothee. *The Matter of Araby in Medieval England.* New Haven: Yale Univ. Press, 1977.

Montgomery, Benilde. "White Captives, African Slaves: A Drama of Abolition." *Eighteenth-Century Studies* 27 (Summer 1994): 615–30.

Moore, John Robert. *Defoe in the Pillory and Other Studies.* Indiana University Humanities Series, no. 1. Bloomington: Indiana Univ. Press, 1939.

———. *Defoe's Sources for Robert Drury's Journal.* Indiana University Humanities Series, no. 9. Bloomington: Indiana Univ. Press, 1943.

More, Thomas. *Utopia.* Trans. and ed. Robert M. Adams. New York: Norton, 1975.

Mullenbrock, H.J. "The Political Implications of the Grand Tour: Aspects of a Specifically English Contribution to the European Travel Literature of the Age of Enlightenment." *Trema* 9 (1984): 7–21.

Namias, June. *White Captives: Gender and Ethnicity on the American Frontier.* Chapel Hill: Univ. of North Carolina Press, 1993.

Nasir, Sari J. *The Arabs and the English.* 2d ed. New York: Longman, 1979.

Netton, Ian Richard. "The Mysteries of Islam." In *Exoticism in the Enlightenment,* ed. Rousseau and Porter, 23–45. New York: Manchester Univ. Press, 1990.

Novak, Maximillian E. *Defoe and the Nature of Man.* New York: Oxford Univ. Press, 1963.

Nussbaum, Felicity. *Torrid Zones: Maternity, Sexuality, and Empire in Eighteenth-Century English Narratives.* Baltimore: Johns Hopkins Univ. Press, 1995.

Oueijan, Naji B. *The Progress of an Image: The East in English Literature.* New York: Peter Lang, 1996.

Pearce, Roy Harvey. *The Savages of America: A Study of the Indian and the Idea of Civilization.* Rev. ed. Baltimore: Johns Hopkins Univ. Press, 1965.

———. "The Significances of the Captivity Narrative." *American Literature* 19 (1947): 1–20.

Person, Leland, Jr. "The American Eve: Miscegenation and a Feminist Frontier Fiction." *American Quarterly* 37 (1985): 668–85.

Peters, Edward. *Inquisition.* New York: Free Press, 1988.

———. *Torture.* New York: Basil Blackwell, 1985.

Pocock, J.G.A. *The Ancient Constitution and the Feudal Law.* New York: Cambridge Univ. Press, 1957.

———. *The Machiavellian Moment: Florentine Political Thought and the Atlantic Republican Tradition.* Princeton: Princeton Univ. Press, 1975.

Pratt, Mary Louise. "Fieldwork in Common Places." In *Writing Culture: The Poetics and Politics of Ethnography,* ed. James Clifford and George E. Marcus, 27–50. Berkeley: Univ. of California Press, 1986.

———. *Imperial Eyes: Travel Writing and Transculturation.* New York: Routledge, 1992.

Prica, Zora. *Daniel Defoe's Robinson Crusoe und Robert Paltock's Peter Wilkins.* Budapest: Serbische Buchdruckerei, 1909.

Price, Lawrence Marsden. *Inkle and Yarico Album.* Berkeley: Univ. of California Press, 1937.

Railo, Eino. *The Haunted Castle: A Study of the Elements of English Romanticism.* New York: Dutton, 1927.

Redford, Bruce. *Venice and the Grand Tour.* New Haven: Yale Univ. Press, 1996.

Rees, Christine. *Utopian Imagination and Eighteenth-Century Fiction.* New York: Longman, 1996.

Richetti, John J. *Defoe's Narratives: Situations and Structures.* New York: Oxford Univ. Press, 1975.

———. *Popular Fiction before Richardson: Narrative Patterns, 1700–1739.* New York: Oxford Univ. Press, 1969.

Richter, David H. *The Progress of Romance: Literary Historiography and the Gothic Novel.* Columbus: Ohio State Univ. Press, 1996.

Rousseau, G.S., and Roy Porter, eds. *Exoticism in the Enlightenment.* New York: Manchester Univ. Press, 1990.

Said, Edward. *Culture and Imperialism.* New York: Knopf, 1993.

———. *Orientalism.* New York: Vintage, 1979.

Sayre, Gordon Mitchell. *Les Sauvages Américains: Representations of Native Americans in French and English Colonial Literature.* Chapel Hill: Univ. of North Carolina Press, 1997.

Schofield, Mary Anne. *Eliza Haywood.* Twayne's English Author Series, vol. 411. New York: Twayne, 1985.

———. *Masking and Unmasking the Female Mind.* Newark: Univ. of Delaware Press, 1990.

———. *Quiet Rebellion: The Fictional Heroines of Eliza Fowler Haywood.* Washington, DC: Univ. Press of America, 1982.

Schonhorn, Manuel. *Defoe's Politics: Parliament, Power, Kingship, and Robinson Crusoe.* New York: Cambridge Univ. Press, 1991.

Secord, Arthur Wellesley. *Robert Drury's Journal and Other Studies.* Urbana: Univ. of Illinois Press, 1961.

———. *Studies in the Narrative Method of Defoe.* Urbana: Univ. of Illinois Press, 1924. Rpt., New York: Russell & Russell, 1963.

Sewell, David. "'So Unstable and Like Mad Men They Were': Language and Interpretation in Early American Captivity Narratives." In *A Mixed Race: Ethnicity in Early America,* ed. Shuffleton, 39–55. New York: Oxford Univ. Press, 1993.

Shuffleton, Frank, ed. *A Mixed Race: Ethnicity in Early America.* New York: Oxford Univ. Press, 1993.

Sieminski, Greg. "The Puritan Captivity Narrative and the Politics of the American Revolution." *American Quarterly* 42 (1990): 35–56.

Slessarev, Vsevolod. *Prester John: The Letter and the Legend.* Minneapolis: Univ. of Minnesota Press, 1959.

Slotkin, Richard. *Regeneration through Violence: The Mythology of the American Frontier, 1600–1860.* Middletown, Conn.: Wesleyan Univ. Press, 1973.

Snader, Joe. "Caught between Worlds: British Captivity Narratives in Fact and Fiction." Ph.D. diss. Univ. of Maryland, College Park, 1998.

Spacks, Patricia Meyer. *Desire and Truth: Functions of Plot in Eighteenth-Century English Novels.* Chicago: Univ. of Chicago Press, 1990.

Spear, Percival. *The Nabobs: A Study of the Social Life of the English in 18th Century India.* Rev. ed. New York: Oxford Univ. Press, 1963.

Starr, G.A. *Defoe and Casuistry.* Princeton: Princeton Univ. Press, 1971.

———. "Escape from Barbary: A Seventeenth-Century Genre." *Huntington Library Quarterly* 29 (Nov. 1965): 35–48.

"The Stolen Wife." In *American Indian Myths and Legends,* ed. Richard Erdoes and Alfonso Ortiz, 285–90. New York: Pantheon, 1984.

Sypher, Wylie. *Guinea's Captive Kings: British Anti-Slavery Literature of the XVIIIth Century.* Chapel Hill: Univ. of North Carolina Press, 1942.

Tanselle, G. Thomas. *Royall Tyler.* Cambridge: Harvard Univ. Press, 1967.

Tilton, Robert S. *Pocahontas: The Evolution of an American Narrative.* New York: Cambridge Univ. Press, 1994.

Ulrich, Laurel. *Good Wives: Image and Reality in the Lives of Women in Northern New England, 1650–1750.* New York: Knopf, 1982.

Vail, R.W.G. *The Voice of the Old Frontier.* Philadelphia: Univ. of Pennsylvania Press, 1949.

Van Der Zee, John. *Bound Over: Indentured Servitude and American Conscience.* New York: Simon and Schuster, 1985.

VanDerBeets, Richard. *The Indian Captivity Narrative: An American Genre.* Lanham, Md.: Univ. Press of America, 1984.

———. Introduction to *Held Captive by Indians,* ed. VanDerBeets. Knoxville: Univ. of Tennessee Press, 1973.

Vaughan, Alden T., and Edward W. Clark, eds. *Puritans among the Indians: Accounts of Captivity and Redemption, 1676–1724.* Cambridge: Harvard Univ. Press, 1981.

Watt, Ian. *The Rise of the Novel: Studies in Defoe, Richardson and Fielding.* Berkeley: Univ. of California Press, 1957.

Weitzman, Arthur J. "More Light on *Rasselas:* The Background of the Egyptian Episodes." *Philological Quarterly* 48 (1969): 42–58.

Wolf, John Baptist. *The Barbary Coast: Algiers under the Turks, 1500 to 1830.* New York: Norton, 1979.

Wood, A.C. *A History of the Levant Company.* New York: Barnes & Noble, 1964.

Zach, Wolfgang. "Mrs. Aubin and Richardson's Earliest Literary Manifesto (1739)." *English Studies* 62 (June 1981): 271–85.

Index